Facing History and Ourselves:
Elements of Time

by Facing History and Ourselves Staff

Mary Johnson
Margot Stern Strom

Facing History and Ourselves

Brookline, Massachusetts

1989

Elements of Time

ISBN 0-9615841-1-4

Printed in the United States of America

This book was made possible by funds granted by the Charles H. Revson Foundation. The statements made and views expressed, however, are solely the responsiblity of the author.

TABLE OF CONTENTS

Montages

Scholars Reflect on Holocaust Video Testimonies

Elements of Time

Preface

If you can have a hundred books in the world today that are all devoted to
teaching that the Holocaust did not happen, imagine the seeds that can fall
on unsuspecting minds. That has to be countered by the full-court press of
teaching history as it happened . . . Unless we keep hammering home the
irrefutable and indisputable facts of the human experience, history as it
was experienced by people, we are going to find ourselves increasingly
unable to draw distinctions between what was and what we think was.

Bill Moyers in an interview with
Margot Stern Strom
Executive Director, Facing History and Ourselves

For well over a decade, Facing History and Ourselves has worked with
teachers, scholars, researchers and students to make history real and connect
the lessons of history to the lives of adolescents and adults today. It is in this
spirit that we are especially pleased and proud to announce the publication of
Facing History and Ourselves: Elements of Time; a resource book of
Holocaust testimonies with extensive commentary by scholars and educators
on their meaning and interpretation.

For the past five years, Facing History and Ourselves researchers have worked
with the unique collections at the Fortunoff Video Archive for Holocaust
Testimonies, Yale University. We have gathered and edited an exceptional set
of materials that can be used in diverse educational settings, middle schools,
high schools, community colleges, universities, adult education programs,
interfaith meetings, and special events sponsored by church and community
organizations. The testimonies described in *Elements of Time* can stand
alone, or be used in conjunction with viewing the video portraits and
montages which are all available from the Facing History and Ourselves
Resource Center and Library.

Elements of Time is itself testimony to how archival materials can become tools of education and provoke the most significant kind of thinking, discussion and analysis. Dr. Mary Johnson, historian and staff member at Facing History who worked most extensively with the collection, is available to speak to interfaith groups, church and temple gatherings, and educators' conferences about this project. She will show excerpts from the videotapes, describe the manual and discuss its connection to unique and universal lessons of the Holocaust. We invite you to call Dr. Johnson at Facing History to arrange a presentation and hear more about *Facing History and Ourselves: Elements of Time*. Call Facing History at (617) 232-1595.

Facing History and Ourselves National Foundation teaches about the dangers of indifference and the virtue of understanding. Through its model program *Holocaust and Human Behavior*, it teaches about prejudice, bigotry, racism, anti-semitism and hatred so that children may learn to care, to be involved and to be just citizens in a democracy. For over a decade, Facing History has offered its unique approach to help adolescents and adults confront the complexities of history and promote critical and creative thinking about the problems facing our society today and the opportunities for positive change.

Facing History teaches these lessons to students when it counts most . . . when they are young and forming values to hold for the rest of their lives. It teaches these lessons in school classrooms, the only place where people of all races, religions, and backgrounds must come together. It provides a setting for these children to share the concerns, fears, ideas, and hopes they experience as they learn and grow together.

Facing History is unique. It is unlike any other citizenship education. It teaches not only about the fragility of democracy but also about the opportunities for civic participation and human rights. It gives new meaning to the question, "Can we learn from the past?"

When students study about the denial and avoidance of the Holocaust, Armenian Genocide, and America's struggle to overcome racism and dehumanization, they begin to see how to make a difference. Facing History is not a media fad, not a one-week curriculum unit nor an assembly topic easily forgotten. It is dynamic, designed to have lasting impact on the life of teachers and their students. It is an active program in which teachers engage students in discussing complex and difficult subjects to achieve knowledge, understanding and commitment.

Introduced initially in the Brookline, Massachusetts school system over a decade ago, Facing History has now been taught to more than 450,000 students annually in public, private, and parochial school settings across the United States and Canada. Over 30,000 educators from 46 states, Canada, and overseas have attended Facing History workshops and conferences held throughout the country.

Teaching methods employ films, readings, class discussion, guest speakers and student journals which promote individual reflection. The program is used in many schools in combination with Art, English, and law classes, stimulating the creative abilities of teachers and students and heightening the significance and relevance of the subject. Teacher training, adult education, and related community activities are unique and essential elements of the program.

Facing History is a program embraced by school administrators, teachers and students. It profoundly moves its participants, and shapes the way they see the world for the rest of their lives. Students eloquently describe changes in their attitudes and their newly formed awareness about the dangers of prejudice and hate. They trace these new values to their involvement with the Facing History program in their classrooms. Facing History is the most powerful tool we have for teaching our nation's children the values of tolerance and justice, thereby ensuring their futures.

Facing History and Ourselves has achieved very special recognition in the professional education community. The U.S. Department of Education has awarded Facing History and Ourselves its highly prized "Certificate of Achievement" and the program is now included in the prestigious *National Diffusion Network* which disseminates information about new and successful curricula. Facing History has also received awards for its work against racism and bias and for its effective programs in moral and ethical education.

Publications

Facing History and Ourselves: Holocaust and Human Behavior
published by Intentional Educations, Inc.

Watertown, MA (1982)

Available from Facing History National Foundation Inc.,

25 Kennard Road, Brookline, MA 02146

This resource book contains the essential materials needed to incorporate the Facing History program into a school or class. Its readings reflect the latest scholarship on the Holocaust and include both primary sources and secondary commentary that give clear examples of abuse of power, violations of human rights and unthinking obedience in response to authority.The book traces the roots of prejudice and discrimination in our own lives and then extensively investigates the history of Nazi Germany. An examination of the Armenian Genocide illustrates the power of avoidance and denial. The final chapter explores how positive participation in a democracy can make a difference in achieving a society of tolerance and justice.

Facing History and Ourselves: Choosing to Participate
published by Facing History and Ourselves

The *Choosing to Participate* resource book is a five-chapter study of citizenship in American democracy. The book is an outgrowth of the last chapter of *Holocaust and Human Behavior*, in which students confront the question of how the lessons of that history can be made part of their lives in America. It includes case studies of individual and groups in the past who tried to make a difference. In examining such studies as the anti-lynching campaign of the nineteenth-century, civil rights movements, or twentieth-century experiments in helping the poor, students are encouraged to ask how they can make a difference in society and to think about their own citizenship responsibilities today.

Facing History and Ourselves: Elements of Time
published by Facing History and Ourselves

This resource text is a companion manual to the Facing History videotape
collection of Holocaust testimonies. It is the result of a five-year collaborative
project between Facing History and Ourselves and the Fortunoff Video
Archive, Yale University. It includes transcriptions of the videos, integrated
with descriptions of the speakers, background information and guidelines for
using them in a classroom. Supplemented essays and readings from scholars
and resource speakers who have addressed Facing History conferences provide
an additional perspective. All materials in the manual are cross-referenced
with readings in *Holocaust and Human Behavior*. All videotapes described in
the manual are also available through the Facing History Resource Center.

Facing History and Ourselves: Annotated Bibliography
published by Walker and Company, NY (1988)

This valuable resource is an annotated listing of works for adults and for
children on the Holocaust and on twentieth-century genocide in Armenia and
Cambodia. Materials are described from several perspectives, including
literary and historical.

Elements of Time

Foreword

Margot Stern Strom

Executive Director, Facing History and Ourselves

The shared experience of listening to a survivor bearing witness is like no other experience. Those of us who have had the opportunity to create such a shared experience for our students and colleagues, as part of a course or workshop on the Holocaust, know that it inevitably affects us deeply and literally changes the way we feel about history and ourselves. Yet this is an experience that only a small proportion of our generation has had, and the option of creating the setting for such encounters is coming to an end. Our children and our children's children will not have it.

The Fortunoff Video Archive at Yale University is one of several centers created to give survivors the opportunity to bear witness. More than 400 interviews had been recorded by the Yale Video Archive by 1984, when the Charles H. Revson Foundation offered Facing History and Ourselves a grant to review the tapes and edit some of them for potential use with student and adult groups.

Facing History and Ourselves: Elements of Time is the outcome of our project to capture some of the power of personal encounters through video portraits and video montages. Integrated with brief descriptions of the portraits and montages are background information and guidelines for introducing them. Supplemental essays, including five essays that reflect the collective thinking of the Facing History and Ourselves staff, are designed to widen the reader's perspective and help the teacher or discussion leader to select among the available testimonies.

Elements of Time has been cross-referenced with *Facing History and Ourselves: Holocaust and Human Behavior*, the core resource book for Facing History teachers and students, and with other resource materials available through Facing History and Ourselves. This enables teachers to enrich assigned readings and class discussions with selected videotapes that illuminate the lives of Jews and non-Jews in the years before and during the Holocaust.

The video portraits and montages are described in sufficient detail to enable educators to incorporate selected tapes into curricula for various age levels and subject areas, in courses that are not necessarily courses about the Holocaust. Thus, a secondary school teacher able to devote only a few class sessions to the Holocaust as part of a course on European history might select part of the montage "Childhood Memories" or use a portrait such as that of Rachel G. A junior or senior high school unit on the Holocaust might include two of the montages, each of which contains several mini-portraits, or a montage and a portrait.

Video montages and video portraits can enrich a wide variety of curricula at the university level. Psychology and sociology classes, courses in human development, legal or medical ethics, all can be illuminated by survivor testimonies. The education of Nazi youth, as described in some of the tapes, is especially relevant for students in teacher education classes.

The more we know about the Holocaust, the more we marvel at the subtleties in the video portraits. Yet we thought it possible that students, with limited factual information about the history of the Holocaust, might react to unedited or lightly edited tapes of individual narratives with stress, confusion, and perhaps even boredom. Without the opportunity to ask questions, without the subtle modifications in presentation made by a witness-bearer interacting with an audience, students' attention might wander or perhaps focus on comparatively irrelevant details. This potential problem led us to the concept of the montage. The montages can partially correct against common misconceptions and the naive assumption that every survivor's experience is like every other survivor's, especially when readings and testimonies on parallel themes are selected for study.

Before we began to screen the testimonies, we wondered how such a vast amount of data would be made accessible to students and adults. Could we single out one survivor's story that would be "everyman's" story? We soon realized that the answer to this question was "no." The experiences of survivors depended on many variables such as their country of origin, how early or late in the war they were apprehended, what work camp or death camp they found themselves in, and what opportunities they had to gain tiny advantages that helped them to preserve their strength.

Ultimately treated like objects and like vermin, most survivors had few choices and no explanations, and for many under conditions of extreme stress their vision of the world shrank to the details of minute-to-minute survival. The testimonies include the kind of telling detail that never gets into written documents. When words fail, the telling gesture and the silences speak for themselves. Yes, the video testimonies are "history," but getting an accurate historical overview of the effect of the Holocaust cannot be achieved by viewing a handful of interviews; the experience needs to be integrated with reading and discussion. As part of a multi-faceted educational experience, viewing testimonials is likely to be the critical experience that moves viewers and listeners to care.

As the Facing History and Ourselves staff began to immerse themselves in the tapes, the cumulative difference between viewing recorded material and the occasional live encounter, or the experience of reading the recollections of a survivor in a book, became very clear to us. Despite all we had read, despite the fact that we thought nothing new could shock us, the stories pierced our hearts and touched our souls. Later, when our staff viewed Claude Lanzmann's *Shoah*, we understood the survivor on the film who warned, "If you would lick my heart, it would poison you."

We became acutely conscious of the role that mere chance played in the survival of the few during the death of the many. It was often chance rather than strategy that saved our witness-bearers, yet we marveled at the variety of strategies for survival they described and recollected for us. Many of these stories were not finally integrated in the edited tapes presented in this manual, but they remain vivid in our minds. Some of these stories involve choice, often between alternatives that made it a "choice-less choice." Thus Rose, a survivor, tells of a conversation with her mother in a cattle car that stopped briefly en route to an unknown destiny. "Jump," urge some of the younger prisoners. "Don't jump," pleads Rose's mother. What to do? Rose's father and brother are already dead; probably they will all die. Should she leave her mother? Rose chose not to jump. Who knows how few survived of those who jumped and those who didn't? Another survivor recalls a moment when moving to the left or to the right, or staying still, all meant death. Which way? A ladybug flew by; the woman moved in the direction of the ladybug—and lived.

Survivors' memories shed light on the incredible varieties of organized and spontaneous resistance—and on the bitter price of reprisals for acts of resistance. One survivor explains how, working in a V2 rocket factory at Dora-Nordhausen, he instructed his fellow workers in ways to sabotage the production of rockets by urinating on the wires. Although he escaped detection, his colleagues were caught and executed for the deed. Victims who had had nothing to do with acts of resistance also were arbitrarily killed to instill fear and passivity into the population. Each act against the Germans, recall numerous survivors, meant that not only you, but also others in your community, would be killed in reprisal.

Touching and shocking as video testimonies may be, we must yet remember that what we come to view and hear are stories that are "self-edited." Bearing witness is a voluntary act; those who have volunteered have struggled to master the past, and in the process, the unconscious has modified, blocked, and fuzzed-over some memories. On a conscious level the witness-bearers can be seen repeatedly trying to spare us some of the horror they recall, although videotapes can be revealing in ways that written material is not. And then, a further softening of the horrors is exercised in the cutting and editing of testimony.

At the same time they try to spare us, some of the survivors despair that their stories will not be believed, or that the act of bearing testimony will make listeners recoil from them in horror. Like Moshe the Beadle, in Elie Wiesel's *Night*, they fear being dismissed as mad by those who do not want to listen to them.

As a rule, witness-bearers put their "best foot forward." They come in their best clothes; many of the women look like they have come directly from the hairdresser. Many look prosperous and successful, so much so that the new generation trained to attend to the video image, rather than the narrative, may be misled into minimizing the survivors' agony. Then, as the interview progresses, some of these witness-bearers "wilt" before our eyes and we catch a glimpse of how the past still ravages them.

What is the effect on a new generation of these personal histories of suffering? Should we "spare" new generations from the pain of witnessing survivor testimonies? We believe that the answer to that question is a resounding "no," based both on our understanding of history and the effect these programs have had on students and their teachers.

During the ten years we have supported teacher efforts to share Facing History and Ourselves with students, teachers have reported that their classrooms are energized and revitalized by the curriculum. Students connect to this material. They are appalled at the way most people in community after community permitted minority groups to be robbed of security, possessions, family, and life itself. They are outraged to learn how children were humiliated in class, how work camp inmates reduced to walking skeletons were herded through streets lined with bystanders to and from the factories where they labored as slaves. They make the connection between scapegoating and peer pressure and the descent into genocide. They vow to reject in themselves the microcosm of the kind of behavior they see in survivors' testimonies about the perpetrators. "This is wrong; this isn't fair; I wouldn't want to be in such a position; no one should be in such a position!" The outrage and the empathy make the students realize that school can teach about "real life," that not everything is a matter of opinion, that civil liberties must be protected and evils resisted.

How can a new generation cope with the pain of having shared some of the survivors' pain? In part, by having the opportunity, however brief, to express grief through words, pictures, and music. The ultimate release, however, may come with the act of judgment. It is the role of future generations not only to remember, but to judge. Hannah Arendt refuted Hegel's assumption that history (success) is the ultimate judgment or action. Rather,

> she would give the last word to spectators, for it is they who make an event at home in history or not. . . . Only the spectators, who constitute the space of history (memory) into which all actions and works of art fall . . . can pass ultimate judgment on an event or action by the quality of their attention.[1]

[1]Denneny, "The Privilege of Ourselves: Hannah Arendt on Judgment," p. 246.

Elements of Time

Introduction

Elements of Time: Exercising the Historical Imagination

Five years ago, Eli Evans of the Charles H. Revson Foundation invited representatives of the Facing History and Ourselves National Foundation to meet with the staff of the Fortunoff Video Archive for Holocaust Testimonies, Yale University, in order to develop a plan for disseminating the video testimonies in the Yale collection to diverse educational settings throughout the United States. At that time, this was a necessary and important project since most of the testimonies in the Archive were unedited and ranged in length from one hour to several hours. Moreover, the great majority of secondary school teachers were unaware of the archival sources; the few that knew of their existence were not trained to use them effectively in their Holocaust courses. After visiting the Archive and discussing its educational potential with the Archive staff, Facing History responded to the Revson Foundation with a proposal for adapting the testimonies for classroom use and preparing appropriate background materials that would provide a context for the videotapes. The dissemination plan as outlined in the original proposal has remained the blueprint for the video testimonies project since its inception.

> Facing History will introduce the testimonies to teachers, students, educators, adults and community leaders interested in the history of the Holocaust as well as bring new communities into the program through the unique presentation of curriculum materials and methodology. Moreover, Facing History has the background and educational expertise to work with eminent scholars to develop original research and written commentaries for especially designed resource materials, new curriculum approaches, and articles for publication.

The manual *Elements of Time*, which has evolved over the last five years, is a key component of the video testimonies project. It incorporates the most recent scholarship on Holocaust testimonies and oral history as well as practical pedagogical suggestions for making video testimonies challenging educational resources. The manual corresponds to videotapes that have been created by the Facing History staff or the Fortunoff Video Archive staff. It also includes other documentary forms, primary and secondary, that can enhance one's understanding of the content of the video testimonies.

Elements of Time serves as a companion to the Facing History video collection of Holocaust testimonies. The companion manual describes the context for and content of video testimonies dealing with a wide range of themes pertinent to the study of the Holocaust and human behavior. Throughout the book are cross-references to readings and topics in the Facing History and Ourselves Resource Book, as well as to other Facing History publications and special information packets and audiovisual materials available at the Facing History Resource Center and Library.

Elements of Time does not attempt to be a comprehensive survey of survivors' experiences in the Holocaust years. Rather, it suggests the types of themes that most engage students' interest and generate worthwhile classroom discussion. It also provides general guidelines for viewing the ever-growing number of video testimonies in cities throughout the United States.

Samuel Bak's painting "Hiding," which appears on the manual cover, features a bird that complements the bird found in the Bak painting on the cover of the Resource Book. It is very appropriate that Bak's works appear on the covers of Facing History publications, especially on the front of *Elements of Time*. A child survivor of the Holocaust, Bak's career as an artist has been devoted towards recapturing scenes from his childhood in the Vilna Ghetto and nearby labor camp.Throughout his works Bak is preoccupied with concepts of time and childhood memories. Broken clocks in his paintings represent moments of fractured time during his days in the ghetto and labor camp. Birdlike figures with wooden wings seeking to fly symbolize that time flies. For Bak, nothing ever truly repairs the fragmented time of his youth—a time that, though flown, will never be totally erased from his memory.

Time is the central theme throughout *Elements of Time*. The video portraits in "Portraits" are chronological studies of individuals who lived through the era of the Third Reich, capturing their important moments of decision-making as well as the moments when fate helped in their survival. In most cases the portraits cover several years of a survivor's life so that audiences can get a sense of the accumulation of humiliations, threats, and physical suffering that survivors endured. Each portrait, except the final one, is between twenty and thirty minutes in length so that a class has an opportunity to discuss the tape immediately after viewing it. The final portrait of Peter Gay is over an hour in length because Gay touches on so many of the critical events of the Weimar and early Nazi eras.

The video montages in "Montages" focus on certain themes of Holocaust history using excerpts from several survivors and witnesses who represent different perspectives on the themes under consideration. The montage "Stories of Separation," for example, highlights the moment in which survivors were separated from their families, showing the variety of separation experiences ranging from brief separations in the ghetto to the permanent severing of family ties. Another montage, "Childhood Memories," concentrates on the period of childhood for Jews and non-Jews growing up during the Third Reich. What is so striking in these memories is the fact that many of the men and women who grew up in these years do not feel they know the true meaning of childhood since they were so rapidly thrust into an adult world. Two montages elaborate on themes in written works on the Holocaust: "Challenge of Memory: A Videotape to Accompany Elie Wiesel's *Night*," and "Friedrich: A Videotape to Accompany Hans Peter Richter's Novel *Friedrich*." Excerpts have been selected that parallel stories found in the literature, and many students report that the testimonies make their reading experience more meaningful.

The third section, "Scholars Reflect on Holocaust Video Testimonies," consists of a series of essays that provide a framework for presenting the video portraits and montages in classrooms. Historians Nora Levin and Martin Gilbert indicate the importance of these testimonies in providing details on incidents omitted or briefly mentioned in traditional written accounts: the more we learn about the events from the victims' perspectives, the more we are able to exercise the historical imagination that is so essential for confronting the Holocaust experience. Lawrence Langer's five essays embody the collective thinking of Professor Langer and the Facing History staff and suggest ways to respond to the questions often asked in classrooms. In Primo Levi's essay the late Holocaust survivor and author documents the questions that students of the Holocaust typically asked him when he met with them. The questions that Levi identifies are similar to questions Facing History students raise in their class discussions.

The video resources listed and described in Appendix I are retrospective. Scholars and educators discuss dominant themes that have appeared in the video portraits and montages and the relevance of these themes for the current generation. For instance, art historians David Joselit and Sybil Milton examine modes of protest in the art of the Third Reich, pointing out how artists in any society have the potential for expressing opposition to dominant values and institutions. Historian Henry Friedlander, who explains the weakness of democracy in Germany of the 1920s and 1930s, singles out certain cues to be looking for to detect weaknesses in democratic societies of the 1980s. Historians Raul Hilberg and Henry Feingold review the long period after the war when people were unwilling to confront the past and pinpoint the specific events in the postwar era that sharpened people's interest in looking at the Third Reich.

Similar information is found in Appendix II, which contains the video proceedings of the Facing History annual conferences. At the First Annual Facing History Conference, "The Impact of Nuremberg: Today and the Future," panelists considered how the Nuremberg trials influence contemporary law and attitudes. The Third Annual Conference, "The Child in War: Seed for the Sowing Shall Not be Milled," examined how the disrupted childhoods of the Holocaust inform us about similar disruptions for children in contemporary war-torn countries such as Cambodia, Vietnam, South Africa, and Nicaragua.

Just as the Resource Book evolved over many years with the input of teachers, educators, and scholars, Elements of Time has grown out of the cooperation of members of the Facing History staff, scholars in Holocaust studies, and teachers using Facing History in classrooms throughout the United States. Among the scholars who have participated in the project are: Geoffrey Hartman, Karl Young Professor of English and Comparative Literature, and Advisor to the Fortunoff Video Archive for Holocaust Testimonies, Yale University; Lawrence Langer, Alumnae Professor of English, Simmons College, and Consultant to Facing History on the Video Testimonies Project; Paul Bookbinder, Professor of History, University of Massachusetts/Boston; Lucjan Dobroszycki, Senior Research Associate, YIVO Institute of Jewish History; Michael Berenbaum, Professor of Jewish Studies, Georgetown University, and Educational Director for the U.S. Holocaust Memorial Museum; Linda Kuzmack, Director of the Oral History Project at the U.S. Holocaust Memorial Museum; Shomer Zwelling, historian and former director of the Learning Center for the U.S. Holocaust Memorial Museum; Nora Levin, Director of the Holocaust Archive and Associate Professor of Jewish Studies, Gratz College; Leo Goldberger, Professor of Psychology, New York University; Carol Gilligan, Professor, Graduate School of Education, Harvard University; and Brana Gurewitsch, Librarian and Archivist, Center for Holocaust Studies, Brooklyn, New York. Also critical in the development of the manual have been Joanne Rudoff and Sandra Rosenstock at the Fortunoff Video Archive.

Among the members of the Facing History staff who have made special contributions to the manual are: Program Director, Marc Skvirsky; Program Associate, Janice Darsa; and Associate Director, Martin Sleeper. Also, several members of the Teacher Training Team—Margaret Drew, Theodora

Kelley, Burt Skvirsky, William Miller, Paul Pickard, and Elly Greene— deserve special mention for piloting the lessons in the manual. Members of the Program Committee offered valuable suggestions; Jacob Birnbaum contributed pertinent documents on ghettos and pre-war Polish communities.

The Pucker-Safrai Gallery in Boston granted permission to use a photograph of Samuel Bak's painting "Hiding" on the cover of *Elements of Time*. The gallery has also granted permission to use other paintings by Samuel Bak on the covers of Facing History's *Annotated Bibliography* and the forthcoming publications *Facing History and Ourselves: Holocaust and Human Behavior* (revised edition) and *Facing History and Ourselves: Choosing to Participate*.

Sharon Rivo and Miriam Krant of the National Center for Jewish Film have provided information on propaganda films and loaned Facing History slides of visual materials used in Hitler Youth training.

Carol Kur and Martha Goodman have given valuable suggestions on the arrangement of materials.

It is important information in using *Elements of Time* to remember that the manual is keyed specifically to Facing History curriculum materials, and the video excerpts described in the manual have been selected to enhance and elaborate upon themes explored in Facing History classrooms. Those for whom *Elements of Time* is the first exposure (or the first intensive exposure) to Facing History materials and methods may find it helpful to learn more about the program and available resources. Introductory Videotapes are helpful entrees to Facing History.

Introductory Videotapes

"A Visit with Facing History," "An Overview of Facing History and Ourselves National Foundation" and "Using *Elements of Time*" are three videotapes which introduce the Facing History and Ourselves National Foundation and this videotestimonies project. (See Appendix for further description of the Facing History and Ourselves National Foundation).

The twelve-minute videotape, "A Visit with Facing History," is a montage of Facing History and Ourselves activity in the classroom, in conferences, and in the national news. Testimonies of students, teachers, administrators and scholars highlight Facing History's successes in bringing excellent educational experiences to adolescent and adult students who are learning that a study of the history of the Holocaust can yield important lessons that affect our society today.

"A Video Overview of Facing History" records the opening talk by Executive Director, Margot Stern Strom, at Facing History and Ourselves' Fourth Annual Human Rights and Justice Conference held at the Harvard Graduate School of Education in 1988. Also available at the Resource Center are video introductions by Program staff and teacher trainers.

"Using Video testimonies in the Classroom" records presentations which describe the *Elements of Time* resource book and the accompanying videos. Presentors highlight key themes and approaches developed by the staff for this program: Mary Johnson outlines *Elements of Time*; Jan Darsa discusses the advantages and limitations of using videotestimonies in the classroom; Professor Lawrence Langer discusses how video testimonies help students and teachers move from the normal world to the abnormal world of ghettos and concentration camps; Elly Green discusses her use of the video montage "Challenge of Memory" in the classroom.

The Fortunoff Video Archive for Holocaust Testimonies, Yale University

Geoffrey H. Hartman

Background

There have been several periods when survivors of the Holocaust recovered their voice and an audience materialized for them. The first came immediately after the war, when the camps were liberated. That period did not last: the survivors could not continue to dwell on the past; a devastated Europe had to be rebuilt; and the disbelief or guilt that cruel memories aroused isolated rather than integrated the survivor. Haim Gouri's remarkable film, *The Eighty-First Blow*, took its title from the story of how a concentration camp prisoner was given eighty blows and left for dead. Miraculously, he survived; but when, after liberation, he told an ignorant world about his experiences, he was not believed. That was "the eighty-first blow," more painful than the rest.

A second wave of interest was created by the Eichmann Trial, and a third came after the airing of the TV series *Holocaust* in 1978. After so many lost their lives, must they now also be deprived of their life story? This was a complaint of the survivors. Many of them wanted to tell stories more true and terrible, more authentic in their depiction of that era.

Thirty-five years, moreover, had elapsed since the war, and the survivors and refugees living in America were settled, with grown families and a third generation in the offing. It was late: now, if ever, was the time to talk; they were less hesitant to be recognized and to transmit their experiences as a "legacy."

A grassroots project developed in New Haven, Connecticut when sensitive neighbors found they knew next to nothing about the survivors in their midst. An interviewer with her own television program, a child survivor who had become a psychiatrist, and the head of a local survivor organization formed a "Holocaust Survivors Film Project." The project hustled local business people for space, equipment, and money, and launched a crash videotaping program that, by the time Yale offered support and helped it to become national, had recorded 200 testimonies in less than three years. The Video Archive for Holocaust Testimonies at Yale opened its doors in October 1982.

Aim of the Yale Archive

The general aim of the Archive can be summarized as the collection and preservation for educational use of eyewitness accounts of the Holocaust. To collect them means conducting sensitive interviews both at Yale and through affiliate organizations elsewhere. This network of affiliates, covered by a formal agreement specifying standards of videotaping and interviewing, has grown to eighteen members and includes such urban centers as Los Angeles, New York, Dallas, Cincinnati, and Tel-Aviv. Preservation means careful storage: the Sterling Memorial Library at Yale has become a central depository (so far the only one) to register and safeguard a copy of every video testimony. Educational use means that the Archive develops outreach programs and that its staff seeks professional advice on the most appropriate way to disseminate these witness accounts. That is how the link with Facing History came about, facilitated by the Charles H. Revson Foundation which funded the Archive from 1982 through 1988.

No single organization can do all the planning in this area: the expertise of Facing History in teacher training and urban school systems, as well as its experience with adult and university audiences, is crucial. For the first time these personal and affecting stories become part of the curriculum, properly keyed to readings and teacher presentations.

Other outreach programs of the Yale Archive include: 1) short documentaries made from its video testimonies and available to schools and communities; 2) assistance to the learning centers and videotaping studios of Holocaust Memorial Museums; 3) analyzing and entering into RLIN (Research Libraries Information Network) over 2,000 hours of testimony, so that major museums and educational institutions will have access to a computerized index summarizing the testimonies; and 4) welcoming scholars and educators to the Archive, which is located in Yale's central research library.

Principles and Procedures

The Yale Archive combines oral history with the needs of the modern museum and public education. We feel that the survivors should be given their own voice, and that academic history, however important, should not speak for them at this point, though it can provide an extension and integration of what these firsthand accounts describe. Instead of statistics and data the testimonies provide living portraits and are the nearest we will come to the actual experiences and thoughts of eyewitnesses.

Nazi photos, moreover, which memorial museums have had to rely on, are triumphal and sadistic: they portray the victim as already a non-survivor, as dead, or degraded to subhuman level. The testimonies help restore the humanity of the persons the Nazis sought to dehumanize. However grim the content of these witness accounts, each speaks to us in a personal voice, and with a relevance that reaches beyond the camps.

If the principle of giving survivors their voice has been a sustaining one, so has that of giving a face to that voice: of choosing video over audio, because of the immediacy, and additionally it adds to the interview. Audiences now and in the future will surely remain audiovisual. By producing video recordings of public broadcast quality, Yale is building up an Archive of Conscience which educators and filmmakers will consult.

Let me emphasize, however, that we are not filmmakers. We are gathering original depositions, as one gathers important draft manuscripts. (Many who testify did not have the chance for a higher or uninterrupted secondary education: this oral history, then, is not just something that duplicates what is written down.) Using the interview in an open, non-directive manner, we capture the everyday and psychological milieu, the annals of those caught up in the Holocaust—not excluding the impact of the interview on both its parties, survivor and interviewer. In all this we consider the *welling-up of memory* as more crucial than the *imposition of a particular research interest*, however important the latter may be for the overall picture. Such interviewing has a chance of releasing detailed memories that flow—often explosively—from within.

Questions Regarding Holocaust Education in General, and the Video Testimonies in Particular

There is a question, first, concerning the exposure of young minds to a terrible and difficult knowledge. Research is needed to determine what is appropriate for each age group. But we have a clear responsibility not to turn away from genocide. The testimonies provide a strong yet sensitive approach. We do not see humiliating photos but persons struggling to recall what they have endured, and sharing their thoughts. Yes, their story has strong emotional impact; but with the aid of a teacher, whose presence is essential, a discussion can be opened about this story, or the teller of it, or the surrounding history. As Lawrence Langer has pointed out, the testimonies are extraordinary texts, and texts require interpretation. He compares oral testimony to a fragile craft that veers through turbulent waters without knowing where the safe harbor lies, or even if it exists. Thus students learn in addition to the basic facts that these experiences have no simple closure.

A related question focuses on the reliability of the testimonies. Are they not vulnerable to the deforming action of emotions and of the lapse of time? But again, they should be approached as revelatory texts, not as depositions concerned exclusively with the exact mapping of the Holocaust and the recovery of historical data. What we have before us are memoirs, not interrogations. The story of the survivor is not over at liberation. The special character of these memoirs is that they include the imaginative and even tendentious reflections of the survivors: a description of the events but also the thoughts and feelings that have accumulated around those events.

The problem, in good part, lies in ourselves: we find it hard to think about history in a context that is so charged. But as Jean Amery writes in protest: "Where is it decreed that enlightenment must be free of emotion?" If we approach the testimonies as texts, if we use them to initiate discussion and encourage reading, then both intellect and empathy come into play. To look at these powerful reminiscences as texts means to become aware of everything in them: the precise words, the rhythms, the gestures, the hesitations, the silences, the changes of affect, even the inconsistencies.

That is another reason why a teacher should be present: to encourage and field questions. These questions may be the ones we often hear. How did they survive? Could I have survived in those conditions? Could I have decided to save my life by running away, when doing so might have weakened or endangered the rest of my family? How could a nation do this to others? How did the Nazis gain the assent or silence of the Germans? Why didn't other nations protest more? Did individuals who had the courage to protest or resist share any characteristics as a group? What early warning system could we set up to prevent a recurrence of genocide? But there may also be less obvious yet troubling questions, because the survivors rarely present themselves as heroic. Moments of startling honesty and self-revelation occur which require thoughtful discussion. Systematically deprived of their human status, the survivors had to make impossible choices. However painful to think about, these aspects too need our response. We become interested, as we should have been all along, not only in what was, but in what is; not only in the grim particulars of survival but in the survivor before us; the person here rather than there, and living among us with that special burden of memory.

For additional information on the Fortunoff Video Archive, contact Joanne Rudof, Fortunoff Video Archive, Sterling Library, Yale University, New Haven, CT 06520
The Accompanying Introductory Videotapes "Seeing" and "Future Imperfect" acquaint one with some of the voices in the Fortunoff Video Archive and are available at the Facing History Resource Center.

Videotapes "Seeing" and "Future Imperfect"

Professor Geoffrey Hartman, Sandra Rosenstock, and Joanne Rudof have prepared the video programs "Seeing" and "Future Imperfect" to introduce the voices of the Holocaust survivors and witnesses in the Fortunoff Video Archive. These programs help us begin to enter the abnormal world of concentration camps that Lawrence Langer and Primo Levi discuss in their essays (**Scholars Reflect on Holocaust Video Testimonies**).

"Seeing"

The videotape "Seeing" has five excerpts from testimonies of Holocaust survivors who try to describe for us moments from their experience that represent a special vision, moments for which we have no analogy in our own experience. They strive to find the language and the imagery to convey to an outside audience like ourselves the painful qualities of those moments. With their help, we enter into some of the more difficult "sights" of the Holocaust, and wonder how to transform them into insights.

Excerpt 1: Father John S. (T-216)

Father John S., a Jesuit seminarian during the period when Jews were being deported from Hungarian-occupied Czechoslovakia to Auschwitz, tells of looking through a knothole in a fence to witness an act of cold brutality by an SS guard against a Jewish man who had jumped down from a boxcar. Father S. seems perplexed by his failure to have done anything at the time in response to this cruel attack, and wonders why. "I just didn't know what to do," he admits. "At that time I was immobilized. . . . It was beyond my experience—I was totally unprepared." The vision seen through the knothole and the subsequent paralysis become a kind of parable for anyone inquiring into the reasons why so little was done to help the victims. This episode can be used as a basis for discussing this issue. Father S. is neither defensive nor apologetic, but genuinely concerned with the question of his own failure to act.

Excerpt 2: Renee G. (T-5)

Renee G. witnessed Nazi atrocities from a very different perspective than Father S. As a young girl, she was in hiding and from behind a concealed entrance watched the roundup of local Jews, including the deportation of her grandfather and grandmother. In learning of what Renee witnessed at a young age, one wonders what the sight of a roundup has meant to her development. How can a person cope with such a memory?

Excerpt 3: Helen K. (T-58)

Helen K. provides an intimate view of being a victim of Nazi atrocities. In contrast to Father S., who watched the scenes of brutality from outside, Helen lived through them: she was on one of the cattle cars destined for the concentration camp of Maidanek. Having had her thirteen-year-old brother die in her arms in the crowded cattle car, Helen resolved that she would live. Helen's story elucidates how difficult it was for victims of the Holocaust to alter circumstances: she was in no position to help her brother, who died of lack of oxygen and overall weakness.

Excerpt 4: Leon S. (T-45)

Sometimes what a person saw during the Holocaust was so different from what was familiar that the person felt as if he or she was entering a realm of nightmare. Leon S. arrived at a labor camp to find himself greeted by creatures with yellow, shrunken faces. This haunting atmosphere resembled nothing he had ever seen before. It must have been a particularly gruesome source of terror and confusion to the prisoner. Leon's description of the explosives factory and of the use of picric acid (a chemical used in shell explosives that makes the skin turn yellow and shrivel) does little to diminish the quality of nightmare in his troubled narrative. In such a place, he says, "Your life span is only three or four months." Leon's testimony makes us aware of the ubiquity of death for inmates in the camps. As one listens to him relive the nightmares of forty-five or fifty years ago, it seems as though his experiences among the dead and dying have had a lasting influence on his life.

Excerpt 5: Edith P. (T-107)

Edith P. tries to describe Auschwitz itself and fails to find adequate words to evoke the terror and unreality of this place. In effect, she says that what she saw was not really what she saw: "The sun was not really like the sun." The Holocaust at first distorts our "sight" and our sense of reality, and then reminds us of the urgency of adapting to its sense of reality. Edith struggles to help us to "see" Auschwitz with new eyes. She says of the sun, our traditional source of warmth and illumination, "It was never life to me. It was destruction." By inverting the traditional associations of common images like the sun (she says the same thing of the moon), Edith exposes one of the fundamental paradoxes of the Holocaust experience—it upsets the values on which we base our instinct toward growth and creation.

"Future Imperfect"

The videotape "Future Imperfect" has four brief excerpts from Holocaust survivor testimonies which illustrate the abyss between traditional experience and the experience of the witnesses. Watching these excerpts, one gains a vivid sense of the limitations of conventional expressions like "learning through suffering," "living for the future," "family unity," and "the joys of parenthood" for describing how Holocaust survivors have "adapted" to life after their liberation. In these testimonies, even the idea of "liberation" assumes an unusual and ironic meaning. They represent sad and painful but utterly honest efforts by survivors to begin to explain how the Holocaust has influenced the "normalcy" of their lives.

Excerpt 1: Helen K. (T-58)

Helen K. admits that the man she married before the war and the husband who survived the Holocaust were not the same person. She assigns no blame; she merely presents truth. She questions traditional notions of suffering by asserting: "I don't know if it was all worth it." If we don't really learn anything from such experience, she implies, what was its value, its point? Her attitude is decidedly skeptical; she seems to feel that whatever gains followed the war did not (and cannot) compensate for the personal losses.

Excerpt 2: Rabbi Baruch G. (T-295)

Rabbi Baruch G. laments the absence of an extended family from "his side." At social events, only his wife's relatives are present. He too undercuts conventional notions about the joys of creating a new family after the war. "You're alone," he insists, even when you are in the midst of a large group of friends and relatives. Although traditionally liberation is considered a high point in the life of the victim, Rabbi G. says that he suffered from loneliness *more* after his liberation, offering some striking testimony on the difficulty of adapting from the "abnormalcy" of the camps to the "normalcy" of the free world. Like Helen K., he exhibits a melancholy side resulting from his experience of the Holocaust. He inhabits two worlds, one in which he wishes he could establish closer ties with his son, and the other marked by the scars that remain from the Holocaust, "and I suppose we'll be buried with them." The issue he cannot resolve is how to keep the scars from marring his efforts to create for himself a normal life. One is left with the feeling that the problem may be insoluble.

Excerpt 3: Shari B. (T-66)

Shari B. reinforces the difficulty of separating the two worlds. When her little son returns from school one day and "innocently" says "Heil Hitler," she is too shocked to do anything but ask him never to say that again. It evokes in her memories that, she believes, she has carefully concealed from her son. But subsequent events prove that the scar has been transferred to her son despite her attempts to protect him. He locks himself in the bathroom and scratches his arm until it bleeds, then tells his mother that he scratched himself to remind himself never to say "Heil Hitler" again. The mother is unable to prevent her painful past from disturbing the next generation. The son's gesture of "Heil Hitler" and the punishment he inflicts on the arm that made that gesture confirm how influences pass unnoticed from one generation to the next.

Excerpt 4: Menachem S. (T-152)

Menachem S. tells of buying many expensive toys, including electric trains and a bicycle, for his newborn daughter even before she has returned with her mother from the hospital.[1] Challenged by his wife with the peculiarity of such purchases for a newborn infant, Menachem suddenly realizes, as he admits, "I was finally buying toys for myself." This leads him to wonder what "we" are doing to the next generation, shedding further light on Shari's desperate recognition that it is impossible to isolate one's Holocaust past from the relationships one develops after that event. All of these witnesses inherit a legacy that creates for them an imperfect future. Is recognition of this fact sufficient compensation and consolation?

---

[1]Audiences should know as background information the circumstances of Menachem's separation from his parents: when he was five years old, he was at Plaszow labor camp with his parents. In order to save their son, Menachem's parents arranged for his escape from the camp, and for three years Menachem fended for himself. He was reunited with his parents at the end of the war.

"This important resource represents what
Facing History and Ourselves does best:
selection, explanation and research which
carefully guides the reader to a confrontation
with the history of the Holocaust."

Carol Gilligan
Author of *In A Different Voice*
Harvard Graduate School of Education

Elements of Time

Portraits

The video portraits of Holocaust survivors and witnesses summarize the experiences of individuals who lived through the Nazi era. The staff of the Fortunoff Video Archive for Holocaust Testimonies has edited three of these portraits—Edith P., Helen K., and Paul D.—into thirty-minute programs from longer interviews housed in the Archive. * Members of the Facing History staff have edited the other portraits, ranging in length from fifteen to thirty minutes, from video testimonies and video presentations housed in the Facing History Resource Center.

These individual stories reveal detail about daily life and decision making among victims of the Nazi regime. In the portrait of Samuel Bak, for example, we learn that his mother decided against his attending a ghetto school, preferring to find a tutor for her artistically inclined son. Her decision had a profound influence on Samuel's development: after the war he continued his art studies and eventually became an internationally recognized artist. Many of his works incorporate symbols that refer to his childhood experiences in the ghetto and labor camp. Bak's drawing on the cover of this manual, for instance, includes a wooden bird that suggests how unnatural elements may enter into the natural world in much the same fashion that the Nazis created an unnatural world, one that contradicted traditional forms of morality and social interaction, in the ghettos and concentration camps. Helen K. (A-35) made the decision, with parental pressure, to marry a baker while living in the ghetto. Although it was not a love match, her father greatly favored the union because he believed it would assure food for his daughter's survival. Edith P. (A-39) bemoans the fact that she, a survivor of the Holocaust, has failed to make a choice to help victims of the Cambodian genocide: she can't understand her impotence since she herself knows what it means to suffer brutality and inhumane treatment.

---

*References for testimonies in the Fortunoff Video Archive for Holocaust Testimonies are as follows: unedited testimonies have "T" before the number; edited testimonies have "A" before the number. Testimonies prepared by the Facing History staff are not referenced by number; they are referred to by the name of the interviewee. Fortunoff Video Archive holdings generally refer to the first name and first initial of the last name of the survivor; in this manual, full last names are only disclosed for those survivors, such as Samuel Bak and Peter Gay, who have presented portions of their testimony in other forums. Throughout *Elements of Time*, all quotes derived directly from video testimonies are shown set off and in italics.

The portraits are organized in accordance with the order of topics in the Resource Book. The first eight portraits—Samuel Bak, Sonia Weitz, Rena Finder, Edith P., Renee Scott, Rachel G., Nechama Tec, and Helen K.—describe conditions before the war and in the ghettos and concentration camps during the war years. The next three portraits—Carl H., Walter Bieringer, and Jan Karski—explain the response of Allied powers to what took place in the Nazi era and raise questions of responsibility. The next three portraits—Leon Bass, Marcus Orr, and Paul D.—reflect on the legacy of the Holocaust and the significance of keeping the world aware of what took place as a way to help prevent future abuses of human rights.

The closing portrait is an in-depth study of Peter Gay. Since Gay is himself a professor of modern European intellectual and cultural history, he is careful to describe how the historical events of the Hitler era influenced decisions he and others in his family made in the 1930s, and he reflects on the impact the Third Reich has had on the evolution of twentieth-century thought. Gay's portrait is longer than others in the manual because of the wealth of detail he provides on the social and cultural life of Berlin in the 1930s.

Material in the "Commentaries" will help put the interviewees into context. In addition to historical information on legislation and the chronology of Nazi occupation, there are descriptions of other survivors and witnesses who come from similar circumstances. There are also cross-references to relevant written and audiovisual resources available at the Facing History Resource Center.

The "Usings" suggest questions and points for discussion to accompany each portrait.

Brief Descriptions of the Portraits

Samuel Bak describes childhood experiences in the Vilna Ghetto and their impact on his career as an artist.

Sonia Weitz from Cracow relates her experiences as an adolescent in five concentration camps and displaced persons camps.

Rena Finder from Cracow explains how the industrialist Oskar Schindler helped protect her and other Jews at Plaszow and Brunnlitz.

Edith P. from Hungary describes life at Auschwitz and her journey in a cattle car to a work camp in Germany.

Helen K. relates her experiences in the Warsaw Ghetto Uprising and in Auschwitz, where she witnessed the execution of women involved in the plot to blow up the crematoria.

Renee Scott from Brussels discusses her life with the French resistance movement and her subsequent imprisonment at Ravensbruck, a concentration camp for women.

Rachel G. from Brussels tells of her girlhood experiences in hiding with Catholic clergy and families during the war and her reunion with her mother at the close of the war.

Nechama Tec from Lublin explains how she and her sister "passed" as Christians with a Polish family in order to survive the Nazi occupation of Poland.

Carl H., from a town in central Germany, relates experiences as a youth attending school in Germany after the Jewish people had been removed from his town.

Walter Bieringer, an American businessman, discusses his efforts to help place German-Jewish refugees in the United States before and after the war.

Jan Karski, who worked as a courier for the Polish underground during the war, describes his efforts to inform Allied leaders of what the Nazis were doing to Jews in occupied Poland.

Leon Bass, a black soldier who entered Buchenwald shortly after liberation, explains how the sights of Nazi atrocities affected his life.

Marcus Orr, professor of history at Memphis State University, describes what he witnessed at Dachau a few days before American troops liberated the camp.

Paul D. relates his childhood experiences in Czechoslovakia and Hungary during the Holocaust and explains how he and his mother managed to survive the war without being rounded up and sent to concentration camps.

Peter Gay describes his adolescence in Berlin between 1933 and 1939, explaining how *Kristallnacht* convinced him and other members of his family that Jews no longer had a future in the Reich.

Samuel Bak (T-618)

Little by little [in displaced persons camps and Israel after the war] I heard so many stories, so many stories [from other survivors]. And with the time it all—somehow settled down. I think I have learned to live with all this as a part of the past which sometimes is very difficult to accept as being part of myself. . . . I don't think that in the wildest novels nineteenth century written by Alexander Dumas or Sir Walter Scott things have happened that come close to what happened to myself. And all this in a certain way has maybe become a nourishing part for what I am doing as a painter in my art.

Samuel Bak

This portrait reviews the boyhood experiences of Samuel Bak immediately before and during World War II in Vilna, Poland. Born in 1933, Samuel was six when the war began in 1939 and twelve when it ended. He spent all of those years in Vilna and a nearby labor camp. Samuel and his mother were among the 200 Jewish survivors of Vilna, a city that had a Jewish population of 80,000 before the war. Afterwards, Samuel and his mother spent three years in displaced persons' camps in Germany before immigrating to Israel. Today, Bak is an internationally known artist who lives in Israel and Europe. As Samuel observes, much of his art is influenced by his childhood experiences in Vilna:

I must say in a certain way that all these experiences [in the ghetto and labor camp] have become the leitmotif—really the leading force—of what I am doing, what I am painting. I certainly do not make illustrations of things that happened. I do it in a symbolic way, in a way which only gives a sense of a world that was shattered, the world that was broken, of a world that exists again through an enormous effort to put everything together.

Although he was a small child, Samuel remembers vividly what his hometown of Vilna was like when the Germans appeared in September 1939. He had been visiting the countryside when the war started, and a relative came to bring him back home. An incident that made the six-year-old painfully aware of wartime occurred after an early bombing raid, when his father found the head of a neighbor girl that had been severed from her body. Although Samuel was spared the sight, he learned of it from his parents. "From that moment," he says, "I became an adult."

From Samuel's perspective as a small boy, the early years of the war were filled with excitement. The Russians occupied his city until 1941, and streams of refugees from German-occupied Polish cities came into Vilna. Many stayed at his home: his father, a dentist, often was called upon to help Jews hide their diamonds and gold in fillings in their teeth. In addition, both sets of grandparents moved in with Samuel and his parents; his maternal grandparents brought along their "large aquarium of fish."

In June 1941, when the Germans invaded Russia and occupied all of Poland, life became increasingly difficult for Jews in Vilna. Samuel's father had to go into a labor camp, and Samuel and his mother had no idea what had become of him. Meanwhile, Samuel's mother tried to manage the family's affairs. She surrendered gold and other valuables to officials from the Jewish community, and as food became more and more scarce, she began selling the family possessions. The first item she sold to a peasant for food was her husband's tuxedo—"the symbol of the peaceful world starting to fall apart."

By the winter of 1941-42, Samuel's father returned to the city and the entire family was forced to move from their home into the Vilna Ghetto. Samuel remembers the bitter cold and chaos that prevailed in the ghetto during these winter months. For a short time he and his parents were able to escape the ghetto, taking refuge in a monastery. The family resided with nuns for about six months, and eight-year-old Samuel was fascinated with the beauty of the residence. However, when it became too dangerous for the nuns to harbor Jews, Samuel and his parents had to return to the ghetto.

By the time Bak's family returned, the ghetto had become more settled. There were schools and cultural activities, and the Jewish Council and Police had begun organizing relief programs for the sick and needy. Samuel's mother decided against having her son attend the ghetto school and arranged for him to pursue his artwork with a tutor at home. Young as he was, Samuel's artistic talent gained recognition in the ghetto. When an art exhibition for children took place, thirty of his works were displayed. Today, as Samuel reflects on the ghetto experience, he thinks of the absurdity of an art exhibition amid the chaos and destruction of the ghetto. At the time, however, he did not think of it in this way. He was considered a celebrity, and he enjoyed the attention. He particularly cherished his prize from the exhibition—a memorial book, known as a "pincus." He painted and drew on the blank pages of this book.

The Bak family escaped the fate of the great majority of Vilna Jews who were shot at Ponary, or transported to extermination camps, or killed by disease and starvation in the ghetto. Instead, the Baks were transferred to a nearby labor camp, where Samuel's father used the manual dexterity he had developed in his dentistry to work as a welder in building railroad tracks. Samuel and other children at the labor camp were not put to work; they were free to roam within the confines of the camp while the adults were working.

Toward the end of the war Samuel and his mother managed to escape from the camp and went into hiding until liberation. Samuel's father was less fortunate; he died at the camp just a few days prior to liberation.

Commentary

There was a long tradition of Jewish culture in the city of Vilna. Many of these cultural activities were continued inside the ghetto, as the following description indicates:

Cultural Activities in the Vilna Ghetto, March 1942

The number of cultural events in March [1942] was exceptionally high, because all existing suitable premises in the ghetto, like the theater, gymnasium, youth club, and school quarters, were used. Every Sunday 6-7 events took place with over 2,000 participants. At the end of the month the Culture Department had to give up to the incoming out-of-town Jews a number of premises like the gymnasium, School No. 2, Kindergarten No. 2, and part of School No. 1. This will greatly affect the work of the schools, the sports division, and also the theater, which had to take into its building the sports division and the workers' assemblies.[1]

On March 29 an art exhibit of paintings, sculpture, graphics, etc., opened in the lobby of the theater. Fifteen artists are represented with a variety of works. Besides the noted Vilna artists. . . , a number of young artists participated. . . . Of special note are the works of three children in the exhibit. S. Wolmark and Z. Weiner sketched ghetto themes (gates of the ghetto etc.). Nine-year-old S. Bock [Samuel Bak] is considered by the jury to be extraordinarily gifted, and the jury selected 30 of his drawings to show.[2]

In his autobiographical essay "Self Portrait of the Artist as a Jew," Bak explains how the preservation of culture enabled him to escape the filth and barbarism of his surroundings:

In the ghetto in the dreadful crowding and the filth in which we lived, imprisoned between walls of brick and barbed wire, I made an attempt to escape: with the help of books. I was eight or nine years old and read for hours and hours, transported to other worlds. In this manner I became familiar with the world which was being destroyed at that very point in time. I became acquainted with the Jewish village, the *cheder*, the *yeshiva* and the *bait midrash*; Jews with beards and sidelocks; religious holidays; the days of the Bible and the history of the Jews in the land of their forefathers, the lands of their exile.[3]

The youth Y. Rudashevski leaves a similar account of education and culture in the Vilna Ghetto, stressing the significance of books and reading as means of escaping the dreary existence of ghetto life:

Thursday, 22 October 1942:

The days pass quickly. Having finished my few lessons, I begin to do a little housework. I read a book, wrote the diary and off to class. . .

Our youth group works and does not perish. Our history group works. We listen to lectures about the great French Revolution, about its periods. The second section of the history group, ghetto history, is also busy. We are investigating the history of Courtyard Shavli 4. For this purpose questionnaires have been distributed among the members, with questions that have to be asked of the courtyard residents. We have already begun to work. I go with a friend. The questions are divided into four parts: questions relating to the period of Polish, Soviet and German rule (up until the ghetto), and in the ghetto. The residents answer in different ways. Everywhere, however, the same sad ghetto song: property, certificates, hide outs, the loss of things, the loss of relatives. I got a taste of the historian's task. I sit at the table and ask questions and record the greatest sufferings with cold objectivity. I write, I probe into details, and I do not realize at all that I am probing into wounds, and the one who answers me—indifferent to it: two sons and a husband taken away—the sons Monday, the husband Thursday. . . And this horror, this tragedy is formulated by me in three words, coldly and dryly. I become absorbed in thought, and the words stare out of the paper crimson with blood. . . .

Sunday the 13th [December 1942]

. . . Today the ghetto celebrated the circulation of the 100,000th book in the ghetto library. The festival was held in the auditorium of the theatre. We came from our lessons. Various speeches were made and there was also an artistic program. The speakers analyzed the ghetto reader. Hundreds of people read in the ghetto. The reading of books in the ghetto is the greatest pleasure to me. The book unites us with the future, the book unites us with the world. The circulation of the 100,000th book is a great achievement for the ghetto, and the ghetto has the right to be proud of it.[4]

Paintings by Samuel Bak:
Elements of Time

Hiding

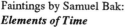

Using

Why do you think Samuel Bak observed that having an art exhibition in the ghetto was "absurd"? How was the activity of an exhibition incompatible with the conditions and daily experiences in the ghetto? Why do you think the Nazis allowed Jews to continue their cultural activities in the ghetto if they considered Jews an "inferior" people that threatened the superiority of Aryan culture?

In a recent interview Bak was asked, "You yourself have wandered a great deal—from Vilna where you were born, through the displaced persons camps of Europe, on to Israel, and then again to France and Italy. When was it during those years that you made a conscious decision to become a painter?"

Bak responded:

> The problem of choosing art as a way of life never existed for me. I was, so to speak, born into it, the ground having already been prepared for me. I was always busy painting and cared for it more than for other activities. My first exhibition took place in the Vilna Ghetto, after my teacher had taken my paintings to the poet Abraham Sutzkever, and also to Kacherginsky. The themes were biblical: The Judgment of Solomon, Moses, and also allegorical motifs.

> In 1944, just prior to the destruction of the Third Reich, Vilna was captured by the Russians. I shall never forget the day I walked through my native town, so much of which had been destroyed by the long spells of bombing and street fighting; the powerful emotions of joy and relief on finding ourselves together with the few surviving Jews, coupled with anguish on discovering that almost our entire family had perished. My father was shot at the camp, only a few days before the Russians took over.

Despite the tragic atmosphere, my mother began, with extraordinary vitality, to build a normal life. One of the first things she did was to take me to a former teacher of the Vilna Academy of Arts. He discovered some broken casts lying among the ruins of the bombed Academy, and these were to be the first models for my professional training. I believe that they explain quite a lot about my art today.[5]

In what ways does Samuel Bak view his works as a means of preserving the heritage of his city that the Nazis tried to destroy?

View the examples of Samuel Bak's art. How do they help to tell the tale of the Holocaust? What symbols does Samuel Bak use? What interpretation do you make of his work?

Study Samuel Bak's "Hiding" on the cover of *Elements of Time*. What are some of the symbols Bak uses? Do any of these symbols remind you of incidents he related in his testimony? In what ways does the drawing reflect Bak's boyhood experiences? If you had an opportunity to meet Samuel Bak, what would you want to ask him about his work?

Is art a way to remember? What does it capture? Can art raise questions? What does it leave out for you?

The Facing History Resource Center has a special information packet on the

works of Samuel Bak, which includes guidelines by Lisa Colt on how to introduce students to Bak paintings and sketches. Colt points out what students should look for regarding content as well as the technical details of form, color and

Descendants I   **Small Landscape**

9

composition. The information packet contains slides of twelve of Bak's works; reprints of Bak's most recent works; Bak's autobiographical essay and a transcript of his unedited interview; and Margot Stern Strom's discussion of how Bak's works encourage students to think in abstract terms.

Samuel Bak's recent paintings and autobiographical sketch appear in the book, *Samuel Bak: The Past Continues.*

YIVO in New York City has a collection of Samuel Bak's drawings as a child in ghettos and displaced persons camps. These drawings show nothing about the reality of the camp: they are still lifes and portraits of family members as well as illustrations for children's stories and copies of classical figures. For many years Bak had not known if these early works had survived. Last year, when he learned that they were preserved in the YIVO collection, he was very eager to see them and made special arrangements to view the collection. Slides of these early works are available at the Facing History Resource Center.[6]

Sonia Weitz

Come take this giant leap with me
Into the other world . . . the other place
And trace the eclipse of humanity . . .
Where children burned while mankind stood by,
And the universe has yet to learn why
. . . Has yet to learn why.

In this portrait Sonia Weitz speaks to a classroom about herself and her sister Blanca, who were the only survivors in a family that once numbered eighty-four. As she tells her story, Sonia incorporates poems that she composed in the ghetto and concentration camps and later reconstructed from memory in displaced persons camps after the war. Today Sonia speaks to adolescent and adult groups about her experiences, urging people to be more sensitive toward one another as they think about the lessons of Holocaust history.

Portraits

Sonia opens her presentation with a rosy picture of a happy childhood in Cracow, Poland, where she was born in 1928. She attended public schools and had many friends, both Jewish and non-Jewish. Once in a while, she relates, she would hear about antisemitism. By the late 1930s, her parents expressed the desire to leave Poland as sentiment toward the Jews grew increasingly hostile.

Sonia Weitz

Still, her young life was relatively peaceful until September 1939 when the Germans invaded Poland. During the first years of occupation Sonia recalls a series of humiliations that made life more and more difficult for Jews, and each day brought news of the death of loved ones.

Sonia especially remembers the first time she saw her father cry. It was in the opening days of the war when he learned that the ashes of a brother-in-law, murdered at one of the early concentration camps, were sent to his sister. Before Auschwitz and other Polish camps became extermination centers in 1941-1942, the Nazis still bothered with "niceties" such as sending ashes to the families.

For a short time in 1940 Jewish families in Cracow, including Sonia's, were sent to the nearby town of Tarnow. The Germans, Sonia explains, were trying to disorient them. However, Sonia's family decided to return to Cracow and enter the ghetto; those families that decided to remain in Tarnow, including many of Sonia's relatives, were shot.

On entering the Cracow Ghetto, Sonia and Blanca followed a custom that was common among sisters in the Polish ghettos. They made their ages as close as possible, hoping that the authorities would allow them to stay together. Sonia pretended she was four years older while Blanca reduced her age by four years. Blanca also secretly married her childhood sweetheart Norbert in a ghetto basement.

Sonia's mother did not survive the ghetto. Unlike her daughters, who had successfully obtained work permits, she was not allowed to work. One day the Gestapo stormed into the apartment and took her away. Sonia's poem "To Tell the World" captures the feelings of a young girl who has lost her mother.

Eventually, Sonia and those remaining in her family were sent from the ghetto to the nearby labor camp of Plaszow. Although there were no gas chambers in this camp, the guards treated the inmates mercilessly. Floggings and beatings occurred daily. In particular, Sonia recalls the day that her friend's mother was working on a road construction detail. The Commandant, Amon Goeth, came by, pulled out a gun and shot the woman. He said nothing, gave no reason. Sonia and her friend were frozen—they did not move. Resistance to such an act would have been a futile gesture, remembers Sonia. "Suppose I decided to confront him. He would have shot others in collective punishment."

Sonia and Blanca remained at Plaszow for more than a year, engaged in various labor assignments. Their work experience contrasted with that of their friend Rena Finder, who was one of the women who worked in the enamel factory of Oskar Schindler, a German Catholic industrialist who sought to protect his workers from the arbitrariness and brutality of the Nazi guards and *kapos*. [See the portrait of Rena on page 25 for additional details on Schindler's factory.]

Sonia last saw her father in Plaszow. They met in one of the barracks, and they danced together while another inmate played his harmonica. Sonia's poem "Victory" expresses the essence of what she felt in these brief moments with her father.

From Plaszow, Sonia and Blanca were sent on a transport to Auschwitz in early January 1945, only a short time before Soviet troops liberated the camp. Their father and Norbert were sent to Mauthausen. While Sonia and her sister spent only a few days at the camp, they will always remember the stench. From Auschwitz, they were sent on a death march: as the liberating forces approached in mid-January, the Nazis tried to remove evidence of the camp, forcing many of the surviving inmates to walk to camps in Germany through the snow and ice. Sonia does not have the language to describe the cold and hunger they experienced during these days. She remembers that all she wanted to do was lie down in the snow and die. Eventually they got on a transport train to Bergen-Belsen.

According to Sonia, conditions at Bergen-Belsen were worse than those at any other camp. There were long waits at the *appel* (count of inmates), no food, crowding, and sickness, especially typhus. Blanca decided that if they were to survive they would have to get out, and so they volunteered, with thirty other girls, to go to a labor camp. On the transport, Blanca contracted typhus. Sonia was terribly worried about her; she thought she would lose her. "I grew up in those weeks when she was dying. I was always worried that they would take her away."

THE POETRY

OF

SONIA
SCHREIBER
WEITZ

The Poetry of Sonia
Schreiber Weitz *(cover)*.

The labor camp was Venusberg, a small camp in Germany where parts were made for German aircraft. Sonia became violently ill with typhus and went into the infirmary. Blanca managed to drag her from the hospital so they could get on a transport for Mauthausen. Sonia remembers how her sister made her appear as though she were healthy. At Mauthausen, she continued to be sick and was still very weak at liberation. After liberation, Sonia and Blanca reunited with Norbert; their father had died in Mauthausen only a few weeks before liberation. The three survivors stayed in displaced persons camps in Austria for three years before coming to the United States and settling on Boston's North Shore.

Commentary

Survivors often tell their stories in classrooms where they lack the time to fill in details of their memories. Sonia, for example, only has time to sketch out her experiences in the ghetto and five concentration camps; specifics about her life during the war years are often omitted or only partially recalled. But Sonia has written a great deal about her Holocaust experience, and these writings supplement her classroom presentation. Particularly useful is her journal, which she discovered recently in an old trunk. Sonia wrote the journal immediately after the war in the displaced persons camp of Bindermichel. Selections from this journal enrich our understanding of her experiences during the Holocaust, providing a wealth of detail on the physical and emotional aspects of life in occupied Poland. The following is a selection from Sonia's journal.

[Sonia describes the day her mother was taken away.]

Suddenly there were heavy footsteps, and we heard the dreaded pounding on the door. The door was forced open and the OD-men were in the room.

"Adela Schreiber, get dressed! Immediately!!!"

I froze. My mother sat upon the edge of the bed, and slowly started putting on her stockings, her shoes. She put a scarf on her head.

"Dress warmly! It's a long journey."

I ran into the yard. I soundlessly screamed for help into the deaf night. My heart was breaking. I must have been screaming. The sound was wild, but it was only in my head. I couldn't cry. I stood there like a stone looking at the sky. I cursed the heavens; I shook with pain, and I trembled, and I trembled.

In reality, the night was quite calm and beautiful. Just an October night in the year of 1942. How was it possible that the sky was so peaceful, and just where was God?

[The police left after Sonia's mother fainted. They were planning to return, but for the time being she lay on the floor.]

My mother had gotten up off the floor, and she was getting dressed. Slowly, deliberately, she was putting on her dress, a sweater, a coat. How carefully she was doing all that. Calmly and with great care, as if she was getting ready to go to a movie, she combed her hair. Then, she took a bag from the closet, and from the cupboard, she took a piece of dry bread and put it into her bag. Dry bread, how horrible! And I was standing there watching her.

Suddenly the door opened, and two men in white coats with a stretcher were looking around asking, "Where is the sick person?"

"Quickly, on the stretcher and let's go!"

"No, thank you," said my mother in a strange distant voice. "I am going to make it on my own. No need for the stretcher." She added with uncommon dignity, "I will walk.

"Come closer, *Sloneczko.*"

I obeyed.

She took something from her bag, some money. She put it into my hand.

"I know you will need this, it may help." She put her arms around me and whispered, "Remember I loved you." The world was spinning in front of my eyes. As if from afar I heard her last words, "and remember to tell the world!"...

Was I ever a child? I guess not. I am old, terribly old. And yet I guess I must have been a child because that's what the world calls a small person who finds joy sitting in the sun looking at flowers, playing with dolls, but cries when her mother is taken away. And I cried too. I cried when my mother was snatched away. Kind people tried to comfort me with words like, "calm down my little girl, don't cry little girl." I responded angrily, "I am not a child. I am very, very old, but I can cry if I want to." After all, my mother was not called a child any longer when her Mamusia was snatched away; she even had me, and yet she cried.

No, I was never a child!!![7]

Historian Michael R. Marrus describes conditions at Bergen-Belsen and other German concentration camps at the close of the war, emphasizing that liberating forces were shocked by their confrontation with "the other world" that Sonia tries to describe in her poetry and stories pertaining to the Nazi era.

As the liberating armies drew close [to German concentration camps], hunger and disease killed a large proportion of the inmate population that had managed, for so long, to survive overwork, torture, and execution. Of the 1.5 million who had passed through their gates, the camps contained only a few hundred thousand living persons at the very end, most of them only barely alive.... During April and May 1945, graphic descriptions of the camps reached the West. The British and Americans were first to enter some of the largest German camps—Mauthausen, Dachau, Bergen-Belsen, Buchenwald, Dora-Nordhausen....

What the soldiers found in these places haunted even hardened military men, presumably inured to the suffering wrought by the war. Bergen-Belsen was one of the largest of these camps, liberated by the British on 15 April 1945. Built for eight thousand, it contained 40,000 skeletal prisoners when the British arrived, plus the corpses of another ten thousand. A medical officer first on the scene observed that "huts which should have contained at the most eighty to one hundred prisoners in some cases had as many as one thousand. Some huts had a lavatory, but this had long-since ceased to function and the authorities had made no provisions outside, so that conditions on the ground were appalling especially when it is realized that starvation, diarrhea and dysentery were rife." Enormous piles of dead lay everywhere. A gallows stood at the center of the camp, and a huge open grave half-filled.... To the Allied troops and to others who saw such sights, the victims were as if from another planet....

In these encounters with liberated victims of concentration camps, Allied authorities had their first direct contact with the tragedy that befell

European Jews. Nearly all the Jews liberated in Central Europe emerged from these camps. So degraded was their condition that communication was obstructed from the start. Richard Crossman, who visited the camps in the spring of 1945 as a member of the Anglo-American Committee of Inquiry on Palestine, noted how an abyss separated a place like Dachau from the rest of humanity. "Even the most sensitive and intelligent people who we met in Dachau seemed to accept it as the only reality, and to think of the outside world as a mirage. Similarly, the incoming troops, after the first rush of indignation, seemed to slump back into accepting Dachau, not as 32,000 fellow human beings like themselves, but as a strange monstrosity to be treated on its own standards." However horrified, the liberators often failed to see the victims as fellow creatures: "One realized how little horror has to do with sympathy, Sympathy demands some common experience."[8]

Dr. Paul Heller, who was an inmate in Buchenwald and Auschwitz from 1939 until 1945, kept a diary of the death march from Auschwitz in January 1945. Heller was involved in a 16-day westward march from Jaworno in Eastern Silesia to the camp of Gross Rosen in Silesia and finally to Buchenwald, near Weimar, where he remained until liberation on April 11, 1945. Dr. Heller's entries for January 19 and 20, 1945 allude to many of the same physical and emotional strains that Sonia and others who survived the death marches have recalled in their memories of the liberation of Auschwitz:

January 19, 1945

Most of us walk in a trance obeying an unknown forceful hypnotizing power. Almost all of us are plagued by unbearable thirst and exhaustion. We swallow snow. I collect my last spiritual strength and attempt rationally to dissect the symptoms of exhaustion. The head hurts, it seems as if all thoughts are in turmoil and one is incapable of putting order into them. All associations seem to fall apart. The past, the present, the future are all in a chaotic mixture. Nightmares in a half-awake state. I feel strong enough to become my own observer and to realize that the organization of my soul and mind is disintegrating. I see all the trouble but I cannot avert it. I cannot help but yield to these powerful forces of inner disorder. I know that I must collect my strength because, if I fall, the SS will kill me. This is how I know I am not yet completely demented; I still know where danger lies. Something inside raises its voice: Collect your strength, you must, you must go on, because next to you is the rifle of an SS soldier.

Daybreak—and we still march, march, march without stopping. Toward noon I really go on but—what a miracle at a critical moment!—we are ordered to halt and take a rest. I have the feeling that I have high fever, I talk nonsense, I know it, but as if there were a spontaneous purgation of the brain, I feel forced to say in full awareness of the nonsense. Like a drunkard I babble irrationally saying, as some prisoners tell me later, that we were going home to the infirmary where I would go to bed. . . . Fortunately, minutes later we entered a large deserted and empty storage shed. There I found sleep that lasted almost 12 hours and helped to restore order in my brain, but when I woke up I realized how horrible the night must have been to others. I tried to reconstruct what happened. We, a crowd of completely exhausted prisoners, hungry, tired, thirsty, most of them with disturbed minds, were driven into the shed where most of us just sank mechanically to the ground. There was no straw, no soft spot; there were a few boards, but most of the ground was frozen earth. When I woke up I could not believe what I saw. Many prisoners were dead, some of them had stab wounds from pocket knives on their hands, necks, and faces. They must have fought for resting places and stabbed each other. It seemed there was an outbreak of mass madness. I was preserved from it in my little corner, where all this turmoil did not awaken me.

January 20, 1945

We were told that 121 prisoners died during the night. More than 100 were severely injured and could not continue the march . . . .

The march continued along the main road westward. We got used to the thirst, to the hunger—the turnip soup could not have stilled it—to the shooting. Most of us somehow converted ourselves into mechanical puppets and switched off all normal responses. The strong will to survive seemed to have produced this kind of defense mechanism. Next to me my friend collapsed. I tried to pull him along to prevent his being shot and he really responded to my admonition. Suddenly, we were ordered to stop. Apparently Russian tanks had overtaken us along a parallel road and the SS leaders had to change their "strategy." After a few minutes we were ordered to leave the road and make for the snowy fields to the south. We still were approximately 2,500 prisoners and 300 SS guards. Everything seemed hopeless. No chance of escaping. We walked up to the knees in snow. Every step was a struggle. In the distance fires became visible. We were told that the retreating German soldiers dynamited bridges. The detonations sounded like continuous thunder. We hoped that the SS would flee and leave us to our fate. It did not happen. . . . On the contrary they became increasingly hostile toward us and shot everybody who, losing his strength stayed behind. Our number shrank within a few hours; toward the end of the night there must have been one SS guard for six or seven prisoners. The temperature must have been several degrees below zero. Our limbs began to feel dead. They seemed to obey the laws of a lifeless machine. The only driving force was the fear of being shot and the hope that the SS would give up. This hope increased when we arrived in a small town where the inhabitants prepared for evacuation. But it looked as if most of them would stay in their houses, after all, as if there was no longer any time left for seeking safety. We were rushed through the town and the

fatigue was getting close to the breaking point. Toward morning we
reached a forest and suddenly saw the electrical fence and the barracks of
the concentration camp of Blechhammer. We were chased into the camp
im laufschritt [at a trot].[9]

In 1986, Sonia joined ninety-four citizens from Boston on a trip through
Poland where she revisited her native Cracow, the site of the former labor
camp at Plaszow, and Auschwitz. Speaking about this experience after her
return, Sonia explained why she believes it is so important for Christians and
Jews to revisit this history and contemplate its lessons:

> My recent trip to Poland with Cardinal Law and one-hundred Catholic
> pilgrims was both a traumatic and yet a truly rewarding experience.
> Returning to my childhood home in Kracow, . . . standing by the ghetto
> wall on the Umschlag-Platz from where my mother was sent to the death
> camp at Belzec, praying upon the hill of the concentration camp Plaszow
> where I last saw my father. . . .
>
> I cannot describe Auschwitz revisited. Tearing at the scars, . . .
> reawakening old nightmares, . . . the agony of standing upon the graveyard
> of my people.
>
> And yet, I am glad I went. As a survivor, I tried to make this piece of evil
> history a little more real for these Christians who sincerely wanted to share
> my pain.[10]

Using

Sonia often begins her presentations with the following poem:
> Come take this giant leap with me
> Into the other world. . . the other place
> And trace the eclipse of humanity. . .
> Where children burned while mankind stood by,
> And the universe has yet to learn why
> . . . Has yet to learn why.

Why does she refer to her years in the ghetto and concentration camps as "the
other world" and "the other place"? How does she attempt to bring her
audience into this "other world"? Has she succeeded in making this leap for
you in her presentation?

Since Sonia's 1986 pilgrimage to Poland with Cardinal Bernard Law and
other civic and religious leaders, she has altered the format of her
presentation: before she describes what happened to her during the war, she
describes how the places of her childhood look today: Cracow, Plaszow,
Auschwitz. According to Sonia, seeing these places triggered memories that
she had forgotten in the postwar decades.

Scenes from the displaced persons camp at Linz, Austria.

"Someone said that it takes 40 years for memories to fade," Sonia reflected in a recent presentation at Trinity College. "I can tell you that the memories and the nightmares became more vivid. When we arrived in Warsaw, it was raining and miserable, and Warsaw is not that beautiful a city anyway. And I thought, 'I have it made. I am emotionally immune.' But we had not yet gone to Cracow. [Upon arriving at Cracow she found it was] beautiful. The sun was shining, and not much had really changed. . . . I realized that I was not made of stone."[11]

Read Lawrence Langer's essay "Interpreting Oral and Written Holocaust Texts" in **Scholars Reflect**

Identity Papers of Sonia Schreiber Weitz.

on Holocaust Video Testimonies. Do you think that Langer's distinctions between oral and written texts are found when comparing Sonia's video testimony and her journal entry?

Rena Finder, Holocaust survivor from Cracow, has been Sonia's friend since their girlhood before the war. The portrait of Rena (immediately following the portrait of Sonia) chronicles her experiences in several of the same places that Sonia spent the war years: the Cracow Ghetto, Plaszow, Auschwitz. Compare the stories of these two women.

Using information from Sonia's testimony, describe conditions for workers at the Plaszow Labor Camp.

Using the following documents pertaining to Sonia's liberation and experience in displaced persons camps, answer the following questions: When and where was Sonia liberated? Why do you think Sonia used her sister's married name (Borer) during the war? What was Sonia's physical appearance when she entered the American zone of occupation? Why is the term "stateless" used to describe Sonia's citizenship in the postwar years? Why do you think she shifted from using her sister's married name to her father's surname (Schreiber) in the displaced persons' camps?

From Sonia's testimony and the testimonies of other survivors, why is it important to know about the immigration process after World War II? What does this process suggest about the willingness of nations to confront the persecution of the Jews and other minorities during the Nazi era and take responsibility for helping survivors readjust to a normal existence?

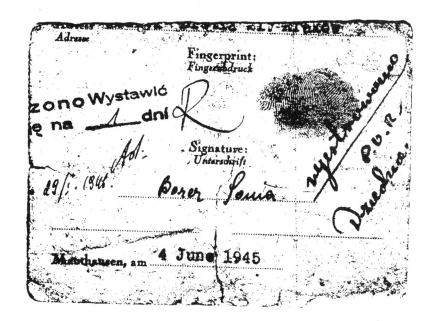

Compare Elie Wiesel's description of his "stateless" years with Sonia's discussion of the war years when she and others in her family were classified as "stateless":

> For years and years [from the time of his roundup in Hungary in 1944 until 1963] I remained stateless. Do Americans, the American-born, know what it means to be stateless? It means to feel unwanted everywhere. It means to arouse suspicion at every border. . . . Like a Kafka character, you feel guilty merely for having undergone the punishment of suffering. Unprotected by any government, the stateless person can be and often is humiliated by anyone. A stateless person is not a person—not in the eyes of bureaucrats.[12]

Poems that Sonia reads in conjunction with her presentations are collected in *The Poetry of Sonia Schreiber Weitz*, available at the Facing History Resource Center. Sonia's poetry can be used in an English or social studies class in conjunction with her personal visit or her video portrait. Chris McDonnell, an eighth grade social studies and English teacher, assigned Sonia's poetry and asked students to write in their journals about their reactions. Sonia made a guest appearance and related her story with selections from her poetry. McDonnell has prepared guidelines, reprinted below, for introducing students to Sonia and her poetry.

Using Sonia Weitz's Poetry in the Facing History and Ourselves Classroom

by Christine McDonnell

In the Facing History and Ourselves program, one of the most difficult sections is that which confronts the experience of the victims in concentration camps. Lawrence Langer speaks of our inability to find words to convey the horror, our need for a new language to express realities that the world had never seen before. Primo Levi speaks of the inadequacies of words like "hunger," "fear," "tiredness," when applied to the camp experience. Zezette Larsen, a survivor of Auschwitz, tells classes that she stopped speaking altogether for four months after being in the camps as a young teenager. Our students themselves are often at a loss for words after they have seen films of the camps, or read first hand accounts. Ordinary words seem insufficient, even trivial.

Poetry, because of its compact intensity and because of the ability of image and metaphor to capture elusive ideas and feelings, is well suited to this section of the course. Poetry can be simultaneously personal and abstract. It can both evoke a specific experience and draw a universal conclusion. It helps us reflect and respond.

Sonia Weitz has written poetry about her experiences in the ghetto and in the five concentration camps she was in. I used Sonia Weitz's poems with an eighth grade class as part of the Facing History course. Different poems touched different students in very personal ways. The class periods that we gave to the reading of the poems had a special quiet, reflective tone. Listening together, sharing the responsibility of reading the words out loud, taking time to note our personal responses and questions for each poem and then sharing these with each other strengthened our feeling of community at this difficult stage of the course.

We prepared for Sonia Weitz's poems by reading several poems by the children in the Terezin concentration camp, from the collection *I Never Saw Another Butterfly*. We talked about the different emotions we heard in the poems: fear, anger, hope, joy, kindness, bitterness, sadness, confusion, despair, etc. At the back of the book there are brief biographies of the different children. I read the biography of each child after their poem. The goal was to accustom the class to simply listening, to have them notice what they were hearing, and to help them realize that each poem was written by an individual. (Many of the children represented in the collections are twelve to fifteen years old.) The class had also seen a videotape of Sonia Weitz speaking at a Facing History and Ourselves institute. As part of her speech, she read several poems out loud.

Sonia's poetry is direct. It is often the content of the poems, the experiences described, that makes them powerful, rather than language or structure. This makes these poems enormously accessible to students. It also makes them tricky to use in class. They are inappropriate for intricate analysis. In any case, it is good to remember that extensive analysis can be dangerous. An author I heard once cautioned [that] the end product of dissection is a dead butterfly.

Rather than analyzing Sonia Weitz's poetry, I asked students to listen carefully, reread, note their reactions and then share them. To help them do this, I asked the class to divide several pieces of looseleaf paper in half lengthwise. On one side of the page they noted parts of the poem that were especially powerful for them personally. On the other half of the page they wrote questions they had about each poem. We went through the poems one at a time. One student read the introduction. Another student read the poem. Then there was time for rereading silently, making notes on their papers. I asked if anyone would like to hear the poem read again. We read most of the poems in class over two or three class periods. Students asked if they had to have questions or things that they found powerful for each poem. I answered no, not all poems will affect us; each of us will find different poems powerful.

The purpose of the two-column sheets was to help students notice and keep track of specific details in the poems so they could refer to these in discussions. When Sonia Weitz visited our class, these notes helped students remember the poems and their questions. Noticing specific details—words, images, comparisons—increases enjoyment and appreciation of the poems. The class as a whole can try to answer the questions that students have about the poems. Their own theories and insights are valuable in provoking thought and understanding.

Students' questions ranged from concrete, practical questions about the content of a poem to abstract discussions of particular words and images. Both types of questions are part of responding to poetry. The following questions raised by the poem "Victory" demonstrate this:

—How did Sonia manage to sneak into her father's barracks?

—How did the boy manage to have a harmonica?

—Why are there quotation marks around the word 'take'?

—What does the last sentence mean: "There are no tools to measure love and only fools would fail to scale your victory"?

—Why did Sonia's father bother to dance with her?

—What does this moment show us about life in a concentration camp?

—What does the title of the poem mean; in what way was this act a victory?

My students found the poems intensely moving. For some, the content was more powerful than the films or accounts that they had seen. They were struck by the images and details. For other, the poems gave an emotional release. For many, the poems were springboards for their own poetry. After reading her poetry, the class wrote letters to Sonia Weitz. They shared the poem that had touched them most, and thanked her for putting her experiences into words. There was a seriousness and depth to their reactions that excited me as a teacher. Her poetry gave them language, reflection, and response.

Poetry is not the only route to understanding this difficult part of the course. For many classes the films and accounts may be sufficient or more appropriate. But I hope that others will consider this poetry as part of the course. It does not require intricate introduction. Often a good poem will spark discussion spontaneously. Poetry doesn't require kid gloves or special language. If you make time for the words to be heard out loud, help students notice particular details and content, and make room for students' personal reactions, the poems will work their own magic.

What can help make the poems even more effective is a visit or video testimony by the poet. Although Sonia was able to visit McDonnell's class personally, using the video portrait including Sonia's reading of several of her own poems can help students connect with the survivor-poet.

Rena Finder

Schindler was like a God to me. He was tall, blond, and handsome. I never got to meet him directly, but I saw him as he came through the factory, and I always felt safe under him.

This tape reviews the wartime experiences of Rena Finder, who spent her adolescence in the Cracow Ghetto and three concentration camps. Although Rena was a friend and neighbor of Sonia Weitz (whose story also appears on page 10), Rena's experiences during the Holocaust differed from those of Sonia. Following the war, Rena met Sonia again and she and her new husband, Mark, emigrated to the United States with Sonia and Sonia's sister and brother-in-law. Today Rena speaks in classrooms and adult education classes about her experiences. Like Sonia, she hopes that her presentations will encourage people to think of ways to prevent abuses of human rights.

Rena was born in Cracow, Poland in 1929 and grew up in a middle class neighborhood living with parents and relatives. Attending a public school just a block from her home, she made close friends among the other Jewish girls in her class and had little to do with her Christian classmates. In these years, Rena developed a tremendous love of learning: she was curious about everything and read whatever she could get her hands on.

Rena's entire lifestyle began to change with the German invasion of Poland in

September 1939. After the Germans imposed a series of restrictions on Jewish economic and cultural life, Jews were forced to move into the ghetto, which was isolated from the rest of Cracow. Rather bitterly, Rena recalls how non-Jews who were able to see all that was happening to Jews did nothing to help their Jewish neighbors. "No one saw anything; no one heard anything; no one said anything."

In the ghetto, the Gestapo took Rena's father away and he never returned to his family. Rena and her mother secured work in the ghetto workshops, and Rena helped care for several younger cousins who had been orphaned.

In time, the SS made plans for the evacuation of the ghetto, ordering all the residents to move up the hill to the Plaszow work camp, located on the site of an old Jewish cemetery. Shortly before departing for Plaszow, Rena and her mother were forced to deposit their young wards at the children's home. The officials promised that the children would receive special treatment in the home. Nevertheless, the children were never again heard from.

Amon Goeth, Commandant of Plaszow.

Like Sonia, Rena remembers Goeth, the commandant of Plaszow, as a sadistic man who seemed to take pleasure in abusing the inmates. Despite the cruel surroundings, Rena points out that Jews did manage to find ways to help one another. For example, she recalls how she and her mother helped hide young children who had been smuggled from the ghetto. They even managed to protect the children when the SS made inspections to disinfect the barracks.

From Rena's perspective, the most hopeful ray of light at Plaszow was Emalia, a ceramics and ammunition factory owned by the German Christian industrialist Oskar Schindler. Unlike other industrialists such as the managers of Krupp and I.G. Farben, who took advantage of slave labor in the SS camps and mistreated their workers, Schindler did everything in his power to provide his Jews with sufficient food and accommodations. Rena and her mother had an influential relative on the Jewish Council, who had them enumerated on Schindler's list. Thus for six months they had the good fortune of being *Schindlerfrauen*, women working at Emalia under far more humane conditions than those in other plants at Plaszow.

However, in 1943 the SS forced Schindler to dismantle Emalia; his male workers were sent to Gross Rosen and Mauthausen, and the *Schindlerfrauen* went to Auschwitz-Birkenau.

The trip to Auschwitz was a nightmare for thirteen-year-old Rena. The four-hour journey took four days in crowded cattle cars with people dying like flies from starvation and sickness. Once at Auschwitz, they were forced to march towards the showers, where they were shaved and sprayed with disinfectant. "I looked around," says Rena, "at the people. I was with some of my friends from Plaszow and with my mother, and I could not believe what I saw. They were all shaved, and so was I. It was at this point that I felt totally humiliated, totally dehumanized. I had disappeared; I wasn't me anymore."

As in the ghetto and work camp, Rena and her mother were able to work in factories and live in the same barracks with other women from Cracow. Rena's greatest fear was that she would be separated from her mother, and on several occasions such a separation was imminent.

By 1944, Schindler had relocated his factory to Brunnlitz, Czechoslovakia and had negotiated with the SS to send his former workers from Emalia to the Brunnlitz plant. The male workers arrived in Czechoslovakia first. Then after months of delicate negotiations with Auschwitz authorities, Schindler arranged for the return of his female workers.

Rena and her mother were among the 180 *Schindlerfrauen* loaded on a train for Czechoslovakia in the fall of 1944. At Brunnlitz they felt as secure as they had felt at Emalia. Schindler spent a fortune negotiating with guards not to harm his workers and obtaining good bread on the black market. "Schindler saved our lives," declares Rena. "Had we gone to Bergen-Belsen where the other women went, we would have surely died. I was so weak and sick at the time, and he [Schindler] gave us more food than others got."

The Russians liberated Brunnlitz in May 1945 and arranged to send the prisoners on a train back to Cracow. After Rena and her mother returned to their native city, they realized how little the Poles wanted Jews.

Unwelcome in Poland, Rena and her mother joined the thousands of other survivors in displaced persons camps located in Germany and Austria. Here, for three long years, they waited for a visa to come to the United States to be with a family friend who had settled in Peabody, Massachusetts before the war. In 1948 Rena moved to the United States with her husband Mark, whom she had married in 1946, and her girlhood friends Sonia and Blanca.

Commentary

Oskar Schindler was an unlikely heroic figure. Although he had an important role in saving the lives of at least 1,200 Jews during the Holocaust, he had a prewar reputation as a womanizer and opportunist and had been known to commit dishonest acts. Born in 1908 in Zwittau, a small industrial city in the empire of Austria-Hungary, Oskar was the son of an owner of a farm machinery plant, and he trained to become an engineer. After World War I, Zwittau became part of the newly created state of Czechoslovakia. Oskar married the daughter of a gentleman farmer and was drafted to serve in the army. After his service, he joined his father to work in the family factory until the business collapsed in the Depression. Oskar next found work as a salesman, and he joined the Nazi Party because this helped when he was conducting business with German companies. When the war broke out, Schindler went to Cracow to take advantage of the profits to be made from the war. He took charge of the factory, Emalia, that was commissioned to supply the German army with mess kits and field kitchenware. Although his original intentions were to reap profits from the military situation, Schindler became more and more hostile to the Nazi regime as he witnessed the persecution of the Jews, and he began to take measures to negotiate for Jews working in his factory. His rescue activities increased as the war progressed, and by the final year of the war he was responsible for saving at least 1,200 Jewish men and women who worked in his plants.

Thomas Keneally's *Schlindler's List* traces Schindler's career, showing the sharp difference between his prewar behavior and his rescue work during the war years. Keneally interviewed many Jews who had been saved by Schindler as well as people who had known him before the war.

Luitgard Wundheiler's "Oskar Schindler's Moral Development during the Holocaust" analyzes the development of Schindler during the war years, showing two main trends: 1) Schindler went from being an impulsive and at times opportunistic helper to one who was a compassionate person and finally a principled altruist; and 2) Schindler evolved from one who helped those he knew directly to helping human beings he did not know at all. According to Wundheiler the transformation of Schindler during the war years was largely due to the fact that he gained a stronger identity of who he was and what he stood for; the stronger his self-identity, the greater his desire to be engaged in acts of rescue.

In addition to the valuable insights Rena provides on life in Schindler's factories, she suggests ways that inmates at Plaszow offered resistance to the Goeth administration. As Rena explains, the inmates cooperated in hiding a baby and protecting young children from roundups. Rena also points out that familial and social connections in the Cracow Ghetto and at Plaszow were important in obtaining certain privileges: in her own case it was the privilege of securing work with Schindler.

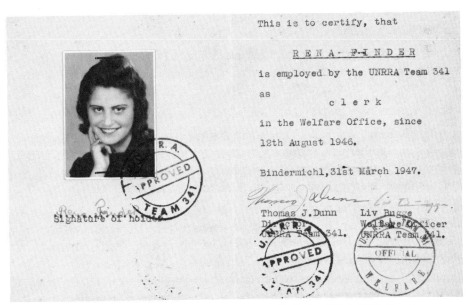

Rena Finder worked as a clerk for the United Nations Relief and Rehabilitation Agency (UNRRA) immediately after the war.

Chronology of the Cracow Ghetto and Plaszow Labor Camp

March 20, 1941: Cracow Ghetto established. All Jews forced to live in the section of Cracow known as Podgorze, surrounded by high walls. Jews no longer able to receive wages for their labor; factory owners have to pay fixed sums to the SS for each Jewish worker used.

March 14, 1943: Cracow Ghetto liquidated. Those Jews still alive after the liquidation sent to the forced labor camp Plaszow or to the newly created mass killing centers.

Summer 1943: Schindler's factory in Plaszow officially designated part of the forced labor system.

January 1944: Status of Plaszow changed from a forced labor camp to a concentration camp under the direct control of General Pohl, centered in Oranienburg near Berlin.

Fall 1944: Orders from Oranienburg call for the disbanding of Plaszow and transport of prisoners to Auschwitz and Gross Rosen.

Using

Describe the incidents in the ghetto when Rena and her mother realized the danger to the children.

Compare Rena's memory of Goeth with Sonia's.

Compare the work conditions for Rena and Sonia at Plaszow. To what extent was Rena privileged to have the opportunity to work for Schindler?

What did Oskar Schindler do for Jews at Plaszow and Brunnlitz? How does his behavior compare with that of other industrialists?

According to Rena, it was very important that she be with her mother and know that her mother was all right. Compare her relationship with her mother to the relationship Sonia Weitz had with her sister during the Holocaust. Do you think these relationships contributed to their survival?

Holocaust survivor Mieczyslaw Pemper said of Schindler, "If there had been a dozen Schindlers, the political situation of the time would have looked different." Another survivor shrugged his shoulders at hearing this and said, "What Schindler did was unrepeatable."[13] Discuss these contrasting assessments: explain your position on Schindler. To what extent did Rena's testimony help you decide your views on the rescue work of Schindler?

From your reading and discussions on the perpetrators and bystanders in the Nazi era, what was the typical response of German industrialists and businessmen to the National Socialist administration and legislation? How does this typical response compare with that of Oskar Schindler?

An article on "Rena Finder: Schindlerfrau" appeared in the *Facing History News* (Summer 1985); copies are available at the Facing History Resource Center.

A thirty-minute television documentary on Wallenberg and Schindler entitled "The Making of a Hero," originally aired on *Chronicle*, is available on half-inch VHS at the Facing History Resource Center.

Copies of Thomas Keneally's book, *Schindler's List*, and Luitgard Wundheiler's article, "Oskar Schindler's Moral Development during the Holocaust," are available at the Facing History Resource Center. These are excellent sources for teachers preparing to discuss rescuers and questions of resistance during the Holocaust.

"Schindler's Jews," Chapter 3 in Milton Meltzer's *Rescue: The Story of How Gentiles Saved Jews in the Holocaust*, is a readable account of Schindler's life for adolescents. Meltzer's narrative emphasizes that Schindler became increasingly involved in rescue work as the war progressed and he learned of the Nazi plans for annihilation of Jews. Meltzer also has a detailed account of the move of Schindler's factory from Plaszow to Brunnlitz.

Birkenau. SS Guardhouse called "Death"s Gate," through which came the trains carrying those destined for extermination.

Edith P. (A-39)

*One day [in June 1944] my father came home and said we had just had a
conference with one of the . . . SS officers and he told us within three days
we had to leave this town and we had to go to a brick factory . . . and we
were going to be leaving for Germany. . . . . In those few days we had to
leave everything that my father worked for [for] 36 years. . . . [T]his was
the last time that our family was together.*

This portrait describes Edith's life from the prewar years in Eastern
Czechoslovakia until her liberation from Auschwitz in 1945. It concludes with
Edith's observations about current events.

Edith, one of six children in a well-to-do Hungarian family, was an adolescent
when the Germans first came to her town. She remembers numerous
incidents, beginning when the Germans initially appeared in her town, that
presaged trouble for Jews. Almost immediately, Jews were required to wear
the Star of David and her father, a devout Jew, was forced to shave his beard.
The drunken German soldiers were rowdy and broke windows and made

Birkenau. Part of the women's camp.

threats, leaving Edith—and all the other Jews—in a constant state of fear. But her most poignant memory is of a friend who visited her one afternoon: Edith showed her two new pairs of shoes. Her friend said that she should get the shoes since Edith would have no use for them anymore where she was going.

Shortly after this incident Edith's entire family, including her ninety-year-old grandmother, were temporarily placed in a brick factory. Terrified and uncertain of their futures, they were treated like animals by their German captors. Next they were herded into railroad boxcars with about ninety people in each car. The heat and lack of air overwhelmed her parents. Today, explains Edith, she understands something of the anguish her mother experienced in that boxcar as she imagined the fate of her six children. Before the family arrived at Auschwitz, Edith's father told his children: "Whoever survives, you've got to go and work right away. Sell your knowledge and go to work. Keep your sanity and keep the principles that you have been taught."

Edith was separated from her parents and brothers and sisters at Auschwitz. By luck, her sister-in-law found her in Block 23 and brought her to block 16 so they could be together. The very next day, Edith learned that all the inhabitants of Block 23 were taken to the crematorium. "From that day on, I knew I'm a survivor."

"Auschwitz," says Edith, "was hell on earth." Like Zezette (a survivor from Belgium whose testimony is found in the video montage "Childhood Memories"), who remembers remaining silent the entire time in Auschwitz, Edith mentions the terrible silence of the days and nights and how she and other prisoners—hungry, dressed in rags, and degraded—suffered the "humiliation of our souls."

Toward the end of the war, Edith and her sister-in-law volunteered to work as cooks for the SS and were sent to the camp at Salzwedel. During this trip Edith remembers looking outside the boxcar where she saw "paradise"—a normal world with women carrying their babies in bright sunshine. This was a world, she recalls, "[where] people were people, not animals."

Edith and her sister were liberated at Salzwedel. Two American soldiers, one white and one black, told them they were free. Edith had never before seen a black man and decided immediately that she loved him. He stood erect "maybe because he understood." Even though she despaired when she realized the loss of so many in her family, she kept in mind her father's words: "Keep all your principles that you brought from home and go work. Sell your knowledge." Having learned English in school, she was able to get a job as an interpreter in the displaced persons camps.

Today Edith is the mother of three children and lives in a suburban Connecticut community. She is plagued by the thought that the world has not learned from the Holocaust; she suffered a deep depression upon learning of the plight of the Cambodians. Why do we do nothing? she asks.

Using

Paul is another interviewee in **Portraits** who, like Edith, was in Czechoslovakia when the German forces occupied the country and began rounding up Jews. Compare Paul's experience with his grandparents with that of Edith and her family.

Silence provided a means of coping with the abnormal world of Auschwitz for Edith and Zezette (Excerpt 8 in "Childhood Memories"). Referring to the testimonies of other survivors, consider the various ways of enduring amid the brutality, death, sadism, and uncertainty of the concentration camps.

What were the "principles" that Edith's father referred to in his parting words?

What skills had Edith developed before the Holocaust that enabled her to find meaningful work in the immediate postwar period? Why were these skills so valued by UNRRA (United Nations Relief and Rehabilitation Administration) and other rehabilitation agencies after the war?

Helen K. (A-35)

I was a very immature, very sheltered little girl. And when the world war came I grew up overnight. I really did.

This portrait traces the Holocaust experience of Helen, a Polish Jew who survived the Warsaw Ghetto and several concentration camps. Helen, born in Warsaw in 1924, was living with her parents, three brothers, and one sister when the Germans invaded Poland on September 1, 1939. By the time her family realized the danger, Helen says, it was too late for them to do anything.

Shortly before the invasion, the Germans and Russians made a secret agreement to divide Poland once the Germans moved into the country. As the Germans moved east, the Russians moved west, stopping at the agreed line of demarcation. Some Jews, fearing the approach of the Germans, fled to the Russian-occupied zone for safety. Although the Russians did arrest and transport eastward some of the wealthy Polish landowners and businessmen, they did not single out the Jews for persecution. Thus some Polish Jews were able to move deep into Soviet territory, where they found work or joined the army. As a result, many of those Jews survived the war.

Helen's two older brothers remained near the line of demarcation. In June 1941, when the Germans broke their treaty and invaded the Soviet Union, the SS caught Helen's brothers. After forcing them to dig their own graves, the SS shot them.

In Warsaw, the Germans established a ghetto to segregate the Jews from the rest of the population. The Warsaw Ghetto was overcrowded from the outset because Jews from all parts of Poland were forced into it. One day Helen's father went out to the nearby pharmacy, and the family never saw him again. The Germans often rounded up Jews on the street and carted them off for labor battalions or to mass executions. Helen's father was killed in this way.

Helen, her mother, sister and remaining brother lived in a ghetto building called Mila 18. (Leon Uris's novel *Mila 18* was named for this building.) Starting in July 1942, the Germans deported more than 300,000 Jews from the Warsaw Ghetto to the death camp at Treblinka. After a brief lull, the Germans resumed deportations in January 1943. There was some resistance, and many Jews were killed. In April 1943, the Germans decided on the total liquidation of the ghetto, where about 50,000 Jews remained. A small percentage of the remaining Jews, mostly young people, formed a resistance group and resolved to fight back with whatever weapons they could secure through purchase from the Polish underground outside the ghetto. The headquarters for the Jewish underground was a bunker in the cellar of Mila 18, Helen's building.

Helen offers eyewitness accounts of the fighting, which lasted for more than five weeks against overwhelming odds. Her mother was taken away first. Helen and her brother and sister were among the last persons to leave the building.

Helen describes the boxcar journey to Maidanek, a large labor camp and death camp in eastern Poland. During the journey her younger brother died in her arms, and when she arrived at Maidanek, she watched as her mother was taken away to the gas chambers.

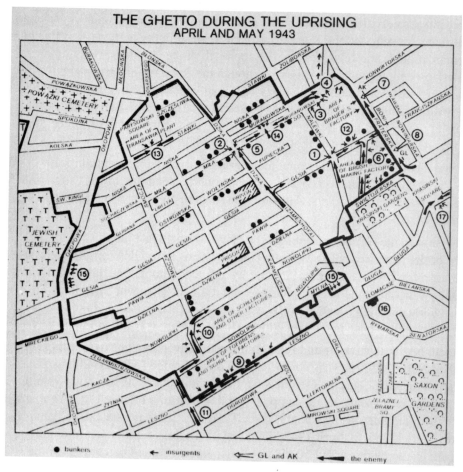

The Warsaw Ghetto during the Uprising, April and May 1943. Note that 14 marks the location of Mila 18 where Helen K. was staying at the end of the uprising.

At Maidanek, Helen shared a bunk with her sister-in-law, who developed dysentery. "I stayed until she became stiff and cold in my arms."

From Maidanek Helen was sent to Auschwitz, where she helped a woman give birth to her baby. She and other prisoners hid the woman's pregnancy since none of them wanted to "oblige" Hitler by dying. (The baby died shortly after birth.) At Auschwitz, Helen lived with several women who worked in a munitions factory at Auschwitz-Monowitz, the labor camp section of the complex that also contained gassing facilities. On one occasion, four of the women smuggled out capsules of explosive powder, which they hid in various parts of their body and then turned over to members of the Jewish underground in the camp. On October 7, 1944, before the gassing facilities were scheduled to be dismantled, this group blew up and destroyed one of the four crematoria and damaged a second one. By tracing fragments of the explosive material, the Germans were able to locate the women responsible for the smuggling. They hanged them publicly and left their bodies on the gallows for three days.

Helen was liberated in Auschwitz by advancing Soviet troops in January 1945. She spent two years recuperating in a sanatorium. She says she lost five years of her life: "I was never young."

Commentary

Mordecai Anielewicz, Warsaw Ghetto Revolt Commander, described the spirit of resistance in Mila 18 (headquarters for the resistance organization heading the revolt) and other hiding places for Jews in his last letter on April 23, 1943:

> What we have experienced cannot be described in words. We are aware of one thing only; what has happened has exceeded all our dreams. . . . Beginning with this evening we are passing to partisan tactics. . . . Jewish self-defense in the Warsaw ghetto has become a reality. I have been witness of the magnificent heroic struggle of our Jewish fighters.[15]

Leon Najberg who, like Helen, managed to hold out in Mila 18 until the end of the uprising, wrote an account on May 19, 1943 which supplements details in Helen's story abut the final hours in the bunker:

> "We are on the third floor and we have done away with the stairs. We go upstairs with the help of a rope-ladder. We are in burnt rooms. . . . One floor lower there is an apartment of Tojst, quite saved and with complete furnishings. I am looking at that apartment and see an analogy to present life of Jews. From among families there are . . . only individuals who saved

their lives, from the whole streets which were occupied by Jews—individuals. From Jewish towns—individuals. From the whole Poland, from the millions—the thousands. And that life of ours is for the present saved by a miracle and overshadowed by the ruins of Polish Jewry. It is useless and incapable of anything and forever unfit for normal life. Though our hearts are still beating, there will never be a joy of life in them. After months of darkness and stuffiness we can again bask in the sun, fresh air and light of day. We are once again people who see sky and sun though sun does not shine for everybody.

"At 4 Walowa Street two bodies of new female victims lie and sun speeds up their decay and ants and crows eat up pieces of flesh from faces. There was a quiet at noon.

"The murderers arrived only at 1 P.M. and uncovered the bunker at 38 Swietojerska Street. After having bored holes, the Huns have let in 'foreign,' that is, poison gas, and smoked out people. Then, after preliminary work, searching the captives and robbery of the properties, they have been forcing victims to confess where Jews are still hidden.

"From among sixty persons they found Moniek K. with a gangrenous leg who was rather like a dead man (eighteen years old). They demanded Moniek to tell them where the other bunkers with Jews are. Moniek categorically stated that he did not know. The murderers were waiting only for that. Riding whips and lead cables were used. Moniek clenched his teeth so as not to betray his brothers. But the Germans contrived everything. One of the SS men shot down Moniek's arm threatening: 'Wenn du zeigst nicht *juden-bunker* schiesse ich dich tot', 'If you don't show us the Jewish bunker, I'll shoot you dead.' Writhing with agony, brave brave Moniek was shouting: 'Murderers, I don't betray! You can kill me!'"[16]

Maidanek, the first camp Helen was sent to, was originally constructed in 1941 for Russian prisoners of war. Between February 1942 and July 1944 Maidanek was used as an extermination center and labor camp for Jews from Poland and other occupied territories. It is estimated that almost half a million Jews were exterminated at Maidanek.

One of the most horrible incidents reported at the camp occurred on November 3, 1943, when approximately 18,000 Jews were machine gunned. Heinz Stalp, an eyewitness of the event, testified at the Maidanek Trial:

> Later on November 3rd there was an operation in which around 18,000 Jews were shot . . . in a large open area near the crematorium. Four big loudspeakers had been set up and played music records—waltzes, popular music, various songs—and you could also see how naked Jews came out of a barracks—men, women, children, all together, about 50 of each—and

38

they ran to an open ditch. A few days earlier four big ditches had been dug, 30 meters long, four meters deep, and three meters wide. And these prisoners, these Jews had to stand naked at the edge of the ditch and were shot from behind with two machine guns.[17]

BBC correspondent Alexander Werth, who had witnessed the mass execution, reported the incident, but BBC refused to release the story, claiming it was Russian propaganda.

Using

Helen mentions that many marriages took place in the ghetto. What might have been the motivations for these unions?

Helen explains that she lost her mother twice. What does she mean here by the word "lost"?

In what ways did Helen demonstrate resistance to the Nazis? Is there any indication in the way Helen tells her story that she considers herself a heroine for her defiance?

Helen suggests that she and her husband have remained together in the postwar era because they share the experience of the Holocaust.

Renee Scott

In the end of 1939 . . . I started to get involved with resistance [activities]
by working between Paris and Brussels. I made false passports and IDs
and found homes for Jewish people until they had their papers. This went
on until 1941 when I was arrested by the Gestapo [with 165 other women
in resistance].

Renee Scott, a non-Jewish survivor of the Holocaust, is a widow who lives in
Boston. She spoke about her experiences to eighth graders in a Facing History
class in Brookline, Massachusetts.

When the war broke out in 1939, Renee, a 35-year-old native of Belgium, was
living with her teenage daughter in the north of France. Her husband, a
soldier, was serving in the Belgian Congo. Renee's father pleaded with her
not to join the underground, stressing that her sole responsibility was to care
for her daughter in her husband's absence. Toward the end of 1939, Renee and
her family moved to Paris where Renee became a secretary for the Belgian
Chamber of Commerce.

In her new job Renee made frequent trips between Paris and Brussels.
Because she was in the process of obtaining papers for a divorce, she did not
mind these expeditions.

Initially, Renee had no idea that the papers she carried on these trips were for
the underground. When she finally realized that she was involved in resistance
activities, she felt it was right to oppose Nazism, and so she continued to
participate in the clandestine activities. In addition to serving as a courier, she
helped forge visas and identity papers and locate hiding places for Jews.

In 1941 the Gestapo rounded up Renee and other women involved in the
Paris-Brussels underground. Renee was placed in solitary confinement for six
months and sentenced to death. Following her incarceration in a Belgian
prison, she was sent in a convoy with Belgian and French women involved in
resistance work to Berlin and confined to the large women's prison of
Moabite. Renee not only witnessed the beheading of her best friend during the
interrogation process, but she also was taken into a torture room and
threatened before she finally was returned to her room. Soon thereafter she
was sent to the men's camp of Mauthausen for ten days, and then to
Ravensbruck where she remained for three and a half years.

Renee was among the inmates who built the Ravensbruck camp. Once they
completed the construction, she began working in the factories. Due to her

manual dexterity, she was selected for indoor work in the Siemens factory and was therefore protected from the elements.

On several occasions she became very ill, once with blood poisoning in her legs and another time with typhus. The camp food did not provide sufficient nourishment—ersatz coffee, stale bread, and soup made from suet were the main ingredients of the camp diet. The brutality of the personnel aggravated camp conditions. Renee most remembers the wife of the commandant, who was fond of leaping out at prisoners, threatening to beat them with her baton.

Renee and other inmates found ways of coping with the awful conditions. She explains that she and other inmates dealt with their hunger by exchanging recipes of their favorite foods, and at night they were so exhausted from their work that they slept even though there were awful screams and people dying in the barracks.

By late 1944 the International Red Cross was coming to visit the camp and providing food packages for the inmates. At liberation the following spring, Count Bernadotte of Sweden negotiated for the release of prisoners by buying their freedom. Later, Red Cross trucks took survivors of the camp to Lubeck, Germany and eventually to Denmark and Sweden. In Sweden Renee, along with many other survivors of Ravensbruck, was sent to a small village for rehabilitation and medical treatment. After several months Renee had regained sufficient strength to return to France, where she rejoined her daughter and parents. Her family was surprised to learn she was still alive; they had had no word about her since 1941.

Commentary

According to historian Vera Laska, women played a key role in the French resistance. In her anthology *Women in the Resistance and in the Holocaust*, Laska explains:

> Women, as well as men, in the resistance had to have courage and daring, nerves of steel and a quick wit; they had to possess endurance, a good memory and the rare gift of knowing how to remain silent. Speaking the native language in the place of operation always meant a multiple insurance for a successful mission. It was to the advantage of women that most of their adversaries were male, and women were less suspected of illegal activities by them—the old male underestimation of the power of a woman. This was especially true in feudalistic regions such as Hungary or the less progressive parts of Slovakia. A smile could often accomplish more than a bribe or a gun.

> Women proved as inventive as men and often more imaginative. They
> played the roles of deception more convincingly. Only a woman could
> have talked her way out of the infamous Star prison of Szeged in Hungary,
> after having been arrested with two dozen or so foreign men whom she had
> been guiding toward the Yugoslav border. . . . Only a woman could have
> had the nerve to slip into a German prison, contact her resistance chief,
> then convince his captors to release him for money and a promise of
> immunity after the war, as Christine Granville . . . did.[18]

As was the case with Renee Scott, it was common for the Nazis to place
female political prisoners in jails under death sentences. Historian Sybil
Milton has observed that these female political prisoners often were kept alive
as long as they could provide labor for the Germans.

Ravensbruck, where Renee was imprisoned for more than three years, was the
largest women's concentration camp. It was located between Berlin and the
Baltic (now a part of East Germany). When it was opened in May 1939 it was
intended for German political prisoners and gypsies, but soon it became an
international camp, housing political prisoners from all parts of Europe.
Included were all women who were considered dangerous to Nazi aims:
members of resistance movements, operators of secret radios, messengers,
female parachutists, Socialists and Communists, patriotic women who
harbored Jews, women caught with illegal pamphlets.

As in other concentration camps, the final months of the war were most
difficult for the inmates of Ravensbruck. The SS made a deliberate effort to
kill their prisoners as rapidly as possible before the liberating forces could
witness what had taken place.

Prisoners such as Renee who had been given death sentences received the
designation NN, standing for *Nacht und Nebel* (Night and Fog). This
expression came from a Wagnerian opera about a figure who could disappear
magically. For the SS, the designation NN meant dangerous prisoners whose
cases had not been investigated. NNs were dispatched to concentration camps
and slated for "disappearance."

Dagmar Hàjkovà, a survivor of Ravensbruck, corroborates Renee's
description of the brutality of the guards in her book on Ravensbruck:

> A much feared and dangerous physical punishment was brought to
> Ravensbruck by Himmler as his personal present at his visit in 1940. This
> was flogging, anywhere between 10 and 25 lashes, in harder cases 50 to 75
> lashes, which were usually administered in installments of 25. It was
> carried out in the presence of the Kommandant, the chief woman
> supervisor and a physician. . . . After the summer of 1943 the Germans
> always assigned Polish and Russian women to do the flogging. . . .

... The hardest punishment in the camp was imprisonment in the Bunker. The Bunker was a jail in the jail, a prison in the prison. Once in the Bunker, it was hard to tell whether a woman would ever leave it alive.[19]

Benjamin Ferencz, a lawyer who helped survivors used as slave labor in the concentration camps receive restitution after the war, learned that women who were chosen to work in the Siemens factories met stiff requirements. They "had to undergo an aptitude test before being selected for work by Siemens. Their vision was tested by requiring them to read small print. To test the dexterity of their fingers, they had to bend a wire with a pliers and cut a paper into a specified pattern...."[20]

Ferencz also sought restitution for survivors of Ravensbruck and other concentration camps who had been used in medical experiments. At Ravensbruck, several dozen non-Jewish women who had been imprisoned for their activities in the Polish resistance movement were subjected to gas gangrene and bone transfer experiments, which were thoroughly documented during the Doctors' Trial at Nuremberg in 1946-47. The summary of a panel on Medical Ethics, presented at the 1985 Facing History Annual Conference (see Appendix 2), includes further details on these experiments and the experiments performed in the other concentration camps. Contact the Facing History Resource Center for the packet entitled "Questions of Medical Ethics Raised by the Nuremberg Trials."

Using

Abraham Foxman, national director for the Anti-Defamation League of B'nai B'rith, defines resistance in the following manner:

The word "resistance" usually connotes an organized, armed, collective action, carried out according to the rules of military strategy. But resistance is a concept which includes persons who resisted passively, who participated in uprisings in ghettos and concentration camps, who fought in partisan units in the forests, who participated in general underground movements. It also includes Jews who fought, knowing that certain death awaited them, but wanted to demonstrate the courage of the Jewish people and were willing to die for "K'vod Ha-am", the honour of the nation. It includes still others who sacrificed their lives to rescue others, those who committed any act plainly against the laws of the German authorities or the goals of the "final solution."[21]

What different forms of resistance mentioned in Foxman's definition did Renee Scott engage in? What type of resistance was she involved with in the underground movement? What type of resistance did she participate in when she was in Ravensbruck?

Did Renee, a non-Jew, have more opportunities than Jewish prisoners at Ravensbruck to oppose Nazi authority?

In viewing the testimonies of female survivors such as Renee, have you found evidence that suggests the experiences of women were different from those of men? If so, what differences have you found? How were the experiences of male and female victims similar?

According to Vera Laska, contemporaries had less suspicion of women being involved in resistance work than men. What were the attitudes towards sex roles in the 1930s and 1940s that might have contributed to the notion that women were less likely than men to participate in resistance?

In the discipline of women's studies there is interest in the types of friendship and bonding among women. Does Renee's testimony suggest that bonding took place at Ravensbruck despite the Nazis' efforts to dehumanize the inmates? Have you heard any testimonies by male survivors that suggest that similar forms of bonding took place among the male inmates?

How does Renee characterize the abilities and behavior of guards and *kapos* (prisoners who served as guards) at Ravensbruck? Does her testimony support Vera Laska's observation that the Nazis in the concentration camps displayed "superorganizational skills"?

According to Nechama Tec and Ervin Staub, who have conducted research on altruism, it is common among people who take risks to help others that they do not deliberate a great deal about their actions: they do what they feel they must as human beings and do not think they could have done otherwise. Does Renee's involvement in French resistance follow the pattern described by Tec and Staub?

What evidence does Renee's testimony offer about the behavior of female *kapos*?

A videotape of storyteller Jennifer Justice relating anecdotes of two women involved in Dutch resistance activities is available at the Facing History Resource Center.

Additional materials on the role of women available at the Resource Center include: Ringelheim & Katz, *Proceedings of the Conference on Women Surviving the Holocaust*; Rupp, "'I don't call that Volksgemeinschaft': Women, Class and War in Nazi Germany"; and Bock, "Racism and Sexism in

Nazi Germany: Motherhood, Compulsory Sterilization, and the State."

Available at the Fortunoff Video Archive for Holocaust Testimonies is the testimony of Marion Pritchard (T-754). Marion, a non-Jew, was twenty years old when the war broke out in Holland, and she was training to be a social worker. Worried about the fate of Jews in Holland under Nazi occupation, she became involved in rescue work between 1940 and 1945. Throughout the interview she comments on how she as a woman was engaged in certain forms of rescue work that men were less likely to do.

Nechama Tec

Some of us [Polish Jews] survived in concentration camps, some of us survived by hiding in the forests. . . , and some of us survived as I did by passing as Christians by living on the Aryan side . . . pretending to be a Christian. For about three years I pretended to be a Catholic girl and lived among Poles illegally under an assumed name.

Born in Lublin, Poland, in 1931, Nechama enjoyed a pleasant childhood in comfortable surroundings. Her father was the owner of a large factory and provided his family with a large, elegant apartment. Nechama and her sister had tutors so that they had an opportunity to learn to speak Polish more fluently than their parents, who had not had the same educational advantages.

The outbreak of war in 1939 brought about immediate changes for Nechama. Although her family had been assimilated with the non-Jewish population of Lublin in the prewar years, Nazi legislation made Nechama's family acutely aware of their Jewish identity. First, the family was forced to surrender its spacious apartment and move

Nechama Tec, a Polish survivor, has done pioneering research on Christian rescuers of Jews in Poland during the Holocaust.

into a cramped apartment in the Lublin Ghetto. Soon thereafter, Nechama and her sister were separated from their parents and placed in Christian homes for protection. These arrangements did not work out, and Nechama and her sister rejoined their parents in the ghetto at the very time that life became increasingly dangerous for Jews.

In 1942 Nechama's father was able to arrange to pay for his entire family to find asylum with a Christian family in Kielce, a town several hundred miles from Lublin, where they would not be recognized. In this hiding place, Nechama's parents remained "hidden" inside the apartment of the host family all the time because their manner of speaking Polish would have betrayed their Jewish identity. Nechama and her sister had blond hair and blue eyes, and proficiency in the Polish language; they "passed" as relatives of the host family of Polish Christians. They assumed Christian names, learned the rituals of Catholicism, and memorized the genealogy and biographical details of their new family. They attended school daily with non-Jews and served as links between their parents and the outside world.

During these months of "passing," Nechama and her sister had to remain silent about their true identity even when they heard slurs about Jewish people. Nechama was so troubled by negative remarks she heard about Jews that on one occasion she asked her father to explain how Christians could believe such things.

Nechama, her sister, and her parents all survived the war and returned to their native Lublin before deciding to leave Poland. There were only three Jewish families in Lublin that managed to survive intact; Nechama's family was one of the three. Although they would have chosen to resume life in Lublin, the omnipresent signs of antisemitism that had survived the war years and Nazi occupation made life so intolerable for Jews that Nechama's family decided to emigrate.

For many years Nechama refused to think or talk about her childhood during the Holocaust. She married, raised a family, and began her career as a sociology professor without ever discussing the subject or conducting research on the Holocaust. Then, in the late 1970s, her memories began to stir: as the stirrings became sharper, she decided to write her memoirs, *Dry Tears*, which appeared in 1982 (a second edition, with an added epilogue, was published in 1984).

As she worked on her personal reminiscences, she became increasingly interested in what motivated people to save Jews. In a systematic survey of several hundred rescuers of Polish Jewry, Nechama developed a profile of the

46

characteristics these individuals have in common. She discussed her findings in her recent monograph, *When Light Pierced the Darkness*.

The final fifteen minutes of Nechama Tec's portrait include her description of her research on rescuers presented at the 1986 Facing History Annual Conference (see Appendix 2). She emphasizes that the majority of interviewees were individualists who did not conform to the dictates of others but followed their own values.

Commentary

It should be noted that Nechama Tec has confined her research to rescuers of Polish Jewry. She opens her monograph with an examination of the cultural traditions of Poland, especially pointing to the role of the church. Dr. Tec also distinguishes between rescuers who helped Jews for money and those who did it for a variety of non-economic reasons.

Whether the motivation was greed or altruism, Tec also points out that the risks were considerable for non-Jews who helped Jews. A 1941 decree demanded the death penalty for all Jews who were found leaving their residential quarters without permission; this decree also specified that "the same punishment applies to persons who knowingly provide hiding places for Jews," and that "accomplices will be punished in the same way as the perpetrator . . . an attempted act in the same way as an accomplished one."[22]

In Kielce, where Nechama and her family "passed" with a Polish family, there had been 19,000 Jews, which represented a third of the total population before the war; 123 Jewish survivors returned to Kielce after the war and forty-three Jews were killed in the pogrom of July 3-4, 1945.

Using

Why does Nechama Tec believe it is important to distinguish between helpers who rescued Jews for money and altruistic helpers?

What were Nechama's first impressions of the Germans when they marched into Lublin?

Compare Nechama's early impressions of the German occupation with those of Samuel Bak. What factors made Tec's initial impressions of the Germans change? Mention some of the legislation and incidents that contributed to her change in attitude.

What steps did her family have to take in order to prepare for passing in the Christian world?

According to Nechama, what were conditions in Poland for Jews who had survived the Holocaust?

Nechama Tec entitled her memoirs *Dry Tears*. What does she mean by this title? What do you learn from her story in the videotape that would help you understand the title to her memoirs?

If you were conducting a survey of rescuers as Nechama Tec did for her research, what questions would you want to ask rescuers?

A summary of Nechama Tec's presentation at the 1986 Facing History Annual Conference is available at the Facing History Resource Center. One question that she dealt with briefly in the conference was whether women helped more than men in rescue work. For a fuller examination of this topic, see her "Sex Distinctions and Passing as Christians during the Holocaust."

Nechama Tec's findings should be compared with those of other scholars on prosocial behavior such as Hunecke, Oliner, Sauvage, Hallie, and Midlarski, whose theories are summarized in *Altruism and Prosocial Behavior*, available at the Facing History Resource Center.

Also available at the Facing History Resource Center are the following articles describing the research on altruism conducted by Oliner and Staub: Goleman, "Great Altruists: Science Ponders Soul of Goodness"; Hillinger, "A Systematic Study of Altruism: Motives of Rescuers Who Aided Jews in WWII Examined"; and Wise, "Making Sense of Risking All to Help Another."

Mordecai Paldiel, director of the Department for the Righteous Among the Nations at Yad Vashem in Jerusalem, argues that the theories for altruistic behavior which focus on a specific group of helpers such as rescuers of the Holocaust are based on too narrow a sample and provide misleading evidence. Paldiel, believing that all individuals have the capacity for performing altruistic acts, suggests that there be a general survey of individuals, not necessarily from a specified group, to determine what would encourage them to demonstrate their altruistic traits. "The task is, hence," explains Paldiel,

> not so much the meticulous search and adulation of the few Righteous persons, so as to be able to honour and salute them . . . from a distance, but rather the no less arduous task of widening the channels through which the altruistic archetype may flow unimpeded. If we are prepared to admit the universality of the altruistic attribute, then the scope of our investigation need henceforth not be restricted to the stuff of the social, psychological, political and religious backgrounds of pre-selected groups of people but, through an introspective exploration into the depths of our soul, rediscover

the magnitude of the hidden altruistic attribute (present in all men) and, arousing it from its enforced semi-slumber, allow it to rise and manifest itself, making us conscious of its presence and permitting it to assume an elevated position and proper role in our lives and behaviour.[23]

The immediate postwar experiences of Polish Jews returning to their native towns and cities after liberation are reviewed in selections in *Witness to the Holocaust*, Azriel Eisenberg, editor, pages 502-523.

For a summary of the postwar situation for surviving Polish Jews, see Marrus, *The Unwanted: European Refugees in the Twentieth Century*, pages 335-336.

For a readable account of a boy "passing," see Kuper, *Child of the Holocaust*, especially pages 139-143.

Rachel G. (T-139)

I was born in Brussels, Belgium. . . . I had a very happy childhood until the Nazis came in. I remember just happiness, just a beautiful family . . . going to school very happily until one day I had to come home from school with a note that I had to show my parents. And that's when the whole thing started. . . . The note said . . . that the Jewish children could not go to school anymore.

This portrait centers on the story of a Belgian Jewish child survivor who spent the three years between 1942 and 1945 among Catholics, separated from her parents.

Born in 1934, the only daughter of Jewish parents, Rachel remembers a happy childhood in which she mingled with Jewish and non-Jewish children. This changed when the Germans came, and she remembers the day in 1941 (she was seven years old) when she came home with a note saying that Jews were no longer allowed to attend school. Things got steadily worse for Belgian Jews, and one day Rachel's mother went to the landlady and pleaded for help. "They are taking away the children. All Rachel's little Jewish friends are going. Can you do something about my daughter? Can you take her, hide her somewhere?"

The landlady did help, calling upon her nephew, a priest, to arrange for Rachel's hiding. Only once after Rachel went into hiding did she see her father—he managed to come to the priest's house with a birthday present for her.

The priest arranged for Rachel to attend a convent school. She adjusted quite well to the Catholic community and remembers enjoying the prayers and routine of the school, although she missed having her parents come on Sundays as the other parents did to visit the non-Jewish students. While Rachel was becoming accustomed to her new life, the landlady betrayed her parents to the Gestapo, who sent them to the transit camp at Malines and eventually deported them to Auschwitz. Rachel's father did not survive the camp years; her mother did not see Rachel until after the war.

The Story of Rachel G. was not atypical. Between 3,000 and 4,000 Belgian Jewish children were rescued by resistance organizations in Belgium. "As If It Were Yesterday" includes the stories of several children who, like Rachel, spent the war years protected by non-Jews.

During the next three years Rachel moved many times. Each time the local officials grew suspicious that the nuns were harboring Jewish children, Rachel and the other Jewish children were walked to another location and given new names. On one occasion the Gestapo almost discovered Rachel, but the nuns quickly stashed their Jewish ward in a large laundry basket so the officials could not detect her presence.

Toward the close of the war Rachel hid with a childless couple in the Ardennes. The husband belonged to the resistance and had an abiding hatred for Nazis and all totalitarian regimes. The couple lavished love on Rachel, whom they called "Marie Rose." After liberation, they wanted to adopt Rachel and began the proceedings. However, regulations required that there be a ten-month waiting period and that children return to the first convent they entered. Thus, if parents survived, they would be able to locate their children.

Nine months after the war, while Rachel was in the convent school, her mother returned. Rachel found it difficult to understand her mother since she felt that her mother had abandoned her. Gradually, however, she grew to realize the tremendous sacrifice her mother and father had made by sending her away. She also learned the full story of the landlady who had turned her parents in to the Gestapo only a short time after arranging to help Rachel go into hiding.

One interesting feature of this interview is Rachel's discussion of her identity. She acknowledges her Jewish origins and recognizes the suffering of her parents and millions of other Jews. She also holds considerable respect for the Christians who took enormous risks to save her. Today she has mixed emotions about her Jewish identity, and she loves and admires the priests, nuns, and Catholic laity who came to her rescue.

Another important element of this tape is Rachel's frank disclosure of her feelings toward her mother after the war. As with other child survivors such as Menachem S. (Excerpt 10 in the montage "Childhood Memories") and Nechama Tec (Excerpt 6 in "Childhood Memories"), Rachel believed that her parents failed to protect her and therefore sent her away. These feelings of neglect and abandonment did not subside quickly after the war, and as she explains, it took a long time for her to "understand" and "thank" her mother.

Sofia Banya arranged for the Rubineks to hide with her family in the Polish countryside during the war. The documentary "So Many Miracles" chronicles the story of Sofia and the Jewish couple she rescued.

Commentary

The Canadian documentary film "So Many Miracles" tells of the reunion forty years after the war of a Jewish couple and the Polish couple who hid them. Like Rachel, the Jewish couple have fond memories of their Christian rescuers.

Historian Saul Friedlander has written a memoir describing what his childhood was like when he left his family and Czechoslovakian homeland to attend a Catholic boarding school in Montneuf, France. Compare his reaction to this move with that of Rachel:

"Paul-Henri," I couldn't get used to my new name. At home, I had been called Pavel, or rather Pavlicek, the usual Czech diminutive, or else Gagl, not to mention a whole string of affectionate nicknames. Then from Paris to Neris I had become Paul, which for a child was something quite different. As Paul I didn't feel like Pavlicek any more, but Paul-Henri was worse still: I had crossed a line and was now on the other side. Paul could have been Czech and Jewish; Paul-Henri could be nothing but French and resolutely Catholic, and I was not yet naturally so. What was more, that was not the last of the name changes: I subsequently became Shaul on disembarking in Israel, and then Saul, a compromise between the Saul that French requires and the Paul that I had been. In short, it is impossible to know which name I am, and that in the final analysis seems to me sufficient expression of a real and profound confusion.

I no longer remember whether I arrived at Montneuf just before or just after my tenth birthday, but it was at Montneuf that I received . . . a letter that my parents had sent me for my birthday. . . . They assured me that they were in good health and that I would soon be with them again; they also said everything that parents can say to their child for his tenth birthday—almost a man now, isn't that right? I was quite aware that there was something strained about this letter. Where were my parents? Were they afraid I might try to run away again? But I didn't have the strength to do it again. In fact, I was at the end of my rope.[24]

The Rescue of Danish Jews, edited by Leo Goldberger, contains a series of essays that explore how an entire society, the Danes, became involved in the rescue of Danish Jewry in 1943. Like Nechama Tec, who has examined rescuers in Poland, the contributors to this anthology believe it is important to consider individual motivations in the context of the national culture, and several of the essays examine the values stressed in Danish religious and secular culture that would have predisposed the society to take risks on behalf of their Jewish brethren. A quotation from Thomas Merton's *The Non-Violent Alternative* sums up the findings of many of the authors in the collection:

Obviously there is no simple answer. It does not even necessarily follow that the Danes are men of greater faith or deeper piety than other western Europeans. But perhaps it is true that these people had been less perverted and secularized by the emptiness and cynicism, the thoughtlessness, the crude egoism and the rank amorality which has become characteristic of our world, even where we still see an apparent surface of Christianity. It is not so much that the Danes were Christian, as they were human. How many others were even that?

The Danes were able to do what they did because they were able to make decisions that were based on clear convictions about which they all agreed and which were in accord with the inner truth of man's own rational nature, as well as in accordance with the fundamental law of God in the Old Testament as well as in the Gospel: thou shalt love thy neighbor as thyself. The Danes were able to resist the cruel stupidity of Nazi anti-Semitism because this fundamental truth was *important* to them. And because they were willing in unanimous and concerted action to stake their lives on this truth. In a word, *such action becomes possible where fundamental truths are taken seriously.*[25]

Using

In reviewing the contents of Rachel's testimony, do you learn anything about the values of the Belgian people that would have encouraged individuals and groups to take part in rescue work? In thinking about this it is important to keep in mind that the Belgian resistance organizations were responsible for saving between 3,000 and 4,000 Jewish children during the Holocaust—there was considerably more resistance work in Belgium than in the neighboring country of Holland.

The Danish people coordinated efforts during the fall of 1943 to transport more than ninety percent of their Jewish population to Sweden in fishing boats.

One of the reasons for the portraits is to enable viewers to become acquainted with the personalities of survivors. What do you learn about Rachel's personality from her interview? What questions would you want to ask Rachel to get to know more about her?

What are some of the long-lasting effects that the Holocaust has had on Rachel? Compare these with effects that Dori Katz relates in her poem "The Return."

Why do you think Rachel has introduced her husband and children to the people who saved her during the war?

Marion Pritchard, a Dutch social worker who helped save Jewish children from the Nazis during the war, participated in efforts to reunite surviving Jewish children with parents and relatives after the war. According to Pritchard, the uneasiness that Rachel felt about reuniting with her mother was not unusual for children who survived the Holocaust.

> I don't know if I could have taken staying with the child search team. Because some children—Jewish children who didn't look Jewish, or children who were maybe half Jewish—were put in German families if they had blond hair and blue eyes. And so you have a baby who has been placed at six months or whatever, and then the war is over, and he's grown up with a German family who may have indoctrinated him as a little Nazi, and he has been brought up as a child in the family. And then these people come in uniform, accompanied by some strange looking people with *payiss* [sidelocks], and they're the real parents, and those children screamed in terror and ran.

> Obviously, when Jewish babies were born during the war, it would have been damn foolishness to register them as Jewish babies, so we used to register them as our own illegitimate children. I once had two in five months, but nobody caught on to that. I don't know what happened to two of "my" children. I don't know whether their parents survived, I don't know whether they're still walking around with my name, or whether they've changed, and their parents could still be looking for them.

> . . . The point was to know as little as possible, so that when you'd placed a child, and done what you had to do, you didn't follow up, because you would have known something that might be better not to know. . . .[26]

The documentary "So Many Miracles" is available at the Facing History Resource Center. Since it focuses on the experiences of Polish Jews rescued by Polish Christians, this documentary will provide a means of comparing rescue experiences of eastern European Jews with those of western European Jews such as Rachel.

The Return *by Dori Katz*
The light I turn on to remember these days
is small and distant in the dark.
I go back very deeply for you, and very carefully.
One false move and I fall off your shoulders
where I placed myself at three to be carried across the
rain puddles; one inadvertent slip and you are gone
while I am waiting for you by the kitchen window,
angry because you promised to be right back,
and I never saw you again.
How you must have felt when they arrested you,
no time to say good-bye, send messages.
They took you to the public square at Malines,
made you line up with other Jews, then climb
into a boxcar; the doors are shut. Back home,
your wife, cursing your fate, burns your pictures,
your documents, packs my clothes in a basket,
then sends me to someone else's house. I squat
in a corner of a strange kitchen, crying for you.

Years pass. Your wife survives by selling your things.
Converted, your daughter goes from house to home,
a different child now, quiet, tamed,
but at night she walks blindly in her sleep,
opening door after door to find you;
you are not there for you are living now in Auschwitz.
Your head is shaved, your hands swollen;
soon they will amputate a leg. You are 177679,
not Moishe Chaim anymore, not anyone, and no one knows what happened when
you disappeared.

I waited for you.
I used to think of accidents, cured amnesia,
a hospital file that would turn up your name,
or that you married again, forgotten us.
I pictured running into you on a deserted street;
you'd be walking against the wind,
dragging your bad leg behind you. As soon as
you'd recognize me, the years would disappear like rain
drying up, or clouds pushed away by strong gusts.
Other times, I saw you as a one legged man hopping around
the house outside, then pressing his face against the window,
against my new life now all patched up.

And so I carried you for years, like salt upon the tongue,
a bitter taste always dissolving, always there;
I was afraid that you were lost, afraid you'd return,
old, crippled, gray and we'd be singled out again.
Today, it doesn't matter what I want, you have been dead
so long there's nothing left that could come back;
you are not flesh, not bone, not even dust of dust;
you are a light behind that kitchen window now,
behind that glass—a light that comes and disappears.

Carl H.

"Okay folks," ordered an American soldier on May 8, 1945 in our town, "go down into your basements. The war is almost over." . . . An American tank went by our house. . . . I looked up through the basement window and suddenly some GI boots went by . . . and the war was over. It was 11:45 A.M.

In this portrait, Carl describes life in his small central German town at the close of the war. Carl's father had joined the Nazi Party in the 1930s, and Carl's three older brothers served in the German air force throughout the war. Carl, who was an elementary school student during the war, had regular lessons in race science and took part in paramilitary exercises. Since most of the Jews who lived in his town before the Nazis came to power had fled by the 1940s, Carl had no way to confirm what he was being taught about the Jews and other so-called "inferior peoples."

One event in the closing months of the war that remains vivid in Carl's memory concerned the fate of a twelve-year-old who had been drafted into the German army. The young recruit had deserted, and the Gestapo forced the entire town to watch as a firing squad shot the boy. Carl, who was nine at the time, marched with the other boys in his class to witness the execution. The officials wanted to assure that they set an example for German boys who soon would be eligible for military service.

Before this, Carl had been aware of death, but it had not affected him directly. The sight of the boy slumped over, a boy he had known, made the horrible effects of war real to him. And as the war came to an end, there were other people he knew personally who died.

As the defeat of the Nazis became apparent, social structures began to crumble. In Carl's town in the final days, the inhabitants tried to salvage whatever they could; typhus was rampant, constant strafing left buildings in shambles, and it was dangerous to walk in the streets because anything that moved became a target for the American planes. Yet, Carl observes, the townspeople remained consistent to the end: school went on as usual until the American troops moved into the town, the Nazi Party continued holding its meetings, and housewives made sure that the one remaining German tank protecting the town was cleaned regularly.

Just before the Americans took possession of the town, they deluged the streets with leaflets threatening to bomb everything. Although the townspeople considered resistance, it soon became clear that this would be impossible against the strength of the troops. Suddenly there was tremendous noise as American tanks rolled in. Carl, who was in the bunker with his parents and friends, remembers peering through one of the small cellar windows at the street level:

> *I looked up . . . some G.I. boots went by and a voice [screamed] "move your ass." And, at that point the war was over. It was 11:45 A.M. [May 8, 1945].*

Because Carl's father was a member of the Nazi Party, he had to undergo a program of denazification. He was stripped of the position he held as a party member and educated in the principles of democracy. Further, he was imprisoned for a year and a half because he had been mistaken for a high-ranking Nazi with a similar sounding last name. For Carl, postwar adjustments were not particularly dramatic. He remembers being placed on a restricted diet of 900 calories a day because there were tremendous shortages of food. In addition, he recalls alterations in textbooks to remove all references to war and martial behavior.

What is most evident in his final remarks about the American occupation of his town is that Americans treated the local residents fairly and without vengeance. In 1953, Carl became an exchange student in the United States, where he remained. Today he teaches social studies in Albuquerque, New Mexico.

Commentary

Historian J.W. Wheeler-Bennet describes the condition of Germany at the end of the war, after Hitler's suicide:

> The end thereafter was speedy. Grand-Admiral Doenitz, named a *Führer* by Hitler, at once initiated negotiations with General Eisenhower for an armistice on the Western Front. The reply was a demand for Unconditional Surrender to all the Allies, and on May 7, at half-past two in the morning, the instrument of Unconditional Surrender was signed at Rheims by a weeping Jodl.

> It was the end. There was no negotiation; there was no haggling. There was no repetition of the conditions of November 1918 when the German High Command was to disclaim responsibility for the acceptance of the Armistice Conditions. This time there was no doubt that the Nemesis of Power had overtaken the German Army. There was no equivocation about this instrument:

"We the undersigned, acting by the authority of the German High Command, hereby surrender unconditionally to the Supreme Commander, Allied Expeditionary Forces, and simultaneously to the Soviet High Command, all forces on land, sea and in the air, who are at this date under German control."

The proportions of the German defeat were gigantic. For the first time in modern history the entire armed forces of a State, officers, non-commissioned officers and men, became prisoners of war, and for the first time in modern history the national sovereignty of the state ceased to be exercised by its citizens and was thrown into commission under the authority of the Occupying Powers. The position of the German military was, moreover, infinitely more precarious than at the close of the First World War, since President Roosevelt, Mr. Churchill and Marshall Stalin had repeatedly emphasized that it was among the most salient of their war aims that Prussian militarism should be destroyed along with the iniquities of National Socialism, and they were now in a position to make good these statements.[27]

Milton Mayer, professor of English at the University of Massachusetts, visited Germany in 1935 and again in the postwar years. His book, *They Thought They Were Free*, describes his observations of the German people and their reactions to Nazism and the postwar Allied occupation. In the following passage from his book he offers his insights into what denazification meant for Germans living in the American zone of occupation:

Why should America have undertaken, in 1945, to export freedom, above all to a people who had habitually squandered their own and eaten up other people's? The question may or may not have had merit, but it was too late, in 1945, to ask it. The American Occupation had added something new to the history of occupations: idealism. It had undertaken to do something more than punish, collect, and control: it had undertaken to civilize the Germans. . . .

Still, as the American Occupation learned that what was done in ten centuries cannot be undone in ten days, some small progress might have been made in time. As the sting of punishment, collection, and control was relieved, receptivity to the American world revolutionary effort might grow in Germany, and the effort itself, if only it were not abandoned in a new isolationist temper in America, might become more imaginative. By 1948 there were signs of hope. No West German would have said, outside an official statement, that his government was free, much less democratic; but words like "freedom" and "democracy" were everywhere heard, especially among the rising generation.

The public schools were full of free books, free movies, and free lectures in praise of freedom and free enterprise, in praise, above all, of peace. And the pupils were memorizing the blessings of democracy as assiduously as their older brothers had memorized the blessings of National Socialism. More significantly, the private elementary and secondary schools, from which public school reform had always emerged, were alive again in the land.[28]

Historian Michael Kater, who has analyzed the teaching tools in the postwar years, points out that history texts failed to make German students confront the fact that Nazism was a popular movement and not just a freak result of Hitler's madness. On the one hand, the glories of Germany in past centuries under such leaders as Frederick the Great and Otto von Bismarck are overemphasized, while the Third Reich is covered in a cursory manner, with only fleeting references to Hitler's crazy behavior. The fourth edition of the upper school text *Grundriss der Geschichte* (1965 edition) contains the following passage on the young Hitler and the origins of National Socialism:

> Hitler was gifted in a variety of ways, but he was lazy, capricious and without stamina. Full of ideas, he was too flighty to make anything of them. His only passions were reading the papers and politicizing. Although he read much, he did so indiscriminately and unsystematically. In any discussion he would scream as soon as he got agitated and would berate his opponents endlessly. Even in that early period, he was showing his manic tendency toward monologues, as well as a one-sidedness that bordered on the psychopathic.[29]

German historian Friedrich Meinecke wrote that Germans in the postwar decades should regard their history in light of the atrocities of the Third Reich and not treat it as uncritically as in history textbooks.

> The radical break with our military past that we must now accept faces us with the question about what is to become of our historical traditions in general. It would be impossible and suicidal to throw them wholesale into the fire and behave as apostates. But our customary picture of the history under which we grew to greatness needs at any rate a fundamental revision in order to discriminate between what was valuable and what was valueless. To do this, according to our conviction, only that type of historical thinking is adequate which perceives the close demonic connection between the valuable and valueless in history. To 'the eternal, iron, great laws' of our existence, of which Goethe spoke in his ode *Das Göttliche*, belongs, we believe, our impression that good and bad, divine and demonic, so often seem to grow into one another. Goethe said in the ode: 'Man alone is capable of the impossible. He discriminates, chooses, judges.' How the apparently impossible nevertheless becomes possible, how we in our observation so often see good and evil growing into one another and in our moral actions are able to discriminate and work for the good—that can never be fully comprehended through logic, but must be

experienced in life in order to be understood. If then observation ventures the task of discriminating between the good and the bad, between the higher and the lower in our historical past of replacing traditional accounts of the past by new evaluations, then the observer must remain aware that he is dealing with the work of mortal man and that he is bound by the momentary spirit of the age. And yet the venture must be made! Made with a sense of responsibility, with a pure, humane, and patriotic feeling.[30]

Thirty-five years after Meinecke's observations about how Germans should view their past, Richard von Weizsäcker, president of the Federal Republic of Germany, commemorated the fortieth anniversary of the end of World War II with an address in which he emphasizes that Germans must continue to confront their past without becoming paralyzed with a collective guilt for the crimes of the Nazi era.

The vast majority of today's population were either children then or had not been born. They cannot profess a guilt of their own for crimes they did not commit. No discerning person can expect them to wear a penitential robe simply because they are Germans. But their forefathers have left them a grave legacy. All of us, whether guilty or not, whether old or young, must accept the past. We are all affected by its consequences and liable for it. The young and old generations must and can help each other to understand why it is vital to keep alive the memories. It is not a case of coming to terms with the past. That is not possible. It cannot be subsequently modified or made undone. However, anyone who closes his eyes to the past is blind to the present. Whoever refuses to remember the inhumanity is prone to new risks of infection.[31]

Using

Why did the German Army take in boys as young as twelve years old by the closing year of the war?

What effect did the public execution of the boy-soldier have on Carl and his classmates? Why did the local officials make certain that Carl and other schoolboys would be present at the execution?

Recent studies of society in Nazi Germany indicate that it was easier for non-Jews to help rescue Jews in large cities like Berlin than in smaller towns and villages. What factors would facilitate helping Jews in the larger urban centers? ("Childhood Experiences of German Jews," in **Montages**, addresses this question, comparing the stories of German Jews growing up in large cities like Berlin and in smaller towns; Gross's *The Last Jews of Berlin* contains an important discussion of how Jews in large urban centers had a greater chance of evading arrest than their counterparts in less populated areas.)

Sociologist Frances Henry, who has studied rescuers during World War II in the small German town of Sonderberg, explains that those who became involved in rescue had to know what was going on with regard to Jews and had to perceive Nazi actions as threatening to the Jewish minority. From Carl's description of his childhood and community, is there any indication that he or his neighbors were in a position to witness and understand what was happening to the Jewish minority?

In several testimonies of child survivors of the Holocaust the interviewees have remarked that they lost their childhood by being thrust into the abnormal world of ghettos and concentration camps. Is there any indication in Carl's testimony that the wartime situation shortened childhood for non-Jewish children forced to take on adult responsibilities?

According to Carl's testimony, what was the reaction of his neighbors to the German defeat in World War II? How did their reactions in 1945 compare with reactions of the German people at the close of World War I?

According to Carl, how did he and his neighbors feel about their treatment by the American occupation forces?

Professor Lucjan Dobroszycki, a scholar for YIVO Institute and editor of *Chronicle of the Lodz Ghetto*, has suggested the following combination for a class focusing on the educational policies and propaganda of the Third Reich: using selections of Frank S. and Carl H. in "Childhood Memories" in conjunction with readings and illustrations from *The Poisoned Mushroom* (sometimes called *The Poisonous Fungus*), a children's book published by the editor of the newspaper *Der Stürmer*, Julius Streicher. According to Dobroszycki the combination of the video testimonies and the antisemitic literature for children will provide some insights into the types of images and stereotypes that permeated the culture for children growing up in the Third Reich. While Frank S.'s testimony offers a firsthand account of a victim of antisemitic propaganda and laws, Carl H.'s testimony reveals how German schoolboys attending Nazi elementary schools interpreted lessons on racism and antisemitism and how their interpretations affected their attitudes and behavior during and after the Nazi era. The children's book *The Poisoned Mushroom* illustrates the types of negative stories and visual images of Jews that influenced children's attitudes. At the Nuremberg Trials *The Poisoned Mushroom* was entered in evidence against publisher Julius Streicher to illustrate how Streicher's antisemitic publications for children and adults helped to create an atmosphere in which neighbor turned against neighbor.

The following story from *The Poisoned Mushroom* exemplifies the tone throughout the story:

> Inge, that is the girl—Inge sits in the reception room of a Jew doctor. She has to wait a long time. She looks through the journals which are on the table. But she is much too nervous to read even a few words. Again and again she remembers her talk with her mother. Again and again her mind reflects on the warnings of her leader of the League for German Girls. A German must not consult a Jew doctor. And particularly not a German girl. Many a German girl who went to a Jew doctor to be cured met with disease and disgrace. When Inge entered the waiting room, she experienced an extraordinary incident. She heard the voice of a young girl saying: "Doctor, doctor, leave me alone." Then she heard the scornful laughter of a man. And then all of a sudden all became absolutely silent. Inge had listened breathlessly. What can be the meaning of all this? she asked herself and her heart was pounding. And again she thought of the warning of a leader of the League of German Girls.
>
> Inge had already been waiting an hour. Again she takes the journals and endeavors to read. Then the door opens. Inge looks up and the Jew appears. She screams. In terror she drops the paper. Horrified she jumps up. Her eyes stare into the face of the Jew doctor. And this face is the face of the Devil. In the middle of the devil's face is a huge crooked nose. Behind the spectacles gleam two criminal eyes. Around the thick lips plays a grin, a grin that means, "Now I have you at last you little German girl." And then the Jew approaches her. His fat fingers snatch at her. But now Inge has got hold of herself. Before the Jew can grab hold of her, she smacks the fat face of the Jew doctor with her hand. One jump to the door. Breathlessly Inge runs down the stairs. Breathlessly she escapes from the Jew house.[32]

The International Military Tribunal at Nuremberg found Streicher guilty of "breaking the moral backbone" of a nation with his antisemitic publications. Streicher was one of twelve defendants sentenced to death by hanging by the IMT.

The documentary film "Now After All These Years," available on half-inch VHS at the Facing History Resource Center, examines the reactions of inhabitants from a small German town and the fate of the Jews who had been forced to leave.

The television documentary "Force of Evil," prepared by WNEV-TV, Boston, to accompany the 1989 Facing History exhibition "The Trial of Adolf Eichmann: Evil, the Media and Society," and currently available on half-inch VHS at the Facing History Resource Center, explores the variety of ways that European Jews and non-Jews responded to Nazism and reports of the Final

Solution. "Force of Evil" also considers the lasting effect of this era on their lives. Included in this documentary are: an interview with a German Jew remembering how his office colleagues turned against him; a German ex–soldier recalling how he came to question Nazism after he witnessed a comrade being shot; and a former Dutch social worker remembering how her friend was persuaded by the antisemitic message in the German propaganda film *The Eternal Jew*.

Another source available at the Resource Center is "Dark Lullabies," on half-inch VHS, in which contemporary Germans indicate how they think about the Nazi era and deal with the German past in their present lives.

See the testimony of Robert Spaetling, available at the Facing History Resource Center, for another account of a German adolescent who was attending school during the Nazi years.

Peter Sichrovsky's *Born Guilty* contains a series of interviews of contemporary West German youth whose parents or grandparents were Nazis. Each of the fourteen interviewees deals differently with his or her heritage: one wonders why he was not killed along with his parents in a car accident; another married a Jew who is completely the opposite of her father, a former Nazi; and a brother and sister hold opposing views of their parents. What comes across so forcefully here and in Carl's testimony is the fact that German youth during and since the Holocaust cannot be free of the Nazi past—it is either seen as a period of great glory for the Reich or as a time of such immense shame that Germany will never be able to atone for its evil deeds under Hitler.

Jan Karski

For 30 years [after the war] I wanted to lead a normal life [not speaking of war experiences]. Then I felt disgust when I read in the press that generals, ambassadors, bishops, Eisenhower [said] they didn't know. . . . Hypocrisy! They knew! They knew!

Jan Karski, a non-Jew born in 1914 in Lodz, Poland, has lived in the United States since 1944, and is now professor of government at Georgetown University. His testimony focuses on his experiences as a political courier for the Polish Government-in-Exile in 1942-43, when he alerted Allied leaders to events in Nazi-occupied Poland.

In September 1942 the Polish underground had begun preparing for courier Jan Karski to visit western Europe with information about the situation in Poland under Nazi domination. Believing that Karski would be more credible if he had first-hand information on the Polish situation, members of the underground and Polish Jewish organizations decided that Karski should witness directly what was taking place. Thus plans were made for him to enter the Warsaw Ghetto and Belzec concentration camp in October 1942.

At that time there was apparently not much danger involved with Karski's entry into the Warsaw Ghetto. Certain houses in the ghetto formed part of the ghetto wall and members of the underground and the Zionist organizations regularly used tunnels in these houses to get in and out of the ghetto without incident. Leon Fajner, a Jewish lawyer working with the Bund, escorted him into the ghetto and there was no particular incident. When Karski and his escort entered, the ghetto population was between 50,000 and 60,000. (The original population had been 450,000.) The majority of Jews had been transported to death camps during the preceding summer.

Karski and his escort walked through the ghetto. When a commotion took place in the street they went inside one of the houses and, from a window, observed some members of the Hitler Youth playing with guns. Then Karski and Fajner left. After getting outside, Karski decided to enter the ghetto a second time; this time he entered alone.

As Karski emphasizes, he remembers little difficulty for someone non-Jewish to get in or out of the ghetto. When Jews left, their major problem was where to go. Polish citizens, either out of fear of punishment from the Nazis or because of their own antisemitic feelings, would not help Jews. The only way a Jew could survive outside the ghetto was to have friends and money. For Jews, Karski explains, there were two ghettos: the actual ghetto and the ghetto of society.

After Karski made his inspections of the ghetto, Leon Fajner took the initiative to plan Karski's entry into the concentration camp of Belzec. This venture was more dangerous than the escapades in the ghetto. Karski journeyed by train from Warsaw through Lublin toward his destination of Belzec. Once at Belzec, he entered a hardware store where he donned the uniform of an Estonian militiaman and was instructed to speak neither German nor Polish. This disguise was thought to be safe because the Nazis did not use Poles as guards in the death camps—they used foreigners so they would be able to preserve the secret of the death camps from the Polish people.

Having entered the camp, Karski immediately became aware of the chaos and confusion that prevailed. He ventured as close as possible to the main gates and was surprised to see that Jews were not taken in the main gates but pushed out and placed on a train platform. It was only years later, in reading historical studies of Belzec, that he learned that the commandant had been sending Jews to nearby Treblinka because his camp could not accommodate the numbers of Jews sent there.

Several weeks elapsed after Karski left Belzec before he was prepared to leave for the west with information on the Polish underground and the treatment of Jews. Finally the underground arranged to have forged papers made for Karski. The Polish Home Army arranged for his trip to London via Warsaw, Berlin, Brussels, and Paris. Once he made contact with the Polish underground in Paris, he was not able to proceed directly to London. Rather, he had to take a circuitous route through Spain and Gibraltar. Finally, by late November 1942 Karski arrived in London where he met with leaders informing them of the state of the Polish Government-in-Exile and delivering his Jewish report. He had about twenty minutes with Anthony Eden. The following July the Polish Ambassador to the United States arranged for Karski to meet with Roosevelt and leaders of American Jewish organizations.

For more than thirty years after the war Karski refused to speak of his experience as a wartime courier. He just wanted to forget about the whole thing and his disappointment that leaders of Allied nations did nothing to stop the persecution of Jews. He only began speaking about these experiences in the late 1970s when filmmaker Claude Lanzmann asked to interview him for the movie *Shoah*. Since then Karski has been speaking throughout the country and thinks it is essential that he tell how his messages were ignored. That leaders such as Eisenhower and Churchill would say immediately after the war that they had never known about the atrocities against Jews and other minorities appalls Karski. "Hypocrisy," he exclaims. "They knew. They knew."

Commentary

On October 14, 1944, *Collier's Magazine* included an article by Jan Karski containing details on his visit to Belzec concentration camp. As an introduction the editors of *Collier's* wrote a biographical note of Karski's early wartime experiences:

> Karski was brought up in a well-to-do middle-class Polish family, attended the University of Lwow [Lvov], and studied in Geneva and London with the idea of pursuing a diplomatic career.
>
> As a reserve officer in the horse artillery, he was called into action against the invading Germans in September, 1939. His regiment was destroyed, and he fled eastward. He was stopped by the Soviet Armies and taken as a prisoner to Russia. He won his release by posing as one of the Poles of German origin, who at that time were being exchanged and sent to work in Germany. During the transfer of prisoners, he jumped out of a moving German prison train into a forest and walked for twelve days back to Warsaw. He found that many members of his family had been killed. He joined the underground and became a courier.
>
> From 1940 to 1943 he covered dangerous routes between Poland and Paris, Berlin and London, serving as a liaison officer between the underground state in Poland and the Polish government-in-exile. The Gestapo caught him as he traveled through the Slovakian mountains, and tortured him. He tried to commit suicide—and woke up in a Gestapo hospital, from which, eventually, he escaped with the help of nurses and doctors who were, of course, underground workers.
>
> When Karski left Poland finally [in the fall of 1942], he carried with him 1,200 pages of underground documents recorded on microfilm. He was authorized by the Polish Prime Minister, Mikolajczyk, to "tell everything." "Give all the information as calmly and objectively as you did in your official reports to us," Mikolajczyk instructed him. "Tell everything you experienced—what you saw, what you heard. Convey the facts and let the people draw their own conclusions."[33]

In the 1944 *Collier's* article, Karski described vividly what happened to Jews loaded on freight cars outside the main gate at Belzec, whom he briefly alludes to in his portrait.

> The SS man turned to the crowd, planted himself with his feet wide apart and his hands on his hips and loosed a roar that must have actually hurt his

ribs. It could be heard far above the hellish babble that came from the crowd:

"*Ruhe, ruhe!* Quiet, quiet! All Jews will board this train to be taken to a place where work awaits them. Keep order. Do not push. Anyone who attempts to resist or create a panic will be shot.". . .

For a moment the crowd was silent. Those nearest the SS man recoiled from the shots and tried to dodge, panic-stricken, toward the rear. But this was resisted by the mob as a volley of shots from the rear sent the whole mass surging forward madly, screaming in pain and fear. The shots continued without letup from the rear and now from the sides too, narrowing the mob down and driving it in a savage scramble onto the passageway, . . . trampling it so furiously that it threatened to fall apart. . . .

"Order, order!" The two policemen echoed him hoarsely, firing straight into the faces of the Jews running to the trains. Impelled and controlled by this ring of fire, they filled the two cars quickly.

And now came the most horrible episode of all. The military rule stipulates that a freight car may carry eight horses or forty soldiers. Without any baggage at all, a maximum of a hundred passengers pressing against one another could be crowded into a car. The Germans had simply issued orders that 120 to 130 Jews had to enter each car. Those orders were now being carried out. Alternately swinging and firing their rifles, the policemen were forcing still more people into the two cars which were already overfull. The shots continued to ring out in the rear, and the driven mob surged forward, exerting an irresistible pressure against those nearest the train. These unfortunates, crazed by what they had been through, scourged by the policemen and shoved forward by the milling mob, then began to climb on the heads and shoulders of those in the trains. . . .

The floors of the car had been covered with a thick, white powder. It was quicklime. Quicklime is simply unslaked lime or calcium oxide that has been dehydrated. Anyone who has seen cement being mixed knows what occurs when water is poured on lime. The mixture bubbles and steams as the powder combines with the water, generating a searing heat.

The lime served a double purpose in the Nazi economy of brutality: The moist flesh coming in contact with the lime is quickly dehydrated and burned. The occupants of the cars would be literally burned to death before long, the flesh eaten from their bones. Thus the Jews would "die in agony," fulfilling the promise Himmler had issued "in accord with the will of the Fuehrer" in Warsaw in 1942. Secondly, the lime would prevent the decomposing bodies from spreading disease. It was inexpensive—a perfectly chosen agent for its purpose.

It took three hours to fill up the entire train. It was twilight when the forty-six cars were packed. From one end to the other the trains were packed. From one end to the other the train, with its quivering cargo of flesh, seemed to throb, vibrate, rock and jump as if bewitched. There would be a strangely uniform momentary lull and then the train would begin to moan and sob, wail and howl. Inside the camp a few score dead bodies and a few in the final throes of death remained. German policemen walked around at leisure with smoking guns, pumping bullets into anything that moaned or moved. Soon none were left alive. In the now quiet camp the only sounds were the inhuman screams that echoed from the moving train. Then these, too, ceased. All that was now left was the stench of excrement and rotting straw and a queer, sickening, acidulous odor which, I thought, may have come from the quantities of blood that had stained the ground.

Having left the camp and returned to the hardware store, Karski continues:

> Then I collapsed. I was completely, violently, rackingly sick. Even today, when I remember those scenes, I become nauseated.[34]

Historian Martin Gilbert, who has done research in the British Archives in the postwar era, traced the impact of Karksi's report that arrived at the office of the Polish Ambassador in London on November 25, 1942. It was only with the publication of Gilbert's book *Auschwitz and the Allies* in 1981 that Karski learned that the British government had been so well informed before he met with Eden and other leaders. In 1942, explains Karski, he had no way of knowing what was going on in British governmental and diplomatic circles.

> "There is no doubt that his visit prompted us to act," the Polish Ambassador in London, Count Raczynski, later recalled. And indeed, on the evening of November 25, the Polish Government-in-Exile handed Karski's report to A.L. Easterman, the Polish Secretary of the British Section of the World Jewish Congress. Easterman at once telephoned the Foreign Office, and asked if he and Sydney Silverman, the Labour Member of Parliament, could show the report to Richard Law, the Under-Secretary of State for Foreign Affairs, and Eden's deputy. The meeting took place on November 26. Easterman handed Law a copy of the report, which told a tragic story. . . .
>
> The Polish report of November 25 ended with a reference to a pamphlet circulating inside Poland which contained "a strongly worded protest against the terrible extermination of Jews," and estimated that the total number of Jews murdered in Poland since the outbreak of war "exceeds one million."
>
> Such was the information which two British Jews, A.L. Easterman and Sydney Silverman, put before the Under-Secretary of State for Foreign Affairs, Richard Law, on November 26. Law himself recorded the course

of their conversation. Whatever the British view might be, Silverman said, "it was now clear" that the State Department "accepted the substantial truth of these stories." But Law replied that he did not think that the State Department "had any more evidence than we had," although, he added, on the State Department's knowledge "of the German character and of Nazi ideology," it probably seemed to them that there was "nothing intrinsically improbable about the story."[35]

In 1944, soon after the *Collier's* article on Karski's mission, Karski completed *Story of a Secret State* describing his experiences with the Polish Underground and visits to Allied leaders. Briefly, but vividly, Karski wrote of his interview with President Franklin Roosevelt after a series of meetings with members of the U.S. State Department in the summer of 1943.

> The White House looked to me like a country mansion, new and well-built, surrounded by trees and silence. . . . My heart beat rapidly when I entered the White House with my Ambassador who was to introduce me. This was the very citadel of power. I was to meet the most powerful man in the most powerful nation of the world.

> President Roosevelt seemed to have plenty of time and to be incapable of fatigue. He was amazingly well-informed about Poland and wanted still more information. His questions were minute, detailed, and directed squarely at important points. He inquired about our methods of education and our attempts to safeguard the children. He inquired about the organization of the Underground and the losses the Polish nation had suffered. He asked me how I explained the fact that Poland was the only country without a Quisling. He asked me to verify the stories told about the German practices against the Jews. He was anxious to learn the techniques for sabotage, diversion, and partisan activity.

> On every topic he demanded precise and accurate information. He wanted to know, to be able to realize, not merely imagine, the very climate and atmosphere of underground work and the minds of men engaged in it. He impressed me as a man of genuinely broad scope. Like Sikorski [head of the Polish Government-in-Exile], his interests embraced not merely his own country but all humanity. When I left, the President was still smiling and fresh. I felt fatigued.[36]

Using

What does Karski mean by a "second ghetto," a ghetto of society that prevented Jews from finding haven outside the ghetto walls? What led to the creation of this form of ghetto?

Describe in detail how the Polish underground obtained false papers for courier Karski. In order to prepare such papers, what types of supplies and technology did the underground need? What form of technology borrowed from the United States was important in the process of creating false papers?

The Jewish Report made up a small portion, perhaps twenty to twenty-five percent, of the information Karski imparted to Allied government and religious leaders. What other aspects of Polish life under German occupation did Karski discuss with Allied leaders?

From the interview do you gain any clues as to what motivated Karski to risk his life for the Polish underground? What information is left out of the interview that you would like to obtain in trying to determine his motivations for risk-taking? (If time permits, review the commentary which contains biographical information on Karski's early wartime career. Is there any information in his pre-1942 activities that helps explain his underground work discussed in the interview?)

Why does Karski express disgust with the reception he received from Allied leaders?

What could Eden, Roosevelt, and other national leaders have done once they had learned the situation of occupied Poland in 1942-43? What could leaders in the Jewish community have done?

Would you call Karski a hero?

How do you define a "hero"? According to your definition of "hero," would you consider Jan Karski a hero? Explain your answer using specific examples from his career as courier to support your argument.

According to the Polish historian Josef Garlinski, Karski's report in the fall of 1942 prompted the following declaration from the governments of twelve countries, including the United States, Great Britain, and Soviet Russia, on December 17, 1942:

> We condemn in the strongest possible terms this bestial policy of cold-blooded extermination. We declare that such events can only strengthen the resolve of all freedom-loving peoples to overthrow the barbarous Hitlerite tyranny. We reaffirm our solemn resolution to ensure that those responsible for these crimes shall not escape retribution, and to press on with the necessary practical measures to this end.[37]

Given that the Allied nations responded with such a strong statement, why does Karski express disgust with Allied leadership at the close of his testimony? What was the effect of the twelve-nation declaration? Was it well publicized at the time? Is there any indication from Karski's testimony that he knew of the declaration when he met with American leaders?

Jan Karski

With regard to my mission in the U.S.A., in June 1943, at the suggestion of American Ambassador Biddle, I was sent to Washington, still secretly, under a false name—Jan Karski. I stayed there until August 1943, living on the premises of the [Polish] embassy. The Polish Ambassador, Jan Ciechanowski, supervised my activities and organized my contacts.

I reported [on what I had seen in the Warsaw Ghetto and Belzec Concentration Camp] to the following individuals: Franklin Delano Roosevelt, President of the United States; Cordell Hull, Secretary of State; Henry Stimson, Secretary of War; Francis Biddle, Attorney General; Colonel Donovan, Chief, Office of Strategic Services; Apostolic Delegate, Cardinal Ameleto, Gionvanni Cicognani; Archbishop Mooney; Archbishop Spellman; Archbishop Strich; Dr. Nahum Goldman, President, American Jewish Congress; Rabbi Stephen Wise, President, World Jewish Congress; Waldman, American Jewish Congress; Felix Frankfurter, Justice of the Supreme Court; and Mr. Backer, Joint Distribution Committee.

Jan Karski, 1981

Walter Bieringer

You ask me what has kept me interested in refugees all these years. . . . I take pride in having the opportunity to get involved in this work. This [becoming a refugee] could happen to almost anybody. . . . So it is important for those of us who are aware of this sort of thing to do something about it and help. . . And I got my satisfaction out of the happiness that this gave a number of those people. I think it is because of selfishness to some degree. I put myself in their position. This thing could happen to me. A man passes a blind man with a cup and puts ten cents in the cup. He feels he is the one holding the cup.

Walter Bieringer founded the Boston Refugee Committee in 1934 to help German and Austrian Jews immigrate to the United States.

This portrait reviews the efforts of Walter Bieringer to help refugees from Germany and Austria seek asylum in the United States before and after World War II. Bieringer, a businessman from Massachusetts, has made a difference in his community and nation by using his time and energy as a volunteer in assisting those in need. Like other rescuers during the Holocaust era, Bieringer did not deliberate about his actions on behalf of refugees. He recognized their plight and felt it was his obligation to respond to their needs.

Bieringer's concern for refugees began in January 1933 when he was on a business trip in Germany. A German salesman in a Nazi uniform met him at the station and encouraged Bieringer to take part in the victory parade for the National Socialists. Bieringer was struck immediately by the degree to which the German people were mesmerized with the Nazi pomp and circumstance. In the following days, as he toured other parts of Germany and Austria, he noted the same sort of fanaticism, and he became increasingly distressed by the signs of blatant antisemitism. The intensity of anti-Jewish sentiment in Vienna strengthened his own identity as a Jew. When he left

Europe in the winter of 1933, he vowed to do something to help those who wished to escape the persecution and oppression.

Upon returning to Boston he organized the Boston Refugee Committee, which became a prototype for 900 similar committees in communities throughout the United States. The refugee committee not only organized ways to help Jews leave Germany and Austria with appropriate papers, but also located employment and lodging for newcomers. Bieringer spoke to local community and religious groups pleading for support of Jewish refugees, and he made seven return trips to prewar Germany where he arranged to sneak out money belonging to Jewish families.

Although there was minimal immigration during the war, in the postwar years thousands of Jews entered the United States under the Displaced Persons Act. Bieringer resumed his prewar activities as the president of United Service for New Americans (1950-1954), and he actively sponsored more liberal quotas to enable additional refugees to settle in the United States. He also worked on the Massachusetts Commission for Refugees and represented the U.S. State Department in 1950 on an inspection of the displaced persons camps in Germany.

New Neighbors reported on the activities of the United Service for New Americans (USNA) and carried updates on immigration legislation. Bieringer's annual presidential addresses (1950-1954) were reprinted in this magazine.

By the mid-1950s the flow of Jewish refugees had subsided and Bieringer began using his experience to help other refugee groups from Communist countries. Now in his late 80s, he retains his interest in helping foreigners seeking asylum in the United States. When asked why he has devoted so much of his life to working with refugees, he mentions two principal motivations: 1) the personal satisfaction derived from work with refugees; and 2) self-interest (because circumstances that force people into refugee situations could happen to almost any group).

Commentary

As Bieringer remembers in his interview, it was not until he witnessed persecution of Jews in Germany and Austria during 1933 that he "became a Jew." In previous years he had grown up in an assimilated German-Jewish family of Boston; his parents did not observe Jewish rituals, nor did they participate in activities of their temple. Rather than engage in religious activities and organizations, both of his parents were active in social movements: his mother was a suffragist committed to pacifism, and his father was a socialist who was active in labor unions.

Bieringer was so appalled by the intensity of antisemitism in Hitler's Germany that he collected copies of *Der Stürmer*, a pro-Nazi newspaper published by Julius Streicher, and smuggled them out of the country as proof of what he had witnessed. In Austria before the *Anschluss* (the German occupation in March 1938), recalls Bieringer, antisemitism was even more intense than what he had witnessed in Germany.

Aware of the imminent danger posed for Jews in the Third Reich, Bieringer took considerable risks to smuggle money out of Germany for Jewish friends and acquaintances. According to historian Raul Hilberg, there were twelve ways to transfer money abroad in the prewar years and these methods became increasingly difficult as the 1930s progressed. Among the methods that Bieringer refers to in his testimony were:

1. The so-called *Freigrenze* (free currency zone). Each emigrant, including a Jew, was permitted to take out of the country the sum of 10 reichsmark in foreign currency . . . and twice that amount if the point of destination was a country with which Germany had no border. In other words, a family of three traveling to the United States could take along $24. . . .

3. Each emigrant could also take out of the country his *personal belongings*, including furniture. However, emigrants were required to submit to the authorities lists of all items intended for removal. The purpose of the lists was to screen the shipments, with a view to preventing the export of jewelry and valuables. There was, of course, a tendency to smuggle such items out of the country, but the bureaucracy did its best to frustrate transfer of that sort. On February 21, 1939, the Jews were directed to surrender their gold, platinum, silver, precious stones, and art objects to purchasing offices of the Economy Ministry, "compensation to be fixed by the ministry." . . .

9. The *smuggling out of currency* in contravention of the law was practiced by some poor Jews who had only a little money and who wanted to exchange it quickly, without middlemen. Since money smuggled out in

cash had to be smuggled back to be of use to anyone except a souvenir hunter, the exchange rate of such transactions was only 10 to 13 cents per mark. The Czech crown, which was worth 3.43 cents before the Germans marched into Prague, was sold in New York banks a week later for less than 1 cent.[39]

In addition to helping German Jews smuggle their money out of Germany in the prewar years, Bieringer helped them locate relatives and friends in the United States who would guarantee they would not become a public burden. One of the most successful methods for doing this was to have a German Jew locate a namesake in an American telephone book and write the person,

"John W. Gibson (center), newly appointed chairman of the U.S. Displaced Persons Commission, yesterday, Sunday, January 21st, pledged an all-out effort to speed up immigration under the Displaced Persons Act at a National Annual Conference of United Service for New Americans, major immigration and resettlement agency, and a beneficiary of the United Jewish Appeal. Shown here with Mr. Gibson are; Arthur Greenleigh (left) Executive Director of the Agency, and Walter Bieringer, of Boston, re-elected President of United Service at the conference." [Original photo caption]

requesting their support and promising not to be a financial burden. Bieringer used this technique and drafted a letter that potential refugees would send their American namesakes.

The Boston Refugee Committee that Bieringer founded worked with religious and governmental agencies to help refugees once they had arrived in the United States. This committee and similar ones formed in American cities before and immediately after the war eventually became the organization known as United Service for New Americans (USNA). In 1954 USNA merged with the Hebrew Immigrant Aid Society (HIAS) in order to make refugee services more efficient.

The transcript of Dr. Rosa Feri's request for help that Bieringer reads in his portrait is reprinted below because it exemplifies the types of requests Bieringer and others involved in refugee work received in the 1930s.

Dear Sir,

Informed about the great help and aid your committee rendered already to many people, I take the liberty to appeal for your help for two sons:

George, 26 years old, chemist who worked already practically. He would do his best at every post he could find. He speaks English, Dutch, Italian and a little French.

Otto, 22 years old, was student at the High School of commerce. The new organisation in our country stopped him to finish his studies. He used the time for learning some useful things and so he became a spectacle cutter, and a photo assistant, and he knows to drive a motor car. He speaks English and a little French.

That is a matter of course that both my sons will do every work they could find.

I think you will be amazed that it is the mother who writes you this letter but not my sons themselves. It would be my most ardent desire that my sons could write you a letter. But, alas, both my sons are in the concentration camp, at first at Dachau and not at Weimar-Buchenwald, where they were put in 21 weeks ago with several thousands for nothing than being Jews. In order to prove their integrity I add my sons certificates of the Federal Chief Police Officer at Vienna.

All pains and efforts for delivering our poor boys were in vain till now. Recently we were told that they could be delivered, when they show a visa. But as we have no relations abroad I was not able procure then the visa, indispensable for their deliverance. and now I am so glad that one of my friends gave me your address today and told me of your goodworks of charity. All my hope is now based on your kindness and I hope instantly that your readiness to help the unfortunates one will save my sons too. You can't imagine how grateful we should be, when, by your help, my sons would find the way from the concentration camp into the freedom of your country. You may be sure they will do their best for being faithful citizens of their adoptive country as good as reliable friends of their helpers.

Both my sons are sound and strong boys, kind and intelligent.

I beg your pardon, dear Sir, for this long letter and for my request, but we are in such a deep despair.

I hope from the bottom of my heart to receive soon your affirmative answer and remain [Yours sincerely,]

An organization that worked closely with the Boston Refugee Committee was the Window Shop, originated in Cambridge in the late thirties. German and Austrian refugees, working with volunteers from the Cambridge community, operated a bakery-tea shop; refugees earned income from working in the shop and profits were used to educate refugees' children. Eventually a dress store and crafts shop were added. The Window Shop was a business success and it managed to continue in operation until the 1960s, when it sold its businesses and devoted its efforts towards providing grants for needy foreign students. The organization continues to this day, and several of the members are currently writing an organizational history.

Despite the efforts of individuals such as Bieringer, there was widespread antisemitism in the United States prior to the war. Bieringer himself encountered it when he spoke to local Christian clubs about the plight of German Jews and when he attended business meetings and conventions. He was particularly troubled by it when he suggested to officials of the Olympic Committee that Americans not participate in the 1936 games (to be held in Berlin) as an expression of American disapproval of the Nazi treatment of Jews. Members of the Olympic Committee dismissed his plea, saying, "You Jews tend to exaggerate things."

Three major indications of antisemitism in the United States in the 1930s and 1940s were Father Charles E. Coughlin's Social Justice movement, William Dudley Pelley's Silver Shirts, and the German-American Bund.

"Indication that hostility toward Jews was reaching an ominous level," writes historian David Wyman,

came from a series of ten surveys conducted between 1938 and 1941. These polls found that a consistent 12 to 15 percent of the people questioned were ready to support a general anti-Semitic campaign. From 1939 through 1941, an additional segment of about 20 percent expressed itself as sympathetic toward such a venture. Surveys made in 1940 and 1941 showed that approximately 30 percent of the respondents would actively have opposed such an undertaking. These results point to the alarming conclusion that as much as one third of the American population was prepared to approve an anti-Jewish movement, nearly the same proportion would have stood against such action, and the remainder would have been little concerned.[40]

Policies of the U.S. State Department and Congress were other indications of antisemitic attitudes. Although President Roosevelt had initially called for the international conference at Evian in 1938 to deliberate on solutions for the Jewish refugee problem, the United States did not offer to liberalize its quota for German immigrants. Had the United States shown willingness to open up its quota, historians such as Henry Feingold and David Wyman argue, then other countries might have followed. Similarly disappointing was the decision by Congress to reject the Wagner–Rogers Bill, designed to offer temporary asylum to 20,000 French Jewish children. The refusal of the government to allow the SS *St. Louis* to land on American shores with 930 German Jewish refugees in June 1939 was one more striking example of antisemitic bias in leading political and diplomatic circles of the United States.

In the postwar era it took three years for the U.S. government to enact the Displaced Persons Act of 1948. Between 1948 and 1952 this act enabled approximately 340,000 non-quota Jewish immigrants to enter the United States, along with thousands of non-Jewish immigrants from western and eastern Europe. Anti-Jewish biases were built into the legislation so that it was easier for non-Jews who may have collaborated with the Nazi regime to enter the U.S. than it was for Jews who suffered persecution in the Nazi ghettos and camps. Despite these obstacles to Jewish immigration, the Displaced Persons Act provided a legal basis for non-quota Jewish displaced persons to enter the U.S., and agencies such as USNA and HIAS, along with Christian organizations, provided services for the new Americans. In 1952, however, the proposed McCarran-Walter Act threatened to interrupt the flow of Jewish refugees.

As president for USNA, Bieringer took a leading role in opposing the McCarran-Walter Act. In the annual meeting held in January 1953, Bieringer warned against the implementation of this legislation:

> In the last few months, the flow of immigrants of all faiths to our shores has been sharply curtailed. This is due to the termination of the major

sections of the Displaced Persons Act, the ensuing shortage of available visa numbers, and to enactment of the restrictive McCarran-Walter Immigration and Nationality Act. Unless there is new legislation removing quota barriers, hundreds of thousands of prospective immigrants of all faiths will have to wait years to enter this country.

Last year at this meeting, the McCarran-Walter Immigration Bill was a threat. As we commence 1953, it is a terrible reality. *No words could better depict the meaning to us of this legislation than those of President Truman included in his recent budget message to Congress. The President called for additional funds for the administration of the McCarran-Walter Immigration Act, indicating that the government must be prepared in following its provisions, to arrest more aliens, deport more and check into the lives and backgrounds of many more applicants for citizenship. The budget forecast some 86,000 more arrests of aliens in the next fiscal year than in the last, some 70,000 more court appearances and more than an additional 100,000 individual naturalization investigations.*

Though we recognized the threat posed by this restrictive legislation, we did not fully realize how much it would complicate the work of our agencies. Its enactment has had, as we would naturally expect, a deteriorative effect on immigration, not only to the United States, but to other countries who follow our lead.[41]

A year later, Bieringer reaffirmed the need to combat restrictive immigration legislation:

Changing the McCarran-Walter Immigration Law will require a long and bitter fight. Our ally will be the American people and our major weapon will be education. It is a fight demanding full dedication of our energies and resources. But we will win it. We must win it for the sake of American democracy and for the sake of homeless people all over the world.[42]

Using

What specific events that Bieringer witnessed in his 1933 trip to Germany and Austria made him much more strongly identify with his Jewish heritage?

According to Bieringer, what factors in German life of the 1930s were responsible for the virulent antisemitism he witnessed?

Why did the Nazis impose such severe monetary restrictions on Jews who tried to leave Germany?

What indications did Bieringer give that there was antisemitism in the United States?

"I got angry at what I observed in Germany [in 1933]," exclaimed Bieringer fifty years later. "I knew that something had to be done to help the Jews.

There were signs everywhere that more trouble was ahead and they needed to get out." What does Bieringer mean by the word "angry"? Have you ever become "angry" about a social injustice? If so, what did your anger motivate you to do?

Has your community been involved in the sanctuary movement for helping illegal aliens? What have been some of the major obstacles for these foreigners gaining legal status in the United States?

Who was Father Charles E. Coughlin? What techniques did he use for popularizing his views? When did he have the greatest following and what eventually happened to his movement? What were the social and economic circumstances of the United States in the 1930s that might have fostered the growth of Coughlin's movement?

Do you think Walter Bieringer has made a difference in his community? Discuss, indicating what you mean by the term "making a difference." Also, point out what traits in Bieringer's character may have helped him persist with his work despite many disappointments and setbacks.

Students might want to explore local response to refugees by studying organizations designed to help immigrants in the prewar and war years. For example, Boston students who are interested in the local response to refugees might visit the Schlesinger Library in Cambridge to examine the papers of the Window Shop. Documents in this collection provide insights into the backgrounds of refugees and the ways refugees assimilated into the Boston community. Since many of the workers and volunteers of the Window Shop are still alive, students may want to interview some of them.

Anti-foreigner attitudes of Americans are manifest in U.S. immigration legislation. Students might review the major acts between 1924 and 1952, noting the biases embraced in these laws.

The Facing History Resource Center houses materials pertaining to the career of Walter Bieringer. These include newspaper clippings of his work with refugees in the 1930s; reports of his speeches to local Christian organizations in the 1930s and 1940s; letters to Bieringer from German Jews seeking assistance; reports and official papers on Bieringer's visit to displaced persons camps in 1950; copies of *New Neighbors* (the USNA magazine), 1950-1954, including several addresses by Bieringer on the McCarran-Walter Act; photographs of Bieringer with local and national political figures; audio interviews of Bieringer by Facing History and Ourselves, 1984-1985; and an article on the life and times of Walter Bieringer in *Facing History News* (Summer 1985).

For a summary of the postwar immigration legislation and its impact on the fate of thousands of displaced persons seeking entry to the United States, see Ryan, *Quiet Neighbors*, available at the Facing History Resource Center. Ryan fundamentally argues that it was easier for former Nazis to gain admission to the United States than it was for the Jewish victims of the Holocaust in the years immediately following World War II. He estimates that at least 10,000 former Nazis, including individuals on the lists of war criminals, obtained visas to enter the United States in these years. Many of these visas were obtained under false pretenses, but it takes years for the Departments of Justice and Immigration to take any action in these matters and in many cases it is now too late to obtain the necessary proof for initiating deportation and denaturalization proceedings.

Additional books on the American response available at the Facing History Resource Center include: Breitman & Krant, *American Refugee Policy and European Jewry 1933-1945*; Feingold, *Politics of Rescue: The Roosevelt Administration and the Holocaust*; Feingold, "The Government Response," in *The Holocaust Ideology, Bureaucracy and Genocide: The San Jose Papers*; Lipstadt, *Beyond Belief: The American Press and the Coming of the Holocaust*; Lockstein, *Were We Our Brothers' Keepers? The Public Response of American Jews to the Holocaust, 1938-1944*; Morse, *While Six Million Died: A Chronicle of American Apathy*; Wyman, *The Abandonment of the European Jews: America and the Holocaust*; and Wyman, *Paper Walls*.

For additional information on Father Charles Coughlin, see "The Radio Priest," an episode of the PBS documentary series *The American Experience*. A copy of this episode is available at the Facing History Resource Center.

Leon Bass

[I]t was 1945, and the war appeared to be over, and our unit went to a place called Weimar . . . . Immediately about five or six of us took off with one of our officers to a place called Buchenwald . . . Buchenwald was a concentration camp. I had no idea of what kind of camp this was . . . But on this day in 1945 I was to discover what human suffering was all about. . . . It is not just relegated to me and mine; it touches us all.

Leon Bass entered Buchenwald with comrades in the the 183rd Unit a few days after the camp was liberated in 1945. Today he tells students how his experience influenced his life and convinced him of the need to combat racism and prejudice everywhere.

Dr. Leon Bass, a former history teacher and principal at Benjamin Franklin High School in Philadelphia, recalls his experiences as a black American soldier in World War II and describes what he witnessed at Buchenwald concentration camp just a few days after American troops had liberated the camp.

Bass grew up in the South. When he was eighteen he enlisted in the army and trained in camps in Georgia and Mississippi. He served in a black unit because the army still maintained a policy of segregation. His happiest memories of the war years focus on the two months he and his unit spent in Liverpool, England, before going to the Continent in 1944. He felt no sense of being discriminated against by the English—they respected all soldiers, whatever their color, who were taking part in the effort to destroy Hitler.

Crossing the English Channel to Le Havre, France, Bass's 183rd Unit was attached to General Patton's Third Army during the Battle of the Bulge. After this encounter, the 183rd was stationed in various cities throughout Germany. In April 1945, Bass's unit bivouacked outside the town of Weimar. Several days after Buchenwald was liberated, Bass and some members of his unit visited the camp.

Bass was only nineteen years old when he entered Buchenwald. He and his comrades were completely unprepared for what they saw. Witnessing the starving inmates, the piles of human corpses and the unspeakable conditions, Bass realized that human suffering was not limited only to his people. As he told the students at English High School in Boston:

[I]t was 1945, and the war appeared to be over, and our unit went to a place called Weimar. Weimar today is in East Germany, but at that time there was no East Germany—just Germany. So we put up our tents and bivouacked in the area.

Immediately about five or six of us took off with one of our officers to a place called Buchenwald . . . Buchenwald was a concentration camp. I had no idea what kind of camp this was. I thought it might have been a prisoner-of-war camp where they kept soldiers who were captured. But on this day in 1945, I was to discover what human suffering was all about. I was going to take off the blinders that caused me to have tunnel vision. I was going to see clearly that, yes, I suffered and I was hurting because I was black in a white society, but I had also begun to understand that suffering is universal. It is not just relegated to me and mine; it touches us all.

An ex-inmate of Buchenwald showed American journalists how the Nazis beat dying prisoners over the head with a club.

And so I walked through the gates of Buchenwald, and I saw the dead and the dying. I saw people who had been so brutalized and were so maltreated. They had been starved and beaten. They had been worked almost to death, not fed enough, no medical care. One man came up and his fingers were webbed together, all of his fingers together, by sores and scabs. This was due to malnutrition, not eating the proper foods. There were others holding on to each other, trying to remain standing. They had on wooden shoes; they had on the pajama-type uniform; their heads had been shaved. Some had the tattoos with numbers on their arms. I saw this. I saw them with the wooden bowls. Some of them were standing waiting for food and hitting on the fence, this was wire fence, and making guttural sounds; not words—just sounds.

I said, "My God, what is this insanity that I have come to? What are these people here for? What have they done? What was their crime that would cause people to treat them like this?" You see, I wasn't prepared for this. I was only nineteen. I had no frame of reference to cope with the kind of thing that I was witnessing.

For more than twenty years after the war Bass did not speak of what he had witnessed at Buchenwald. Then in 1968, while he was principal at Benjamin Franklin High School, his silence ended. He entered a classroom where a Holocaust survivor was trying to tell the class of her experiences. The students were being rude and inattentive. Bass reprimanded the students and informed them that what this woman was telling them was the truth—he had seen it for himself at Buchenwald. The students were moved by these words from their principal, and they began to listen to the survivor's story.

Bass realized how important it was for him to share his story, especially with young people, and since that day in 1968 he has spoken to audiences of youth and adults throughout the country. He recounts the details of what he witnessed to help people consider the repercussions of racism, discrimination and dehumanizing policies. As he concluded his presentation at English High School:

I didn't come up to Boston just to tell you the horror story; as horrible as it is, the story must be told. History cannot be swept under the rug. It shouldn't be and you must not permit it to be. We have things in our history that are ugly; slavery was ugly. I don't care what anybody tried to tell me when I was young, like Gone With the Wind; everybody is happy on massah's plantation. That's for the birds; that wasn't so.

It was an evil, horrible institution and the Holocaust is just as evil, if not more so. There was a planned, organized, systematic approach to annihilating a whole group of people. They killed not only six million Jews,

*but millions of others. There were Gypsies there, there were Catholics
there, there were communists, trade unionists, homosexuals, anyone who
didn't fit the scheme of things for the Nazis was in Buchenwald and all the
other camps to be annihilated. They came pretty close to doing it too. But
somebody had to stand up, somebody had to dare to be a Daniel and walk
into the den and say, "This evil cannot continue." This is what brings me
here to Boston to talk to you.*

Commentary

Buchenwald was one of the German camps built in the prewar years for the
detention of political prisoners. During the war years when extermination
camps were established in Poland, Buchenwald remained a labor camp, not
expressly set up to kill Jews and other victims of the racial policies of the
Third Reich. Buchenwald, which had a number of subcamps in the area
around Weimar, supplied slave labor for the Nazi regime.

By 1945, conditions at Buchenwald—never particularly "good"—had
deteriorated dramatically. The population of the camp had increased to around
50,000 and had become a society of extremes. The relatively favored group of
prisoners—non-Jewish Germans and western Europeans—were at the top;
less-privileged prisoners—Jews, Gypsies, and eastern Europeans—were at the
bottom in the "Little Camp."

Between April 3 and 10, 1945, with the approach of American troops, the
commandant ordered that more than 20,000 inmates be shipped out to other
camps. On April 11 a team of the 6th Armored Division accidentally
discovered Buchenwald. Shortly thereafter the 4th Armored Division and 8th
Infantry entered the camp. The liberators found the sharply divided society:
the healthier prisoners—Communists and other political prisoners who were
in the main camp—were able to greet the liberators and wreak revenge against
the ex-guards; the weaker inmates—primarily Jews, Gypsies and little
children—in the little camp were too sick and emaciated to greet their
liberators and lacked sufficient strength to contemplate revenge.

John Glustrom of the 333rd Engineers reports the suffering and bewilderment
of inmates during the days of liberation:

> My first impression of it was the odor. The stench of it was all over the
> place and there were a bunch of very bewildered, lost individuals who
> came to me pathetically at the door in their unkempt uniforms to see what
> we were doing and what was going to be done about them. They were
> staying at the camp even though their guards and staff had fled because
> they didn't know where to go or what to do. They had heard news that the

Americans had taken over that area and they were waiting for somebody to turn their lives back straight again and they were just lost souls at that time.

Well, my feeling was that this was the most shattering experience of my life.[43]

The American correspondent Percy Knauth, who entered the Little Camp a few days after liberation—about the same time that Bass and his comrades visited Buchenwald—reports seeing men

emaciated beyond all imagination or description. . . . Their eyes were sunk so deep that they looked blind. If they moved at all, it was with a crawling slowness that made them look like lethargic spiders. Many just lay in their bunks as if dead.[44]

General Eisenhower, commander of the Allied Forces in Europe, reported how the scenes at Buchenwald shocked him into the reality of Nazi barbarism:

I have never felt able to describe my emotional reaction when I came face to face with indisputable evidence of Nazi brutality and ruthless disregard of every shred of human decency. Up to that moment I had only known about it generally, or through secondary sources. I am certain, however, that I have never at any time experienced an equal sense of shock.[45]

As in the liberation of other camps, the American soldiers entering Buchenwald developed coping mechanisms for dealing with the atrocities they witnessed. Some denied what they had seen or focused on only one thing because their minds were unable to absorb the enormity of the atrocity. According to psychologists who visited Buchenwald shortly after liberation, it was not uncommon for American soldiers to adopt the Nazi point of view about the inmates in the Little Camp, regarding them as somehow subhuman and deserving of their treatment.

Survivors of the Holocaust had rarely, if ever, seen a black person in the European communities from which they had come. For this reason the sight of a black American soldier such as Leon Bass at the time of liberation was associated with the joy of being freed from the horrors of Nazism.

Sonia Weitz, a survivor who was liberated at Mauthausen (and whose story also appears in **Portraits**), described reaction to the sight of a black liberator in her poem entitled "Liberation Day":

Liberation Day

A black G.I. stood by the door
(I never saw a black before)
He'll set me free before I die,
I thought he must be the Messiah.

A black Messiah came for me. . .
He stared with eyes that didn't see.
He never heard a single word
Which hung absurd upon my tongue.

And then he simply froze in place
The shock, the horror on his face,
He didn't weep, he didn't cry
But deep within his gentle eyes
. . . a flood of devastating pain,
His innocence forever slain.

For me, with yet another dawn
I found my black Messiah gone
And on we went our separate ways
For forty years without a trace.

But there's a special bond we share
Which has grown strong before we dare
To live, to hope, to smile . . . and yet
We want Not Ever to Forget.[46]

Using

In studying World War II, we often focus attention on racism taking place in totalitarian regimes, Nazi Germany in particular. From Bass's description of his experiences as a soldier in the American army, what indications do you have that racist policies existed in American society?

What does Bass mean by the comment that before he entered Buchenwald he had had "tunnel vision"?

Why does Bass say that he questioned risking his life in the European theater of battle?

In Bass's description of Buchenwald, which aspects of the concentration camp most affected him? Why do you think he recalls these features so vividly?

Compare Bass's reactions with those of Marcus Orr, who entered Dachau shortly before liberation.

Discuss ways that Bass developed of coping with scenes he found so hard to understand at Buchenwald.

Compare Bass's description of Buchenwald forty years after liberation with excerpts from the eyewitness account by war correspondent Edward R. Murrow on April 15, 1945, four days after liberation:

> Permit me to tell you what you would have seen and heard had you been with me on Thursday. It will not be pleasant listening. If you are at lunch or if you have no appetite to hear what Germans have done, now is a good time to switch off the radio, for I propose to tell you of Buchenwald.
>
> It is on a small hill about four miles outside of Weimar, and it was one of the largest concentration camps in Germany. And it was built to last.
>
> As we approached it, we saw about nine hundred men in civilian clothes with rifles advancing in open order across the fields. There were a few shots. We stopped to inquire. We were told that some of the prisoners had a couple of SS men cornered in there. We drove on, reached the main gate. The prisoners crowded up behind the wire. We entered.
>
> And now, let me tell this in the first person, for I was the least important person there, as you shall hear. There surged around me an evil-smelling horde; men and boys reached out to touch me. They were in rags and the remnants of uniforms. Death had already marked many of them, but they were smiling with their eyes.
>
> I looked out over that mass of men to the green fields beyond where well-fed Germans were plowing. A German, Fritz Kersheimer, came up and said, "May I show you around the camp? I've been here 10 years." An Englishman stood to attention saying, "May I introduce myself? Delighted to see you. And can you tell me when some of our blokes will be along?" I told him, "Soon," and asked to see one of the barracks. It happened to be occupied by Czechoslovakians.
>
> When I entered, men crowded around, tried to lift me to their shoulders. They were too weak. Many of them could not get out of bed. I was told that this building had once stabled 80 horses; there were 1,200 men in it, five to a bunk. The stink was beyond description. . . .
>
> I asked how many men had died in that building during the last month. They called the doctor. We inspected his records. There were only names in the little black book, nothing more. Nothing of who these men were, what they had done or hoped. Behind the names of those who had died there was a cross. I counted them. They totalled 242—242 out of 1200 in one month.[47]

Alan Filreis, Professor of English at the University of Pennsylvania, teaches a course on Literature of the Holocaust. As part of the course, students make distinctions between written memoirs and oral testimonies and determine what each form contributes to their understanding of the Holocaust experience. One recurring topic was how witnesses who tell of their experiences repeatedly can retain their true memory of the event. As Professor Filreis put it, "How can one reach back and twice effect the same fresh recovery?"

Leon Bass, who has told his story in many different educational settings, visited Filreis's class where he recounted his wartime experiences in the same manner he does in his portrait. Professor Filreis reported how he and his class reacted to Bass repeating an oft-told memory.

> Leon Bass makes no effort to hide the fact that what he has to say he has said many times before, though for him as for many others, there was a time when he could not speak. Indeed, at the center of his testimony is the "story" of how he learned that when one has something to say one must tell it, disregarding the risk that the words will become "used" and that the original horrifying experience will fade and become secondary to the words used to describe that experience. To Leon Bass, the meaning of the story is the very reason for telling it. To him, repetition is a risk worth taking, because the alternative is silence. So what would we have wanted Filip Muller to say in describing those impacted bodies at Auschwitz? Would we have him go silent at that point in his story, or whenever new words simply did not come to him at the moment? Or leave a nonliteral experience nonliteral? Teaching us a last lesson about literature, Leon Bass—neither a novelist, poet, nor playwright—taught us this: "Never again," one of those icons the students came with, inherently means repetition, a repeated message, even down to the words a set of often-used signs. One student was so moved by Leon Bass's willingness to repeat his story at the risk of seeming "merely" to repeat it, she wrote him a letter after his visit. Here is a portion of it:

> *Dr. Bass, I found your courage very moving. Your message was so perfect, so simple. You put it in such a way that a young child as well as a college senior could hold onto each word that you said and be equally affected . . . Right now, I am in the process of thinking what I can do for two years to be helpful in Philadelphia. I have the strength to contribute more than I have already. [For a year she has worked with black teenage girls in the community.] Thank you for coming to Penn and speaking to us. After you were done, I was wishing I could package you up and distribute you all over the country. I know how difficult it is to do what you do, but please keep on doing it. It makes a huge difference. We students need all the words of encouragement we can get our hands on today.*[48]

Marcus Orr

Just after mid-April 1945 [I and two others from 8th Infantry Division of the American Army were sent on a reconnaissance of the city of Dachau]. So we approached Dachau. We had a very strange experience . . . we saw a railroad yard. Boxcars were pulled up there. I saw to my amazement and horror they were all full of dead and dying people in all states of dishabille and disarray.

Marcus Orr, professor of history at Memphis State University, recalls his experiences as an American soldier in World War II. This selection focuses on the closing weeks of the war when he and two companions inspected the German camp at Dachau.

Several months after the attack on Pearl Harbor, 17-year-old Marcus Orr enlisted in the 8th Infantry. During training he was selected to study ammunition because he had a strong background in chemistry and physics. He was later assigned as an aide to the major general whose task was to keep the infantry regiments supplied with ammunition under all sorts of conditions.

Orr's division trained in Oklahoma until 1944, when it was sent overseas to take part in Operation Over, in the southern part of the Bulge. Following this encounter, the 8th Infantry moved into Germany and by the spring of 1945 was settled near Munich in the Bavarian region.

In mid-April the division prepared for a possible battle for control of Munich. Orr and two others were dispatched on a scouting expedition to locate spots for depositing ammunition. The trio, disguised as Germans and driving a captured German vehicle, explored the area of the town around Dachau, which had a population of approximately 15,000. They were especially interested in checking the accuracy of aerial photographs of the I.G. Farben chemical plant and the camp, which they assumed was an army camp.

The three scouts made their reconnaisance only a few days before the liberation of the concentration camp at Dachau. It was cold and rainy and all the bridges in the area had been blown out. They were constantly on the alert because enemies lurked everywhere. When they arrived at the camp, they realized it was much larger than they had anticipated.

The size of the camp was not the only surprise. They were amazed to find the gates of the camp open and unguarded. Disorder was everywhere. Just to the left of the entrance, they saw barracks and inmates in striped uniforms. Orr wanted to go inside because he believed that captured American soldiers were there. In fact, there were very few Americans in the camp, and only a small

At Dachau Concentration Camp M.E. Walter of the Houston Chronicle (in civilian clothes with back to the camera), a member of the group of editors and publishers investigating POW atrocities after liberation, inspects one of the prisoner's living quarters while the prisoners crowd around him.

percentage of the 35,000 inmates were Jews. All the other Jewish prisoners had already been killed.

As the scouting party drove out of the camp to rejoin their unit, Orr was hit and wounded by shrapnel from bombs that had been dropped from a German jet. Orr was removed to a hospital, where doctors told him that his injuries would leave him with both legs paralyzed.

From others in the 8th Infantry who took part in the liberation of Dachau at the end of April, Orr learned that the camp was a detention camp, not just an army camp, and that the I.G. Farben complex had been a labor camp. He also discovered that the boxcars he had seen came from Buchenwald—the dead and dying people were to have been sent to the crematoria and mass open graves at Dachau.

Recently he has learned more details about the closing days of the camp from Dr. Marcus J. Smith's *Dachau: The Harrowing of Hell*. Dr. Smith entered Dachau two days after liberation as the doctor accompanying Displaced Persons Team 115; he remained there until August 1945, treating survivors and reporting on their condition in letters to his wife, also a physician. Almost thirty years after the war he decided to publish these letters in an effort to counter claims by the revisionist movement, which he feared was gaining momentum.

In the postwar years, Orr has reflected frequently on the scenes of April 1945. As he recalls, he and the other soldiers knew almost nothing of what was occurring to the civilian population in the Third Reich. Officials in intelligence and governmental circles might well have been informed, he explains, but "we [enlisted men] were innocent and naive in that we did not have the proper perspective or the true scope of the Nazi experience." But, he adds sadly, even after the American public did know about the atrocities of the Holocaust, little was done to help the displaced persons.

Commentary

On March 21, 1933, Heinrich Himmler, then Police Commissioner of Munich, announced that the first concentration camp for functionaries of the Social Democratic and Communist parties was to be opened at Dachau on March 22. The original camp, designed to hold 5,000 prisoners, was intended to eliminate all political opposition. In time, it also held Jews, Gypsies, and anti-Nazi clergymen, and many citizens whose views made them unpopular.

The changes in the ratio of the various nationalities from 1939 to 1945 reflected the course of the war. When the German army invaded a country, the first prisoner transports began to arrive. In the occupied nations, the Germans sought to stifle all opposition by deporting intellectual and political leaders. Jewish citizens were persecuted everywhere. Deportation was greatly accelerated during the last years of the war, since it provided the basis for a slave labor force necessary for the German armaments industry.

Between 1942 and the spring of 1945 transports of slave laborers and prisoners were constantly sent to Dachau. For the most part the camp had been able to absorb these arrivals and maintain a semblance of order. In the last months of the war, however, "with supply lines endangered, and the arrival of ever-increasing trainloads of disease-ridden prisoners, the camp began its inevitable slide into uncontrolled death and decay."[49] Orr's repeated references to disorder and disarray in the camp during mid-April resemble accounts of survivors and other eyewitnesses.

On April 29, 1945, the liberators of the Dachau camp found more than 30,000 survivors of thirty-one different nationalities, in the overcrowded and filthy barracks in the subsidiary camps attached to Dachau. During its twelve years of existence, 206,000 prisoners were registered in Dachau; it is impossible to determine the number of nonregistered arrivals.

The present memorial site at Dachau was opened on May 9, 1965. Attached to the museum are a cinema, archives, and a library for Holocaust scholars.

Benjamin Ferencz, a prosecutor at the Nuremberg Trials and later the director of the restitution program for victims of the Nazi labor camps, recalls the final days of the war when he, like Marcus Orr, witnessed the condition of German camps:

> As a war crimes investigator, I gathered evidence of German atrocities that had been committed in areas which were being liberated by the advancing American army. The retreating Germans frequently murdered French and Belgian civilians; for the first time, my knowledge of French and my training in the laws of war were put to use as I reported on the crimes and tried to apprehend the criminals. As we entered Germany, the army began to receive reports about wholesale murder of Allied flyers who had been shot down over German territory. My duties required that I disinter and try to identify the bodies of young aviators who had been beaten to death by enraged German mobs; yet the depth of Nazi criminality did not strike me full force until I joined the troops advancing into some of the German concentration camps.
>
> What I recall most vividly—in Buchenwald, Mauthausen, Dachau, and the surrounding camps—are the carts loaded with skeletons and the mounds of emaciated bodies covered with lye, piled up like cordwood before the crematoria. It was difficult for me to tell whether the hundreds of inmates who were lying in the dust were dead or alive. Those who had been able to walk had been whipped out of the camps by the retreating SS. As we pursued the fleeing camp guards through the woods, the path was marked by a trail of corpses. The bedraggled prisoners who could not keep up with the retreat had been shot by the SS and left dead or dying along the way. Occasionally we would come upon a ditch filled with ragged bodies or a mass grave that had been covered with a light layer of dirt. The American soldiers rounded up the townspeople, male and female, and ordered them to dig up and carry the cadavers to the nearest cemetery for proper burial.[50]

93

The Report of the 7th Army in May 1945 contained details on the conditions and appearance of the camp at Dachau. The description of malnutrition provides insights into what American soldiers like Orr and Ferencz witnessed upon entering the camp in the spring of 1945:

> Although the many thousands of prisoners at Dachau underwent various and different forms of torture, punishments, and executions, there was one experience they shared in common and that was an existence in a state of semi-starvation. Probably the largest number of deaths from any one cause were those due to malnutrition. Thus, 7,000 autopsies performed at Dachau during the years 1942-1945 demonstrated that the great majority died of hunger and the remainder of diseases such as tuberculosis, typhus, and dysentery, the progress of which was directly related to the poor nutritional state of the victims. The daily ration was fairly well standardized. The basic menu consisted of 1/2 litre of synthetic coffee for breakfast, 3/4 litre of soup in which a few cabbage leaves or rotten potato peelings floated for a noon meal, and a slice of bread (150-300 grams), a thin slice of sausage or a bit of cheese or margarine, and a litre of soup for the evening meal. The very maximum caloric content of these meals was 1,000 calories per day, but often running as low as 500 to 700. All those at hard labor, that is, all but the priests, received the additional so-called "Brotzeit" which was an extra slice of bread with a slice of sausage or a piece of margarine.
>
> The worst cases of malnutrition and gross starvation were seen on the transports to and from Dachau. These transports would arrive with hundreds of dead and dying of starvation. Thus, one transport from Buchenwald had been 21 days enroute during which the prisoners had had nothing but a half a loaf of bread and four potatoes. Water on such trips was either insufficient or omitted entirely. Another transport arrived at By-camp No. 3 with 120 dead, the prisoners having had no food for four days. They were then placed in an encloure and given one loaf of bread for each 10 men.[51]

Using

What details of Dachau most surprised Orr and his companions when they entered the camp?

Why was it dangerous for American soldiers to appear in their own uniforms in areas around Munich and other German cities in the period before liberation?

Why were Hitler and other Nazi officials insistent that Germans continue to fight despite the inevitability of defeat in the spring of 1945? What other testimony in **Portraits** discusses this phenomenon?

Why were American soldiers so naive about what was happening in the concentration camps even though reports had reached Allied powers with details of the mass killings and Nazi brutality as early as the summer of 1942?

Why did the Nazi guards try to remove prestigious prisoners from Dachau before liberation? Who was Martin Niemoeller whom Orr mentions? Can you name other prestigious prisoners at Dachau?

Why do you think Dr. Orr has carried out research on Dachau in the postwar decades? How might his research affect his memory of the event?

Two testimonies in the Fortunoff Video Archive for Holocaust Testimonies elaborate on themes discussed by Marcus Orr: Daniel F., a survivor of Hungary, describes himself as a Musselmanner (a person in a stage of such starvation that he appeared ghostlike) at Dachau—he weighed 55 pounds at liberation; and David C., an American physician who entered Dachau two days after liberation, provides clinical details of what happened to prisoners suffering from starvation and malnutrition.

"You Are Free," a 20-minute film, contains testimonies by men and women involved in liberation. The film is available at the Facing History Resource Center.

See Lewis Weinstein's article, "The Liberation of Nazi Death Camps by American Army—1945: The Report of a Witness," for his description of how he encouraged General Eisenhower to visit Ordruf concentration camp after liberation.

Paul D. (A-41)

*When I was down in the chasm [very ill a few years ago], the feeling that
overwhelmed me was that there were people who only lived in my memory,
that I was the only link to the world for these people. . . . And the feeling
was so awful that what I did was that I called in my son . . . and I said what
I want you to do is hear about the shochet [ritual slaughterer who makes
meat kosher] of Hummene so that you will also remember him . . . and my
son said to me, "Okay, I will remember him." . . . And my daughter also.
She . . . said, "I will also remember him."*

This portrait describes the life of a young Jewish boy from eastern Europe
who managed to escape arrest and deportation throughout the war. Like other
Jewish children during the war years, Paul D. lived with uncertainty and
fear—no sooner did he get used to one place than he was forced to move on.
Even more frightening, for ten months he lived in an orphanage, completely
separated from his family.

Paul D. was born in 1935 in Moldava, Czechoslovakia. Paul's paternal
grandparents, Orthodox Jews, lived close by, and Paul's first years were
steeped in traditional Jewish culture. Paul's father died in 1938 when he was
three years old, and with his mother he moved to her hometown of Hummene
in Slovakia. Soon thereafter, Paul's mother married a man who treated Paul as
his natural son.

Slovakia became a German satellite in 1939, but the local officials were not
rigorous about enforcing anti-Jewish legislation in the first years of the war.
Paul and his parents spent the early war years in relative safety because they
had declared themselves converted to Christianity. However, in 1941
converted Jews were no longer exempt from anti-Jewish legislation; all Jews
were being identified, rounded up and deported. While several of Paul's close
relatives were deported to Lublin, Paul and his parents secured false papers
and went into hiding with non-Jewish friends.

They stayed together in Slovakia until 1942 when it became increasingly
dangerous for Jews. At this point, Paul's mother arranged to send Paul to live
with his grandparents in Moldava, which had become part of Hungary in
1939. Jews in Hungary were not being rounded up in 1942 and Paul's parents
felt he would be safer outside of Slovakia. Paul's journey turned into a
nightmare. His grandparents did not pick him up at the train station in Kosice
and local authorities placed the Jewish boy in an orphanage. Ten months went
by before his grandparents were finally able to claim their grandson and take
him back to their home in Moldava.

In March 1944 Paul's life was again disrupted. Germans began the roundup of Hungarian Jews and he and his grandparents were deported to a ghetto in Kosice. Paul's stepfather managed to have his son rescued from the ghetto, and by the summer of 1944 Paul was reunited with his parents in Slovakia. But the reunion was brief. Paul's stepfather was separated from his wife and son, and Paul spent the duration of the war with his mother, always on the run from one town to another to escape being rounded up by the Nazi authorities.

Paul ends his testimony by explaining the importance of insuring that his own son and daughter know what happened to him and to the culture of Orthodox Jews in eastern Europe.

Commentary

The prologue to the memoir *Gizelle, Save the Children!* provides an outline of political events in Hungary during World War II that is useful in following the details of Paul's boyhood during this era:

August 30, 1940

As he stood in a luxurious conference room in the Belvedere Palace in Vienna, staring down at a map spread on the table before him, Mihai Manolescu, the foreign minister of Rumania, fainted. He fell heavily on top of the map, which he had seen for the first time. The Germans had decreed, in the so-called 'Vienna Awards,' that one half of the Rumanian province of Transylvania must be ceded to Hungary.

Thus, overnight, some 150,000 Rumanian Jews became Hungarian Jews. . .

November 20, 1940

As "repayment" for the German gift of northern Transylvania, Hungary became an official ally of the Germans. And seven months later Hungarian forces joined with the Nazis in their invasion of Russia. Some 130,000 Hungarian-Jewish men, up to the age of sixty, were drafted into 'auxiliary army service' (forced labor battalions) and sent to the Russian front to clear mine fields and serve in other ways as cannon fodder. In addition, thousands died from hunger, typhus, and murder by Hungarian soldiers.

January 1942

Seeking to prove Hungary's "trustworthiness" in solving the Jewish question, the pro-German prime minister Laszlo Bardossy, offered to deport 300,000 "new" Jews obtained during his country's recent acquisitions, which included not only parts of northern Transylvania, but also southern Slovakia, as well as sections of Yugoslavia. The German Foreign Office was delighted with the offer. Eichmann, however, declined, for technical reasons. "It was," he said, "too costly to set in motion the whole machinery for evacuation for only one category." He preferred to wait until the country was "ready for the entire solution to the Jewish problem in Hungary."

March 1942

Miklos Kallay became the new prime minister, and the reprieve of Hungarian Jews was extended for another two years. Not only did the courageous Kallay resist ever-mounting German pressure to deport Hungarian Jews, he also dragged his feet on the matters of depriving Jews of their livelihood.

With good reason. Although Jews comprised only 5 percent of the total population, they were the backbone of the Hungarian middle class. . . .

March 1944

The fragile safety bubble suddenly burst. The two years of Kallay's regime had coincided with the roaring heights of the holocaust as millions of European Jews were murdered. However, in Hungary there still existed the largest concentration of Jews in the German sphere of influence. The Germans needed the vital Hungarian network of railroads, needed Hungarian foodstuffs and equipment, needed the Hungarian open plains for access to Russia, Rumania, Yugoslavia. And because of these needs the Nazis had allowed Kallay measures of liberty. But now, with defeat looming on all fronts, the Nazis decided that their most important mission must be fulfilled before it was too late. *Vernichtung.* Annihilation of European Jewry. All of Hungary's Jews must be murdered. In a matter of months.

Kallay was ousted; a pro-Nazi prime minister put in.

On March 19, two divisions of the German Army occupied Hungary, together with German policy makers, supervisors, coordinators, and advisers.

And Adolf Eichmann moved into the Majestic Hotel in Budapest with his *Sondereinsatzkommando*, the Eichmann Special Operation Unit. The work of these high-ranking murder specialists was all but finished in the rest of Europe. Their experience and well-honed efficiency could now be concentrated on Hungarian Jews. . . .

It was decreed that all Jews must wear the yellow Star of David when appearing outside their homes. . . .

All stores, offices, and warehouses still owned by Jews were closed. . . .

Jewish journalists, civil servants, notaries, accountants, lawyers, were dismissed from their jobs. Jewish bank accounts were closed.

Property owned by Jews was turned over to Hungarians. This included cars, radios, books, paintings, clothing—and over 600,000 acres of land. . .

It was decided that Jews who lived in the recently annexed territories would be deported first. All Jews in these areas would be rounded up and transferred to ghettos. Those who lived in villages or towns of less than 10,000 would be transferred to ghettos in larger cities and camps. . . ."[52]

Using

What factors led Paul's parents to believe he would be safer with his grandparents in Moldava than in Czechoslovakia in 1942?

Why does Paul believe it is so important for his children to hear his story of the *shochet*?

Holocaust survivors often mention that luck played a major role in their survival. What incidents in Paul's story suggest that luck was a critical factor in his survival and that of his mother?

The filmstrip "The Life that Disappeared," available at the Facing History Resource Center, provides information on traditional Jewish life in Eastern Europe.

Paul's testimony touches briefly on the attitudes among Hungarian Jewry before the Nazis occupied the country and began a systematic roundup and deportation of Jews in the spring of 1944. Additional insights into the Hungarian attitudes—especially the belief among Hungarian Jews that they would be spared the fate of Jews in other countries—are found in the montages "Imagining the Unimaginable" (Excerpts 4 and 5) and "Challenge of Memory: A Videotape to Accompany Elie Wiesel's *Night*," (Excerpt 2), and "Childhood Memories" (Excerpt 10).

Braham's *The Politics of Genocide: The Holocaust in Hungary* is the most comprehensive study of the subject. For additional insights on attitudes among Hungarian Jewry, see Bauer's *The Holocaust in Historical Perspective*, pages 106-107, and Marrus's *The Holocaust in History*, pages 150-151.

For additional testimonies on Hungarian Jewry, see the ninety-minute videotape "Witness to the Holocaust," available at the Facing History Resource Center. Testimonies included in this program come from the originally-videotaped proceedings of the trial of Adolf Eichmann.

Peter Gay (T-51)

*One had an ongoing set of experiences which . . . culminated in things . . .
[we had not anticipated]. For example, even Kristallnacht, which I went
through . . . was not exactly something that in 1933, 1935, or even 1936
that we expected necessarily.*

This portrait covers the adolescent years of Peter Gay, the Sterling Professor
of History at Yale University. As a teenager, Peter lived with his parents, Mr.
and Mrs. Moritz Fröhlich, in Berlin, Germany, during the early years of the
Nazi regime, 1933 until 1939. The family emigrated to Cuba in the spring of
1939; two years later the Fröhlichs obtained visas to enter the United States
and settled in Denver, Colorado, where the family officially anglicized the
name Fröhlich to Gay. Professor Gay's experiences as a youth are not
necessarily typical of the Jewish experience in the Third Reich. Yet they
provide important insights into the impact of Nazi antisemitic measures on
some assimilated Jews in Berlin during the prewar years, particularly the
effect of *Kristallnacht* and its aftermath on Jews who had regarded themselves
loyal German citizens. The following description of Gay's video portrait is
longer than preceding descriptions in order to illustrate how Gay, in relating
his own adolescence, shows the relationship between crucial historical events
of the 1930s and their impact on ordinary men and women residing in Berlin.
As Gay himself has argued in several of his works, it is possible for subjective
experiences to become the basis for an objective study of an historical era.

Peter was born in 1923 as the only son of Moritz Fröhlich, a commercial
agent who had come to Berlin from Kampen (a small town in Upper Silesia),
and his wife, who had been born in Breslau, the Silesian capital. Although not
wealthy, the Fröhlich family enjoyed prosperity in the mid-thirties. Moritz
owned a car for business purposes and in the spring of 1936 the family took a
motor trip through the country. Peter attended a *gymnasium*, a private school
that prepared many of its graduates for university education.

Whereas other German Jewish refugees have recalled suffering antisemitic
persecution, even violence, during their school years, Gay remembers
encountering very little discrimination. Peter and his Jewish classmates were
not allowed to attend the ceremonies to commemorate the occupation of the
Saarland; there were occasional anti-Jewish remarks by a French and a history
teacher. "But," Gay insists, "they were very isolated, very rare."

Peter's headmaster made a point of acknowledging young Fröhlich's
academic excellence. In the spring of 1935, it came time for Peter to decide

whether to take the Latin classical track preparing for university education and a professional career or to take the English track in preparation for a career in business and commerce. While Peter had indicated a preference for English, the headmaster called in Peter's father, suggesting strongly that Peter study the classics. Peter thus joined his classmates in following the Latin curriculum.

As Gay explains in his portrait, the incident with the headmaster was a microcosm of his experiences during the 1930s. "There were lots of incidents like this," he remarked,

> *which suggest something that is extremely important in the history of this period, namely how unbelievably complicated it was, or to use more popular language, how conflicting the signals were. You got all kinds of signals. Obviously, the government said you are . . . scum and you can't do this and you can't do that. On the other hand, a great many other people said: "Nonsense, I don't believe in this." It is that kind of thing that one should keep in mind.*

Peter also remembers how he exercised caution during his *gymnasium* years. While he was perhaps the most intelligent student in his class, he did not seek to stand out. Rather, he hung back slightly, allowing another classmate to gain prominence as the top student. Peter explains that his prudence was instinctive. However, he had witnessed the type of persecution that his cousin suffered for speaking out against the antisemitic atmosphere of Hitler's Germany.

For the most part, the antisemitic policies of the early Nazi administration did not affect the Fröhlich family. Peter's parents were *Konfessionslos* (without denomination)—this was a classification in German law that meant that no portion of their taxes could be applied to support a religious community. Moreover, Mr. Fröhlich was a wounded veteran of World War I who had been awarded the Iron Cross and received a pension. As a veteran he was entitled to certain privileges, such as traveling in first class train cars with second class tickets. During the early Nazi era, Jewish veterans such as Fröhlich were exempted from measures in antisemitic legislation. For instance, the children of Jewish veterans were not subject to the rigid school quotas placed on Jewish students, and this is why Peter was able to pursue his education in a German *gymnasium*.

The assimilated and nonreligious way of life of Moritz Fröhlich's family contrasted with that of other members of the family who observed major Jewish holidays. While Peter and his father had no problem attending sports events on Saturdays or high holidays, Peter's aunt and uncle sharply criticized Moritz when their sons sneaked out of services to accompany Peter to a soccer game. Clashes of this sort led to minor tensions in the extended family and created different perspectives on the meaning of Nazism for the whole family.

Peter's encounters with the Nazis were minimal up to 1938. Although cognizant of the parades and rallies that took place in Berlin, Gay's most prominent memory is that of being told by the troop leader of his Jewish boy scout troop to remove his identifying scarf and go home quietly one weekend in 1934—it was the weekend of the Night of Long Knives when Hitler stripped the SA (the Brown Shirts) of power.

The Nuremberg Laws of September 1935, which many historians today cite as the first clear demonstration of the Nazis' intention to eliminate Jews, scarcely affected the Fröhlichs. While they had to dismiss their German maid who was

"Kristallnacht was a night when the Nazis attacked the most central institution of Jewish life—the synagogue." Photo shows the destroyed interior of the Fassanenstrasse Synagogue, Berlin.

102

under forty-five years of age in compliance with the regulations in the Law to Protect German Blood and German Honor, they did not feel as though they had been relegated to inferior status in the community. Peter and his father attended major soccer games, and since Moritz had obtained tickets in Budapest for the 1936 Olympics, Peter was able to sit in the Hungarian section and watch the games. The normal pattern of life that the Fröhlichs followed leaves Gay with little patience for those who blame German Jewry for not anticipating the course of Nazi persecution before escape became impossible.

Shortly after Peter attended the 1936 Olympics, however, members of the extended Fröhlich family decided that there was no long-term future for them in Germany. Peter's uncle (who had emigrated to the United States after marrying an heiress to a hardware store in Florida) visited Germany, and a family gathering took place. Present at the conclave were Peter and his parents; his aunt and uncle, who were small shopkeepers; and the uncle visiting from the States. The family planned to leave Germany according to the following time schedule: Peter's eldest cousin Hanns, who was about to graduate from the *gymnasium*, would leave in 1937; Peter and his cousin Edgar would leave in 1938 or 1939; and the adults would leave after the youth of the family had settled in their respective communities. Hanns did leave as scheduled, settling with his uncle in Florida and returning during World War II as an American soldier. Events overtook the rest of the plan.

Although Peter and his father continued to attend soccer games after the Olympics, opportunities for normal participation in the German community narrowed considerably by 1938. Peter was forced to leave the *gymnasium* in the spring; he took some vocational training and found a job as an errand boy apprentice for a deaf-mute couple who worked as dental technicians. In November, the prosperity that Moritz Fröhlich had enjoyed for several years came to an abrupt end. Throughout the year there was intensified pressure from the Ministry of Economics to tighten the policy of Aryanization making it mandatory for Jews to give up their businesses for minimal compensation. Peter's father was among these victims; his partner Pelz cut him out of the firm without a penny, leaving Moritz to live off his savings and the sale of stamps he had purchased in his lean years.

Kristallnacht was the most memorable episode of antisemitism for Moritz Fröhlich and his family. On the morning of November 10, after Peter had biked to his job three miles from home, Mr. Fröhlich called his son, asking him to return home because there was trouble. Peter told his employers that something was wrong and began cycling home. He remembers riding through the Berlin business district and seeing the shards of broken glass and the wrecked displays of Jewish-owned stores. He was especially struck by the sight of shambles at one of the largest department stores in the city. Forty-five years later, as he recalls the events of that morning, he points out that there had been preparation for the destruction of Jewish property several weeks before *Kristallnacht*: the regime had ordered that all Jewish storeowners have their names written in large white letters in front of their stores. The Nazis' rationale for this, explains Gay, was that they suspected Jews of hiding under neutral gentile names to evade legislation earlier in the year requiring them to register property worth 5,000 marks or more.

Gay not only recalls the details of his bike ride on November 10, but he remembers arriving home. The Fröhlichs lived in a typical Berlin apartment house, designed like a square doughnut with a courtyard in the middle and apartments in the front, back and sides. Upon entering the house, he saw the superintendent's wife crying, and upstairs in the family apartment he learned that his father had gone into hiding with a former employee. Mr. Fröhlich stayed out of sight for at least a week until he was certain that the disturbances were over. He was more fortunate than thousands of Jewish males who had been arrested during *Kristallnacht* and detained at concentration camps.

On the afternoon of November 10 the extended Fröhlich family held another meeting: Peter and his mother joined other members of the family living in the capital. It was now decided that the family would need to seek emigration at the earliest possible moment. The more leisurely plan for emigration was totally scrapped; young people and adults would have to leave together. Peter became convinced that emigration was imperative when he visited the store of his aunt and uncle and saw with his own eyes the shop in ruins. Windows were smashed and things thrown around and a shelf full of buttons had been turned over. "It was a piece of exemplary vandalism," exclaims Gay.

Quite clearly, *Kristallnacht* marked a point of crisis for this particular Berlin family. While Nazi persecution of Jews had become increasingly harsh between 1933 and 1938, it had taken place within an ongoing context of fundamentally normal life. Those events that students of the period regard as indicative of a long-term program leading to the destruction of German and European Jewry—the April 1933 boycott, the purge of Jews and anti-Nazis from the civil service, arts, and journalism, and the Nuremberg Laws—did not have the same ominous portent at the time. *Kristallnacht* was different because it marked the advent of government-sanctioned and -organized physical violence against the Jewish community. Not only was the long-term prospect bleak, the short-term outlook was imminently dangerous.

Emigration became considerably more difficult in the aftermath of *Kristallnacht*. Increasing numbers of Jews within Germany were seeking emigration, as were those in recently annexed areas—Austria (in March 1938) and the Sudentenland (in October 1938). These swelling numbers coincided with more stringent regulations by the Nazi bureaucracy: Jews had to register their possessions and obtain appropriate identification and proof of sponsorship in countries of immigration as well as surrender the major portion of their wealth to the state.

Gay enumerates the steps his family went through between November 1938 and March 1939 in order to obtain passports and other documents necessary for emigration. First, the Fröhlichs had to have proof that they had turned in all their property to the government and that they had paid their part of the billion-dollar fine imposed on the Jewish community for allegedly provoking *Kristallnacht*. During these same months Moritz desperately sought to find a country that would receive his family. The United States, which was the preferred destination of the Fröhlichs and many other German Jews, had a limited number of spaces: the quota for German and Austrian Jews was about 28,000 (after the *Anschluss*), and after November 1938 approximately a quarter of a million Jews were seeking to emigrate to the United States. The Fröhlichs speculated that it would take them at least seven or eight years before their number would be reached. Thus, they began looking for alternatives. They tried England, but just before Christmas 1938 they were turned down since the British did not want competition for the unemployed in their own country.

As immigration possibilities declined in western European states, more and more German Jews looked to places such as Cuba and Shanghai as temporary havens until they could obtain visas for one of the preferred countries. Peter's father was willing to try any place that was willing to receive refugees. With the help of American relatives who made an intensive search for places with "openings," Moritz learned of the possibility of Havana and pursued it, booking passage for his family on the SS *St. Louis* leaving for Havana in mid-May. However, he began to think that this was too late a date for departure and altered the papers declaring the date of departure to read April rather than May. In doing this, he had taken considerable risks. It was not certain that his friend could secure passage on an earlier ship. Moreover, he gambled on the fact that no one in the bureaucracy would note the changed date. Fortunately, his deception worked: his friend managed to secure passage for the family on the *Iberia* leaving in April, and a month before departure the family applied for passports.

Gay remembers the voyage on the *Iberia* as subdued but uneventful. To be sure, it did not end as tragically as that of the SS *St. Louis*, the liner that the family had originally planned to take.

The Fröhlichs spent two years in Cuba. During that time the war broke out in Europe, and the United States belatedly became a belligerent. These events led to the closing of most U.S. consulates and embassies in Europe, with the consequence that the immigration quotas for the affected countries could not be filled and those quotas were redistributed. The Fröhlichs left Havana for Atlanta in 1941, and shortly thereafter they moved to Denver where Peter's mother received treatment for tuberculosis. Contrary to stories of the insensitivity of U.S. State Department officials to the plight of Jewish refugees, the doctor at the consulate permitted Mrs. Fröhlich to enter the United States with a respiratory ailment so severe that it could be detected without a stethoscope, despite statutory regulations to the contrary. Once again, a detail in Gay's story reminds us that knowledge of statutes and legislation regarding emigration and immigration does not provide the full picture of the refugee experience. One must account for certain acts of humanity or human error in implementing the regulations.

Peter and his parents assimilated rapidly into American society. Moritz Fröhlich changed the family name in 1943, as Peter's cousin had done earlier. The anglicization of the name was for the convenience of Americans who did not speak German and therefore for whom the name would be difficult to remember and to spell. It was also the Fröhlichs' symbolic dissociation from the country that had driven them into exile. Peter worked at a number of minimum wage jobs and earned his bachelor's degree at the University of Denver. He later completed doctoral work at Columbia, which in the late forties and early fifties was a haven for German intellectuals who had fled Hitler's Reich. For more than thirty years, Professor Gay has pursued a distinguished academic career as one of the foremost historians of modern European intellectual history.

Peter Gay's memories of Berlin in the years 1933 to 1939 offer one view of an immensely complex picture of the Jewish community's response to Nazism. The experience of the Fröhlich family was not typical of German Jewry: they lived in Berlin which, according to some historians and contemporaries, never became thoroughly Nazified during the Third Reich; they were totally assimilated according to their own lights; they had some financial resources and connections to the non-Jewish community; they had relatives in the United States willing to sponsor them; and they escaped. One must remember, however, that the experience of any one person or family is never typical and never serves properly as the basis of generalization. Yet these memories do provide a human dimension to what can too easily become an impersonal history and give us some better insight to the pivotal nature of the pogrom of November 1938.

Commentary

The video montage "Childhood Experiences of German Jews," which appears in the next section, suggests that there were differences in the implementation of antisemitic legislation in urban and rural areas. Jews living in Berlin and other large cities could remain anonymous if they did nothing to call attention to their Jewish identity; even in the war years, approximately 5,000 Berlin Jews who received help from non-Jewish neighbors and friends were able to avoid being rounded up and imprisoned by the Nazi regime. Leonard Gross's *The Last Jews of Berlin* suggests that Berlin Jews benefited from the fact that the non-Jewish population of the capital had never been completely Nazified and therefore there were Berliners willing to take risks to oppose Nazi antisemitic legislation. Moreover, Jewish self-help organizations located in Berlin and other large cities had the resources to assist indigent Jews. By contrast, Jews in the smaller towns and villages were easily identified by the local population and generally they were entirely removed from the area before the war years. In the portrait of Carl, for example, we learn that Carl's town had been *Judenrein* (free of Jews) for several years before the war and many of the children had never known or seen Jews.

Gay also emphasizes how difficult it was for him and other assimilated Jews to anticipate the Final Solution: while there were antisemitic measures and violence against Jews in the 1930s, there were non-Jews such as Peter's headmaster who disregarded or derided the Nazi policies.

Moreover, as Gay explains, it was impossible to expect something like the Final Solution since there had never been a precedent for such a program. The montage "Imagining the Unimaginable" develops this theme, considering the attitudes of German Jews and Jews in Nazi-occupied territories of eastern and western Europe.

The portrait of Walter Bieringer and the montage "Flight from Destiny" supplement Gay's discussion of his family's effort to emigrate after *Kristallnacht*.

In the United States Gay has become a recognized authority in modern intellectual and cultural history. Throughout his works on the eighteenth, nineteenth and twentieth centuries, he seeks to trace the evolution of modern thought. Among his best known works are *The Enlightenment*; *Weimar Culture*; *The Outsider as Insider*; *Freud, Jews, and Other Germans* and *Freud for Historians*.

Using

Compare the schooling experience of Peter Gay with that of Walter K., described in the montages "Childhood Experiences of German Jews" (Excerpt 5) and "Childhood Memories" (Excerpt 5). How do you account for the differences?

Why do you think that Gay says it is unhistorical for people to blame German Jews for not leaving in the first years of the Nazi regime?

What do you learn about *Kristallnacht* from Gay's account that you had not heard or read about in other accounts? From Peter's testimony, what features of *Kristallnacht* so frightened him and the rest of his family that they decided to hasten plans for emigration?

What were the principal obstacles to emigration for Jews after *Kristallnacht*?

What advantages did the Fröhlichs have in planning their emigration? What were their connections with the United States? What connections did Moritz Fröhlich have with non-Jews in Germany?

Name some significant events that have taken place in the last five years. How did you react when you first learned of these events? Did you think of them as watersheds, or were you unaware of their significance at the time?

Peter Gay describes how his parents treated him as an adult, asking him to make important decisions himself rather than deciding for him. For instance, they left it up to Peter to decide whether or not he should have a *Bar Mitzvah*. Why do you think that Gay, thinking back on his upbringing, is critical of the burden of decision making that adults imposed on him? Have you ever felt that your parents or adult relatives have left you with responsibility that was too much for you to handle?

Select some examples in Gay's stories of the inconsistency and inefficiency of the Nazi administration. To what extent do these examples alter your view of the Nazi regime?

Short excerpts of Gay speaking of his youth are found in **Montages** ("Flight from Destiny" and "Childhood Experiences of German Jews").

Facing History has prepared a study guide on *Kristallnacht*, available at the Facing History Resource Center. An abbreviated version of this guide is found in *Dimensions* (October 1988).

1. Dawidowicz, ed., *A Holocaust Reader*, pp. 208-209.

2. As quoted in Dawidowicz, ed., *A Holocaust Reader*, p. 212.

3. Bak, *Self Portrait of the Artist as a Jew.*

4. Rudachevski, *Diary of the Vilna Ghetto*, p.72-73.

5. Kaufman, "Conversation With the Artist," p. 37.

6. For further information about works of the young Bak, contact Dr. Marek Webb, archivist at YIVO, 1048 Fifth Avenue, New York, NY. YIVO references for the Bak drawings are: (a)**Still lifes**—33/61(175), 33/62(175), 25 921(175); (b)**Two Gentlemen**—2.5 919(175); (c)**Facial Studies**—5.17 1064(175), 5.17 1065(175), 5.17 1066(175); (d)**Classical head**—2.5 920(175); (e)**Landscape**—5.17 1068(175).

7. Weitz, "Flashbacks of Darkness: Journal at Bindermichel," pp.13-15, 19-20.

8. Marrus, *The Unwanted*, pp. 306-308.

9. Heller, "A Concentration Camp Diary," pp. 31-32. Heller encouraged American journalist Edward R. Murrow to visit Buchenwald just after liberation. For an excerpt of Murrow's comments on his visit, see the portrait of Leon Bass.

10. Weitz, "Speech to the Anti-Defamation League of B'nai B'rith."

11. Fry, "Holocaust Survivor Shares Memories of Concentration Camp."

12. Wiesel, "What it Means to Be Stateless."

13. As quoted in Wundheiler, "Oskar Schindler's Moral Development During the Holocaust," p. 350.

14. Stille, "Primo Levi: Reconciling the Man and the Writer," p. 5.

15. As quoted in Ainsztein, *Jewish Resistance in Nazi-Occupied Eastern Europe*, p. 643.

16. As quoted in Gilbert, *The Holocaust*, pp. 566-567.

17. Testimony at the Maidenek trial as quoted in *Majdanak 1944*, a documentary film by Bengt and Irmgard von zur Mühlen, Block 53. Transcript available at the Facing History Resource Center.

18. Laska, *Women in the Resistance and in the Holocaust*, pp. 7-8. For an example of women who took part in resistance activities, see Fourcade, *Noah's Ark.*

19. Hàjkovà, *Ravensbruck*, as translated by Vera Laska and cited in Laska, ed., *Women in the Resistance and in the Holocaust*, pp. 211-213.

20. Ferencz, *Less Than Slaves*, p. 124.

21. As quoted in *Together*, October 11, 1987, p. 8.

22. Tec, *When Light Pierced the Darkness*, p. 22.

23. Paldiel, "The Altruism of the Righteous Gentiles," p. 195.

24. Friedlander, *When Memory Comes*, pp. 94-95.

25. As quoted in Goldberger, ed., *The Rescue of the Danish Jews*, pp. 207-208.

26. "An Interview With Marion Pritchard," p. 31.

27. Wheeler-Bennet, *The Nemesis of Power*, pp. 697-698.

28. Mayer, *They Thought They Were Free*, pp. 306-310.

29. As quoted in Kater, "Problems of Political Reeducation in West Germany," p. 109.

30. Meinicke, *The German Catastrophe*, pp. 106-107.

31. von Weizsäcker, Speech during a commemorative ceremony (May 8, 1985), p. 62.

32. As quoted in International Military Tribunal: Nuremberg, *Official Text*, pp. 115-116.

33. Introduction to Karski, "Polish Death Camp."

34. Karski, "Polish Death Camp," pp. 60-61.

35. Gilbert, *Auschwitz and the Allies*, pp. 93-95.

36. Karski, *Story of a Secret State*, p. 38.

37. As quoted in Garlinski, *Poland in the Second World War*, p. 168.

38. Koslowski, "The Mission That Failed," p. 334.

39. Hilberg, *The Destruction of the European Jews*, Vol 1, pp. 140-142.

40. Wyman, *Paper Walls*, p. 22.

41. Bieringer, "Demands Better Immigration Laws," p. 9.

42. Bieringer, USNA Annual Address, p. 8.

43. As quoted in Abzug, *Inside the Vicious Heart*, p. 53.

44. As quoted in Abzug, p. 56.

45. Eisenhower, *Crusade in Europe*, pp. 408-409.

46. Weitz, *The Poetry of Sonia Schreiber Weitz*, inside back cover.

47. As quoted in Chamberlin & Brewster, *The Liberation of the Nazi Concentration Camps, 1945*, pp. 42-45.

48. Filreis, "Learning to Hear a Voice," p. 4.

49. Abzug, *Inside the Vicious Heart*, p. 89.

50. Ferencz, *Less Than Slaves*, p. xiv.

51. U.S. Army, *Report on Dachau Concentration Camp*.

52. Hersh & Mann, *Gizelle, Save the Children!*, pp. 7-10.

Montages

Arranging Memories to Gain Perspective

The selections in the montages for this manual are arranged to create a variety of perspectives on certain themes in the history of the Holocaust or on certain works of Holocaust literature. The opening montage, "Challenge of Memory: A Videotape to Accompany Elie Wiesel's *Night*," contains testimonies which describe memories similar to those in Wiesel's kingdom of *Night*. The memoir and its author have awakened the twentieth century conscience to the history of the Nazi genocide, and both serve as symbols for this watershed event in modern times.

The other montages elaborate on themes introduced in *Night*: the experiences of children during the Holocaust; the difficulty of anticipating the Final Solution; the separation of families and friends during the Holocaust; and the response of the outside world to news of Nazi atrocities.

The montages appear in the following order:

"Challenge of Memory: A Videotape to Accompany Elie Wiesel's Night"

This 22-minute montage is designed for junior high and senior high school students who are reading Elie Wiesel's *Night*. Each of the testimonies elaborates on a theme in the memoir. For example, the testimony of Helen supplements the discussion of resistance in *Night*, while the testimony of Leon provides additional insights into Wiesel's description of his liberation from Buchenwald. The montage is accompanied by suggestions for class discussion. Students report that this montage makes the memoir *Night* and the history it describes more accessible to their inquiry and provides a basis for discussion on many of the themes explored in the study of the Holocaust.

"Childhood Experiences of German Jews"

This 23-minute montage contains memories of German Jewish childhood in Nazi Germany of the 1930s. The testimonies provide perspectives which indicate the diversity and complexity of the German Jewish population. This montage premiered at the program for the "Jews in Germany" exhibition at Brandeis University. It supplements material in the Resource Book.

"Friedrich: A Videotape to Accompany Hans Peter Richter's Novel Friedrich"

This 13-minute montage is designed as a companion to the novel *Friedrich*, a story of two adolescents, one Jewish and one Christian, who have been friends and neighbors for many years. The novel details Nazi legislation and social policy and traces their impact on the two boys and their parents. Testimonies in the montage illustrate topics from several chapters in *Friedrich*. For example, in one testimony a young Jewish girl tells of her attraction to the glitter and excitement of Nazi parades. Her testimony can be compared with the incident in the novel in which Friedrich eagerly anticipates a meeting of the *Jungvolk*. Like the montage for *Night*, the *Friedrich* montage has been piloted in a variety of educational settings. It generates discussions on the nature of friendship, the abuse of power, peer pressure, and obedience to authority.

"Imagining the Unimaginable"

This 23-minute montage incorporates selections from video testimonies that illuminate the near-impossibility of anticipating the "Final Solution." Professor Lawrence Langer introduces each testimony with background on the interviewee and pertinent questions raised by the excerpt. In addition to the video testimonies, documentary photographs of the ghetto and camp life illustrate certain themes mentioned in the testimonies.

"Flight From Destiny"

This 30-minute montage (the first half of a one-hour documentary film) chronicles the history of the voyage of the SS *St. Louis* in May-June 1939, when over 930 German Jewish passengers made futile efforts to land in Cuba and Miami. The montage includes interviews with former passengers of the *St. Louis* and agents of American Jewish organizations who sought to aid the refugees. It supplements materials in the Resource Book. (The second half of

114

the documentary traces the story of German Jewish refugees who fled to Shanghai in the later 1930s and early 1940s.) The documentary was produced by the Holocaust Survivors Film Project and its co-founder, Laurel Vlock.

"Stories of Separation"

This 12-minute montage includes excerpts from interviews of three women who recall how they were separated from their parents during the Holocaust. It explores reasons that parents were willing to sacrifice family unity and the effects the separations had on the children. This montage, which has been piloted in junior high and senior high school classrooms, college settings, and adult education courses, generates discussion on the painful and complicated decisions that confronted Jewish parents during the Holocaust.

"Childhood Memories"

This 57-minute montage includes excerpts from eleven video interviews of Jews and non-Jews, who recount their experiences growing up in western and eastern European countries during the era of the Third Reich. The selections reflect on the day-to-day events of children and adolescents during the period of political, social, economic, and diplomatic upheaval of the 1930s and 1940s. There are recollections of life in Nazi Germany before the war, hiding during the war years, and imprisonment at Auschwitz. Key issues covered are central to the interests of youth: what was it like to grow up in the totalitarian regime of the Third Reich? How did Nazi ideology influence schooling? Selections from this montage can be used throughout the unit, but it is not appropriate to use the entire, lengthy montage in one class meeting. The manual contains historical background for each excerpt as well as suggested topics for discussion.

Challenge of Memory: A Video Montage to Accompany Elie Wiesel's *Night*

The video montage to accompany Elie Wiesel's *Night* provides a framework with which to explore a number of episodes recorded in the memoir. The testimonies in the montage include seven excerpts from Holocaust survivors and witnesses whose experiences paralleled closely those described in *Night*.

Wiesel's first book, *Night*, published in 1956, is widely read and is often used in conjunction with high school and college courses on twentieth-century genocide. It is a memoir of Wiesel's experiences as a boy during the

Holocaust. He and his entire family were taken from their home in the small village of Sighet in Transylvania (Rumania) and sent to Auschwitz during the spring of 1944. Almost immediately, Elie's mother and younger sister were taken to the gas chambers. Elie remained with his father and worked in the labor camps at Auschwitz located in the area known as Buna-Monowitz. At Auschwitz the young Wiesel learned about the world of death created by the Nazis and the SS. He witnessed the sadistic behavior of guards and *kapos* and the executions of victims who tried to resist, as well as the humiliations daily inflicted on them. He also witnessed the erosion of civilized behavior among the victims, who

Elie Wiesel.

subsisted on starvation rations as they endured the harsh physical conditions of the camp. The world at Auschwitz that had been created by the Nazis was another world, Wiesel observes, totally different from the one he had known as a young boy in Sighet.

In early January 1945, with Allied forces closing in, the SS guards at Auschwitz sent Elie and his father, along with other prisoners, on a forced march to the German border. There they were loaded onto boxcars and transported to Buchenwald. The bitter cold and lack of food made conditions so unbearable on this journey that Elie thought death would be a welcome release. Day after miserable day, Elie watched the steady deterioration of his father and others who had been his friends, making the ordeal even more horrible.

Soon after the prisoners arrived at Buchenwald, Elie's father contracted dysentery. Weak and exhausted, he died in his sleep on the night of January 28, on a bunk just below Elie.

Three months later, in April 1945, American forces liberated Buchenwald.

Many of the survivors, physically and emotionally sapped, showed little emotion, displaying neither elation about freedom nor desire for revenge. Elie recalls most vividly the days just after liberation and his first look into a mirror. "From the depths of the mirror," he writes, "a corpse gazed back at me. The look in his eyes as they stared into mine never left me."[1]

Excerpt 1: Introduction to the Video Montage "Challenge of Memory"

In this opening clip, Elie Wiesel speaks to a group of students from schools in the Boston area. [Just days before Wiesel made this presentation, he had received international media coverage for his criticism of President Reagan's plans to tour the Bitburg Cemetery in Germany where Nazi soldiers were buried.] Many of the students have read about Wiesel's protest and have read his memoir *Night*, and they are eager to meet the author whom they assume will tell about his experiences as a Holocaust survivor. Initially, Wiesel does not meet the students' expectations.

Instead of speaking about his experiences immediately, Wiesel asks his friend Rabbi Joseph Polak, Hillel director at Boston University, "to tell a story." Polak, surprised at the request, steps to the podium and gradually begins to tell a story of his early childhood. Polak's story has a surprise ending.

After Polak finishes his story, Wiesel returns to the podium and connects Polak's story to the message he wants to convey to the students. "These stories," he begins, "are to sensitize people . . . to make you more sensitive. . . because whatever happens today is always related to what happened then [during the Holocaust]."

Commentary

Egil Aarvik, Chairman of the Norwegian Nobel Committee, introduced Elie Wiesel as the 1986 recipient of the Nobel Peace Prize. Aarvik began with an explanation of Wiesel's mission to sensitize people to the suffering of others and then related the details of Wiesel's life during the Holocaust.

> His [Wiesel's] mission is not to gain the world's sympathy for the victims or the survivors. His aim is to awaken our conscience. Our indifference to evil makes us partners in the crime. That is the reason for his attack on indifference and his insistence on measures aimed at preventing a new holocaust. We know that the unimaginable has happened. What are we doing now to prevent it happening again? . . .

> Through his books Elie Wiesel has given us not only an eyewitness account of what happened, but also an analysis of the evil powers which

lay behind the events. His main concern is the question of what measures we can take to prevent a recurrence of these events.

The terrors he encountered in the death camps, which were slowly revealed to the rest of the world, were something which was qualitatively new in the history of mankind. The Holocaust was a war within a war, a world in itself, a kingdom of darkness where there existed an evil so monstrous that it shattered all political and moral codes. It represented a new dimension. According to its theoretical basis, which could only have been the product of sick minds, it was a capital offense to belong to a certain race. This was previously unimaginable, but now the unimaginable was happening.

It is true that previous regimes had used brutal punishment against real or imagined opponents, but behind such measures there was always an element of logical—though perverted—reasoning. The punishment was the result of some injury or offense, either actual or potential.

But for the Jews—and, to a certain extent, the Romanies—the situation was different. Among the relics of the Nazi regime have been found registration forms used when arresting Jews. The usual details were noted down: name, age, sex, religion, address and, of course, reason for arrest. In the last case only one word was entered, the word Jew. . . .

Elie Wiesel's sojourn in the death-camps ended in Buchenwald in the spring of 1945, when the prisoners were liberated by American troops. Together with a group of other Jewish children he was sent to France. His stay in France was part convalescence, part study: he learned French and studied at the Sorbonne before becoming a correspondent with a Tel Aviv newspaper. He traveled to the United States as a journalist, became a correspondent with a New York Jewish paper, and took American citizenship in 1963. In the meantime, he had published a number of books, of which *Night* (1956) was the first. His writings which have been translated into many languages, now include 26 full-length books, together with a large number of articles, essays and lectures. He has been awarded a number of honours and prizes.[2]

Using

After reading *Night* and studying about the Holocaust, do you agree with Elie Wiesel's observation that those who study the Holocaust become "inhabited by its fire"?

Wiesel believes once one has been "inhabited by the fire" then that person will be sensitive to all potential victims in the world today. How do Wiesel's observations affect your understanding of his plea for students to become "more sensitive"?

Using Wiesel's comments after Rabbi Polak's story and the following selections from his Nobel Peace Prize interview, develop a definition for "sensitive" that you think Wiesel would approve.

> Some people [today] are sensitive only to one category of victims and not to the others. That is wrong. I believe that what we are teaching is sensitivity, period. If one is sensitive to one injustice, one must be sensitive to all injustice, which will never be at the expense of others. For two thousand years the Jewish tragedy was singled out as one that people could not pay attention to. For two thousand years there were great humanists who were humanists and at the same time remained anti-Semitic. Knowing but not knowing what they were doing or saying or writing. To me it was one of the great shocks of my adult life when I discovered that people who used to be my heroes, Voltaire, Kant were anti-Semites. It was possible then to be treated as human, to even aspire to elevate themselves, to portray themselves as humanists and at the same time to hate Jews. A child said, "When I suffer don't I cry, don't I bleed?" What does it mean? It means "Why aren't you sensitive to my pain?" People were not sensitive to pain. The culmination of all this was, of course, Auschwitz.[3]

Excerpt 2: Early Warnings

The second excerpt in the montage focuses on Shari B. (T-66), a native of Hungary who was a teenager during the Holocaust. Shari recalls a time after the war started when her father brought a Polish Jew to their home. The visitor spoke of how he had escaped from the concentration camp and of *Mein Kampf* and the Nazi plans to exterminate Jews. People could not believe what they were hearing, Shari explains. "It was so terrible I could not believe it, and my father's reaction was, 'But the Germans, they're a country with a culture.'"

In a section which does not appear in this excerpt, Shari relates what happened after the visitor finished speaking. She asked her father for

Elie Wiesel's Night *[cover].*

permission to go to the movies. She simply was not able to grasp the implications of what the man had said.

In the opening chapter of *Night* Wiesel tells a similar story of Moshe the Beadle, a caretaker for the synagogue in Sighet and a devout Jew who had introduced him to many of the secrets of the Talmud. In 1941, Jews not native to Hungary (Sighet had been incorporated into Hungary early in the war) were rounded up and deported to Polish concentration camps; Moshe the Beadle was among these victims. Late in 1942 he managed to escape and return to Sighet where he tried to alert the Jews to the horrors that he and his companions had endured in Poland. Wiesel's neighbors were unable to take Moshe's warnings seriously. They considered him a "madman" and resented his efforts. Moshe himself realized how futile his efforts were when Wiesel asked him why he was so anxious for people to believe what he was saying:

> "You don't understand. . . . You can't understand. I have been saved miraculously. I managed to get back here. Where did I get the strength from? I wanted to come back to Sighet to tell you the story of my death. So that you could prepare yourselves while there was still time. To live? I don't attach much importance to my life any more. I'm alone. No, I wanted to come back and to warn you. And see how it is, no one will listen to me."[4]

Commentary

Political scientist Helen Fein makes the following observation of how people deal with news of impending disaster:

> Investigations of how people respond to warnings of disaster reveal that they weigh the likelihood of the threat against the anticipated costs of accepting a new definition of the situation: how it will disrupt their lives, what access routes are open, what unprecedented actions coping will entail, and what people and resources they can count on for assistance. Apprehension both leads to increased vigilance (sensitivity to warning cues) and raises the need for reassurance. When the source of the danger is clear, and people can anticipate what to do to avoid it, their perception is sharpened and their energy released: they are not immobilized by anxiety but mobilized to avoid danger. But if the costs of accepting a new definition of the situation call for discarding one's social identity and disrupting one's way of life while the nature of the threat cannot be determined with certainty, people are more likely to perceive the threat as overwhelming and either to react with terror or to defend themselves against threat by denial. Since information sources available to Jews in the ghettos always conflicted—the Germans propagated reassuring messages that contradicted the rumors and direct reports—selective perception,

120

Buchenwald. A section of the hospital cribs. The patients in the upper cribs were unable to go to the latrine, making the sanitation in this section intolerable. [Original photo caption]

denial, and distortion were probable. In ghettos in which extermination came in successive waves of "selections," the constant adjustment to attrition and mourning itself promoted demoralization and misperception of the scope of threat.[5]

Even in cases where Jews did realize that they were in imminent danger, they had relatively few opportunities to escape. As the danger to Jews increased in the middle and late 1930s, it grew more and more difficult to emigrate due to domestic policies of the Nazi regime and restrictive immigration legislation throughout the international community. During the war years, immigration came to a standstill. And among those German Jews who had emigrated when the Nazis first came to power, many had settled in countries that were occupied by the Nazis during the war so that they were subjected to antisemitic measures in their new homeland. There were also emigrants of the 1933-34 period who decided to return to Germany by the mid–1930s, believing that the worst of the antisemitic excesses and legislation had passed.[6]

Using

What reasons does Shari give for disbelieving the stories of the Polish Jew who visited her father after the war began? How did Shari's reaction to the news of planned extermination compare with the reactions of Jews in Wiesel's hometown, Sighet?

Elie Wiesel mentions in the opening clip how important the stories of the Holocaust are for "sensitizing people" to the potential for evil. Why do you think that the stories of the Polish visitor in Shari's home and of Moshe the Beadle in Sighet failed to sensitize the Jews adequately? Can stories ever be expected to be effective in convincing people of the "unimaginable"?

The video montage "Imagining the Unimaginable" documents survivors from several countries who testify that it was impossible for them to anticipate the Final Solution. There had been no analogy, no way for imagining the systematic extermination of human beings.

Excerpt 3: The Outside World

In this excerpt Edith P. (A-39) describes the transport from Auschwitz to a labor camp in northern Germany. She has been in the concentration camps for so long that she has almost forgotten the existence of the normal world in which there is a sun and in which people show love and concern for one another. From the transport she looks out between the wooden slats and sees the sun shining and the people going about their normal activities. "I looked out," she exclaims, "and there I saw paradise. The sun was bright and vivid. There [was] one woman with a child. People were people not animals. I forgot how normal people looked."

Wiesel describes a similar experience in *Night* when, as a prisoner in the abnormal world of Auschwitz, he gazes at the world that lay beyond his grasp:

> We marched on. Doors opened and closed again. On we went between the electric wires. At each step, a white placard with a death's head on it stared us in the face. A single caption: "Warning: Danger of death." Mockery— was there a single place here where you were not in danger of death?

> The march lasted half an hour. Looking out around me I noticed that the barbed wires were behind us. We had left camp. It was a beautiful April day. The fragrance of spring was in the air. The sun was setting in the west.[7]

Using

Based on the descriptions that Edith P. and Elie Wiesel give of seeing the normal world from the abnormal world of the concentration camp, what changes do they appear to have undergone as a result of their experiences?

Compare Edith's description of seeing the sun during the Holocaust with the description found in Wiesel's *Night*. Which description did you find most vivid? Explain your response.

In other video testimonies, survivors mention that the sun they saw in concentration camps like Auschwitz was not the same sun they knew from normal life. Why do you think some survivors refer to the unreal quality of the sun in describing their life in the concentration camps?

Auschwitz survivor and author Primo Levi has explained that for prisoners in the concentration camps the abnormal became normal. Discuss this observation with respect to the testimonies of Edith and Elie.

What questions do the descriptions of abnormal life in the concentration camps raise about the role of bystanders?

Historians and filmmakers continue to collect testimony from citizens who lived near the extermination camps. In preparing his film *Shoah*, filmmaker Claude Lanzmann sought out Polish civilians and interviewed them about the Holocaust years. (*Shoah* is now available on videotape.) Social historian Gordon Horowitz is currently conducting systematic interviews of people who lived in the villages around the camp of Mauthausen near Linz, Austria, and a preliminary report of his findings is available at the Facing History Resource Center. How else might the historian find out what the bystanders were thinking during the Holocaust when prisoners in transports passed by?

Excerpt 4: Resistance

In the fourth excerpt, we learn about a major incident of resistance at Auschwitz. Helen K. (A-35), who was a prisoner in the camp, describes an act of sabotage in which women workers in an armaments plant at Buna smuggled gunpowder to male prisoners who were working in the area of the crematoria. With the women's help, the men were able to blow up one of the crematoria. The Nazis traced the gunpowder to its origins and subsequently hanged five or six young girls who worked in the Buna plant. Associated with this action was an attempted breakout by the Jewish *Sonderkommando* in Auschwitz on October 7, 1944. They were all caught and killed.

(Helen describes how women smuggled gunpowder. Before showing this clip, a teacher might want to warn students that explicit reference is made to a part of female anatomy.)

Wiesel speaks of a similar execution in *Night*. Prisoners managed to blow up an electric power station at Buna. The SS suspected a child who had been a servant for a member of the Gestapo as well as two other adult prisoners; the three were hanged in a public execution while the other prisoners were forced to watch.

Commentary

Individuals or groups of people contemplating resistance in the ghettos and camps had to consider that their actions might endanger individuals and groups of people not directly involved in their activities. According to Michael M. Marrus, the Nazis' tactic of "collective responsibility" in which entire groups or their leaders were taken hostage and punished for acts of resistance meant that

> resistance was guaranteed to punish Jews, rather than assist them. Fearful of massive German retribution, resisters everywhere waited until what they felt was the last moment—the final extinction of hope—for only then could they justify the reprisals that followed.[8]

In the Fortunoff Video Archive, the testimony of Max B. (T-94) contains a poignant example of the reprisals the Nazis took against individuals and groups engaged in resistance during the Holocaust. Max, acting as an electrician at Dora, an outcamp of Buchenwald located in the Harz Mountains near the city of Nordhausen in Central Germany, discovered how to rewire a V2 rocket so that it would not work and convinced members of a Ukrainian Kommando unit to do the rewiring of a rocket. The prisoners in question were caught and the Nazis responded by hanging all the members of the unit. Max made a second effort, asking members of another unit—this one Jewish—to blow up a rocket. The members attempted to destroy the wires by urinating on them. As with the Ukrainian unit, the sabotage effort of the Jewish Kommando failed, and again, the Nazis responded by hanging all the members of the unit. Max did not try sabotage a third time.

Dov Frieberg, a survivor of Sobibor, recalls the Nazi response to an attempted revolt in May 1942:

> "[T]here was a captain from Holland, a Jew. He headed an organization, secret organization. It was a period when there were difficulties among the Ukrainians and we thought maybe we could get in touch with them. We heard stories about the partisans from them and some contact was established between this Dutchman and the Ukrainians for a revolt.

> "They began plotting an uprising. And then one day in a roll call they took him out, this Dutchman, and began questioning him. 'Who were the ringleaders?'

> "This man withstood tortures and endless blows and he never said a word. The Germans told him that if he does not speak they would give orders that the Dutch block would be ordered to move to Camp III and they will be beheaded in front of his eyes. And he said, 'Anyway you are doing what

you wish, you will not get a word out of me, not a whisper.' And they gave the orders to this Dutch block to move, all of them, about seventy people, and they were brought to Camp III. On the next day we learned that the Germans kept their word.

"They beheaded the people. Yes, they cut off their heads."[9]

Using

What is meant by resistance in the concentration and death camps? Should the definition be limited to acts of organized resistance involving the use of arms and military strategy, or should the definition be broad enough to encompass acts of defiance by individuals? Did refusal to eat constitute resistance? Historians themselves have differing interpretations of the meaning of resistance. Raul Hilberg insists upon a narrow definition: armed resistance is the only form, or almost the only form, of "legitimate resistance." On the other hand, Michael Marrus accepts a broader definition to include all forms of "armed, unarmed but organized, semi-organized or semi-spontaneous" resistance.[10]

The girls hanged for helping provide rebels with ammunition were involved in an organized military resistance. What type of preparation was necessary for prisoners to plan such resistance? Why do you think that such resistance activities largely involved young people?

How do you think that the Nazi threat of collective punishment might have influenced individual decisions to carry out acts of private resistance?

Compare Wiesel's reaction to witnessing public executions at Auschwitz with the following reaction recorded in the memoirs of Mel Mermelstein, a Hungarian Jew who was at Auschwitz in the same months as Wiesel:

> I stood close to the gallows and could see the life drain from the faces of Ivan and Fedor [the victims of execution for an escape attempt]. Their necks broken, their tongues hanging from their mouths, their bodies swaying from side to side, all of us watched as they died a violent but heroic death.
>
> I could not eat my meager rations of bread that evening. Neither could anyone else. I saw my own inner torment reflected in the faces of every prisoner I encountered.
>
> The bodies hung loosely all evening as a display for all to see, for all to take note of. Standing in the shadow of the gallows, the dangling men, the Kapos' lust for murder—everything burned itself into my mind. For a moment I felt old, beaten and dead.[11]

In the selection below, two survivors discuss the importance of prisoners taking collective action. How did the hangings described in Helen's excerpt and *Night* discourage prisoners from working collectively?

> Unlimited egoism and a consuming desire to save their own lives at the expense of their fellows were common phenomena among prisoners who were politically backward, for such people were quite incapable of realizing that in this way they merely strengthened the hand of the SS against the prisoners. . . . Our experience of other concentration camps [prior to Auschwitz] had taught us the vital need to live collectively. Political consciousness and contact with others in the struggle against Nazism were necessary conditions of success; it was this that gave people a sense of purpose in life behind barbed wire and enabled them to hold out.[12]

Excerpt 5: Hunger

In the fifth excerpt, Hannah F. (T-18) discloses how she stole a piece of bread from her bunkmate. Extreme hunger drove her to do this, although under normal circumstances she probably would not have considered such an action. In watching the testimony, note how Hannah struggles for the right words.

In *Night*, Wiesel describes a man in Auschwitz as "a starved stomach." In Chapter 7, he offers a particularly vivid example: one day a German workman threw a piece of bread into the transport carrying Wiesel and other prisoners. The train had stopped just long enough for the dead to be removed. When the bread was thrown in, "[t]here was a stampede," explains Wiesel. "Dozens of starving men fought each other to the death for a few crumbs." As German workmen witnessed this spectacle with "lively interest," others began dropping pieces of bread into a wagon and a son fought his own father to the death for a crumb of bread.[13]

Commentary

Auschwitz survivor and author Primo Levi reflects on the limits of traditional vocabulary for describing experiences in the concentration camp:

> Just as our hunger is not that feeling of missing a meal, so our way of being cold has need of a new word. We say "hunger," "tiredness," "fear," "pain," we say "winter" and they are different things. They are free words, created and used by free men who lived in comfort and suffering in their homes. If the lagers (camps) had lasted longer, a new, harsh language would have been born; and only this language could express what it means to toil the whole day in the wind, with the temperature below freezing, and wearing only a shirt, underpants, cloth jacket and trousers, and in one's body nothing but weakness, hunger and knowledge of the end growing near.[14]

The Ghetto Anthology gives the following facts about the diet of prisoners in Auschwitz:

> The prisoners received each day three meals that had the total caloric count well below that required by a person in a complete state of repose. In camp jargon, starving prisoners were called "muslims." A prisoner who was systematically underfed could live from three to six months depending on the nature of his or her work. When the camp was liberated, the majority of prisoners were in a bedridden state. They looked like skeletons covered by earth-colored fistulas and adults weighed an average of 30-35 kilograms [66-77 pounds], 50-70% below normal adult weight. A special legal-medical commission which examined 2,819 prisoners in February and March of 1945 attested that 2,189 of them were sick as a result of the exhaustion and hunger and that 233 had tuberculosis. Autopsies performed on 536 corpses indicated that in 474 cases, death had occurred from emaciation. Of the estimated 3,000 children born in the camp, 1,000 died of hunger and the rest were murdered. Only 180 children were liberated by the Soviet Army.[15]

Since bread was so crucial to survival in the camps, the prisoners themselves adhered to the "bread law." As Terrence Des Pres observes, the "bread law" is aptly defined by a survivor of Sachsenhausen:

> Thefts occurred continually in the prisoners' barracks, ours as well as others. Hunger tormented us all incessantly and transformed men into irresponsible beasts. Even those who had formerly passed for honorable men stole from their comrades the bits of bread that many had laid by from their evening ration for the next day. By day, all with one voice condemned the theft. By night, the stealing was repeated, just the same. In our conversation periods we sought counter measures. We knew that the thieves did not realize the crime they were committing, for hunger had driven them nearly out of their senses. But we knew also that these bits of bread were the life-preserver by which we might keep ourselves afloat until the longed-for moment of freedom. And when we caught a bread thief, we punished him so severely that he lost his taste for stealing."[16]

Des Pres also argues that had the Holocaust gone on longer, a new vocabulary would have had to be invented in order to describe such feelings as hunger in a new frame of reference—that of the victims.

Fred Wander's *The Seventh Well* contains a story entitled "Bread," which suggests just how vital bread was to the survival of inmates.

> Bread is life. He who steals the other's bread, steals his life. . . .

> Most prisoners eat the bread immediately. They tear it into pieces with their hands and devour them with greedy exhaustion. Besides, then it can't

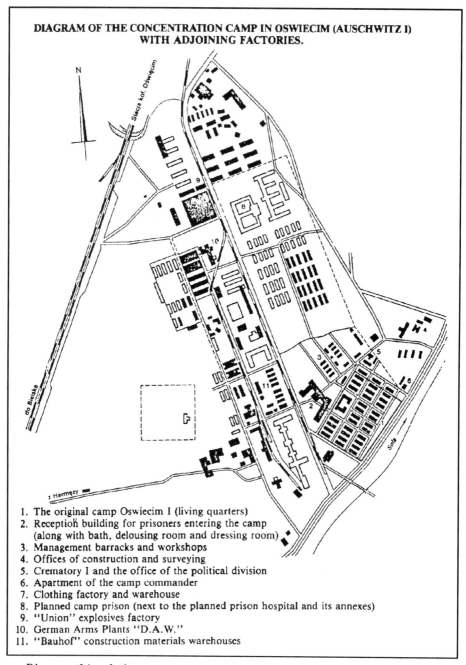

**DIAGRAM OF THE CONCENTRATION CAMP IN OSWIECIM (AUSCHWITZ I)
WITH ADJOINING FACTORIES.**

1. The original camp Oswiecim I (living quarters)
2. Reception building for prisoners entering the camp
   (along with bath, delousing room and dressing room)
3. Management barracks and workshops
4. Offices of construction and surveying
5. Crematory I and the office of the political division
6. Apartment of the camp commander
7. Clothing factory and warehouse
8. Planned camp prison (next to the planned prison hospital and its annexes)
9. "Union" explosives factory
10. German Arms Plants "D.A.W."
11. "Bauhof" construction materials warehouses

Diagram of Auschwitz.

be stolen from you. There's one loaf of bread per six—sometimes eight men—and on a few good days for four! Why is that? Several prophets claim to be able to know the position of the fronts by the size of the bread ration. If the rations increase, they say, this means the victorious advance of the Allies, if it looks bad for the Nazis, then they tremble for fear of the world. Others assert the opposite.

So the bread comes, the six men crawl into a corner and buckle down to the holy procedure of distribution. There are various recipes. For example, you can draw lots. The bread is quickly cut into six parts and the differently sized pieces are drawn by slips of paper or numbers. Everyone has an equal chance, no one can complain. Whoever draws the biggest piece tries to conceal his joy so as not to offend his mates, makes a grab for it and if he knows what's good for him disappears under the covers. Whoever gets the smallest piece also goes to bed, only sleep can console him. When you wake up, hunger, cold and all the biblical plagues of a long day swoop down on you. The normal way of divvying up proceeds like this: a crossbar hanging in the middle on a string, two pegs on the ends which you stick in the rations; this is the complicated way the parts are weighed out until all six rations are equal. Six morbidly widened pairs of eyes observe the ritual. This method also has the advantage that it takes a long time and the bread still has to be weighed while the others have already devoured theirs! If the bread crumbles while being divided and weighed, everyone holds out his cap and receives the crumbs. But I still must mention the masochists, the members of a secret bread cult. They stick their ration in a bag which they always carry about with them, and torture themselves with. The bread, outside on the body nourishes perhaps the fantasy but undermines the last strength. They die more quickly than the others.[17]

Charlotte Delbo describes how water was more precious for inmates than bread.

I now have my bread in my hand, my piece of bread and the few grams of margarine that constitute our evening ration. I hold them in my hand and I offer them from cell to cell to anyone who would swap their portion of tea for them. I dread that no one will do this. There is always someone who takes it. Every evening I exchange my bread for a few gulps. I drink it straight down and I am still more thirsty.[18]

Using

Can we understand what Hannah means by hunger? How does Hannah judge herself regarding the incident? How do we respond to her story? Is "theft" an appropriate term to describe her action? What other ways might we describe it? According to the "bread law," would Hannah be regarded a thief by the other prisoners?

Holocaust survivors and scholars have written about the failure of traditional vocabulary and systems of decision-making to describe the experience in the concentration camps. Primo Levi writes:

> From the standpoint of communication—indeed, of failed communication—we survivors have known a peculiar experience. It is an irksome habit of ours to intervene when someone (our children) speaks about cold, hunger, or fatigue. What do you know about it? You should have gone through what we did. In general, for reasons of good taste and good neighborliness, we try to resist the temptation of such *miles gloriosus* interventions; nevertheless I find it imperative to intervene precisely when I hear people talking about failed or impossible communication. "You should have experienced ours." There can be no comparison to the tourist in Finland or Japan who finds interlocutors who do not speak his language but are professionally (or even spontaneously) polite or well intentioned and make an effort to understand and help him. Besides, who, in what corner of the world, cannot string together a few words of English? In any event the questions of tourists are few, always the same, hence uncertainties are rare, and almost understanding each other can even be as amusing as a game.[19]

Lawrence Langer suggests that prisoners in the concentration camps often were confronted with "choiceless choices" in which the alternatives were impossible.

Was Hannah confronted with a choiceless choice? Do we judge her action using traditional ethical standards or should we suspend our moral judgment of her action?

From Hannah's testimony, what do we learn about mechanisms some victims developed in order to improve their chances for survival? In what ways were newcomers in the concentration camps at a disadvantage?

How would Wiesel's description of an Auschwitz inmate as a "starved stomach" affect traditional notions of what it means to be a human being?

Excerpt 6: Liberation

In this excerpt, Leon Bass, an American soldier who served with a black unit in World War II, describes what it was like when he and his fellow soldiers entered Buchenwald after the liberation in April 1945. Bass was only nineteen years old, and the sites of Buchenwald, he remembers, "removed my blinders," making him vividly aware of the depths of human depravity that had been reached in the concentration camps. Upon entering the camp, he says, he had no "frame of reference" for what he was about to witness. Once inside the camp he came to the realization that "suffering was universal."

Black Americans like himself were not the only minority to endure persecution and discrimination. Today Bass speaks to audiences throughout the United States about what he saw at Buchenwald in 1945.

In the final chapter of *Night*, Wiesel writes about his own liberation at Buchenwald. Rather than detail the horror and pain of the final days in the camp and the illnesses that many of the survivors endured in the weeks following liberation, Wiesel relates what it was like to look at his emaciated face in the mirror. Just as Bass had been haunted for decades by the skeletal figures in the camp after liberation, Wiesel has never forgotten the image of himself after months of starvation and cruelty under the Nazis.

Commentary

See Sonia Weitz's poem "On Liberation," in the portrait of Leon Bass.

Using

Bass said that he had no frame of reference for what he witnessed when he was nineteen years old. Today those of us looking back at the history of the Holocaust also lack a frame of reference. Can we ever completely understand what it was like to be a victim of Nazi persecution? Can we understand what prompted the perpetrators to treat human beings as subhuman? In what ways do literature and video testimonies help us come closer to the experience?

What experiences do we still have after reading the memoir *Night* and listening to the testimonies of Allied soldiers like Bass who entered the camps at the close of the war?

Why do you think that Bass takes such efforts to tell contemporary audiences about his experiences in Buchenwald?

Leon Bass's video testimony is described in **Portraits**. When Bass entered the camp his first reaction was to ask "What had they [the victims] done to deserve this?" Without discussion, some students may make a similiar judgment.

Also in **Portraits** is the description of the video testimony of Marcus Orr, which offers the perspective of an American soldier who entered Dachau just prior to liberation.

Available at the Resource Center are: "You Are Free," a twenty-minute film containing interviews of liberators and survivors remembering the period of liberation and its effect on their postwar lives; Weinstein, "The Liberation of Nazi Death Camps by American Army—1945: The Report of a Witness"; and the transcript of Leon Bass's video testimony.

Excerpt 7: Memory

In the concluding excerpt, Elie Wiesel returns to Auschwitz in 1985 with Peter Jennings, anchorman for ABC News. It is forty years after Wiesel's liberation, and Wiesel and Jennings walk through the snow-covered remains of the camp, with Wiesel pointing out the location of the bunks and gas chambers. The Germans, explains Wiesel, created a "universe with rules totally different from those we had known before." The German order "worked and was efficient. . . . I was convinced that I would never leave Auschwitz." Jennings then showed Wiesel a photograph of prisoners in a bunk at Buchenwald at the time of the liberation on April 16, 1945. Wiesel indicates where he is in the photo and recalls the many members of his family who did not live to see the day of liberation.

Wiesel ends the interview saying, "[Auschwitz] should be the greatest warning against indifference."

Commentary

Auschwitz is often thought of as a metaphor for the Holocaust since the camp complex included both the facilities for killing millions of Jews and non-Jews and the factories where thousands of inmates were used as slave labor. As Yitzchak Mais, Director of Yad Vashem Museums, explains in a brochure about the recent exhibition "Auschwitz: A Crime Against Mankind":

> Auschwitz, the German name for the Polish city Oswiecim, has come to mean much more than a geographic location. It has become a symbol of the Holocaust—a metaphor for systematic mass murder. Before Auschwitz, "western civilization" could, on the whole, describe itself as a world in which there was advancement, progress and achievement in science and technology that improved the human condition—a world which allowed the human spirit to flourish.

Using

How is our understanding of the Holocaust experience enhanced by reading *Night* and viewing the video excerpts of Holocaust survivors and witnesses? What differences have you found in the written memoir and in the video testimonies? How do the two types of sources complement one another?

How does Wiesel respond to Jennings' question of why Jews submitted so easily during the Holocaust? What problems surface as Peter Jennings tries to enter into the world of the survivor Elie Wiesel? What problems exist for you?

If you had the opportunity to walk through Auschwitz with Wiesel today, what questions would you ask?

"Challenge of Memory" has been used in a wide variety of educational settings. Responses of teachers throughout the Facing History network who have piloted this montage are similar to those of Elly Greene, a ninth grade social studies teacher and a member of the Facing History Teacher Training Team, who reported on her experiences using the montage in conjunction with Elie Wiesel's *Night* at the Fourth Annual Facing History Conference. Greene found the montage especially helpful because students were able to connect video testimonies with stories in Wiesel's memoir and once they made the connection they found it easier to discuss passages they were reading. Also, like so many of the teachers who piloted the video materials, Greene observed that the testimonies personalized the history of the Holocaust for her students. See "Using Video Testimonies in the Classroom" in the summaries of the annual conferences in Appendix 2.

Program Associate Jan Darsa has piloted "Challenge of Memory" in adult education classes, junior and senior high school classes, and college courses. Before showing the excerpts, she reminds students of the passage or passages in *Night* that parallel the video testimony. After viewing an excerpt, students have ample opportunity to discuss their reactions and elaborate on themes suggested in the montage.

Darsa has learned from experience that the montage engenders thought and discussion on three major themes of Holocaust history: the dichotomy between existing in the abnormal world of Auschwitz and living in the normal world; modes of resistance in the Third Reich; and coping with memories of atrocities that occurred more than four decades ago.

The opening excerpts of Rabbi Polak, Shari, and Edith sharpen awareness of the chasm between survivors' experiences in the Nazi era and the everyday lives of those who did not live through the Holocaust. How, students wonder, can it be possible that people survived in a universe of death? What sustained them? Why were some able to survive? Shari's testimony raises discussion about the difficulty students have in making the leap into comprehending the Holocaust, since she herself admits that she denied the Final Solution even after an eyewitness came to her home and reported the mass murders occurring in Polish camps.

The powerful imagery of Edith's description of the sun helps students comprehend how greatly the world of concentration camps differs from their own world in a free society in the late twentieth century. "It was almost like two worlds," one student explains. "The world inside the camps and the world outside the camp." Other students are intrigued with Edith's reference to the sun. Ninth grade students speculated on why Edith continually refers to the sun: Did her references mean she was expecting to survive? Why did she keep thinking of life-giving forces like the sun amidst death? Did Edith have hope that sustained her through the ordeal of the concentration camps? Was she angry to think the warmth of everyday normal existence was denied her and other inmates at Auschwitz?

At times some students find it impossible to comprehend the distant universe no matter how powerful the story of the speaker. In one ninth grade English class some students reported that they could not comprehend what Edith was talking about. "It's too remote and removed from my life." "I just couldn't relate to her."

The excerpt of Helen K. inevitably leads to a discussion of resistance. Students at Tufts University inquire about the difficulties of organizing an act of resistance: how much planning was needed and how could they meet? Why were only some of the participants in the plot to blow up crematoria hanged?

The closing excerpts lead to discussion about the power of memory and the importance of bearing witness. Leon Bass raises questions about the role of racism in the United States and Europe in fostering violence, brutality, and senseless murder. How can this chain be broken? How can knowledge of Nazi atrocities help prevent present and future violations of human rights?

Elie Wiesel's reminiscences with Peter Jennings at the site of Auschwitz evoke observations about the importance of keeping history of the Holocaust forever alive. Students report that the Wiesel-Jennings clip is the most memorable excerpt in the montage because it allows them to envision the real Auschwitz through the eyes of a man who lived to bear witness. "Seeing Auschwitz after reading what happened there, you feel like everything around there is dead. When you see it you feel like this is not a safe place to be even though there are no more people there. Seeing how Elie Wiesel was affected by going there made you feel like you shouldn't be there, it was like being in someone else's graveyard." "The Jennings interview of Wiesel," explains another student, "touched me where I was scared to be touched. It scared me in a way I was feeling emotional for everyone. I recommend this to anyone old or young. *It taught me.*"

College students are more critical of Jennings. They wonder why he pushes Wiesel on the issue of resistance. Is Jennings presuming that inmates should have done more? Is he aware of the Nazi use of reprisals and the many obstacles to any form of resistance?

Childhood Experiences of German Jews

The montage "Childhood Experiences of German Jews" contains five excerpts from the testimonies of men and women who recall growing up in Jewish homes in Nazi Germany between 1933 and 1939. From the very outset of the Nazi regime in January-February 1933, Jews were designated among the "enemies of the state" along with dissident political and religious groups such as the Communists, Jehovah's Witnesses, Freemasons and Catholics. The Enabling Decree of February 28, 1933 gave the Nazi government legal sanction for the arbitrary imprisonment of all suspected enemies of the new regime. By the following July, more than 27,000 "enemies" had been arrested and placed in detention camps.

Approximately 525,000 Jews lived in Germany in 1933; this figure represented less than one percent of the total German population. By the outbreak of the war six years later, more than half of German Jewry had emigrated. Many who relocated in western European countries such as France and Holland, as well as those Jews who remained in Germany, were rounded up by the Nazis during the war and deported to concentration camps in eastern Europe. This was the fate of Anne Frank and her family, who left Frankfurt, for Amsterdam in 1933 and were taken from their hiding place in the fall of 1944. Only about 10,000 German Jews survived the war years in hiding or in the camps.

The excerpts in this montage shed light on what conditions were like for Jewish children in the first years of the Nazi regime. They reveal how antisemitic measures were applied differently in different geographic areas, as well as the variety of responses among Jewish families to the harsh legislation against Jews. Some families made plans for emigration while others adopted a "wait and see" attitude of choosing to remain in their homeland in spite of the new antisemitic laws.

In four of the five excerpts, the witnesses explain why their families stayed in Germany until 1938. In the remaining excerpt, the witness explains what happened to her family, who waited until it was too late to contemplate emigration.

This montage may be used in conjunction with readings and discussions on the ways in which the Third Reich consolidated its power in the 1930s. Chapter 5 ("Nazi Philosophy and Policy") and Chapter 6 ("Preparing for Obedience") in the Resource Book examine this subject. Also useful for background is Lucjan Dobroszycki's "Unit on the Destruction of European Jewry, 1933-1945," coordinated by the American Association for Jewish Education and available at the Facing History Resource Center.

This montage can also accompany the readings and discussions of Hans Richter's novel *Friedrich*, which focuses on the lives of two youths, a Jew and a non-Jew, growing up in the 1930s.

Two other montages that complement this material are "Imagining the Unimaginable," about Jews who could not imagine the "Final Solution," and "Flight from Destiny," about German Jewish refugees seeking asylum in Cuba and Shanghai.

Excerpt 1: Peter G. (T-51)

Peter Gay was born in Berlin and was attending a *gymnasium* in the 1930s when the Nazis came to power. He was a member of an assimilated family that did not feel the need to emigrate in the early and middle 1930s. In fact, Peter experienced relatively little antisemitism in his school prior to *Kristallnacht* in November 1938. Peter and his parents were fortunate enough to obtain visas to enter the United States, where they joined family members living in Baltimore. Today Peter is a distinguished professor of history who specializes in cultural and intellectual history of modern Europe.

Excerpt 2: Eva S. (T-29)

Eva was born in Berlin and enjoyed the life of an upper class assimilated Jewish family. She was used to having servants and to attending good schools. Before the rise of Hitler she had very little awareness of her Jewish heritage; her parents did not emphasize religion, and Eva and her brother actually celebrated Christmas. It was only with the establishment of the National Socialist regime in 1933 that Eva became more acutely aware of her Jewishness and of the antisemitic feelings among the German population. Despite growing signs of anti-Jewish feeling after 1933, Eva's father opposed emigration. He felt he had too much to lose if he left his business in Germany. As it turned out, after her parents emigrated to America, Eva's father could never again establish a successful business. Eva and her brother did not emigrate with their parents. They were sent to Great Britain during the war years, and the whole family, so closely knit before 1933, never reunited.

Excerpt 3: Walter K. (T-97)

Walter was born in the region of Silesia near the Polish border. In contrast to Peter Gay, Walter was the victim of explicit antisemitism after 1933. He was beaten in school by a Nazi teacher, and he was humiliated by his German classmates. He and his family were among the passengers on the ill-fated voyage of the SS *St. Louis*; on the return voyage the family took refuge in France. While Walter and his brother managed to survive the Holocaust in a school for boys and later as members of the French resistance, their parents and sister were captured and sent to concentration camps, where they died.

Excerpt 4: Hilda G. (T-96)

Hilda was born in a village in southern Germany near the city of Frankfurt. Before Hitler came to power, Hilda did not experience much antisemitism in her neighborhood and school, and she had many non-Jewish friends. Unlike more urban Jewish families such as those of Peter Gay and Eva S., Hilda's family did observe Jewish traditions, and Hilda was proud of her Jewish culture and customs. It was only with the emergence of the Nazis in 1933 that her Jewish identity marked her as a victim of discrimination in the village. The children in the schools, she explains, were taught to hate Jews after 1933. Later, in the war years, Hilda and other members of her family were deported to the Lodz Ghetto where Hilda's grandparents and parents died of disease and starvation. Hilda survived the ghetto and was sent in the last transport from Lodz to Auschwitz, where she was reunited with her sister. The two sisters remained together in several camps until the end of the war.

Excerpt 5: Frank S. (T-30)

Frank was born in Breslau, the capital of Silesia, and from the outset of the Nazi era he was the victim of discrimination. He tells of his treatment as a Jew in a public school, where he was held up for ridicule as the example of a Jew in "raceology" classes. His classmates made fun of him for having a "Jewish-looking mother." In the late 1930s, Frank was able to leave Germany and join his aunt in England; his parents remained in Germany until 1941 when they managed to escape to Shanghai.

Commentary

Conditions for German Jews in the 1930s

From the time Hitler became chancellor of Germany on January 30, 1933, until the outbreak of the war in September 1939, the situation of Jews in Germany steadily deteriorated. Increasingly, legislative measures interfered with the ability of Jews to earn a living and to exercise their rights as citizens.

As early as the spring of 1933, there were signs that the Nazi state would discriminate against its Jewish minority. On April 1, 1933, a boycott of Jewish stores took place. Although not all Germans participated in the boycott, it was frightening for Jews to see how vulnerable they were in the new regime.

Following the boycott the Nazis implemented a series of economic measures to destroy Jewish economic life. These measures, known as Aryanization, gave power to individuals loyal to the Nazi regime to take charge of Jewish enterprises.

A Nazi stationed outside a Jewish store on Boycott Day in 1933. The sign reads: "Germans! Defend yourselves! Don't buy from Jews!"

During the first months of Nazi rule, Hitler met with several major industrialists and bankers who were hesitant to endorse an all-out assault on the Jewish minority— they did not approve the brutal tactics of the Storm Troopers and were reluctant to be associated with blatant acts of violence. By the middle 1930s, the squeamish attitudes among German business and banking communities disappeared and they offered little or no objection to unfair treatment of Jews. This was largely due to the fact that German entrepreneurs and financiers had benefited from Aryanization measures which had enabled them to acquire Jewish businesses and properties at low prices. Moreover, by 1938, Nazi government ministers who had advocated moderation in treatment of Jews, such as Hjalmar Schacht, were replaced by more zealous antisemites. These developments led to an accelerated effort to eliminate Jews from the German economy. By early 1939, the large Jewish firms with international connections and extensive resources were forced to sell out to Nazi industrialists at vastly undervalued prices.

Concurrent with the declining economic opportunities for Jews in the Third Reich, the Nazis enacted a series of laws that stripped Jews of their rights as German citizens and excluded them from protection of the law. (See "Regulations and Laws of the National Socialist State Against German Jews," below.)

Following the *Anschluss* (German occupation of Austria) in the spring of 1938, mistreatment of Jews in both Germany and Austria was part of everyday life. After the Munich Agreement (September 1938) in which Western powers permitted Hitler's Germany to determine the fate of Czechoslovakia, Czech Jews were exposed to the same sort of political and economic discrimination practiced against Jews in Germany and Austria. Thus, in 1938, approximately 400,000 Jews from Austria and Czechoslovakia were added to the German Jews seeking refuge from the antisemitic environment of the Nazi government.

On the night of November 9-10, 1938—known as *Kristallnacht* (the Night of Broken Glass)—carefully orchestrated riots throughout the Reich led to the destruction of some 7,000 Jewish shops and 280 synagogues. Approximately 25,000 to 30,000 Jewish men were arrested and detained in concentration camps until their families could provide proof that the detainees had a means of emigration. Meanwhile, the Reich held Jews responsible for the destruction of property on *Kristallnacht* and fined the Jewish community one billion Reichsmarks for the restitution of property.

The statistics of the German Jewish population between 1925 and September 1, 1939, suggest the increasing pressure on Jews to leave Nazi Germany. The majority of those who fled Germany in the 1930s were young people under twenty-five years of age, who in 1933 comprised approximately 27% of the Jewish population; by 1939 young Jews under twenty-five years of age comprised only about 14% of German Jewry.

The Disappearance of German Jewry

Date	Jewish Population
1925 census	564,000
January 1933 (estimate)	525,000
June 1933 (not incl. the Saar)	499,628
September 15, 1935 (estimate)	450,000
September 1937 (estimate)	350,000
May 17, 1939 (unpubl. census)	235,000
September 1, 1939 (estimate)	215,000

Source: Eisenberg, ed., *Witness to the Holocaust*, p. 115.

In the first years of the Nazi regime there were no serious legal obstacles to emigration. Nevertheless, as greater numbers of Jews sought to emigrate in the late 1930s, they found it more and more difficult to obtain the necessary papers. The United States and other nations throughout the world refused to liberalize immigration quotas even after reports of abuse towards the Jewish population in the Third Reich appeared in the newspapers and magazines.

During July 1938, thirty-two nations met at Evian to discuss the fate of German Jewish refugees. None of the participating nations, with the exception of the Dominican Republic, was willing to extend its quota for German Jews. In the United States, for example, the quota for the German nationality remained unchanged, even though it was recognized that Jews were being persecuted in Germany and the existing quota would be insufficient to accommodate the growing number of German Jews seeking asylum. The Dominican Republic opened its doors because it needed additional agricultural workers to fulfill its plans for economic recovery. In the months following the Evian Conference, as the number of Jews seeking to leave Central Europe swelled, Britain, Palestine, and the United States adopted even harsher regulations for admission; four South American countries—Argentina, Chile, Uruguay and Mexico—also adopted laws that severely restricted admission of Jews eligible to enter.

A particularly graphic illustration of the indifference of the world community toward the plight of German Jews was the incident of the liner, the SS *St. Louis*. In May 1939 the ocean liner set sail from Hamburg with 907 Jewish passengers. The passengers had visas for Cuba, and many were planning to head to the United States from Cuba as soon as their papers were in order.

However, when the *St. Louis* arrived in Havana, Cuban authorities refused to let the passengers disembark. The ship then took its passengers to Miami, where again officials rebuffed their entry. Finally, the *St. Louis* headed back to Germany. At the last moment, four European nations—Great Britain, France, Holland and Belgium—agreed to accept the passengers.

Although the international community did not make a determined effort to solve the problem of Jewish refugees in the Nazi state, it was not totally unresponsive to the pressure of Jews in Central Europe seeking asylum.

Absorption of Jewish Refugees, 1933-1943

Country	Number Admitted	Percentage
Total	811,000	100.00
United States	190,000	23.5
Palestine	120,000	14.8
England	65,000	8.1
France	55,000	6.8
Holland	35,000	4.3
Belgium	30,000	3.7
Switzerland	16,000	1.9
Spain	12,000	1.4
Other Eur. Countries	70,000	8.8
Argentina	50,000	6.2
Brazil	25,000	3.1
Bolivia	12,000	1.4
Chile	14,000	1.7
Uruguay	7,000	0.8
Other Lat. Am. Countries	20,000	2.4
China	25,000	3.1
Australia	9,000	1.1
South Africa	8,000	1.0
Canada	8,000	1.0
Other Countries	40,000	4.9

Source: Eisenberg, ed., *Witness to the Holocaust*, p. 117.

The greatest percentage of refugees came from the population of young Jews. Two organizations that proved particularly helpful were Youth Aliyah, a Jewish organization founded in 1932 to help young men settle in Palestine, and the World Movement for the Care of Children from Germany, established in England in response to the events of *Kristallnacht*.

Gisela Wyzanski, a volunteer for Youth Aliyah, recalls the innumerable technical details involved in securing visas and other official papers for children emigrating to Palestine between 1935 and 1938. "I spent hours with Nazi officials, consuls," she explains, "to obtain the necessary papers and on the long distance telephone with parents all over Germany to assemble the missing papers." Even more difficult, however, was the separation of children from their parents.

> The farewell scenes in Berlin I shall never forget. On the one hand the families, mothers, brothers and sisters, and fathers, if they had not disappeared, and friends seeing these children off with a very fair premonition that they would never see them again; and on the other hand the happiness . . . with a sort of hope against hope that you would see them again in Palestine and that at least these children were starting out on a better future.[20]

While youth left and organizations like Youth Aliyah facilitated their departure, older Jews tended to remain in the *Vaterland*. In addition to the political and legal impediments to their departure, other considerations entered into their decision to stay in Germany. Some lacked the economic means and were unable to arrange for visas and transportation abroad for themselves and other members of their family. Others who had the economic wherewithal felt too attached to their homeland to leave: those who had served in World War I could not imagine that their country would betray them with abuse and persecution. For example, Otto Frank, the father of Anne Frank, was so proud of his wartime service that he paid for a dress uniform and had himself photographed in this attire.

Older Jews who had extended families in Germany and were unwilling to leave their familiar surroundings often felt there was no cause for alarm at anti-Jewish legislation. While younger Jews sought a new life outside Germany, other older Jews "hoped against hope that their fellow citizens, among whom they had lived for so many centuries, would not throw them to the wolves. Every time there was a pause in persecution, they would breathe easier."[21]

With the outbreak of the war in September 1939 the situation for Jews in Germany worsened rapidly. Prewar legislation enacted to expel Jews from the Reich was replaced by police measures in the war years, with special police agencies established to rid the Reich of Jews. During the war, sixty-three transports to the east of German Jews claimed 35,000 victims, and 117 transports of the elderly claimed 15,000 victims. In total, 123,000 German Jews perished in the concentration camps. Transports in these years was a term referring to trainloads of victims who were forcibly rounded up and deported.

According to historian Karl A. Schleunes, German Jewish businesses that lacked foreign investments and contacts were the earliest victims of Aryanization:

> The number of Jewish firms which were liquidated in one form or other in the first two years of Nazi rule is impossible to assess, although one estimate puts it at about 75,000. Such estimates, however, are no more than educated guesses. In fact, only one clear pattern emerges between 1933 and early 1938: The larger and more complex the Jewish firm, the greater were its powers of resistance. These powers alone seem to be responsible for the framework into which the anti-Jewish assault on the economic front can be fitted. By the Nazis' own estimate in April 1938, there were still some 39,532 Jewish business establishments in Germany, and many of these were in one way or another critical to rearmament or to the import-export trade. As early as 1936, on the other hand, many of the smaller businesses, especially those associated with agriculture, were declared to be judenrein.[22]

Douglas Miller, an American emissary, sent a report on Aryanization to the government via the U.S. diplomatic pouch. In his report he quoted the following letter that had been written to a Jewish businessman in Germany:

> "Dear Sir:
>
> "Your letter of the 21st of this month to the chief of the Department of Egg Wholesalers, Eugene Fuerst, has been turned over to me with the request to give my opinion and prepare an answer.
>
> "I wish to state right now, that it is no part of the duties of the German Labor Front to give advice or guidance to non-Aryans. If, however, I do answer your letter, it is only in the interest of your employees, for I wish to prevent German fellow countrymen from losing work and bread, i.e., to turn it over into Aryan ownership while this still remains possible; it is well known that with the existing shortage of supplies Aryan firms are given the preference in having their orders filled. In this way, it would also be made possible for your employees to continue receiving wages. Of

course, I must reserve the right to withhold my approval of such a sale in order to make absolutely sure that the business actually becomes Aryan. Also, I must reserve my approval regarding the person of the buyer. It will not have escaped your notice that in recent times with the co-operation of the German Labor Front very many non-Aryan plants have been turned over to Aryan control with a turnover amounting to millions.

"If today, in the entire country, the Aryan import trade and the Aryan wholesale trade refuse to sell to Jews, this is accounted for by various reasons, and there can be no possibility of raising a claim of interference in the business rights of non-Aryans. The unwillingness to deliver goods is based upon the fact that the present food stuff trade is well aware that for military and political reasons this trade must be in Aryan hands. Furthermore, the supplies of fresh goods are actually very short and one cannot blame the trade if they think first of their Aryan customers. There is no sense in your pointing to the Nuremberg Laws and the regulations which had been published in connection with them. I refer you to the leading article in Voelkischer Beobachter of November 22nd of this year, entitled 'Unwritten Laws.' In recent times it has been repeatedly stated by the Fuehrer and by other persons that the Party rules the State. If a member of the Party enters into business relations with a Jew, he incurs the danger of coming into conflict with the written and unwritten laws of the Party and accordingly of being called upon to assume the responsibility for his acts. Neither the Ministry of Economics, the Agricultural Ministry, the German Labor Front nor any other Government office can compel an Aryan importer or wholesaler today to sell goods to German firms, or particularly, in view of the above-mentioned facts.

"When you refer to the fact that you were a front fighter, let me remind you in this connection that this was the self-understood duty of every able-bodied man. I have become acquainted with your activities on the front and know that they did not continue for four years even if you did wear a uniform of a front fighter for four years. Your main service was passed in Belgium behind the lines and in Berlin in the hospital service. You even had the opportunity during the war to look after your business in Berlin.

"Your wish to be allowed henceforth to receive goods cannot be granted on account of the reasons which I have just given. In the last paragraph of your letter you refer to the regulations regarding the citizenship laws of November 14th, 1935, as they affect Jewish officials who were front fighters. This law removes from public employment the last remaining Jewish front fighters, but all of them are to retain their pensions. But you were not an official but are in business for yourself and revolutions have always had their effects upon certain types of business, and, in this particular case, upon non-Aryan firms in the foodstuff industry.

"I can only advise you to sell your business immediately, as long as it has any value at all; for when you have once lost your customers to those Aryan firms which are able to deliver goods, your business will depreciate or become completely valueless.

"Signed Hoffheinz"[23]

The Process of Stripping Jews of Their Citizenship

Besides the Nazi measures to remove Jews from their role in the German economy, a series of legislative measures between 1933 and 1939 removed Jews from the protection of the law and denied them their rights as German citizens. (See "Regulations of the National Socialist State," below, for a fuller listing of these measures).

Within the first year of power, the Nazis began excluding Jews from the life of the nation:

April 7, 1933: The Law for the Restoration of the Professional Civil Service and Supplementary Decrees deprived Jews of their positions in the state bureaucracy.

April 25, 1933: The Law against the Overcrowding of German Schools and Institutions of Higher Learning denied children of German Jews the right to higher education.

September 1933: The Reich Chamber of Culture was established and the Press Law laid the basis for excluding Jews from literary and cultural institutions and professions.

In the fall of 1935 more sweeping measures were enacted. The Nuremberg Laws (see pages 155-156) first announced at the Nazi Party Convention in September 1935 identified Jews according to their racial and religious heritage and forbade Jews from marriage with "Aryans" or from employing "Aryan" maids under the age of 45.

The Nuremberg Laws made Jews pariahs in the German state. Not only were Jews prohibited from sexual or social intercourse with Aryans, but Julius Streicher's newspaper, *Der Sturmer*, daily vilified the image of Jews with grotesque cartoons and banner headlines reading, "The Jews are our Misfortune." Since Jews were no longer considered citizens, the Gestapo and local police could treat Jews in a brutal fashion with impunity.

Scenes from Carnival in Cologne. Men dress up as Jews, 1934. "The last Jews disappear. We're only on a short trip to Lichtenstein or Jaffa."

Carnival wagon with men in concentration camp uniforms: "Away to Dachau." Nuremberg, 1936.

At the Nuremberg carnival in 1938. "National enemies." A puppet at the gallows wearing a Star of David.

During the months of the Olympic Games in 1936, the government did not harshly enforce the Nuremberg Laws and other anti-Jewish measures in order to avoid criticism from abroad. Once the Olympics ended, however, the Nazis resumed their assault on the Jews, exacting harsher taxes on Jewish wealth and enforcing civic restrictions with greater rigor than previously. Martin Gilbert records the story of Helmut Hirsch, which captures some of the despair Jews experienced in the hostile environment of Germany in 1937:

> In Germany, a young Jew of twenty, Helmut Hirsch, in despair at the unyielding pressures against his people, had been caught with a revolver and a suitcase of bombs. He was charged with intending to assassinate Streicher. Hirsch was then tried and sentenced to death. As Hirsch was technically an American citizen, although he had never been to America, the American Ambassador, William Dodd, appealed to Hitler to commute the death sentence. But Hitler's reply, Dodd told the American journalist William Shirer, "was a flat negative." Dodd then sought a personal interview with Hitler to plead the case; he was "rebuffed". [24]

At dawn on June 4, Helmut Hirsch was executed with an axe. Eight days later, a number of Jews accused of "race defilement" were sent to Dachau Concentration Camp, where some three hundred Jews were being held.

The increasingly antisemitic environment in Germany between 1933 and 1938 is mirrored in photographs of public events in these years . [25]

1934: Carnival in Cologne in which the wagons bore the sign: "The last Jews disappear; we're only on a short trip to Lichtenstein or Jaffa."

1936: Carnival wagon in Nuremberg with the sign, "Away to Dachau."

1938: Carnival at Nuremberg in which "National enemies" are displayed hanging with a windmill and wearing Jewish stars.

Decisions at the Evian Conference: The World Stands By

The decisions announced by the Evian Conference on July 14, 1938, indicated that the world community was not willing to take any extraordinary measures on behalf of the Jews:

1. Considering that the question of involuntary emigration has assumed major proportions and that the fate of the unfortunate people affected has become a problem for intergovernmental deliberation;

2. Aware that the involuntary emigration of large numbers of people, of different creeds, economic conditions, professions and trades, from the country or countries where they have been established, is disturbing to the general economy, since these persons are obliged to seek refuge, either temporarily or permanently, in other countries at a time when there is serious unemployment; that, in consequence, countries of refuge and settlement are faced with problems, not only of an economic and social nature, but also of public order, and that there is a severe strain on the administrative facilities and absorptive capacities of the receiving countries;

3. Aware, moreover that the involuntary emigration of people in large numbers has become so great that it renders racial and religious problems more acute, increases international unrest, and may hinder seriously the process of appeasement in international relations;

4. Believing that it is essential that a long-range programme should be envisaged, whereby assistance to involuntary emigrants, actual and potential, may be coordinated within the framework of existing migration laws and practices of Governments;

5. Considering that if countries of refuge or settlement are to co-operate in finding an orderly solution of the problem before the Committee they should have the collaboration of a country of origin and are therefore persuaded that it will make its contribution by enabling involuntary

emigrants to take with them their property and possessions and emigrate in an orderly manner. . .

7. Bearing in mind the resolution adopted by the Council of the League of Nations on May 14th, 1938, concerning international assistance to refugees . . .

Recommends:

. . . c. that in view of the fact that the countries of refuge and settlement are entitled to take into account the economic and social adaptability of immigrants, these should in many cases be required to accept, at least for a time, changed conditions of living in the countries of settlement;

d. that the governments of the countries of refuge and settlement should not assume any obligations for the financing of involuntary emigration;

f. that there should meet at London an Intergovernmental Committee consisting of such representatives as the Governments participating in the Evian Meeting may desire to designate. This Committee shall continue and develop the government of the Intergovernmental Meeting at Evian. . . .[26]

While the world community did not take determined measures to meet the needs of Jewish refugees, the efforts of the World Movement for the Care of Children from Germany, founded in London after *Kristallnacht*, illustrate the type of response that was still possible. Between November 9, 1938, and the outbreak of the war in September 1939, the World Movement in conjunction with Jewish organizations in Germany and the British Home Office arranged for 9,354 Jewish and non–Jewish children to settle in England. Eva S. was among the youth who benefited from the efforts of the British organization.

Regulations of the National Socialist State 1933

April 7: Law for the Restoration of the Professional Civil Service

May 10: Burning of books whose contents had been declared un-German by the Nazis

1934

February 5-December 8: New rules on government state examinations for physicians, lawyers, and pharmacists; non-Aryans are excluded from these examinations

1935

July 25: Non-Aryans are not permitted to serve in the armed forces

September 15: The Nuremberg Laws, the Reich Citizenship Law, and the Law for the Protection of German Blood and German Honor legalize the Nazis' antisemitic policies

1937

April 15: Jews of German nationality are no longer allowed to receive doctorates

1938

July 25: Jewish physicians lose their licenses

August 17: Second regulation for the implementation of the law concerning the alteration of family names and first names—"As of January 1, 1939, Jews whose first names differ from those permitted under paragraph 1 are required to accept an additional name which will be Israel for males, Sara for females."

September 27: Jewish lawyers lose their right to practice

October 5: The marking of Jewish passports with the letter "J"

November 9-10: *Kristallnacht*

November 12: "The totality of Jews who are German subjects will pay a fine of one billion Reichsmarks to the German Reich"

November 15: Jewish children are excluded from state schools

December 3-6: Jews are not allowed to own or to drive cars, to enter theatres, cinemas, cabarets, public concerts, libraries, museums, public and private swimming pools, and sports grounds. In addition, they are not permitted to enter the government district in Berlin. Jews can be ordered to sell their businesses and they have to deposit their stocks and bonds in specified banks

December 8: Jews are excluded from universities.[27]

Using

What do you learn from the excerpts about differences in the implementation of Nazi legislation in urban and rural communities? Why do you think that Hilda was more immediately affected by antisemitic measures than Peter Gay? What factors exist in an urban community that might have mitigated the impact of Nazi antisemitic legislation?

What varying reactions to Nazi legislation were illustrated by the excerpts?

Why were youth (as the young men and women described in the excerpts of "Childhood Experiences of German Jews"), especially male youth, so highly represented in the emigration statistics of the 1930s? What factors made it easier for this age group to leave? What institutions existed to help this age group relocate outside Germany?

From your readings and discussions about bureaucracy, in what ways does bureaucracy in a modern nation state affect the identities of individual citizens? In studying the identity papers of Sonia Weitz and in hearing the testimonies of survivors, what have you learned about the nature of Nazi bureaucracy? Did it resemble other bureaucracies in modern nation states? What was unique about the Nazi bureaucracy? Can Nazi bureaucrats in the immigration office be held accountable for administrative delays of German Jews seeking to leave before 1941?

In current events, what difficulties do refugees encounter in trying to obtain papers for emigration?

Students often ask why Jews in Germany failed to leave in the years before the war. The memories on these tapes and the information in *Elements of Time* illuminate how complex it is to answer this question. Jews, especially younger ones, did leave when they could. Using the table "The Disappearance of German Jewry," point out when the Jews left. What years witnessed the largest exodus? How do you explain the relative slowup in the period from May until September 1939? What was taking place between September 1937 and May 1939 that would help explain the increased pace of emigration?

Look at the table "Absorption of Jewish Refugees." Which countries absorbed the greatest percentage of Jews? The smallest percentage? How do you account for the large number of nations that maintained stringent restrictions against immigration in the 1930s? Why do historians like David Wyman and Henry Feingold so sharply criticize the American response to the "Jewish Question" when the United States admitted a higher percentage than the great majority of states in the prewar international community?

Judy Hudson uses the Facing History unit to introduce her world history course to seniors at a parochial high school for girls. Since Hudson begins her world history survey with Facing History, she stresses four themes in the unit that she plans to elaborate upon in subsequent units on Modern China, Soviet Russia, and the Third World: (1) the concept of freedom—what does it mean in a democratic society?; (2) patterns of education and how they mirror dominant values of their respective societies; (3) the role of propaganda in modern society; and (4) the impact of war on modern society.

Hudson has little difficulty selecting materials in the chapters of the Resource

Book dealing with Society and the Individual, Prejudice and Antisemitism, Preparing for Obedience, and Judgment. She is familiar with these topics and can choose readings and films that best illustrate her four principal themes. However, she finds the chapters on "German History" and "Nazi Philosophy and Policy" most challenging. Since her students have so little background in European history, she grapples with the question of where to begin. What facts are necessary for students to understand the rise of Nazism? What history can be deleted without distorting the context of Nazism? She is constantly wrestling with these questions while teaching this section of the course. Other teachers who have had similar concerns have had a member of the Facing History staff or the Teacher Training Team versed in European history give a lecture on the interwar years. Steve Cohen, for instance, often visits classrooms to present the history of Weimar and early Nazism, examining the conundrum of economic, social, and political factors that contributed to the popularity of the Third Reich. In conjunction with Cohen's visit, teachers commonly assign the novel *Friedrich* that chronicles the erosion of a friendship between two boys, a Jew and non-Jew, between 1933 and 1942. Another option for approaching this material is to use the video montage "Childhood Experiences of German Jews," in which the lives of the interviewees intersect with the principal historical events of the early Nazi years.

Hudson chose the latter option because she believed that her seniors would find *Friedrich* too simple for their reading level. As it turns out, her choice was successful. In viewing the five excerpts of German Jews recalling their school years in the 1930s, the students raised a series of questions that, in turn, provoked them to look more closely at the historical roots of Nazism: Why was Nazi legislation implemented differently in different areas of Germany? Why was the Berliner Peter able to remain in German schools for several years after rural students like Hilda were forced to leave their public schools? Why were Frank and Hilda attracted to the pomp and circumstance of Nazi parades? Why didn't Jewish families flee Germany once the Nazis revealed their anti-Jewish policies? Why did the parents of Eva and Peter believe their service in World War I would protect them from anti-Jewish measures under the Nazis?

Students' comments suggested that the montage opened up new areas of thought and offered a context for studying daily life under Nazism. Several said that the video helped them realize that antisemitic legislation was imposed with varying levels of intensity in different locales and that it took several years for the legislation to affect Jews throughout Germany. During a class discussion one student explained why she found it so useful to hear a range of voices:

> I never really thought about the impressions children received through elementary education. I found it interesting to hear the perspectives of German-Jewish school children. Listening to them speak about their experiences made the idea of the Holocaust and Nazi Germany a reality, because it gave the millions of persecuted peoples names, faces and identities.

Toward the close of the discussion, another student noted an omission in the videotape. "It is interesting," she said,

> the way history suddenly becomes 'real' when you hear someone who lived through it. . . . As we discussed the tape ["Childhood Experiences of German Jews"], I realized we had not seen anything about the other side of antisemitism in Nazi Germany—the people who did the hating. I would have liked to hear a former non-Jewish German school child explain how he or she was educated to hate Jews.

To fill this void Hudson was able to use the excerpt Carl in "Childhood Memories." She also referred students to readings in the Resource Book which compare experiences of Jewish and non-Jewish youth in school settings and extracurricular activities.

Henry Friedlander's presentation "The Rise of Nazism" discusses Nazi legislation with regard to the property of Jews sent to concentration camps. Given the bureaucracy of a modern state like Germany, it was necessary to develop the legal procedures for disinheriting Jews before they were sent for extermination. Friedlander's presentation is described in Appendix 1.

Friedrich: A Video Montage to Accompany Hans Peter Richter's Novel *Friedrich*

The video montage "Friedrich" has been designed to accompany Hans Richter's novel of the same name. The video excerpts enhance Richter's story by illuminating certain historical and emotional issues raised throughout the novel. All of the witnesses in the video excerpts were children or young adolescents during the Nazi era, and as they look back forty-five to fifty years, they recount events that parallel those in Richter's story.

Friedrich is the story of two young boys caught up in the events of Germany during the Weimar and Nazi eras. It opens in 1925 and traces the lives of the

Hans Peter Richter

Friedrich

Winner of the Mildred L. Batchelder Award

Friedrich *(cover)*.

two protagonists until the death of Friedrich in 1942.

Friedrich is told from the perspective of a first person narrator, a non-Jew who never discloses his name. The narrator's close friend and neighbor is a Jewish boy, Friedrich. The story of the two boys captures the time in history when neighbors turned against one another. Because each chapter in the novel begins with a date and incident that chronicles the gradual deterioration of conditions for German Jews between 1933 and 1942, this story becomes a history lesson as well as a lesson in literature. It reminds students that society does not change overnight; events occur one by one, and slowly individuals make choices as they respond to what is happening around them. The timeline provided at the end of the novel will help remind students of the dominant political events that took place each year during the period.

At the outset of this story it is of little consequence that Friedrich Schneider is a Jew and his friend is not Jewish. The two, born within a week of one another in 1925, grow up in the same apartment building and develop a close friendship. As small children they play in each other's homes, and they start school together in 1930.

During these years, the major difference between the two families is economic: Herr Schneider, a civil servant in the post office, makes a comfortable living while the narrator's father is unemployed and has to rely on support from a relative. Although the children are oblivious to the differing circumstances, the narrator's parents are keenly aware of the greater economic security enjoyed by the Schneider family and are embarrassed by their own impoverished situation.

Relations between the two friends become more complex after Hitler's rise to power in January 1933. Beginning that year and continuing during the six years that follow, the Nazis impose a series of restrictions against the Jews that culminate with *Kristallnacht* (the Night of Broken Glass) on November 9-10, 1938. On that evening, a series of violent demonstrations takes place in which Jewish businesses, shops, and synagogues are looted and destroyed and thousands of Jewish men imprisoned.

Of course, these restrictions have a direct impact on the Schneider family. In 1933, Herr Schneider is dismissed from his position with the post office. Fortunately he is able to find work at a Jewish department store. The quotas which limit the number of Jews in public schools mean that Friedrich has to leave his public school to attend a Jewish school. The Schneiders' maid explains that she can no longer work for Jews on account of the Nuremberg Laws (September 1935). By 1938, the year of *Kristallnacht*, Friedrich is reminded daily of his inferior status. At a neighborhood swimming pool, for example, he is humiliated because he is identified as a Jew. He and his friend, the narrator, have to meet secretly so no one will know a Jew is speaking with a non-Jew. Friedrich's parents suffer as well. Herr Schneider loses his job at the department store, and Frau Schneider becomes one of the thousands of victims of the *Kristallnacht* violence. She dies soon thereafter of her wounds.

For Herr Schneider and Friedrich, the months that follow bring hardships. They eke out a meager living by repairing lamps in the kitchen of their apartment. Rarely do they have enough food for a meal. One day, the landlord Herr Resch, reports his Jewish tenants to the Gestapo; Herr Schneider, along with a rabbi who is hiding there, are taken away. Friedrich is out at the time; when he returns, he discovers Herr Resch rummaging through his apartment, taking whatever he can fit into his wife's large shopping bag.

Friedrich, now all alone, goes into hiding. One day in 1942 he risks visiting the narrator at the very time of a threat of an air raid. The narrator and his parents leave Friedrich in their apartment while they seek protection in a shelter. They know that Herr Resch, in charge of the shelter, will not allow Friedrich in. When the family returns, they find Friedrich fatally wounded.

The Nuremberg Laws (the Reich Citizenship Law and the Law for the Protection of German Blood and Honor) were announced at the Nazi Party rally of September 15, 1935. As Holocaust survivors in the montage "Friedrich" indicate, these laws had an effect on all aspects of Jewish life.

The Nuremberg Laws

Reich Citizenship Law

The Reichstag has unanimously enacted the following law which is herewith made public:

paragraph 1

(1) A subject of the State is anyone who enjoys the protection of the German Reich and who therefore is especially obligated to it.

paragraph 2

(1) Only the state citizen of German or kindred blood who by his conduct proves that he is willing and able to serve loyally the German people and Reich is a Reich citizen.

(2) Reich citizenship is acquired through the granting of a Reich Citizenship Certificate.

(3) The Reich Minister of the Interior, in co-ordination with the Deputy of the Fuehrer, will issue the Legal Administrative orders required to implement and complete this law.

Law for the Protection of German Blood and German Honor

Moved by the understanding that purity of the German Blood is the essential condition for the continued existence of the German people, and inspired by the inflexible determination to ensure the existence of the German Nation for all time, the Reichstag has unanimously adopted the following Law, which is promulgated herewith:

paragraph 1

(1) Marriages between Jews and subjects of the State of German or related blood are forbidden. Marriages nevertheless concluded are invalid, even if concluded abroad to circumvent this law.

(2) Annulment proceedings can be initiated only by the State prosecutor.

paragraph 2

Extramarital intercourse between Jews and subjects of the State of German or related blood is forbidden.

paragraph 3

Jews may not employ in their households female subjects of the State of German or related blood who are under 45 years old.[28]

In meetings of the Hitler Youth, members learned that National Socialism intended to restore the Reich to glory, health, and strength. Above are samples of photographs used in Hilter Youth training.

Excerpt 1: Defining the New German Society

Janet B. (T-227), the daughter of a Jewish mother and a non-Jewish father, was born in Berlin in 1935. By the outbreak of the war her parents had divorced. Although she lived with her mother and had to wear the Yellow Star of identification as a Jew during the war years, her father was responsible for her well-being. In this excerpt Janet recalls an incident when she was five years old. A non-Jewish neighbor decided to take her to a Nazi parade and removed Janet's yellow star for the occasion. Janet remembers how delighted she was: the parade and the color and noise were exciting and had a momentum all their own. Janet felt totally involved in the celebrations. When she got home, however, her mother was upset that Janet had been taken to the parade.

In *Friedrich* there is a similar account of a Jewish child eager to be involved with the activities of the new Germany. Friedrich accompanies his friend, the narrator, to a meeting of the Jungvolk, the organization preparing German boys for participation in the Hitler Youth. Friedrich likes the idea of belonging to such a group and hopes his father will let him go to the meetings. As the two walk to the meeting, Friedrich confides:

> "I'm so glad you know [about the meeting]. . . . But you mustn't tell my father. He doesn't like my going there. You know, I saw you all marching through town with your flag and singing. I think that's really great. I'd love to take part, but Father won't let me join the *Jungvolk*. Still, maybe he'll change his mind after a while."[29]

As it turns out, Friedrich is to change his mind about wanting to belong to the youth organization. His disappointment with the meeting will be discussed in conjunction with the next excerpt.

Commentary

The Nazis revived the Yellow Star that Janet refers to in her story. The Yellow Star originated in the Middle Ages as a means of identifying and isolating the Jewish minority. It was made of yellow material on a black background with the word *Jude* (Jew) written in black lettering; the Nazis stipulated that Jews six years and older must wear the Yellow Star sewn on the left breast of their outer garment so it would be fully visible.

Many accounts of Germans and non-Germans in the 1930s allude to the impact of rallies and parades organized by the National Socialists. The reminiscences of the German brother and sister Hans and Sophie Scholl suggest how these activities excited and inspired them.

> "One morning, on the school steps, I heard a girl from my class tell another: 'Hitler has just taken over the government.' And the radio and all the neighbors proclaimed: 'Now everything will improve in Germany. Hitler has seized the helm.'

> "For the first time politics entered our lives. Hans at the time was fifteen years old: Sophie was twelve. We heard a great deal of talk about Fatherland, comradeship, community of the Volk, and love of homeland. All this impressed us, and we listened with enthusiasm whenever we heard anyone speak of these things in school or on the street. For we loved our homeland very much . . . And every square foot of it was well known and very dear to us. Fatherland—what else was it but the greater homeland of all who spoke the same language and belonged to the same people! We loved it, but were hardly able to say why. Until that time we had never lost many words over it. But now it was written large, in blazing letters in the sky. And Hitler, as we heard everywhere, Hitler wanted to bring greatness, happiness, and well-being to this Fatherland. . . . We found this good, and in whatever might come to pass we were determined to help to the best of our ability. But there was yet one more thing that attracted us with a mysterious force and pulled us along—namely, the compact columns of marching youths with waving flags, eyes looking straight ahead, and the beat of drums and singing. Was it not overwhelming, this fellowship? Thus it was no wonder that all of us. . . joined the Hitler Youth."[30]

During the war the Scholls and other students at the University of Munich grew so disillusioned with Nazi leadership that they organized a widespread distribution of anti-Hitler pamphlets in the winter of 1942-1943, following news of the defeat of the German Sixth Army at Stalingrad. The Scholls and other leaders of the protest were arrested and executed in February 1943.[31]

American journalist William Shirer, who was in Berlin between 1934 and 1940, observed many of the parades and the pageantry that captured the imagination of the German people. From his description below of the Nuremberg Party Rally in 1934, we can begin to understand why a child such as Janet would have been so excited by the Nazi festivities.

> [A]fter the events of the first day of the party rally had come to an end, I had "begun to comprehend," I boasted in my diary, "some of the reasons for Hitler's astonishing success." Borrowing from the Roman Church, I noted, he was restoring pageantry to the drab lives of Germans. The morning's opening meeting in the huge Luitpold Hall on the outskirts of Nuremberg was more than a colorful show. It had something of the mysticism and religious fervor of an Easter or a Christmas Mass in a great Gothic cathedral.

> The hall was a sea of brightly colored flags. Suddenly the band stopped playing. There was a hush over the thirty thousand people packed in the immense arena. Then the band struck up the "Badenweiler March," a rather catchy tune and played only, I learned, when the Leader made his big entrances. Hitler appeared in the back of the auditorium, dressed in a brown party uniform, and followed by his aides, Hermann Göring, Joseph Goebbels, Rudolf Hess, and Heinrich Himmler, all in brown uniforms except Himmler, who wore the black garb of the S.S. He strode slowly down the wide center aisle while thirty thousand pairs of eyes were turned toward him and as many hands were raised in salute. It was a ritual, I was told, that had been followed at the opening of the party meetings for years.
> . . .

> It was in such a hushed atmosphere that Hitler sprang his Proclamation to the People, which the Nazi press office had tipped us off the evening before would be the most important pronouncement ever made by the Führer. . . .

> The words of the proclamation I never forgot. They kept coming back to me in the ensuing years, a reminder of the way history turns out differently than some, even the mightiest have planned.

> "The German form of life is definitely determined for the next thousand years. For us, the nervous nineteenth century has finally ended. There will be no revolution in Germany for the next one thousand years!"[32]

From the mid–1930s on, the Nazi administration began to ostracize Jews from the community by prohibiting them from participating in patriotic ceremonies and rituals.

It was customary in Germany, especially in the big cities, to hoist the red-white-black flag from the windows on holidays (more ardent Nazis put colored pictures of Hitler in their windows), to wear Nazi insignia and swastika armbands, and to give the "German salute": the *deutscher Gruss* (outstretched arm and "heil Hitler"). All these manifestations of membership in the German community were successfully denied to Jews. The Blood and Honor Law (September 15, 1935) prohibited Jews from displaying the Reich colors. The decree of November 14, 1935 regulated the use of insignia, medals, titles, and so on. Finally, a ruling of the Justice Ministry, dated November 4, 1937, deprived those Jews who were prone to give the "German salute" of a chance to hide their identity.[33]

Patriotism was integral to the training of boys between ten and twelve years old. The following procedures were set forth for membership in the Deutsches Jungvolk, the junior branch of the Hitler Youth (April 1940). The following is a text of a speech of the Hitler Youth Leader to be read in all branches.

"Dear boy! Dear girl!

"This hour in which you are to be received into the great community of the Hitler Youth is a very happy one and at the same time will introduce you into a new period of your lives. Today for the first time you swear allegiance to the Führer which will bind you to him for all time.

"And every one of you, my young comrades, enters at this moment into the community of all German boys and girls. With your vow and your commitment you now become a bearer of German spirit and German honour. Every one, every single one, now becomes the foundation for an eternal Reich of all Germans.

"When you too now march in step with the youngest soldiers, then bear in mind that this march is to train you to be a National Socialist conscious of the future and faithful to his duty.

"And the Führer demands of you and of us all that we train ourselves to a life of service and duty, of loyalty and comradeship. You, ten-year-old cub, and you, lass, are not too young nor too small to practise obedience and discipline, to integrate yourself into the community and show yourself to be a comrade. Like you, millions of young Germans are today swearing allegiance to the Führer and it is a proud picture of unity which German youth today presents to the whole world. So today you make a vow to your Führer and here, before your parents, the Party and your comrades, we now receive you into our great community of loyalty. Your motto will always be:

"'Führer, command—we follow!'

"(*The cubs are asked to rise.*) Now say after me: 'I promise always to do my duty in the Hitler Youth in love and loyalty to the Führer and to our flag.'"[34]

Using

What would have been appealing about the Jungvolk for Friedrich? In the novel, why does Friedrich say he is so eager to attend a meeting of the Jungvolk? Why do you think his father would object?

From the point of view of Nazi ideology, why was it not permissible for Jews to participate in various organizations of the Hitler Youth? How did Nazis define the status of Jews in the German citizenry?

Why do you think Janet's mother was so upset about her daughter witnessing a Nazi parade?

Excerpt 2: Racial Tensions in Schools and Extracurricular Activities During the Nazi Era

In this excerpt, Walter K. (T-97) speaks of an incident in his childhood in which he experienced discrimination by his teacher and his peers. Walter was a student in a public school in the Silesian town of Pieskretscham. His teacher, a member of the Nazi Party, wore a uniform to school. Short in stature, the teacher exhibited cruel and violent behavior when he forced his Jewish student, Walter, to stand in front of the class and receive a beating for no apparent reason. Walter recalls that there was nothing anyone was willing to do to help him. The principal, he explained, was a nice man, but he could not help; he was not a member of the Nazi Party, while the teacher was. Walter's parents were powerless: the police certainly were not interested in intervening on behalf of the Jews. Adding to Walter's humiliation was his treatment by his non-Jewish classmates. These students remained passive when the teacher beat Walter; later, they taunted him, called him names, and spit on him.

Friedrich's situation in school differs considerably from the one described by Walter. Before he is forced to leave the public school in 1934, Friedrich's non-Jewish teacher is kind and understanding and explains in a gentle voice to his Jewish student that he will have to attend an all-Jewish school.

However, Friedrich encounters similar discrimination in extracurricular affairs. One evening he attends a meeting of the Jungvolk with his friend, the narrator. Here he incurs the wrath of a fanatical Nazi, a short hunchback man who never tires of berating Jews. During the meeting he forces Friedrich to repeat, "The Jews are our affliction." When Friedrich refuses to comply, the Nazi leader grabs him and threatens to hit him. Friedrich manages to escape from the clubhouse unharmed.

Later that year, Friedrich is playing with the narrator when he is blamed for breaking a shop window. Both boys try to explain that the break is an accident and that Friedrich is not responsible for the damage. Nevertheless, the owner of the shop refuses to believe that Friedrich is innocent. Even the policeman on the scene seeks to blame Friedrich. "Believe me," he says to the narrator, "we grown ups have plenty of experience with Jews. You can't trust them. They're sneaky and they cheat." Friedrich sobs at the indignation of being falsely accused and of having nowhere to turn for assistance. Like Walter, Friedrich is hurt most by the humiliation and unfairness marking the Nazi era.

Commentary

Hitler made a major effort to integrate Nazi ideology in the curriculum of the schools. Soon after Hitler acceded to power, teachers in primary and secondary schools and universities had to take an oath of loyalty to the new regime, and quotas were established for the number of Jewish students that could attend public schools. Jewish teachers were dismissed from the public schools; some found positions in the all-Jewish schools that Jewish organizations established to accommodate those students forced to leave the public schools.

According to Raul Hilberg, the effort to remove Jewish students from the public schools was part of the overall Nazi program to prevent the mixing of the races.

> The most important of those antimixing ordinances was the Law Against the Overcrowding of German Schools on April 25, 1933, which reduced the admission of non-Aryans to each school or college to the proportion of non-Aryans in the entire German population. The acceptance quota was accordingly fixed at 1.5 percent, while enrollment ceilings were devised with a view to the progressive reduction of the Jewish student body as a whole. By 1936 more than half of the Jewish children in the age group of six to fourteen years were being accommodated in schools operated by the Jewish community. There were, however, no Jewish technical colleges or universities, and the position of Jews enrolled in German institutions of higher learning was becoming more and more tenuous. As of November 1938, the remaining Jewish students in the German school system were expelled. From that date, Jews were permitted to attend only Jewish schools.[35]

Using

In the novel, Friedrich is forced to leave his public school in 1934. Walter K. remained in his school in Pieskretscham (a town of 18,000) until 1937-1938 before his family finally decided to try to emigrate. How can you explain why Jewish students would have left their public schools at different times? Why weren't measures against Jews carried out uniformly throughout Germany?

How do you account for the differences among non-Jewish teachers? Why was Friedrich's non-Jewish teacher so much kinder and more understanding than Walter's was? What words and actions did Friedrich's teacher take to make his Jewish pupil less anxious about the transfer to a Jewish school?

Front page of Der Stürmer, an antisemitic newspaper that appeared in Germany in 1934. The headline accuses the Jews of murdering non-Jews as part of their religious ritual. The botton line reads: "The Jews are our misfortune"—a quotation from the German historian Heinrich von Trietschke, which was adopted as an antisemitic slogan.

Compare the stories of Jews told by the Nazi leader at the Jungvolk meeting and the teacher in Friedrich's public school. How does the picture of Jews differ in the two? In what ways do the stories by both the teacher and the leader of the Jungvolk contribute to antisemitic views and stereotypes of Jews?

It should be noted that the teacher's lesson on the history of Jews, while intended to give students compassion for their Jewish classmates, had the potential for reconfirming stereotypes of Jews as outsiders in German society.

Using the illustration from the front page of *Der Stürmer* (the magazine edited by Julius Streicher, an ardent antisemite), discuss how the cartoon with the caption *Die Juden snd unser Unglük* (the Jews are our misfortune) depicts the antisemitic attitudes expressed in the Jungvolk meetings and public schools.

See the readings in the Resource Book entitled "Through the Nazi Streets Walks the Nazi Child," "Home is not the most important place," and "The Birthday Party" ("Preparing for Obedience"). Consider how the upbringing of non-Jewish children described in these readings contributed to the treatment Walter K. and Friedrich received from their peers inside and outside of school.

Fred Uhlman's novella *Reunion* provides additional insights into discriminatory practices in Nazi schools and their effect on Jewish students. The narrator, a Jewish boy named Hans, befriends a Christian boy of noble heritage, Konradin von Hohenfels. While their friendship flourishes in 1932, it deteriorates significantly after Hitler's rise to power. Hans becomes the victim of continuous assaults and insults from the Christian students in his *gymnasium*; his closest friend, Konradin, does nothing to come to his defense. When Hans decides to emigrate to America in 1934, Konradin does not publicly bid his old friend goodbye but writes a letter expressing his regret. Their friendship notwithstanding, the farewell letter makes it plain that Konradin has placed his primary allegiance with the Führer.

My dear Hans,

This is a difficult letter. First let me tell you how very sad I am that you are leaving for America. It can't be easy for you, who love Germany, to start a new life in America—a country with which you and I have nothing in common, and I can imagine how bitter and unhappy you must feel. On the other hand it's probably the wisest thing you can do. The Germany of tomorrow will be different from the Germany we knew. It will be a new Germany under the leadership of a man who is going to determine our fate and the fate of the whole world for hundreds of years to come. You will be shocked when I tell you that I believe in this man. Only he can save our beloved country from materialism and Bolshevism, only through him can Germany regain the moral ascendancy she has lost by her own folly. You won't agree, but I can't see any other hope for Germany. Our choice is between Stalin and Hitler and I prefer Hitler. His personality and sincerity impressed me more than I should ever have thought possible. I met him recently when I was in Munich with my mother. Outwardly he is an unimpressive little man, but as soon as one listens to him one is carried away by the sheer power of his conviction, his iron will, his demonic intensity and prophetic insight. When my mother left she was in tears and kept on repeating: 'God has sent him to us.' I'm sorrier than I can say that for a time—perhaps a year or two—there won't be a place for you in this New Germany. But I can't see any reason why you shouldn't come back later. Germany needs people like you and I am convinced that the Führer is perfectly able and willing to choose between the good and the undesirable Jewish elements.

For that which dwells near its origin is reluctant to leave the place.

I am glad your parents have decided to stay here. Of course nobody will molest them and they can live and die here in peace and security.

Perhaps one day our paths will cross again. I shall always remember you, dear Hans! You have a great influence on me. You have taught me to think, and to doubt, and through doubt to find our Lord and Savior Jesus Christ.

Yours, Konradin von H.[36]

Excerpt 3: Assimilation—The "It Can't Happen to Me" Syndrome

In this excerpt, Eva S. (T-29) tells us how assimilated her father, a Jew, felt in the German capital of Berlin, where the largest community of German Jews resided before the Third Reich. Quite emphatically, he told his daughter that what Hitler was saying about the Jews not belonging in Germany was wrong. He himself was a veteran of World War I; he had fought and risked his life for Germany, and Germany was his country. He insisted to his daughter and wife that he could not leave Germany. He was German. He belonged in Germany with his family and livelihood.

Eva's father was not alone in his views. There were slightly more than half a million Jews in Germany when Hitler came to power as chancellor in 1933, about half of whom emigrated in the years between 1933 and 1939. Those who decided to remain believed, as did Eva's father, that they were Germans and that the current demonstrations against Jews were temporary. After all, antisemitic demonstrations were hardly a new phenomenon in Germany. They had happened in earlier eras. Moreover, the Jews felt they had no real options. Their jobs and homes were in Germany. There were numerous difficulties involved in securing the necessary papers for emigration and adapting to a new culture. Added to these obstacles, there were very few countries willing to take in German Jewish immigrants in the 1930s. Emigration quotas and bureaucratic red tape served as potent deterrents to many German Jews who may have contemplated uprooting themselves and their families from German soil to start anew.

The fate of Eva's father illustrates just how problematic emigration was for German Jews. When the family finally secured the necessary papers to go to the United States, Eva's father could not adjust. He was unable to find work as fulfilling and remunerative as his business in Germany had been; he never learned to speak the language, nor to enjoy the culture of his new country.

In *Friedrich*, in the chapter entitled "Reasons," the narrator's father invites Herr Schneider to his apartment. It is 1936. He has just come back from a Nazi Party meeting and wants to warn his neighbor of the dangers for Jews who remain in Germany. Herr Schneider thanks his neighbor for his "frankness," but he argues that there are many reasons why he has to stay in Germany. "I am German, my wife is German, my son is German, all our relatives are German," he declares. Herr Schneider also points out that the persecution of Jews has eased during 1936 in anticipation of the Olympic Games. And he seems to feel that patience is preferable to panic. "'There has been prejudice against us for two thousand years,'" Schneider explains. "'No one must expect this prejudice to disappear in a half a century of living together peacefully.'" The narrator's father responds, "'You talk as if all you had to fear was a small group of Jew haters. But your oppressor is the government.'"[37]

Ironically, Herr Schneider feels reassured by this observation. He replies:

> "But surely that's our good fortune! Our freedom may be curtailed, and we may be treated unfairly but at least we don't have to fear that the people will murder us pitilessly. What you envisage cannot be, not in the twentieth century."[38]

Commentary

The reactions of Eva's father and Friedrich's father to the antisemitic measures of the Nazis were based largely on their status as German citizens. After all, weren't they entitled to the rights and privileges of all Germans?

Historians of the Third Reich frequently allude to the Jewish presence in Germany. Jews had been well assimilated into German life since the early nineteenth century. The Jews had made major contributions to German art, music, and literature and had won distinctions in the professions of law, medicine, and science. Moreover, Jews participated with honor in the German army of World War I. As Henry Friedlander has observed, Germany appeared to be the least antisemitic country in Europe in the early decades of the twentieth century. More blatant demonstrations of antisemitism had occurred in France, Austria, and Poland.

166

Nevertheless, antisemitic feelings did not disappear, especially among the right-wing political groups that blamed Jews for the defeat in World War I. Consequently, many German Jews in the interwar years tended to look upon their religion as a private matter. The following excerpt from the Exhibit Catalogue "Jews in Germany" further provides historical context.

Like their non-Jewish countrymen at the beginning of World War I, the majority of German Jews was swept along by enthusiastic patriotism. They hoped that the last barriers to complete emancipation could be overcome. Many Jewish volunteers heeded the call of Jewish organizations to give themselves completely in their services to the fatherland. These hopes, however, were not fulfilled. Anti-Semitic groups accused Jewish citizens of war-profiteering and of evading military service. In 1916 a Jewish census was taken by the Prussian Ministry of War to assess the extent of Jewish military participation. The results, however, were never published. According to data compiled in 1932 by the National League of Jewish War Veterans the share of Jewish soldiers, officers, medal winners, and casualties exactly matched that of non-Jews. Nevertheless, the legend of the Jewish draft dodger was never contradicted by the authorities.

After the November Revolution in 1918, anti-Semitism became even more acute. Demands for pogroms and the murder of Jews were openly voiced. Jews were accused of enriching their coffers through the misery of the German people, of causing the loss of the war and of having brought about the November Revolution. The racial right wing propagandists began to equate Communism and Bolshevism with international Jewry. During this time, anti-Semitic publications defamed the Jews and held them responsible for all political misfortune. Thus, by fanning anti-Jewish hysteria, a climate was created which the National Socialists could utilize to further their aims.

The basic rights statute in the Weimar Constitution opened all state offices de jure to Jewish citizens. Walter Rathenau, for instance, became the first Jewish Minister of Foreign Affairs. His position exemplifies the ambiguous situation of Jewish citizens in the Weimar Republic: high public offices were open to them, yet the threat of militant anti-Semitism continued to grow. Rathenau's murder by right-wing nationalists underscored the precariousness of Jews in the Republic.

Religion was of little concern to Jews who participated in public life as politicians, artists, journalists, merchants, or scientists. Yet, when they defended themselves against anti-Semitic accusations, they acted as Jews. Many Jewish organizations co-operated: educational meetings were arranged, pamphlets distributed and defensive organizations established to protect Jewish culture from encroachments upon their rights. German Jewry, in response to anti-Semitic accusations, always pointed out that they belonged much more to Germany and German culture than to Judaism.

The demand that Jews should abandon their identity as Jews in order to be accepted by German society had been nearly realized by the end of the Weimar Republic. Most Jewish citizens considered their religion as a private matter. Germany was their homeland, and they lived as Germans in Germany[39]

Even after the Nazis came to power in January 1933, many German Jews persisted in the belief that their status as German citizens would ultimately protect them from real harm. Accordingly, although Zionist organizations helped young people to emigrate to Palestine, many young Jews chose to remain in Germany. They did not feel the need to leave their homeland. Historian Nora Levin points out that the flight of adults was also limited:

> Adults, too, left Germany but the panic emigration in 1933, involving a total of 37,000 German Jews, had left a train of disappointments and failures which slowed down the process for the next few years. Moreover, other strong pulls among German Jews slackened the exodus. Many believed, particularly in the early years of the regime, that it would be possible to work for a renaissance of Jewish culture in Hitlerized Germany. They believed that they had time for a reconstruction, that reasonable discussions could still be had with government officials, as in the past. Like a sick man fighting death, unaware of the nature of his struggle, German Jews experienced a new strength before the end, magnificent bursts of spiritual renewal on the eve of extinction. At the same time, this retrieval of old buried Jewish springs delayed recognition of the doom facing them. For some, it meant stoically meeting the fate they only dimly comprehended.[40]

Using

Listings of the anti-Jewish legislation enacted in Nazi Germany between 1933 and 1943 appear in the commentary for the montage "Childhood Experiences of German Jews" and in the Resource Book. As you review these measures, in particular the sections of the Nuremberg Laws of 1935, how can you explain the continued optimism expressed by Friedrich's father and Eva's father? What indications did they have that the persecution of Jews would abate?

Martin Gilbert describes conditions for Jews in Germany of 1935, prior to the promulgation of the Nuremberg Laws that elevated random discrimination against Jews into a system.

> Inside Germany [in 1935], at least a quarter of the Jews who remained had been deprived of their professional livelihood by boycott, decree, or local pressure. More than ten thousand public health and social workers had been driven out of their posts, four thousand lawyers were without the right to practise, two thousand doctors had been expelled from hospitals and

clinics, two thousand actors, singers and musicians had been driven from their orchestras, clubs and cafes. A further twelve hundred editors and journalists had been dismissed, as had eight hundred university professors and lecturers, and eight hundred elementary and secondary school teachers.

The search for Jews, and for converted Jews, to be driven out of their jobs was continuous. On 5 September 1935 the SS newspaper published the names of eight half-Jews and converted Jews, all of the Evangelical-Lutheran faith, who had been "dismissed without notice" and deprived of any further opportunity "of acting as organists in Christian churches". From these dismissals, the newspaper commented, "It can be seen that the Reich Chamber of Music is taking steps to protect the church from pernicious influence."[41]

What evidence do you have that Eva's father and Herr Schneider had not encountered such economic hardships by the mid-1930s? Do you think that they would have been more eager to emigrate had they been unable to secure employment?

Does Eva's testimony and the following description of Herr Schneider confirm the conclusion of historian Karl A. Schleunes?

In many respects, though, the most basic impediment to emigration was the deep attachment most German Jews felt for their country. Germany was their fatherland. The Jewish emancipation in Germany had coincided with the developing nationalism of the nineteenth century. Jews had shared in Germany's growth and died in her defense in World War I. Their deepest political allegiance was to Germany. To leave would be to break irrevocably the bonds of that allegiance. In their own image they were German and all of Hitler's fulminations could not shake the foundations of that self-image. Hitler's attacks were vicious, but they were also patent nonsense. Given a choice between staying in Germany or accepting the insecurities of emigration, most of them preferred to stay in Germany. Germany at least was home.[42]

Excerpt 4: Kristallnacht (The Night of Broken Glass)

In this excerpt Joan B. (T-82) of Mainz, Germany, recalls *Kristallnacht*. She was twenty-nine years old and still living with her parents. Although Joan was not assaulted, her parents were beaten. As a result of the attack, her father contracted a liver ailment and suffered for nine months after *Kristallnacht* before he died. Her mother, unable to live without her husband, died six weeks later.

The chapter "Pogrom" in *Friedrich* contains the narrator's description of his own experiences during *Kristallnacht*. Amid the violence and destruction, he is also swept up in the actions against Jews. Joining the mob that ransacks the house of Jewish apprentices, the narrator becomes almost drunk with the excitement of smashing T-squares and blackboards. Only after he returns to his apartment and realizes that the crowd has invaded the Schneider apartment does the narrator fully realize the horror of the actions against the Jews. Peering inside the Schneider apartment and seeing how Frau Schneider has suffered, the narrator begins to weep.

Commentary

Bernt Engelmann, who was growing up in a liberal anti-Nazi family in Germany during the 1930s, spoke to his friend Peter about the reaction of his cousin Klaus-Gunter, a staunch supporter of the Nazi regime, to the pogrom. Klaus-Gunter's attitudes, as reported by Peter, offer insights into how Nazis and their sympathizers rationalized and sustained the actions taken in the November pogrom:

"When I described these incidents [of Kristallnacht], my cousin Klaus-Gunter said, 'What are you making such a fuss about! These things are trivial. You have to perceive the larger historical context and accept the idea of political necessity! When we annexed Austria and the Sudetenland, we picked up almost half a million more Jews—and they're nothing but parasites! One decisive stroke is preferable to a hundred-year struggle. Besides, these Jews have thick hides. Some of them still don't realize that this was an ultimatum . . .' Then he boasted of how magnificently the operation had been organized, and praised Hermann Göring for having the brilliant inspiration that the Jews themselves should pay for the property damage. 'Now they have to come up with a billion marks! We're going to keep the rich Jews in concentration camps until they cough up the money. Just think—a billion! That will come in handy. It'll pay for the West Wall! Now do you understand how valuable it was?'"[43]

According to Peter, whom Engelmann interviewed in the 1980s, Klaus-Gunter's views of *Kristallnacht* never changed, even after he had been imprisoned after the war for his involvement with the Nazi regime.

"[Y]ou're mistaken if you think he [Klaus-Gunter] might have seen the light or felt guilty. I ran into him in the early sixties—it just happened to be November 9, and I reminded him. He wasn't the slightest bit embarrassed. 'I didn't harm a hair on anyone's head,' he said, 'and none of us believed in that racial nonsense anyway. We were just little cogs in a huge machine—important cogs, true, but on the whole we did nothing different from any general staff officer. . . .' He told me that he's now a director of a large industrial enterprise, and remarked, 'People with technical expertise are always needed.' And I'm afraid he was right."

". . .Types like my cousin can cold-bloodedly murder tens of thousands—from their desks, issuing orders on official stationery in standard memorandum form; and they take great pride in their efficiency. But don't think for a moment Klaus-Gunter would have been capable of beating an old man unconscious and dragging him onto the streetcar tracks, or attacking women and children and driving them into the streets. I'm sure he would have found it extremely difficult even to smash up an apartment or plunder a synagogue. He knew how to issue orders, but he and his ilk left it to the rabble to carry them out. You'll always find people willing to lend themselves to any atrocity anywhere. And in those years the gangsters and murderers were given a free rein. On Kristallnacht the police had orders to protect the criminals and not worry about the victims. The patrolman who helped me carry the old man to the hospital was terrified that he might be punished. Thousands of SA, SS, and Vehicular Corps men—all pretense of law enforcement abandoned—became accomplices to the squads of attackers. Even Hitler Youths were delegated to plunder synagogues and desecrate Jewish cemeteries."[44]

For many Jews still living in Germany in 1938, *Kristallnacht*, on the night of November 9-10, 1938, served as a stern warning that the persecutions of Jews in the Nazi regime were not temporary and sporadic. Although the German press and the Minister of Propaganda, Goebbels, referred to the actions against Jews as "spontaneous demonstrations" in response to learning that a Jewish boy had killed a German diplomat in the Parisian embassy, documents indicate that the action had been carefully planned by the Nazi administration.

The Resource Book contains readings by Jewish and non-Jewish eyewitnesses of the destruction of Jewish property and persons during the riots.

For a narrative account of *Kristallnacht*, see Thallman and Feinermann, *Crystal Night*. Articles and a documentary discussion guide to the Nazis' "Night of Broken Glass," relating the events of the pogrom and their significance for present and future generations, are found in *Dimensions: A Journal of Holocaust Studies*, Vol. 4, No. 2.

Using

In 1936, two years before the November Pogrom, there had been an incident in which a Jew killed a German official, but this had not triggered widespread anti-Jewish demonstrations. However, a similar incident occurred in October 1938 when a Jewish student in Paris killed a German embassy official. The young man had just learned that his father had been deported back to Poland. It was this young man's action that provided a convenient pretext for *Kristallnacht*. What factors does Nora Levin point out that distinguished circumstances in 1938 from those of 1936?

The timing of the Crystal Night pogroms is significant. Pretexts for anti-Jewish actions were never in short supply in Nazi Germany. There had even been an earlier assassination of a Nazi by a Jew. In February 1936, David Frankfurter, a Jewish youth, had killed the Nazi Gauleiter in Switzerland, Wilhelm Gustloff, but there were no serious repercussions at the time. The destructiveness of November 1938 could be dared and carried off because now Hitler had nothing to fear—from Germans, from Jews, or from the world. His successes were dazzling enough to give triumphant assurance to any intuition or excess. In the spring of 1936 he had carried out the military occupation of the demilitarized Rhineland without opposition. . . . In 1937, the Rome-Berlin Axis was forged while both partners were expanding their military power. The world watched. In 1938, Germany absorbed Austria without hindrance and bullied the Western powers into sacrificing Czechoslovakia at Munich. The Evian Conference in July had failed dismally to provide refuge for the harassed Jews of Germany. Hitler could dare to go on to ever more radical pitches of destruction. There was nothing to stop him.[45]

Compare the account of *Kristallnacht* by the narrator of *Friedrich* with Joan's description. How do the Jewish and non-Jewish accounts differ? How does Joan's account compare with the accounts by Jewish eyewitnesses from Cologne and Kassel cited in the Resource Book?

Compare the account by the narrator in *Friedrich* with the description by a German Catholic in the Resource Book. What do both accounts tell about the role of fear in getting Germans to comply with the Nazi Party?

Some scholars of the Holocaust have suggested that *Kristallnacht* was the precursor to the Final Solution. Discuss what aspects of this event anticipate the brutality and scope of violence which appeared in later years during the Holocaust.

Excerpt 5: Jack G.—Neighbors During the Third Reich

In this excerpt Jack describes an incident that occurred in Poland during his childhood. In the fall of 1939, two hours after the Germans marched into his town, a female neighbor who had known his family for years walked into their apartment without knocking. According to Jack, this was not unusual. The woman was a close friend of his mother and customarily came in unannounced. On this particular occasion, however, the neighbor displayed no friendship. She told Jack's mother that in a few weeks everything Jack's family owned would be hers. "The party is over for you Jews," she boasted. Jack said that he never would be able to forget the shock on his mother's face when she asked the "friend" to leave her apartment at once.

Friedrich's friends and neighbors do not turn against the Schneiders in the same way. Although the narrator's father joins the Nazi Party, the narrator and his parents remain sympathetic and supportive of Friedrich's family. For instance, the narrator risks meeting Friedrich even after the Hitler Youth warns him against fraternizing with Jews. And when the Schneiders harbor a rabbi in their apartment, the narrator refrains from reporting them to the authorities even though he jeopardizes the safety of his own family. Toward the end of the story in 1942, Friedrich finds temporary asylum with the narrator's family.

Nevertheless, the narrator and his parents are unable to provide sufficient protection to save Friedrich. They cannot risk taking the Jewish boy to the air raid shelter when the apartment building is in imminent danger of air attack because the outspokenly antisemitic landlord, Herr Resch, is in charge. Consequently, Friedrich remains in the apartment and is fatally wounded when the air raid occurs.

In Friedrich's case, then, his non-Jewish neighbors try to assist and protect him as Nazi persecution of Jews intensifies. Nevertheless, Herr Resch, the landlord, behaves in much the same manner as the neighbor described in Jack's testimony. After Friedrich's father is taken away by the Gestapo, Herr Resch descends on the Schneider apartment and fills his wife's shopping bag with the Schneiders' personal belongings. Just as the woman in Jack's story took advantage of her neighbors during the Nazi era, so too does Herr Resch seek to capitalize on the suffering and misfortune of his Jewish tenants.

Commentary

Raul Hilberg describes the pattern of housing restrictions imposed on German Jews after 1938:

> The actual implementation of the housing restrictions was a very slow process. A great many Jewish families had to be evicted, but eviction was no solution so long as these Jewish families had no place to go. It was practicable only if the homeless family could be quartered in another Jewish household or if there was a vacancy in a house designated for Jewish occupancy. The first eviction regulation against Jews is to be found in the decree of July 25, 1938, which allowed German landlords to terminate leases for Jewish doctors' apartments. The year 1938 was a period of very loose court interpretation of tenancy regulations and leases. During that year many Jews emigrated, and consequently there were vacancies. In a decision dated September 16, 1938, a Berlin court went so far as to rule that the tenancy laws did not apply to Jews at all. Inasmuch as Jews were not members of the people's community (*Volksgemeinschaft*),

they could not be members of the housing community (*Hausgemeinschaft*). This decision anticipated matters a bit, but in effect it was put into a decree dated April 30, 1939, and signed by Hitler, Gurtner Krohn (Deputy of the Labor Minister), Hess, and Frick. The decree provided that Jews could be evicted by a German landlord if the landlord furnished a certificate showing that the tenant could live somewhere else. At the same time, the decree stipulated that homeless Jewish families had to be accepted as tenants by other Jews still in possession of their apartments.

Now the crowding of Jews in *Judenhauser* could begin. Selecting the houses and steering the Jews into them was the job of the local housing authorities (*Wohnungsämter*). In larger cities the *Wohnungsämter* had special divisions for the movement of Jews (*Judenumsiedlungsabteilungen*). By 1941 the movement had evidently progressed far enough to entrust the remaining apartment allocations to the Jewish community organization, which kept close watch on vacancies or space in the *Judenhauser*. The Jewish bureaucrats worked under the close supervision of the State Police (Gestapo).[46]

In considering the treatment that individuals like Herr Resch gave their Jewish neighbors, it is significant to note that at the Nuremberg Trials Julius Streicher, the editor of *Der Stürmer* and other antisemitic publications, was convicted of having contributed to the poisoning of minds with hatred.

It may be that this defendant is less directly involved in the physical commission of crimes against Jews. The submission of the prosecution is that his crime is no less the worse for that reason. No government in the world, before the Nazis came to power, could have embarked upon and put into effect a policy of mass extermination without having a people who would back them and support them. It was to the task of educating people, of producing murderers, educating and poisoning with hate, that Streicher set himself. In the early days he was preaching persecution. As persecution took place he preached extermination and annihilation; and, as we have seen in the ghettos of the East, as millions of Jews were being exterminated and annihilated, he cried out for more and more.

That is the crime that he has committed. It is the submission of the prosecution that he made these things possible—made these crimes possible—which could never have happened had it not been for him and for those like him. Without him, the Kaltenbrunners, the Himmlers, the General Stroops would have had nobody to carry out their orders. The effect of this man's crimes, of the poison that he has injected into the minds of millions and millions of young boys and girls and young men and women lives on. He leaves behind him a legacy of almost a whole people poisoned with hate, sadism, and murder, and perverted by him.[47]

Julius Streicher edited virulently antisemitic publications for both adults and children. Since 1925, Streicher had advocated extreme measures to eliminate the Jews from Germany. After the Nazis came to power in 1933, he openly vowed that he stood at the head of a struggle to expose Jews who had been "blood suckers" and "extortioners" in Germany for centuries. On the night of November 10, 1938, just after *Kristallnacht*, Streicher announced his antipathy for Jews:

> From the cradle the Jew is not taught, as we are, such texts as "Thou shalt love thy neighbor as thyself" or "Whosoever shall smite thee on the right cheek, turn to him the other also." No, he is told "With the non-Jew you can do whatever you like." He is even taught that the slaughtering of a non-Jew is an act pleasing to God. For 20 years we have been writing about this in *Der Stürmer*; for 20 years we have been preaching it throughout the world, and we have made millions recognize the truth.[48]

In *Der Stürmer* Streicher enunciated his antisemitic views on a regular basis. He purchased the magazine in 1935 when the circulation was about 28,000; the circulation grew to over 200,000 in the late 1930s and perhaps twice that figure in the war years. Vicious antisemitic stories and illustrations peppered every issue. For instance, Streicher frequently blamed the Jews for committing "ritual murders" of Christians:

> The Archbishop of Canterbury therefore sides with the money bags, with the lying world press, with the Jewish crooks and financial hyenas, with the Jewish-Bolshevist mass-murderers. It is a fine company which the Archbishop of Canterbury has joined. They're flayers of mankind, criminals, gangsters, murderers. In short, they are Jews. By choosing their side, the Archbishop of Canterbury committed a further, even more contemptible crime. He committed the crime of betraying Christianity. The crime of betraying non-Jewish mankind.[49]

Using

Examine the behavior of the landlord Herr Resch. How does he show his antisemitic views from the outset of the novel? At what point in the story does he begin to take more overt measures against his Jewish tenants? How does Nazi legislation in the late 1930s and the war years assist Herr Resch in his discriminatory policies against Jewish tenants?

Compare and contrast the behavior of neighbors in *Friedrich* and in Jack's video testimony (Excerpt 5). How do you explain that the neighbors in *Friedrich* were more willing to take risks for the Schneiders than the neighbor who insulted Jack's family?

Discuss how hate literature has the potential for poisoning people's minds and for encouraging people to persecute those who do not hold the same views and values. You may want to refer to the selection from Streicher's *Der Stürmer* quoted above. You may also want to refer to samples of hate literature that may have come to your home.

Streicher was one of the 12 sentenced to death at the International Military Tribunal at Nuremberg, 1946.

Excerpt 6: Differing Responses to Anti-Jewish Laws in the Nazi Era

In this excerpt Rachel G. (T-139) describes an incident that occurred more than nine months after the war had ended. Rachel and her mother returned to their old apartment to pick up some valises that contained family mementos and valuables. Three years earlier the landlady of this apartment had helped Rachel, the daughter of a Jewish couple, find a hiding place in a convent. Between 1942 and 1945 Rachel moved from place to place, always protected by Catholics who trained her as a Catholic child. Throughout these years she was completely unaware that her parents had been deported to Auschwitz. In the camp Rachel's father died, while her mother managed to survive. Mother and daughter were reunited nine months after the war had ended.

It was only on the day that Rachel and her mother went to their former apartment that Rachel learned how her parents had been captured by the Nazis. As soon as the landlady saw them at the door, she fell on the floor and kissed Rachel's mother's feet, saying, "I did that to you. I denounced you. Will God ever forgive me?"

When Rachel's mother asked her for the valises that had been left behind, the landlady responded, "Oh, I'm sorry. We gave it all to the nuns in the convent so that they would help your daughter." According to Rachel, this was false. "No one ever got anything for helping me," she exclaimed. "They never got anything. They did it out of the goodness of their heart."

The landlady showed pity for the plight of the little girl, Rachel, and expressed her regret at having betrayed Rachel's parents to the Gestapo. Nevertheless, the fact remains that she betrayed her former tenants and then took part in looting their belongings.

Commentary

Raul Hilberg explains how Holocaust survivors attempted to gain restitution for the losses and suffering of the Holocaust era. In addition to the type of disappointment Rachel and her mother experienced at the landlady's home, survivors had to deal with an immense bureaucracy, and the process of restitution often took years.

From the very start the Jews asked for three things: they insisted on the restitution of all Aryanized and confiscated Jewish property; they wanted indemnification for survivors who had suffered damage and injury; and they claimed reparations for the rehabilitation of the displaced. In all these demands the Jews confined themselves to the needs of victims who were still alive. For all those who had gone down with everything they had there was no further claim. Though European Jewry had for centuries been the fountainhead of all that mattered in Jewish life, the Jews of the world did not step forward now as its heirs in laws. One might say that the Jewish organizations were reversing the inherent proportionality between infliction and adjustment: their claim was like a salvage operation in which recovery is inversely proportional to the depth of the loss. In a sense, the perpetrators were asked to pay for the incompleteness of their job. Yet even this bill was not paid in full.

The Jews could expect their earliest success in the battle for restitution. However, this contest became at the very outset the struggle for two objectives: the return of property values to individual survivors and the recovery of assets that had no heirs. The first objective was much easier to achieve than the second. At that, the difficulties within the realm of individual restitution were already quite formidable. Some of these obstacles were the project of intrinsic factors; the others were the outcome of extraneous causes.

The inherent limitations in the individual procedure were three-fold. In the first place, the restoration of a property right was feasible only to the extent that the object was identifiable: that is, it had to be something that could be spotted in the hands of a wrongful possessor. Little could be done, for example, to effect the return of movables that had long been in non-Jewish homes. Second, the restitution laws did not lend themselves to the recreation of an asset that had disappeared, such as a liquidated business or a job that was no longer in existence. A third limitation was generally the repossession of something that had only been rented, such as an apartment. Clearly, these were natural limits. The very idea of the restitution process did not encompass the solution of such problems. However, the Jews were also confronted with the complications that were not rooted in the administrative characteristics of the operation but were the result of outside forces. These factors, which effectively blocked or impeded the return of tangible property, could be found primarily in Eastern Europe and in occupied Germany.[50]

Using

How would you distinguish the actions of the landlady in Rachel's story from those of Herr Resch, Friedrich's landlord?

Teachers who use the novel *Friedrich* and the accompanying montage find them helpful for introducing students to the series of antisemitic laws passed between 1933 and 1942. Asking students to read and describe the laws deepens their understanding of the chronology of the Third Reich. Virginia Ordway, a ninth grade social studies teacher in a dropout prevention program, asked students to write about the following questions before a class discussion of *Friedrich*:

Virginia Ordway, a ninth grade social studies teacher, uses Friedrich *in her Facing History unit. She finds this novel effective for engaging students' interest in the history of the interwar years.*

1. In 1933 what laws were created that were directed against Jews? What potential did these measures have for affecting Jews living in Germany?

2. Compare the 1933 laws with those of 1935.

3. Using the dates and events listed in the chronology at the back of *Friedrich*, discuss the time period in which it became very difficult for Jews to leave Germany. Review the chapter "Reasons." If the Schneiders had taken the advice of the narrator's father, would the Schneider family have been able to escape?

4. What were the provisions of the Nuremberg Laws passed in September and November 1935? In what ways was this legislation more threatening to the safety of Jews in Germany than preceding legislation?

5. When did the deportation of German Jews begin? Where were they sent?

6. Among the antisemitic measures passed in the 1930s, which ones seem most harsh for the Jewish minority? Why?

178

7. Review the chronology at the end of *Friedrich*. Describe the process of antisemitic legislation under the early Nazi administration, 1933-1939.

8. If you were a non-Jew living in Germany in the 1930s, at what point would you have spoken out against Hitler's laws? What options were available for objecting to legislation?

Ordway finds that using the chronology that accompanies *Friedrich* helps her students trace the evolution of events in the early Hitler era. She is able to refer to incidents in the novel as a frame of reference for discussing the escalation of antisemitic legislation and the deepening separation between Jews and non-Jews in German society. Moreover, Ordway has found that the novel helps her students imagine themselves living in Hitler's Germany: they can identify with certain characters and speculate on how they would have acted in similar circumstances. Many educational theorists believe the ability to think hypothetically and speculate about historical incidents enables students to broaden their perspectives and to consider the various factors that affected the decision making of individuals in the past. Adolescents are preoccupied with questions of identity, and as they consider how other people think and act they also make connections to their own lives, wondering what they would have done in similar situations and asking what they should do when confronted with moral choices. This process, in turn, helps students recognize that individuals in the Hitler era did not have simple clear-cut choices: political, social and economic factors impinged on their decision making.

In her final assignment for *Friedrich*, Ms. Ordway encourages her students to exercise their skills in speculating about the past and recognizing the complicated situations that confronted individuals living in the Hitler era. Students are asked to write five pages in their journals on one of the following three choices:

1. You are an investigative reporter. Conduct an interview with one of the following people: Herr Resch, Herr Schneider, the narrator's father. The time of your report is after the war. Ask the interviewees about the following: (a) looking back on the 1930s, would you act differently now knowing what happened during the war?; (b) what are your opinions of the behavior of Friedrich, Mrs. Schneider, the narrator, and the narrator's mother?; (c) how do you explain the increasing hatred and violence against Jews that resulted in the Final Solution?

2. Write a series of letters from Friedrich to an American cousin who is Friedrich's pen pal. The letters must be written between 1933 and 1942. Select at least five crucial events to describe. Capture the changes in the

situation in Germany, and the changes in Friedrich himself as he grows. Describe Friedrich's hopes and fears, his happy times and his sorrows. What are his dreams as a teenager? His hopes for the future? Use your imagination to develop his character as fully as possible.

3. In the novel *Friedrich*, the narrator does not tell us his feelings. Pretend that he is keeping a diary in which he is writing his feelings and reactions to the events in the book. You are the narrator. Write diary entries describing events and feelings. Explore the character of the narrator. What are his hopes and fears, his dreams? Entries should span the era between 1933 and 1942. You may go beyond 1942 if you want to, using your imagination and knowledge of the history to make up events in his life. There must be entries describing "The Jungvolk," "The Encounter," "The Pogrom," and "In the Shelter."

Imagining the Unimaginable

"Imagining the Unimaginable" begins with a German Jew recalling the incomprehensibility of the Final Solution, reiterating many sentiments described in the montage "Childhood Experiences of German Jews, 1933-1939." Subsequent excerpts illustrate how Jews in nations that were occupied during the war were incredulous of a systematic plan for extermination. In contrast to the situation for German Jewry, however, the imposition of Nazi antisemitic legislation was so rapid in occupied countries that Jews in these areas had very little time to realize the extent of the discrimination and react to it.

Bad news is never welcome. In ancient literature, messengers who brought ill tidings were often punished. Witnesses in some of these testimonies preferred to call the modern equivalents of such messengers madmen. Others refused to believe that members of German society, with its long cultural tradition, could be capable of atrocities like those reported. The Germans themselves took advantage of this skepticism by developing a special vocabulary designed to conceal the truth. They spoke of "resettlement to the east" when they meant "deportation to the camps." In the creation of euphemistic terms such as "showers" and "delousing operations," they capitalized on their victims' desire to accept anything except reality.

These excerpts reveal how geography, chronology, and sources of information all conspired to undermine the sense of urgency for those potential victims in locales far away from the killing centers. However, as the excerpts illustrate, an underlying reason for the failure of those further west to foresee the danger was the passive nature of what we might call the imagination of disaster. Even

180

with the evidence before our eyes, we hesitate to accept the worst. When the evidence is founded on unconfirmed rumor, we hesitate even more. For—as we see in this montage—psychological, economic, historical and cultural information prevented people from imagining the worst. One woman insists that even when an escapee from the camps warned her father, he refused to accept the truth: "It was too terrible to believe," she says. Later, she adds, "I was very naive." This simple remark offers eloquent testimony about the mindset of those who still lived according to the beliefs of a so-called enlightened civilization.

The six excerpts comprising the video montage are taken from testimonies of Jews living in different parts of Europe during the Third Reich. Despite the diversity in backgrounds and social circumstances of the interviewees, the theme that runs through all the excerpts is that the "Final Solution" was something that could not be imagined.

The descriptions include information on the contents of each excerpt as well as a brief note on the subsequent experiences of the interviewee.

Excerpt 1: Eva S. (T-29)

Eva, the daughter of assimilated Jewish parents, recalls her childhood in Berlin during the Nazi era. Her father repeatedly reminded her of his military service to Germany in World War I. He could not take the Nazi threat against Jews seriously because of his veteran status. Even when Eva's mother pressed for the family to flee Germany, her father held out to stay where he made a good living.

In the late thirties Eva and her brother left Germany for England, where they married and began raising their families. Their parents emigrated first to Portugal and later to the United States. Eva's father, who had been so reluctant to leave his native land, was unable to build a new life in the United States and it fell upon Eva's mother to earn a living and manage the household.

Excerpt 2: Menachem S. (T-152)

In this excerpt, Menachem speaks about his early childhood in Cracow shortly after the Nazi occupation. His grandfather had the wealth needed for the family to emigrate, but he would not consider such an action since the family had lived in Cracow for generations.

Following the family's decision to stay, they were rounded up and sent to the ghetto. When the ghetto was destroyed, Menachem and his parents were relocated to the nearby labor camp of Plaszow. In order to save their son, Menachem's parents arranged for him, then only five years old, to escape from the camp, and for the duration of the war Menachem survived on his own.

Excerpt 3: Eva L. (T-71)

Eva L., who was born in Lodz, entered the ghetto with her parents in 1943. Her father died in the ghetto; she and her mother were deported to Auschwitz in 1944. Before they arrived at the concentration camp, they had never heard of it. Nobody knew, she maintains, about the extermination process. Moreover, they did not want to believe it.

Excerpt 4: Shari B. (T-66)

Shari, who was born in Czechoslovakia in 1927, was twelve when the war broke out. Early in the war years a Polish refugee visited her father and spoke of the gas chambers and the extermination program against Jews. Shari and her father thought the visitor must be exaggerating his story. Shari refused to believe what she was hearing because she could not imagine such a thing.

In 1944, when the Nazis began the roundup of Hungarian Jewry, Shari posed as a non-Jew to avoid deportation. Nevertheless, she was detected and deported to Thereisenstadt, where she remained until her liberation by Soviet forces in the spring of 1945.

Excerpt 5: Daniel F. (T-153)

Daniel, who was a teenager in 1944 when Nazis occupied his Hungarian homeland, recalls how he had not had the slightest idea that there was a Final Solution. His father saw himself as a patriot who had served in World War I and did not believe that Hungarians would do anything to harm him. Even when there were rumors of mass killings of Jews, Daniel remembers that he refused to deal with it. "I really didn't want to believe it. I don't think I wanted to deal with that. I just assumed it was rumor."

Daniel only began to comprehend the magnitude of the threat when he and others in his family were gathered in the ghetto. He saw an armed Hungarian soldier shove his grandmother in a truck. Then, he explains, he was alerted to the fact that "things were bad."

Excerpt 6: Selma E. (T-42)

In this excerpt Selma, a Dutch Jew who was deported to Sobibor in 1943, explains how she and other prisoners refused to believe that exterminations were taking place even when they could see the fire and smell burning flesh in the camp. She remembers how she and others went to work; she even danced with a man who was later to become her husband.

During the Sobibor Uprising in April 1943 Selma managed to escape with her future husband. They remained in hiding until July 1944 when they were liberated by Soviet forces.

Commentary

Until October 1941, Nazis encouraged Jewish emigration. Why, then, did Germany's Jews not simply leave? It is important to understand that the Nuremberg Law of 1935 imposed many restrictions on Jewish professional and financial life. Oppressive as this legislation might have been, however, it was still not life-threatening. *Kristallnacht* in November 1938 represented a more vivid and obvious threat: Jewish synagogues all over Germany and Austria were destroyed while thousands of Jews, males over 16 years of age, were arrested and sent to concentration camps. After that date Jewish attempts to emigrate increased significantly. But Jews needed money and visas to get out of Germany; by that time, these were not readily available.

At the outbreak of the war in September 1939, Germany and the Soviet Union divided Poland: the Soviets occupied the eastern part of Poland while the Germans made the Silesian region part of the Greater German Reich and created the administrative district of the General Government for much of central Poland. Many Polish Jews fled from German-occupied areas to zones under Russian control and most of these emigrants managed to survive the war. However, there were those who could not bear to remain in areas controlled by the Russians. They had left family members behind in the German zones and wanted to reunite with their loved ones.

At first these returnees had no way of knowing that they were endangering their lives. The Warsaw Ghetto was not established until the end of 1940 and other ghettos in the General Government did not emerge until 1941. Just as German Jews living in Germany in 1935-1936 could not have anticipated *Kristallnacht*, Polish Jews, based on their experiences in 1939 and early 1940, could not have anticipated the killing centers.

To understand better why Jews behaved as they did, consider what our reactions would be to the possibility of nuclear war, based on our experiences in the 1970s and 1980s (or even our memories of Hiroshima and Nagasaki). Should such a war occur, survivors of the catastrophe might look back on our generation and ask the same question we ask about Holocaust victims: "Why didn't they believe?"

Despite the blatant antisemitism of the Third Reich, the Germans did not publicize their intentions to exterminate European Jewry. No "official" policy was ever announced, and in fact no documents signed by Hitler authorizing the program exist. When the first large-scale killings of Jews began in the Soviet Union after the invasion in June 1941, it was too late for most of Soviet Jewry because the retreating Soviet army had left them defenseless. Moreover, most of these Russian Jews had nowhere to flee. Cut off from the west, Soviet citizens were ill-informed about Nazi policy against Jews in Germany and other occupied countries between 1933 and 1941.

We have few video testimonies from survivors of the Nazi mobile killing units in the Soviet Union. Without their memories to guide us, it is important to try to imagine the surprise, confusion, and terror that must have overwhelmed the victims when they found themselves staring, without warning, into huge mass graves. Throughout the summer and autumn of 1941, mass shootings of Jews and Soviet communist officials went on. It was impossible to conceal these large-scale killings, many of which were carried out on the outskirts of cities and towns; thus, more than a million Jews were able to flee with or be evacuated by the retreating Soviet army before the Germans arrived. The threat to life here was not based on rumor, but on widely reported eyewitness accounts. Still, even this knowledge did not help the million or more Russian Jews who had no time to escape.

One of the most melancholy stories is the fate of Hungarian Jewry. Until the spring of 1944, Hungary was an ally of Germany and hence not an occupied country. As the Russians drew closer to the Hungarian border and it became clear that the Nazi cause was lost, Hungary became less cooperative, and the Germans moved into the country. Thus the roundup of Hungarian Jewry did not begin until after most of European Jewry had been murdered. However, witnesses insist that they knew virtually nothing about the fate of their fellow Jews. The newspapers did not report it; most Hungarians did not have radios, and accounts that did leak through were received with skepticism.

By 1944, the war had been going on for nearly five years, and Hungarian Jews were lulled into a sense of false security, believing that they were safe. Just as they were unable to grasp what was really happening, the rest of the world also remained unconvinced of the coming doom. In April 1944, two Jews escaped from Auschwitz, hoping to warn the world that the gas chambers were being prepared for the extermination of Hungarian Jewry. Their report, transmitted to the Vatican and to leaders in England and America, did little to slow down the process of extermination. Throughout the spring and summer of 1944, 300,000 Hungarian Jews were killed.

Using

Yehuda Bauer makes the distinction between knowing about the atrocities and internalizing that knowledge so people would recognize that the extermination of Jews and other minorities was not only taking place but in fact threatening people in all societies. From the testimonies in "Imagining the Unimaginable," do you find Bauer's distinction applicable? How do you think this process of moving from "knowledge" to "internalizing knowledge" takes place?

Discuss a contemporary issue that you learned about from the news. Have you ever moved from the stage of "knowing" about an atrocity to "internalizing knowledge" of it? What factors sharpened your awareness and empathy for victims of the atrocity?

One of the first questions students in Holocaust courses ask is: "Why didn't they [the victims] do more to help themselves?" The first answer is that when they could, they did; the second is that often it was not possible, or it was too late. But a third answer is that before we are able to protect ourselves, we need to recognize a threat. From our vantage point, as we examine this history fifty years after the fact, the escalation of events seems clear. Between 1933 and 1943, however, many Jews and other victims of the Third Reich were unable to confront the possibility that Nazi policy mandated their extermination.

The excerpts in "Imagining the Unimaginable" illustrate this premise. We learn that factors such as chronology and geography are crucial. One witness, for example, speaks of expectations: early in the 1930s in Germany, Jews had no reason to believe that discrimination against them would lead to gas chambers.

It is natural and normal to wonder at the disbelief of potential victims: after all, we have the advantage of retrospective vision. However, the subjects of these video testimonies did not have that advantage. We need to exercise historical imagination, slipping back in time to view the experiences through the feelings and attitudes created by what was happening then. Furthermore, even now that we know what happened, many of us still have great difficulty believing it because the information presented to us violates everything we have ever learned about community, civilization, and moral behavior. If we have trouble accepting the truth of extermination today, with the evidence before us, how much more impossible it must have been then for the potential victim, whose sense of possibility was not confirmed by hindsight.

Professor Lawrence Langer sensitizes students to these issues and encourages them to listen to each of the excerpts in the montage, discerning similarities and differences among the survivor testimonies and trying to explain the differences. For example, the speaker in the first episode left Germany shortly before the war and escaped to England. The last two witnesses endured the ordeal of death camps at Auschwitz and Sobibor. The time factor, Langer reminds students, is critical here. Evidence of the danger of extermination accumulated as the months passed. The spectacle of relatives forced to emigrate appeared less threatening than the deportation of friends or family who were never heard from again. Langer also points out the importance of recognizing the source of the information: rumors are more easily ignored than eyewitness warnings, but as seen in the montage it was also possible for Jews to disbelieve or belittle eyewitness accounts.

Langer believes it is worthwhile for students to watch each excerpt separately and discuss it. For example, they should watch the first excerpt of Eva S. and discuss why it was so difficult for her and her family to decide to emigrate. Such a discussion gets into the subject of the assimilation of German Jewry: unlike Jews in other European states, German Jews were so attached to their German identity that they minimized the importance of their Jewishness in Nazi ideology.

The issue in viewing all of the excerpts in the montage is not to discover the "correct" reasons for not recognizing the danger, but the "reasons," good or bad. Were there signals that one might have recognized? Were there "sound" arguments for not having recognized them? Students might discuss the role of fear in blocking out or denying possible threats, as well as the role of clinging to the familiar (one's home, one's belongings, one's neighborhood, etc.) as long as possible. Eva S. (Excerpt 1) mentions several of these. As it turns out, her family is the only one represented in the montage that took deliberate steps to emigrate in time. However, her father's reluctance to leave was ironically "justified," since (as he predicted) he was unable to adapt to a new environment and in America never regained his old assurance. In other words, when you know what you may lose in the present and are uncertain about the price the future may exact from you, you may choose to trust the present despite the ominous clouds looming on the horizon.

A full discussion of the excerpt of Eva S. can establish a procedure for examining the others. Menachem's testimony introduces important issues that Eva S. scarcely mentions. What makes us so prone to disbelieve the unfamiliar, the untraditional? What possible truths make us feel uncomfortable? Why did the family defer to the grandfather's will while ignoring rumors of danger and accepting belief in their own security? Today, many refer to the chiefs of the death camps as "madmen"; Menachem says that townspeople used that same term for his father when in 1940 and 1941 he tried to alert them to what lay ahead. This raises the interesting question of whether naming a phenomenon defines it or obscures it.

All of the excerpts in the montage show how language can be used to clarify or evade an issue. Langer asks his students how this principle applies to these excerpts, and to the study of the Holocaust in general.

When the Germans told the Jews that they were being "resettled" in "labor" camps, the words themselves were reassuring. Such use of language helps to explain how Eva L. could insist that there were no rumors, not the slightest suspicions of any peril (Excerpt 3). Otherwise, she argues, people would have committed suicide. She says that people just did not want to believe that such horrors exist. It would be useful to ask students to describe the unwillingness Eva L. mentions. They should be able to explore the verbal possibilities: fear? ignorance? tradition? Then students should consider the ideas and feelings behind these words, and compare them with the realities they seek to avoid.

Eva L. (Excerpt 3), who came from Lodz, Poland (near the death camps), maintains that she had no specific evidence of their existence. Shari B., who lived in an area of Czechoslovakia that had been ceded to Hungary by Hitler (and who therefore was safe from deportation until the spring of 1944, when the Germans marched into Hungary), says that her father brought home a Polish Jew who told them about the ghettos and the camps. If students have been watching carefully, they will note that her language is more precise than that of her predecessors: "I couldn't imagine that people could act this way." By adding that she was very naive, she simply defines the usual human situation: we are trained to believe that unimaginable horror is the province of entertainment, not real life. Was it otherwise in western Europe before and during World War II? At this point, Langer recommends asking students to sum up the reasons why the first four witnesses and their families were so reluctant to believe in the possibility of the "worst."

The fifth excerpt is of Daniel F., who contends that the notion of the gas chambers was so "remote," so "unthinkable," and so "unbelievable" that it was not considered factual. He refers to place (remote), mind (unthinkable), and faith in truth (unbelievable), thus creating for students a framework for analyzing victims' responses to the impending catastrophe.

In discussing the Daniel excerpt, Langer introduces the concept of the imagination, a faculty that traditionally enables us to gain access to areas of reality we may not have experienced directly. It is clear from the testimonies in the montage that potential victims were given no opportunity to experience directly the carefully orchestrated program of extermination that lay before them until it was too late to do anything to save themselves. Daniel admits that when he saw an SS man shoving his frail grandmother, who was boarding the boxcars about to take them to Auschwitz, something "awakened in me that things were very bad." Why should this particular episode alert him to the gravity of his situation? His confession that until then, "I really didn't want to believe it. . . . I don't think I wanted to deal with that," frankly acknowledges the difficulty, not to say the impossibility, of imagining at least two prospects: not only the gas chambers, but also seeing one's grandmother mistreated and being unable to do anything to help her.

Some students ask why Jews were not alerted to the dangers of extermination before the war, since there had been incidents of Jews being maltreated and murdered years before deportations began. In response to these inquiries, Langer asks students to prophesy future disasters—such as nuclear war—based on present evidence. He has found that students quickly perceive how meager is the evidence of future disasters and how the imagination often is prone to turn away from thinking about the worst. "How many students," Langer asks, "could imagine graphically what we know about 'nuclear winter'? How many would prefer to imagine something else—anything but that?"

The final excerpt touches directly on the heart of the unimaginable—the Sobibor death camp. Selma says that even when she arrived at Sobibor, she still did not "know." What does she mean by that? How does one internalize experience so that it becomes more than information, more than mere facts? Standing before the fires of the crematorium and hearing what they meant, Selma recalls, "I think it took a few days before I really believed it."

The closing image of this montage is a visual reproduction of what the six witnesses have called the "worst." Who "believes" it today? We look at the bones and ashes of a human being inside a crematorium and recall the decision of Eva S.'s father in the first excerpt to "wait and see," to measure against emigration the value of "what you had to lose," and we understand that the psychological process of the potential victim in the beginning was totally out of touch with the chaos of this end.

The purpose of this montage is not to award commendation or blame to alert heroes or passive victims, but to shed some light through the observations of survivors themselves on the dilemma of anticipating the gas chamber and crematorium as one's final destiny—and of taking action against it.

Flight from Destiny, Part 1 (A-30)

This half-hour videotape, taken from a longer videotape prepared by the Holocaust Survivors Film Project (the organization which preceded the Video Archive for Holocaust Testimonies at Yale University) and by Laurel Vlock (the co-founder of the original project), is a documentary of the voyage of the SS *St. Louis* in May-June 1939. The ocean liner left Hamburg, Germany, for Cuba on May 13 with 937 passengers, 930 of whom were German-Jewish refugees. Among these Jewish passengers, 734 had fulfilled the immigration requirements and quota numbers that would permit them to enter the United States. The Hamburg-American Line sold each of the passengers $150 landing certificates signed by Manuel Benitez, the Cuban director general of immigration. While most of the passengers felt confident that the passes were sufficient for their landing, twenty-two of them were skeptical about the validity of the passes and paid an additional legal fee of $500 to obtain landing certificates authorized by the Cuban government.

When the ship landed in Cuba on May 27, the Cuban government refused to allow the passengers with the landing passes signed by Benitez to disembark, even after officials from the Joint Distribution Committee offered to pay for each passenger (guaranteeing that the refugees would not impose a burden on the Cuban welfare system). The only passengers who were allowed to land were those who had paid for the authorized Cuban passes and six non-Jewish passengers—a Cuban couple and four visiting Spaniards.

After several days of fruitless negotiations between members of the Joint Distribution Committee and Cuban President Federico Laredo Bru, the *St. Louis* proceeded to American shores. Here, too, officials refused to allow passengers to disembark.

American newspapers, which daily reported on the ship, expressed sympathy for the refugees but emphasized that the United States must retain stringent control of immigration policies to prevent a drain on the American economy.

> Editors repeatedly stressed that there was a limit "beyond which no nation may go." Fears that the St. Louis represented a Pandora's box were again expressed: One such "influx" is sure to be "followed by other ship loads." Letting this one dock would set a most "dangerous precedent." Another argument was that trying to aid Jews would be an incentive to the Germans to subject them to even worse treatment. In this case it might prompt Germany to "dump its Jewish population upon other nations without regard for any international law or regulation."[51]

And so the ocean liner headed back to Europe, and four western European countries—France, England, Holland, and Belgium—agreed to take the passengers so they would not be forced to return to Germany. However, after the outbreak of the war and the spread of Nazism throughout Europe, many of the refugees of the *St. Louis* were swept up and deported to the extermination camps. It is estimated that at least eighty percent of the passengers did not survive the war years.

Excerpt on Historical Background, Peter G. (T-51)

The videotape opens with historian Peter Gay, himself a refugee from Germany in 1939, describing the circumstances of German Jews between 1933 and 1939. As he explains, the situation for German Jews, at least those he knew in Berlin, did not become intolerable until *Kristallnacht* in November 1938. Prior to that incident, many non-Jewish industrialists told Hitler that they did not endorse Nazi antisemitic legislation. Further, many German Jews, according to Gay, felt they had time to plan their departure.

Kristallnacht made it clear that there was no more time. The rush of 350,000 to 400,000 desperate people, all trying to leave at the same time, created a major problem for those countries that would accept German Jews. America had a quota system; France and England agreed to take the refugees but wanted to be careful not to antagonize their native populations by creating too much competition for jobs.

Excerpts of St. Louis Passengers and Eyewitnesses

Following Gay's background information, several men and women who were passengers on the *St. Louis* voyage—Herbert and Walter Karliner, Marianne Vargish, Fred Hilb, Fred Buff, and Hans Fisher—describe why they and their

The SS St. Louis carried 937 Jewish refugees to Cuba, where they were denied entry although they had visas. The ship sailed along the U.S. coast for two weeks but was again denied permission to dock, forcing it to return to Europe.

families sought to leave. Herbert Karliner, for example, recalls how his father had been brutally mistreated during *Kristallnacht*. Vargish explains that her parents had left in 1937 to set up residence in Cuba so they could apply for the immigration quota to the United States from Cuba rather than deal with the quota from Germany.

These same passengers describe the exhilaration many felt as they set sail for Havana, and the tremendous disappointment when they learned that the Cuban officials refused to honor their landing passes. According to the Karliner brothers, several passengers contemplated—and even attempted—suicide.

Heightening the tension of the days in Havana harbor were the daily visits of Milton Goldsmith, a representative of the Joint Distribution Committee, who kept the passengers abreast of the complications that prevented their disembarkation. Laura Margolis, a social worker with the Committee, tried to solicit assistance for the refugees but was rebuffed by three levels of Cuban bureaucracy.

The sadness and tension continued to mount when the ocean liner failed to find a landing place on American shores and was forced to head back to Europe. Although England, France, Holland, and Belgium eventually agreed to offer asylum to passengers, the behavior of the United States—a land so many of them had hoped to make their own—was a devastating disappointment.

A representative of the Joint Distribution Committee pinpoints the significance of the *St. Louis* incident:

> [The St. Louis] was the first alarming sign that no one wants us [Jews]. That made the St. Louis a chapter of shame for America, for Roosevelt, for Jewish organizations. It was surely a signal of the world to take notice.

Commentary

Ten months before the SS *St. Louis* set sail, an international conference took place at Evian, France to consider where Jews from Germany could be relocated. Of the sixty nations represented, only one—the Dominican Republic—agreed to take in additional Jewish refugees. Even though the delegates at the conference had been told that Jews were being persecuted in Germany and Austria, most were not sympathetic. The Australian delegate, for example, said there were no racial problems in his country and Australians were not interested in importing such problems. And later in the summer, as the numbers of Jews seeking to leave Germany and Austria grew, Britain,

Palestine, and the United States each tightened their rules for admission. Four South American countries—Argentina, Chile, Uruguay, and Mexico—adopted laws severely restricting the number of Jews who could enter. In the case of Mexico the number was limited to one hundred per year. And during the war years, even while the "Final Solution" was being implemented, there was no improvement. In Hungary, for instance, where the policy to exterminate native Jews did not go into effect until the spring of 1944, Jews and non-Jews alike generally did not believe stories of exterminations of Jews in Poland and Russia.

Kristallnacht marked a turning point in the history of German Jews: the vandalism and destruction of November 9-10, 1938, convinced those German Jews who previously had wanted to stay in their homeland that Germany was no longer a safe place for Jews. Thus there was an enormous increase in numbers of Jews from Germany and Austria seeking to leave the Reich after November 1938, and the existing bureaucracy was unprepared to handle the upsurge of requests for visas. Michael R. Marrus describes the impact of *Kristallnacht* on trends in emigration:

> Kristallnacht sent a tremor through refugee organizations, which mobilized for what now seemed to them an emergency emigration. Everywhere under Nazi rule the story was the same. In Austria and the incorporated Sudetenland, the German masters pressed the Jews to emigrate. Kristallnacht had its equivalent in Danzig, the supposedly Free City under the League of Nations where the local Nazi administration introduced the Nuremberg Laws on 23 November 1938. Here, too, there was a crisis—in this case affecting about 15,000 Jews and other "non-Aryans" under direct Nazi threat. Jewish officials throughout Europe began in desperation to cut corners, often under direct pressure of the Gestapo. They sent refugees abroad with incomplete documentation, obtained other papers through dubious channels, and connived to dispatch emigrants illegally into Palestine. Chartered vessels left German ports with uncertain destinations; sometimes these went from port to port in Central and South America trying to find a chink in the bureaucratic wall that prevented the passengers from landing. One famous ship, the *St. Louis*, left Hamburg with 930 passengers in May 1939, heading for Cuba. At Havana, Cuban authorities questioned the validity of the entry documents and refused admission. Eventually, after appeals everywhere fell on deaf ears, the ship finally returned to Europe, and its passengers were dispersed in several countries, most to be swallowed up by Hitler. All previous concerns for orderly emigration and the export of capital now appeared unrealistic: in the desperate rush after November 1938 the overwhelming priority was escape—one way or another.[52]

Henry Feingold and David Wyman point out that American Jews in the late 1930s and war years were themselves divided as to the most effective response to the refugee question. Feingold comments:

> Probably no amount of pressure on the part of Jewish leaders could have succeeded in changing the immigration law or the Administration's Middle East policy; these were fixed. The disunity made a great deal of difference, however, in the area of visa administration and the compilation of special visa lists. Here snarls and blocks and miles of red tape were used by the second-echelon officials of the State Department to keep those refugees who had successfully run the gauntlet imposed by the consuls away from these shores. Leading this group was Breckinridge Long. Appointed Assistant Secretary of State for Special Problems in January 1940, he committed himself to halting completely the flow of refugees. It did not take him long to discover the disunity within American Jewry. Before he surrendered his strategic position in January 1944 he confided in his diary that "the Jewish organizations are all divided amid controversies . . . there is no cohesion nor any sympathetic collaboration—rather rivalry, jealousy and antagonism. . . ." It was a startlingly accurate observation and although at other times Long was inclined to attribute immense power to American Jewry and bewail the absence of a countervailing Arab community in the United States, he was aware that disunity among the Jews was a blessing for his cause.[53]

A resident of Richmond, Virginia wrote the following letter to the *Richmond Times-Dispatch* when he read of how the U.S. Coast Guard established patrols to prevent passengers from the *St. Louis* from coming ashore:

> [T]he press reported that the ship came close enough to Miami for the refugees to see the lights of the city. The press also reported that the U.S. Coast Guard, under instructions from Washington, followed the ship . . . to prevent any people landing on our shores. And during the days when this horrible tragedy was being enacted right at our doors, our government in Washington made no effort to relieve the desperate situation of these people, but on the contrary gave orders that they be kept out of the country. Why did not the President, Secretary of State, Secretary of the Treasury, Secretary of Labor, and other officials confer together and arrange for the landing of these refugees who had been caught in the maelstrom of distress and agony through no fault of their own? . . . The failure to take any steps whatever to assist these distressed, persecuted Jews in their hour of extremity was one of the most disgraceful things which has happened in American history and leaves a stain and brand of shame upon the record of our nation.[54]

Using

Discuss other incidents or events in the immediate prewar years that suggest the United States response to the *St. Louis* refugees was consistent with its general immigration policy of the period. For example, compare the United States response to the Evian Conference to the Wagner-Rogers Bill.[55]

How does the *St. Louis* incident illustrate the significance of having accurate and verified documentation in the 1930s? Are there any contemporary events that suggest a similar emphasis on documentation for refugees seeking asylum in the United States?

Leonard Dinnerstein emphasizes that antisemitism was largely responsible for government policies in the late 1930s.

> In the late 1930s, when the refugee problem became more acute, the President, though aware of antisemitism among State Department career officials, made no attempt to appoint more sympathetic administrators to American consulates where foreigners had to obtain visas to enter the United States. Even Secretary of State Cordell Hull, although married to a woman of Jewish birth, did not interfere in immigration matters.[56]

For additional discussion of the American response to German and Austrian refugees, see the presentation of Henry Feingold in **Resources**, and the testimony of American businessman Walter Bieringer in **Portraits**.

For another account by a passenger of the SS *St. Louis* who ended up in France, see "Judy's Story" in *I Too Had Dreams of a Bright Future*, edited by Yaffa Eliach. A copy is available at the Facing History Resource Center.

Peter Gay and his parents originally had planned to sail on the S.S. *St. Louis* in mid-May 1939. However, Gay's father, who became increasingly worried about the safety of Jews in Germany after *Kristallnacht*, arranged for the family to leave a month ahead of the scheduled departure of the *St. Louis*. See Peter Gay's story in **Portraits**.

Clara Reif and her son and daughter were among the passengers of the SS St. Louis who departed from Hamburg, Germany on May 13, 1939 for Havana, Cuba. In the interwar years Clara's husband had been a successful dentist in Vienna and took pride in having served the Austrian army on the eastern front during World War I.

Zustimmung

zum freiwilligen Eintritte in das Heer (Kriegsmarine, Landwehr).

Ich ertheile meinem minderjährigen Sohne (Mündel) *Gerschon Reif* , geboren im Jahre 18*94* in *Serafince* Bezirk *Horodenka*, Land *Galizien* , heimatsberechtigt in der Gemeinde *Serafince* , Bezirk *Horodenka* , Land *Galizien* *mosais.* Religion, *ledigen* Standes, die Bewilligung zum freiwilligen Eintritte in das Heer (Kriegsmarine, Landwehr).

Serafince am *1 September* 19*15*

Gesehen! Der Bezirkshauptmann:

Unterschrift des Vaters (Vormundes)

Fischel Reif

Pöbenstein.

Von dem Unberzeichneten wird bestätigt, dass laut hieramtlichen Sterbebüches Jahrgang 1938 Re.Zerall 2271 Dr. Gerson Reif, verheiratet, Zahnarzt, geboren am 9.VII. 1894 in Serafince, zuständig nach Wien, wohnhaft in Wien, I. Reichsbrückenstrasse 28, in Wien, II. Schmelzgasse 4 an Schädelbruch, zahlreiche Rippenbrüche

am 30. IX. 1938 (dreissigsten September) im Jahre Eintausend neun hundert achtundreissig starb und am 4ten Oktober 1938 auf dem israelitischen Friedhofe in Wien beerdigt wurde.

Wien, am 9. Mai 1940.

Matrikelamt der israelitischen Kultusgemeinde in Wien

Kollationiert.

After the German occupation of Austria (Anschluss) in March 1938 there were increasing restrictions placed on Jews. Dr. Reif was forced to give up his practice in August. A month later while seeking papers for emigration he died from a fall.

When the passengers on the St. Louis were not permitted to disembark in Havana or Miami, the ship returned to Europe where England, France, Holland, and Belgium agreed to grant the refugees asylum. The Reifs went to Loudon, France. Liane Reif (left front) currently lives in Boston and writes about her girlhood memories of the St. Louis.

Stories of Separation: Denying Family and Saving Children

This video montage has three short excerpts of adults—Nechama Tec, Rachel G., and Zezette L.—remembering their childhoods during the Holocaust when they were separated from their parents. The circumstances of separation were different for each of the interviewees, but for all of them the break from their parents was a traumatic experience that has left an indelible imprint on their lives.

Excerpt 1: Nechama Tec

Nechama Tec, from a Jewish family in Lublin, Poland, was only separated from her parents for short periods just after her family moved into the Lublin Ghetto. Then her father managed to find a Polish couple willing to take in the whole family for an agreed sum of money, and Nechama along with her sister and parents moved in with the host family for over two years until the end of the war. Although Nechama was able to remain with her parents in the same residence, she and her sister lived a separate existence from their parents. Nechama and her sister looked Polish and could speak Polish fluently, so they were able to "pass" as Aryans outside the house. They went to school with Polish children, engaged in black market activities, and took part in all aspects of community life. By contrast, their parents, who had characteristics considered Jewish and who lacked facility in speaking Polish, had to remain inside the house. They had to rely on their daughters for news from outside and for goods the girls could procure on the black market.

Initially Nechama found it difficult to "pass" among the Christians of her village, and she complained to her father about the anti-Jewish remarks she heard from girls whom she considered her friends. In time, however, Nechama became used to her role of passing as a Christian and began to identify with members of the Polish family hosting her own family. This, in turn, further distanced her from her own parents and her Jewish heritage.

Excerpt 2: Rachel G. (T-139)

Rachel, a Belgian survivor of the Holocaust, remembers how her parents arranged with their non-Jewish landlady to find a hiding place for their daughter with a priest. She recalls her mother's approach to the landlady:

> *"They are taking away the children, all Rachel's little Jewish friends are going. Can you do something about my daughter? Can you take her, hide her somewhere?"*

And the landlady said, "Yes I have this nephew who is a priest. Yes, I will ask him."

My mother could not take me to those people. My father took me. My mother was crying, crying so and my father took me to the tramway. . . . I remember my father crying like a baby in the middle of the street while he was taking me to those people, to strangers, and he explained to me, "Don't forget, you're a Jewish little girl, and we're going to see you again. But you must do that, you must go away. We are doing this for your best."

Of course, I couldn't understand. My mother was crying and only my father could take me and explain to me: "You've got to go. This is for your good. This is for your good. It's the best for you."

Later, after surviving for three years as a Christian child, Rachel was reunited with her mother and found out then how her parents had been captured and sent to Auschwitz. Following liberation, Rachel and her mother returned to the landlady's home in search of their belongings.

We went back . . . the landlady opened the door. She looked at us like we were ghosts. She fell on the floor. She kissed my mother's feet. She said, "I did that to you. I am the one who denounced you. Will you ever forgive me?"

Her mother responded, "I know it's you who gave us in because one of the Gestapo said, 'We know you're Jews because the landlady said so.'"

When Rachel was asked to describe her feelings about her childhood, she answered:

How on earth this happened. It's beyond me. I can't understand how people went that far to denounce other people, to hurt other people, to build, to actually build things to destroy a human race. And by the way, not only Jewish people suffered, I mean. I can tell you of nuns who were shot.

I'm a little confused. I must admit—not a little, a lot. Because when I found out there is good and bad in all of us . . . if there were a lot more like the gentiles who saved me, this could not have happened. So those people were very unusual people.

Excerpt 3: Zezette L. (T-100)

Zezette, another Belgian survivor, gives an account of her parents who were forced to entrust both their son and daughter to Christians. Her brother stayed with Trappist monks and Zezette hid in a Catholic school where she adopted another name and was told to forget about her parents. Meanwhile, the nuns instructed her in Catholicism: "I got up," she explains, ". . . went to church, opened my mouth . . . got first communion, and [then] kept my mouth shut. . . It was something that happened in an instant [with no preparation]."

Zezette did not see her parents for a year and a half. Then, during Easter break of 1943, she visited her parents who were hiding in Belgium. While she was there, on Easter Sunday, the Gestapo discovered her and her parents. They were eventually transported to Auschwitz. Her parents did not survive. Many years later, Zezette decided to return to Auschwitz to "bury" her parents.

"Obviously we were followed or betrayed," Zezette explains in her testimony. She recalls the sense of fear that she and her parents experienced as the Germans approached and knocked on the door of the house next door. Then she remembers being pushed into a truck along with her parents.

Commentary

The stories of Nechama, Rachel, and Zezette attest to the complex decisions people were forced to make during the Holocaust. Their parents made the painful choice to separate from their children in order to better ensure that someone would survive. As we hear of the specific situations of these families, we wonder what we would have done in similar circumstances. Could we separate, take risks, and place our trust in our neighbors?

These stories also raise a number of fundamental questions about the motives of those who took the risks of helping Jews and other persecuted minorities. Those who helped not only defied Gestapo and neighbors, but they also jeopardized their own lives and those of their relatives and friends. Most perplexing of all is why the very people who helped some individuals escape extermination did not hesitate to turn others over to the authorities. How could noble and brave individuals in one instance convert into compliant subjects of the Nazi regime in another?

The history of the Holocaust offers a wealth of evidence about people who, at one time or another, took risks to save victims of the Third Reich. In the town of Le Chambon, for instance, Pastor Trocme organized efforts to rescue French Jewish children. Janusz Korczak, a teacher and writer of children's books who opened an orphanage in the Warsaw Ghetto, went to his death with a group of orphan children he had been supervising. Oskar Schindler, a wealthy industrialist, bribed SS guards to protect hundreds of workers from destruction. Raoul Wallenberg, a Swedish diplomat, was captured by Russian forces at the close of the war while he was conducting rescue operations of Hungarian Jewry. Other nuns, priests, pastors, and lay persons also performed extraordinary feats of humanity.

An examination of Nazi legislation in occupied Poland suggests how dangerous it was for non-Jews to engage in rescue activities. For example, Hans Frank, the governor of the Nazi puppet state known as the General Government, issued the following decree on October 15, 1941, which specified the death sentence for Jews not living in designated areas as well as for non-Jews who helped Jews hide:

> Pursuant to #5, paragraph 1, of the Fuehrer's decree of October 12, 1939. . . I issue this ordinance:
>
> Article 1
>
> In the Decree on Restrictions of Residence in the General Government September 13, 1940 . . . as modified by the Second Decree on Limitations of Residence in the General Government, on April 29, 1941 . . .
>
> #4b
>
> (1) Jews who, without authorization, leave the residential district to which they have been assigned will be punished by death. The same punishment applies to persons who knowingly provide hiding places for such Jews.
>
> (2) Abettors and accomplices will be punished in the same way as the perpetrator, and an attempted act in the same way as an accomplished one. In less serious cases the sentence may involve penal servitude, or imprisonment.
>
> (3) Cases will be judged by special courts.[57]

Today some scholars are trying to identify any characteristics that distinguish those individuals who took risks to help people during the Holocaust. Did they have a certain training? Did they hold a particular faith? What makes someone save another? What constitutes an altruistic personality?

One of these scholars is Nechama Tec (Excerpt 1), professor of sociology at the University of Connecticut. After relating the story of her own family in a memoir entitled *Dry Tears*, she embarked on a sociological survey of hundreds of men and women involved in helping Jews in Poland during the war. Her book *When Light Pierced the Darkness* is the vanguard of research in this field.

Tec and other scholars of the altruistic personality have made two principal observations. First, there was no prototypical savior. Indeed, people decided to assist those in need for a variety of motives ranging from greed, economic necessity, and fear, to religious convictions and matters of personal conscience.

Second, there is no adequate language to describe the phenomenon of Christians saving Jews and other minorities during the Nazi era. The word "saving" in this context is a term laden with emotional connotations; in its normal use, we do not think of one who saves another as an individual who risks combating centuries of prejudice and hatred to help individuals designated as enemies by the government.

Moreover, saving does not convey the varying levels of help extended to minorities. In some cases, the savior carefully instructed children in hiding about the Christian religion and rituals and showed understanding for children who found it difficult to adjust to a totally different lifestyle and identity. In other cases, the savior did not go beyond providing physical protection for the children in custody and expected gratitude in return. Then there were those who saved in the purest sense of the word; they wanted no recognition or compensation for their humanitarian deeds, and they did not think that what they were doing was anything beyond what individuals should do for one another in desperate situations.

Samuel Oliner, director of the Altruistic Personality Project, points out two principal functions of studying altruism in past and present societies. The first is to elucidate what Oliner calls "pure history: living walking historians describing events of what has occurred." The second "is to find the common threads among those few who have helped, and the differences between the rescuers and those others who might have helped but chose to look the other way."[58]

Pierre Sauvage, a survivor who was rescued as a child in the French town of Le Chambon-sur-Lignon and who has just completed a film of rescuers in France, reinforces Oliner's arguments for studying altruism despite the small numbers of individuals who participated in rescue work.

> There were so few of them. As if moral or spiritual significance is a matter of numbers. As if we even knew the numbers in this largely uncharted chapter of our past. As if we didn't believe, we Jews especially, that even tiny minorities may own important, perhaps divine, truths.

> The late pastor of Le Chambon [Andre Trocme] lived his life, his eloquent pacifist's life, as a demonstration of Christian faith. Yet in his unpublished memoirs, he confided that his faith was, ultimately, in the possibility of good on earth, "without which," he added, "the theoretical existence of God doesn't interest me."

> And I, the father of David, who want to believe in that possibility, too, who want to extend it and pass both the belief and the evidence for it on to my

child and to his, am bound to seek out and to treasure and to learn from the bits and pieces I can find even in the moral rubble of these times— especially in the moral rubble of these times.

That is why, as I tell David of these things, as he learns that there is in all of us a capacity for evil and an even greater and more insidious capacity for apathy, I want them to learn that the stories of the righteous are not footnotes to the past but cornerstones to the future. I owe my life to the good people of Le Chambon. I owe even more that that to my son.[59]

The chronicles and historical monographs that detail the horror of the Nazi era highlight the need to prevent such evils from occurring again. But it is the rescue stories that offer models of noble and courageous individuals, whose stories contemporaries may contemplate as they think about ways to prevent the abuse of human rights and dehumanization characteristic of Nazism and other totalitarian regimes in the 1930s and 1940s and today.

Pastor Andre Trocme organized citizens of Le Chambon to hide Jews. Above is one of the farmhouses that offered asylum to Jews escaping Nazi roundups.

Using

What does the word "altruism" mean? Would you refer to the landlady in Rachel's story as altruistic? Would you consider the priest who took Rachel from her father altruistic?

What would be the motives of priests and nuns in helping to rescue Jewish children? How do you explain the fact that priests and nuns in several occupied countries took a risk of helping Jews even though the Vatican did not take a strong stand in behalf of Jews persecuted in the Third Reich?

How can one explain that some individuals took the risk of helping Jews despite the harsh penalties for such actions while others did not help Jews or other persecuted minorities? Would you call the men and women who helped Jews heroes and heroines?

Rachel mentions how the landlady betrayed her parents to the Gestapo, and Zezette tells how neighbors betrayed her and her parents when they took their fishing trip. What were the conditions in Nazi-occupied countries like Belgium that might have encouraged neighbors to turn against their neighbors?

From the testimonies, can you tell of any major differences between the experiences of the western European Jews (Rachel and Zezette) and the eastern European Jew (Nechama)?

Nechama points out that she was able to retain a sense of her own identity despite the years of "passing" as a Christian because she always had her parents in her midst. How did the presence of her parents help in this process?

The Facing History Resource Center has additional videotapes that pertain to the questions of rescue and altruism: "Motivations for Caring," a 35-minute videotape of Nechama Tec and Ervin Staub talking about their research on altruistic personality, based on the studies of Christians involved in rescue work during the Holocaust; "Anne Frank in the World," a 28-minute dramatic reenactment of the life of Anne Frank in the Annex, with background material on the Nazi Party in Holland and the German occupation; *As If It Were Yesterday*, an 86-minute documentary of the rescue of Jewish children in Belgium; and a thirty-minute documentary on Oskar Schindler and Raoul Wallenberg produced for *Chronicle*, WCVB-TV, Boston, entitled "The Making of a Hero." For additional suggestions on materials pertaining to altruism, see Nechama Tec in **Portraits**.

The testimony of Paul D. in **Portraits** provides an in-depth study of a child separated from his parents and grandparents on several occasions during the Holocaust. Paul describes the fear he felt upon being thrust into an orphanage after being separated from his parents. Another interesting study of separation is found in the story of Menachem S., found in the video montage "Childhood Memories," Excerpt 10. The reminiscences of these two men should be compared with the experiences described by Rachel, Zezette, and Nechama.

Two especially interesting cases of children separated from parents are those concerning the Jewish children who sought refuge in Le Chambon, France, and the twins at Auschwitz who were victims of Mengele's experiments. The experiences of the former are described in Hallie's *Lest Innocent Blood Be Shed*; the latter are described in Segal's "Holocaust Twins: Their Special Bond."[60]

It is not uncommon for Jewish families to have only one survivor of the Holocaust. Rose Murra (nee Rachel Leah Zysman) is the sole survivor of the Zysman family. The photograph above shows a Zysman family gathering just before the war. Seated left to right: Rivkah Zysman, Moshe Y'oel (brother), Rachel Leah Zysman, Sally Gradowczyk (aunt), Shlomo Zalmen (brother), Srul Hersh (father); standing, Minecha Gradowczyk (aunt), Yosef Cooperschmidt (uncle), Eva Gradowczyk Cooperschmidt (aunt).

The last chapter of the Resource Book ("Facing Today and the Future"), which is also the basis for a separate book entitled *Choosing to Participate*, helps students examine the neglected history of how people participate—in community work, in human service, in politics and social activism, and in other kinds of voluntary or nonprofit activity. Lessons confront apathy and helplessness with hope and direction. "Facing Today and the Future" and *Choosing To Participate* respond to students as they question where they fit in society and whether their actions can affect today and the future in a positive way. They demonstrate how caring for others and social change can come about through individual initiative, collaborative action, and enduring commitment. At the same time, they force students to confront the dilemmas that face anyone's efforts of service or advocacy in a democratic society. Contact the Facing History Resource Center for additional information on this material.

Marion Pritchard helped to reunite separated families after the war. Above during the War and recently at the right.

Childhood Memories

"Childhood Memories" includes eight excerpts from testimonies of Jews and three from non-Jews who recall their experiences growing up in various European countries during the Third Reich, 1933-1945. The selections reflect the day-to-day experiences of children and adolescents in a variety of circumstances: some interviewees were able to attend school and continue living with their families; others were compelled to go into hiding with or without their parents; and one spent several years in concentration camps.

The selections focus on issues of central importance to all students of the Holocaust, and most particularly to young students: What was it like to grow up in the totalitarian regime of the Third Reich? Were young people aware of the lack of freedom in their society, or did they accept their closed society without questioning its controls? What did students in elementary and secondary schools study? How did Nazi ideology influence curricula and the organization of the school day? How did Jews react to abusive treatment in the schools of the Nazi era? How did non-Jewish students behave when classmates were mistreated? What were parent-child relationships like during the Third Reich? Did ideological concerns turn children against their parents? What happened when children were forced to separate from their parents? What did Jewish children have to do to prepare for hiding in the Christian world? How did growing up in the Third Reich affect adult attitudes and behavior?

In viewing the excerpts in "Childhood Memories," it is important to note that they are the specific memories of the individuals selected for the montage and are not intended to represent a cross-section of Holocaust experiences of survivors and witnesses. These testimonies of childhood memories are important sources for learning about young people who grow up in a culture of violence, racism, hatred, and oppression. In the milieu of Nazi Germany, "in" and "out" groups were clearly defined; German children learned disdain for "inferior peoples" and were encouraged to turn neighbor against neighbor. The Nazis made a deliberate effort to indoctrinate youth inside and outside of school with their views of race science, foreign policy, and orderly government. By studying the testimonies of individuals who were exposed daily to Nazi ideology, we begin to understand the effectiveness of Nazi propaganda and the ways in which the younger generation responded to Nazi ideals. Such information supplements existing materials written by adults during the Nazi era about the treatment of children in the New Germany.

The interviewees recollect what it was like to witness daily harassment of Jews in the schools and in the streets; many relate personal experiences with Nazi brutality in their communities, in the ghettos, and in the concentration camps. Some of the non-Jewish interviewees represented in the montage belonged to Nazi youth organizations which promoted hatred for "inferior" peoples and emphasized martial values.

During the Holocaust the victims had no outlet for their anger over the abuses they endured. Any public complaint would have jeopardized their own lives and the lives of others. Several witnesses recall instances when they had no place to turn for redressing the wrongs they sustained under the Nazis. In fact, such injustices often became the norm of behavior. The testimonies help us to understand more about life in the totalitarian society of the Third Reich and to learn what happens when generally unacceptable means of relating to other people suddenly become accepted standards of behavior.

The witnesses in "Childhood Memories" recall the Third Reich in a variety of ways. One speaks dispassionately about being abused as the token Jew in a class of non-Jews. Another man from the same town, also the only Jew in a class of fifty-five boys, becomes so emotional as he tells of the discrimination he experienced that words fail: deep sighs and long pauses punctuate his recollections of his school days. Interviewees also display a broad spectrum of emotions. One woman is on the verge of tears as she recounts the separation from her parents. Later, as she speaks of Christians who helped her hide from the Nazis, she smiles and speaks of her love for these rescuers. In another excerpt, we watch as a man recounts the close calls he and his mother had in trying to avoid arrest by the Nazis. As he speaks we can see the emotional toll on his face. Nevertheless, he maintains a smile throughout the interview, speaking often of his cherished memories of traditional Jewish rituals practiced in his family even after the Nazis came to power.

Language itself is a problem for many of the speakers. Normal vocabulary proves inadequate for what they want to convey. At times, when a word used in normal discourse fails to describe an experience adequately, the witness will fumble. At other times a witness will suddenly interrupt the narrative with a silence. A remembered detail will overwhelm the voice and the process of recall and cause the witness to lose control or to turn inward in a way that temporarily breaks the communication with the viewer.

It is important to consider the nature of memory as we listen to the voices of witnesses on this montage. Often, the interviewers allow the witnesses as much time as they need, so that they may remember with deliberate thoughtfulness and analysis. Still, a date or place may be mistakenly recalled. Witnesses are, after all, being asked to recall details from half a century ago. Perhaps, too, the adult memory is perceived through a more powerful lens— some witnesses unconsciously color a moment or enhance a recollection with information they have heard or read in the intervening years. One witness in the montage, for example, remembers the details of his separation from his parents when he was just four years old. Was his memory enhanced by the trauma of the event? Survivor Kati David, who has studied the testimonies of scores of other child survivors, observes that "the single greatest fear for children in the Holocaust years was separation from their families." Most of the child survivors David has spoken with since the war vividly recall the fear of losing their parents and of being taken from their homes. Bombs and Gestapo raids, David continues, were much less frightening for these children, who were accustomed to the noises and tensions of wartime.

The video testimonies excerpted in this montage are valuable sources for information about childhood during the Third Reich. Young people who lived in Germany and in German-occupied areas left fewer written records than adults. Much of what we know about education in Nazi Germany comes from legislation that set forth regulations for students eligible to attend public schools and for establishing curricula, as well as from observations by adults visiting schools and meetings of Hitler Youth organizations. In Nazi-occupied territories, youth who had been keeping diaries often were forced to destroy these records when they were sent into the ghettos and concentration camps in order to prevent Nazi officials and collaborators from taking reprisals against them and their families. Thus the testimonies challenge the interviewees to recall and reflect upon incidents, personalities, and experiences to fill the void created by the absence of written sources.

Finally, these excerpts raise questions about how Allied officials introduced their program of denazification into the German educational system after the war: what kind of curriculum can counteract the twelve years of militarism and racism that pervaded the social structure, including the schools and youth organizations? The excerpts also raise crucial questions for today's society because abuse of children in war-torn countries and in impoverished areas throughout the world continues. What will happen when these children come to maturity? Their own development has been marked only by fear, atrocity, and hatred; where and how will they learn about human dignity and decency?

Arrangement of the Montage

The video excerpts selected for "Childhood Memories" are arranged to focus on the evolution of Nazi legislation and its impact on young people and their families. The first excerpts concentrate on relations dealing with schooling and curricula enacted early in the Nazi regime and their effects on Jewish and non-Jewish students. Subsequent excerpts examine the "Final Solution" and its influence on the younger generation in Germany and the occupied territories. The closing excerpts focus on the legacy of the children of the Third Reich.

The excerpts reveal reactions of children to their hostile environment. It is useful to view one or two excerpts at a time rather than all eleven at once. Thus students will be able to examine and discuss the full range of experiences and reactions of the survivors. The selections vary according to age and nationality of the witnesses. A school-age child in Germany in 1933 has memories very different from schoolchildren in occupied territories during the war years; the youth who survived the labor camps at Auschwitz has memories very different from the child hidden by Christians or partisans. And the children who stayed with their parents during the Holocaust report family experiences that did not exist for the children separated from parents and forced to live among strangers.

Geography, community leadership, and the level of collaboration in an area also affected children's experiences. For example, a non-Jewish German child who attended school in a town in north-central Germany during the war vividly recalls his third-grade lesson in race science, yet another non-Jewish German teenager from the northern town of Lubeck does not recall lessons in race science in these years. Therefore, the manual includes background information on various areas in which witnesses lived during the Third Reich.

The montage is designed to coordinate with the dominant themes found in the Resource Book, as well as with other readings and audiovisual materials available with the program.

Excerpt 1, Frank S., corresponds to themes on Antisemitism , Nazi Philosophy and Policy, and Preparing for Obedience.

Excerpt 2, Carl H., corresponds to themes on Nazi Philosophy and Policy and Preparing for Obedience.

Excerpt 3, Elizabeth D., corresponds to themes on Nazi Philosophy and Policy, Preparing for Obedience, and Victims of Tyranny.

Excerpt 4, Krystyna S., corresponds to themes on Preparing for Obedience and Antisemitism.

Excerpt 5, Walter K., corresponds to themes on Antisemitism and Preparing for Obedience.

Excerpt 6, Nechama Tec, corresponds to themes on Antisemitism and Who Knew.

Excerpt 7, Rachel G. #1, corresponds to themes on Nazi Philosophy and Policy and Who Knew.

Excerpt 8, Zezette L., corresponds to themes on Nazi Philosophy and Policy, Victims of Tyranny, Facing Today and the Future: Choosing To Participate.

Excerpt 9, Rachel G. #2, corresponds to Facing Today and the Future: Choosing To Participate.

Excerpt 10, Paul D., corresponds to Victims of Tyranny and Today and the Future.

Excerpt 11, Menachem S., corresponds to Victims of Tyranny and Today and the Future.

If students want to know more about one of the interviewees, teachers may be able to obtain a longer selection through the Facing History Resource Center or the Fortunoff Video Archive.

Excerpt 1: Frank S. (T-30)

> *And then we had a different curriculum because we had this Rassenkunde, which is raceology. That was a regular subject that we had and we were supposed to learn what an Aryan is. . . . Opposed to the Aryan race we were the Jews.*

In this excerpt, Frank remembers his experiences in Breslau during 1933 as a twelve-year-old Jewish schoolboy, one of two Jewish students in a public school class of fifty-three boys.

Frank recalls that he lived with discrimination all his life. He was born in 1921 in Breslau, Germany, a medium-sized industrial town in Silesia where the Jewish population numbered approximately 23,000. As a young child, Frank experienced antisemitism and sensed that he was somehow different from his non-Jewish classmates.

After the Nazis took power, however, antisemitism became even more open in Breslau. Various economic measures forced Frank's father to close down his restaurant; the family was forbidden, along with other Jewish families of the area, to watch Nazi parades or salute the Nazi flag.

National Socialist parades and rallies engendered enthusiasm among the German people.
Frank S. describes the difficulty of being excluded from such events.

Incidents of violence against Jews occurred daily. The SA were particularly harsh in enforcing the regulations to exclude Jews from the civil service and legal profession. The Brownshirts stormed the local courts, dragging out Jewish lawyers and judges and subjecting them to public humiliation. When the local police tried to intervene, the Nazis quickly silenced the opposition by placing an SA officer in charge of the Breslau police.

Frank's mother repeatedly urged her son not to stand out as a Jew, and although Frank tried to follow her advice, it was difficult to assimilate in his school. Not only did the non-Jewish students beat up Frank and his Jewish classmates, but they also relentlessly insulted the Jewish people and their beliefs. On one occasion in 1933, after Frank's mother visited the school, the non-Jewish students insulted her, telling Frank he should be ashamed of such a mother. Teachers who adhered to the Nazi ideals also made a point of abusing their Jewish students.

In accord with Nazi guidelines for teaching "racial science," Frank's biology teacher designed lessons to heighten student awareness of racial differences.

Frank remembers one class in which the teacher ordered him to the front of the room as the example of a Jew. The teacher pointed to Frank's features, explaining that they marked him as an inferior human being while the features of a blond-haired, blue-eyed student represented the perfect Aryan. In addition to these humiliations, Frank encountered repeated insults from non-Jewish students who wanted to pick a fight with him. The racial tensions at school made it virtually impossible for Frank to remain inconspicuous as his mother had urged.

Further, Frank describes obstacles he confronted when he tried to "blend in" outside the school. The Nazis, he explains, expected citizens to salute the flag with a raised arm and "Heil Hitler" greeting. Since Jews were not regarded as citizens after 1933, they were forbidden from saluting the flag and thus could be identified easily in a crowd when they did not salute. At times Frank tried to hide his non-citizen status and would raise his hand in salute. Sometimes he would try to duck inside a store or house so he could avoid the decision. Frank was especially afraid of being caught violating the flag laws. There was no protection for Jews, he says. "You couldn't complain to the police."

By 1934 Frank could no longer bear to be subjected to the humiliations he describes in the video excerpts. For months his classmates had so harassed him for being a "dirty Jew" that he begged his parents to let him leave the school. He then secured a position as apprentice to an electrician. Although his employer made fun of his "Jew" worker, the other non-Jewish apprentices were "not so bad" to Frank, and he began to enjoy his work.

Kristallnacht in November 1938 completely changed Frank's circumstances. While he managed to escape being rounded up or harmed during the demonstrations against Jews, he was frightened by the excesses he had seen. Following *Kristallnacht*, Frank quit his job and, with other members of his family, began making plans to leave Germany. Early in 1939 Frank joined his aunt in England, who had secured an affidavit for him and guaranteed he would have work there. Frank's parents were unable to leave Germany until 1941, when they took a train through Russia to Shanghai. They remained there under Japanese occupation until the end of the war. (See the second half of the hour-long videotape "Flight from Destiny" for a description of German Jews who sought refuge in Shanghai.)

Commentary

This excerpt links the motivation for Frank's emigration to the experiences he had in school. However, it is important to note that the opportunities for emigration of Jews from Germany in the early years of the Nazi regime were not available by the time Germany occupied other countries during the war.

Frank remembers the "shame and humiliation" he experienced in his school that forced him to leave his formal education in 1934 and begin his four-year training as an electrician's apprentice. This training helped Frank secure papers for emigration to England when it was no longer safe for Jews to remain in Germany.

Nazi educational policies exacerbated the tensions between non-Jews and Jews in the public schools. As early as April 25, 1933, the Nazis enacted measures limiting the number of Jews in public schools and compelling them to attend private Jewish schools.

Nazi curricula stressed the significance of subjects such as "race science," physical education, "Aryan history," and geopolitics. Jacob Graf, a teacher and influential textbook writer, recommended the following assignments to help students learn how to recognize a person's race:

Summarize the spiritual characteristics of the individual races.

Collect from stories, essays, and poems, examples of ethnological illustrations. Underline those terms which describe the type and mode of the expression of the soul.

Collect propaganda posters and caricatures for your race book and arrange them according to a racial scheme. What image of beauty is emphasized by the artist (a) in posters publicizing sports and travel? (b) in publicity for cosmetics? How are hunters, mountain climbers and shepherds drawn?

Observe the Jew: his way of walking, his bearing, gestures, and movements when talking.

What strikes you about the way a Jew talks and sings?

What are the occupations engaged in by the Jews of your acquaintance?

In what stories, descriptions and poems do you find the psychical character of the Jew pertinently portrayed ("The Jew in the Pickle" from Grimm's *Fairy Tales*; *Debit and Credit* by Fritz Reuter; *The Hunger Pastor* by Wilhelm Raabe; *The Merchant of Venice* by William Shakespeare). Give more examples.[61]

Gregor Ziemer, an American educator who lived in Germany during the 1930s, reported similar lessons in classes he observed while touring Nazi schools. His book, *Education for Death*, provides detailed descriptions of the Nazi curriculum, which nurtured attitudes of hatred toward Jews and other minorities.

The emigration of German children to England was organized by the World Movement for the Care of Children from Germany. The organization was set up in response to *Kristallnacht*. When the war broke out in September 1939, 9,354 children had come to England, 7,482 of whom were Jewish. Those like Frank who had relations or friends in England could be sponsored individually and thus were given a guaranteed status. The World Movement itself, in conjunction with local committees, took the responsibility for non-guaranteed children. The numbers of children brought to England by the World Movement declined after April 1939.

The following brief passages come from the reminiscences of individuals saved by The World Movement:

> My mother took me to Berlin; when I left home my father was lying in bed ill, the concentration camp had damaged his health. He held me close and bade me look after my mother when she got to England in case he did not make it. I was then just ten years old. We got to Berlin to learn that I was too late for the first transport, but would be able to go on the second. There was of course no money for me to go back home, so my mother took me to friends in Berlin, who kindly put me up for a fortnight or so. My mother had to leave me there, and the last I ever saw of her was in the Berlin Street, outside the friends' house, walking backward along the pavement to get a last look at me, until she rounded the corner and we were parted.[62]

> Not only had I never been on a large ocean-going ship but I had never even seen the sea. Alas, it was a night-crossing and I saw very little. The ship had been specially chartered for us. The only adults on board were the crew and those in charge of us. While they were busy I explored the ship, top to bottom, bow to stern. I stumbled into the crew's quarters, engine room and all kinds of places I had no business to be. The only place I was denied was the bridge. Everything I saw was new to me, it was fascinating. ... There were about forty or fifty boys, all about fifteen or sixteen years old, in that room [the cabin where we spent the night]. We were all a little over-excited, and for the next hours we exchanged, in the dark, all the political jokes which we had picked up. They were mostly variations of "Hitler, Goebbels and Goering. ..." The jokes, as such, were not memorable, but the occasion was. We did not need to look over our shoulders or lower our voices and the realization that we could say what we liked with impunity engendered an atmosphere of enormous gaiety.[63]

Using

In the last part of the excerpt Frank describes giving a Nazi salute as a parade passed. He suggests that there was no correct or uniform behavior that would have kept him safe. What was correct behavior one day or with one teacher was incorrect on another occasion. How does Frank describe his dilemma with the flag salute? How does Frank as an adult recall this episode? From Frank's view, why did the Nazis place such emphasis on patriotic rituals?

Students might explore the implications of a society in which an individual had "no one to complain to" about wrongs he and the members of his family sustained.

When Frank left school, what options were available to him? How did he deal with the constant harassment and discrimination?

An American eighth grader who recently viewed Frank's testimony commented, "It's bad enough being picked out of a class of twenty for doing something wrong. It must have been horrible to be picked on the way he was. I want to know why he kept going to school like that."

What does emigration mean? What factors in Germany of the 1930s might have prevented Frank and other Jewish youth from leaving their schools and neighborhoods? Are there similar obstacles today for youth seeking to emigrate?

Would you consider Frank heroic for his refusal to remain in a school where Jews were humiliated?

Available at the Facing History Resource Center are two contemporary descriptions of education in Nazi Germany: Ziemer's *Education for Death: The Making of a Nazi*, and Erika Mann's *School for Barbarians*.

Julius Streicher, who published the antisemitic newspaper *Der Stürmer*, also published antisemitic literature for children. For example, *The Poisoned Mushroom* contains stories that depict Jews as the enemies of the German people; accompanying illustrations reinforce the negative stereotypes of Jews. *The Poisoned Mushroom* was entered in evidence against Streicher at the International Military Tribunal at Nuremberg. See Milton's, "The Social Responsibility of the Artist" in **Resources** for further discussion on *The Poisoned Mushroom*.

Historian Whitney Harris summarizes the evidence on Streicher's influence on German children that was presented at Nuremberg:

Streicher spoke to children at every opportunity upon his basic theme, hatred of the Jew, and his single overture—Hitler had been sent to redeem Germany from Jewish oppression. Such a talk was reported as given by him to the children of Nuremberg at Christmastime, 1936: "Do you know who the Devil is?" he asked his breathlessly listening audience. "The Jew, the Jew," resounded from a thousand children's voices.

Streicher demanded that anti-Jewish propaganda be disseminated in the public schools. In the course of a 1935 speech he said: "I repeat, we demand the transformation of the school into an ethno-German institution of education. If German children are taught by German teachers, then we shall have laid the foundations for the ethno-German school. This ethno-German school must teach racial doctrine."

From the offices of *Der Stürmer* Streicher published a book for teachers entitled *The Jewish Question and School Instruction*, in which his anti-Semitic doctrines were expounded. . . . The purpose of the book, which was . . . directed against the Jews at every page, was summarized in this sentence: "One who has reached this stage of understanding will inevitably remain an enemy of the Jews all his life and will instill this hatred into his own children."[64]

Excerpt 2: Carl H.

I was in third grade. . . . We went to class one morning. . . . A strange man arrived . . . [who] was introduced as a professor of the University of Wurzburg from the Office of Racial Research. . . . We were given a lecture on what an Aryan was supposed to be.

"Childhood Memories" includes Carl's testimony, in which he offers a detailed description of one of his third grade classes in "racial science." One day a professor from the University of Wurzburg visited the class. Using a number of charts and graphs, he proceeded to describe the distinguishing characteristics of the ideal Aryan. "We were all very impressed by the figures," recalls Karl. Following the lecture, the teacher instructed the students to go into the town and locate an Aryan, who they would then describe in their notebooks. Carl remembers the obstacles he and his classmates encountered because so few in the town resembled the perfect Aryan described by the visiting professor.

Carl, born in 1935, spent his boyhood with his parents and three older brothers in Wurzburg, a small town of 3,500 in central Germany. Before the outbreak of World War II, Wurzburg was an impoverished agricultural community, and Carl remembers that most of the stucco houses needed paint and repairs. Both of Carl's parents were trained accountants, but they could not find work in their profession during the depression. Carl's father joined the Nazi Party during the 1930s.

Carl was exposed to Nazi ideology from his earliest childhood. He had no direct contact with Jews and did not question the values espoused by the Third Reich. Prior to Hitler's accession to power in 1933, about a quarter of Wurzburg's population had been Jewish, but most of them had fled by the mid-1930s when Carl was growing up. Carl was aware of the existence of one Jew—a red-headed woman—but he never knew her personally.

"All of my memories of my childhood are of wartime," Carl explains. "I had no other frame of reference." Especially vivid are his memories of people who were a part of the war—his brothers when they went off to the Air Force, the return of one brother who was wounded in the Italian Campaign, and the funeral of a former ice-cream man who was killed in action on the Russian front. At the end of the war, as American troops entered Wurzburg, Carl recalls that his family took shelter in a basement bunker. "The war came to an end for me at precisely 11:45 A.M. on May 11, 1945." From the bunker Carl saw large boots pass by the basement window and heard an American officer shouting for people to move along quickly. Then, Carl continues, "all the townspeople had to turn in their arms and cameras." Carl was even ordered to surrender his BB gun.

After the war Carl's father, mistakenly identified as a leading Nazi whose surname was the same, spent a year and a half in prison. After it became clear that he had not served as a major official of the Third Reich, he was released. The detention of Carl's father had been part of the process of denazification—an effort of the Allied powers to replace the economic, intellectual, cultural, and political leaders of the Third Reich with leaders who supported democratic ideals.

During this same period, Carl attended schools in which the curriculum was denazified. Teachers were prohibited from mentioning anything about war or nationalism. "It made studying Latin especially difficult," explains Carl, "since we could not study wars." At age eighteen Carl came to America as an exchange student, and he remained in the States. Today he teaches social studies and classical languages and takes an active part in his community.

Commentary

The Nazis drew considerable support from the German academic community. The professor from Wurzburg University who visited Carl's class was typical of academics who used their scholarship to substantiate the racial theory of the Nazis.

Dr. E. Hartshorne, a representative of American universities who investigated German universities after the war, reported that at least 112 on the staff of Wurzburg University should be dismissed for their support of the Nazi regime. He found that active Nazis dominated the medical faculty and the library staff. He also learned that in the postwar era there remained one member of the liberal arts faculty who continued to teach "Germanics," a "science of mysticism," the basis of the theory of the "Superior Race." This teacher had taught the course throughout the years of the Third Reich.

Hans Gunther, a professor at the University of Jena, provided a description of "the Aryan race" that was widely accepted in the Third Reich and resembles the definition Carl heard in his third-grade classroom:

> The Nordic race is tall, long-legged, slim, with an average height, among males, of above 1.74 meters. The limbs, the neck, the shape of the hands and feet are vigorous and slender in appearance. The Nordic race is long-legged and narrow-faced, with a cephalic index of around 75 and a facial index above 90. As in all races, at least in the medium- and long-headed ones, the female head, in comparison with that of the male, appears to have a higher cephalic index and a lower facial index. The back of the Nordic head characteristically projects far beyond the nape of the neck. The projecting part of the back of the head, however, is comparatively low, so that in Nordic people the head springs backward, as it were, over the part of the neck visible above the collar. The face is narrow, with a rather narrow forehead, a narrow high-built nose, and a narrow lower jaw and a prominent chin.[65]

Using

How might Carl's story be different if he were still a child instead of recalling his experiences as an adult? How might the story change if a victim of the Nazi educational policies were with Carl as he told the story? Imagine how Frank might react to this story.

As an adult, Carl recalls the absurdity of his assignment in his town where no one could be located who conformed to the stereotype of an Aryan. Nevertheless, in a recent interview Carl reflected on the seriousness of the whole incident. He wondered what might have happened if the war had continued and he had undergone the indoctrination process of the Hitler Youth. With more years of Nazi propaganda and education, might Carl have taken his lessons on race science more seriously? What do you think was the impact of Nazi education on those who were in their teens when Hitler came to power?

What was the process of denazification? How do you think people who have been taught to hate can be untaught?

From the perspective of Carl's teacher, what was the goal of the assignment on locating an "Aryan"? What was the impact of such an assignment on Carl and his classmates? Was Carl's assignment compatible with Hitler's education goals set forth in the following excerpt from *Mein Kampf*?

> The whole organization of education and training . . . must take as its crowning task the work of instilling into the hearts and brains of youth entrusted to it the racial instinct and understanding of the racial idea. No boy or girl must leave school without having attained a clear insight into the meaning of racial purity and the importance of maintaining the racial blood unadulterated. Thus, the first indispensable condition for the preservation of our race will have been established and thus the future culture progress of our people will be assured.[66]

What might Carl have thought as he discovered that he could not complete the assignment because there was no perfect "Aryan"?

How do you think that Carl and his classmates dealt with the paradox that neither the Nazi professor who visited their classroom nor the local leader of the Nazi Party possessed the features that were supposed to characterize the perfect Aryan?

See **Portraits** for a description of a longer excerpt of Carl H.'s testimony.

Excerpt 3: Elizabeth D. (T-95)

> *We were living with my grandparents . . . and they told us . . . when people ask you things in school, or anywhere about anything, you don't know anything. You just say I don't know. And it was very difficult for us, my brother and I, to act dumb all the time.*

This excerpt focuses on reminiscences of Elizabeth D., whose parents were Jehovah's Witnesses. During much of the Nazi era Elizabeth attended school in Lubeck, a city in northern Germany where the majority of the population was Protestant.

Elizabeth was born in 1929 in the small town of Sachsenburg in Saxony, a section of north-central Germany that is part of East Germany today. Both parents and all four grandparents belonged to the small Christian sect known as Jehovah's Witnesses. Members of this religion claim their primary allegiance to God and the Bible and refuse to compromise this allegiance with obligations to secular authorities. Therefore Jehovah's Witnesses will not bear arms for their state or swear oaths of loyalty to a secular state. In the Third Reich, Jehovah's Witnesses were suspect because of their religious convictions and their unwillingness to support the armed forces, and they were subject to arrest and imprisonment for their nonconformity to the laws of the National Socialist regime.

In 1935 Elizabeth's father and mother were arrested and sentenced to local jail because of their religious affiliation. Elizabeth's mother received a two-and-a-half year sentence, but she was released early for good behavior. In 1936 her father was transferred to the concentration camp Sachsenhausen, a camp for political prisoners or "enemies of the state." It was only after *Kristallnacht* in November of 1938 that the SS began to place large numbers of Jews in this camp.

Later, after the war began, Elizabeth's father might have been released had he agreed to take an oath to the new regime. He refused. One day in 1941, Elizabeth's mother received a telegram from Sachsenhausen informing her that her husband had died of "heart and circulatory failure." It was signed, "The Commandant." According to Elizabeth, her father was then only thirty-five years old and had always been a very healthy man.

When Elizabeth's parents were imprisoned, she and her brother moved to the home of their maternal grandparents in Lubeck, who arranged for their schooling in a local public school. One day the Gestapo arrived at their house, demanding to know why Elizabeth had not joined the Bund Deutscher Mädel (BDM), the Hitler Youth organization for girls. (In a section of this interview not included in the excerpt, as well as in later interviews, Elizabeth has explained that she then decided to join the BDM in order to keep the officials from suspecting her grandparents of disloyalty to the state.)

Unlike Frank S. and Carl H. (Excerpts 1 and 2), Elizabeth does not recall having school lessons in race science. On the other hand, she does remember the Nazi rituals that were an integral part of school life. Each morning, she explains, the students had to give the "Heil Hitler" greeting to their teacher. While Elizabeth resented this order, she knew that there were consequences if she failed to obey. She faced punishment from her school authorities for her intransigence; even more important, the school authorities would report her behavior to the local Gestapo, who then would be suspicious of the loyalty of

Elizabeth's grandparents. Thus Elizabeth risked not saluting the Führer only occasionally. As she explains, she and others could pretend that they were fumbling on the floor for a dropped handkerchief or a pencil while the oath was recited. But, she continues, there were only so many times one could do this.

Many of Elizabeth's attitudes about truth and authority came from her religious training and early childhood experiences. On the one hand, it was very important in her family to be truthful at all times: her father sacrificed his life to remain true to his convictions. On the other hand, Elizabeth knew that if she revealed her true feelings about the Nazis she would jeopardize her own safety and that of her entire family.

Commentary

Elizabeth D.

During the early years of Nazism, the decision to teach race science or exclude it from the curriculum depended largely on local town and school officials. In towns where the officials and teachers strongly endorsed the National Socialist Party, Nazi ideals were embedded early into the curriculum. However, the Germans were not uniformly enthusiastic and, in the 1930s, certain areas of Germany showed a greater allegiance to Hitler and to his policies than others. Despite the diverse response to Nazi policies in the early- and mid-1930s, official Nazi policy determined curriculum in schools throughout the country by the late 1930s.

A similar process occurred in the judicial system. In the early period of the Nazi regime, some legal decisions were sympathetic to the plight of the victims. However, as the Nazis consolidated their authority over the courts and judicial personnel, judges increasingly rendered opinions in accordance with Nazi guidelines. Evidence of this change is clear in the case (cited later in this section) that deals with the daughter of a Jehovah's Witness. Before the war, the courts were less willing to interfere with parent-child relationships, especially in matters of religion and personal conscience. But during the war, the courts strictly enforced Nazi policies without regard for relations between parents and their children (see the Judge's Letter).

The circular sent to Gestapo offices by the Gestapo chief Heinrich Müller on August 5, 1937, indicated that the courts had no power to protect the rights of Jehovah's Witnesses even if they had been found innocent or had served a stipulated sentence.

A sample of the statement that Jehovah's Witnesses were asked to sign at Dachau Concentration Camp is reprinted below. According to Elizabeth D., her father had refused to sign a similar statement and eventually lost his life because of his religious convictions.

Statement:

I_____born:_____in_____make the following statement:

1. I acknowledge that the International Association of Jehova's [sic] Witnesses advocate a false doctrine using their religious activities as a pretext in the pursuit of their subversive aims.

2. I have therefore totally rejected this organization and have freed myself emotionally from the sect.

3. I hereby undertake never again to work for the International Association of Jehova's Witnesses. I shall report any persons who approach me with the false doctrine of Jehova's Witnesses or those who in any way display sympathy for them. Should I receive any Jehova's Witness literature, I shall surrender it immediately to the nearest police station.

4. I shall in future observe the laws of the nation especially in the event of war when I shall take up arms to defend my Fatherland, and strive to become a whole-hearted member of the national community.

5. I have been informed that I must expect a further term of protective custody if I fail to observe the undertaking which I made today.

Signature[67]

Martin Gilbert describes the fate of Jehovah's Witnesses at Mauthausen shortly before the close of the war.

One of the last concentration camps under German control was Mauthausen, together with its satellite camps at Gusen, St. Valentin, Gunskirchen and Ebensee. In just over four months, more than thirty thousand people had been murdered at Mauthausen, or had died from starvation and disease. Jews and Gypsies formed the largest groups of those killed, but other groups had also been singled out by the Nazis: Homosexuals, Jehovah's Witnesses, Soviet Prisoners of War, and tens of thousands of Spanish republicans.[68]

Using

Elizabeth D. on her mother's lap with father and brother.

What were Elizabeth's conflicts about saluting the Führer? Frank (Excerpt 1) described a memory about saluting the flag. How did the options available to Elizabeth differ from those that Frank had? Were more options available to Elizabeth because she was not Jewish?

What is meant by the term "guilt by association"? How did the Nazis use this technique to control people? Discuss a specific incident in Elizabeth's story where the fear of "guilt by association" had an impact on her behavior.

Compare Elizabeth's decision to comply with regulations to salute the Nazi flag and Führer in her classroom with the decision of the employee in the defense plant in the reading "Do You Take the Oath" (in the Resource Book).

Does Elizabeth think that her compromises in the classroom contributed to the evil of the Nazi state? Does Elizabeth indicate that her education prepared her to resist supporting the Nazi regime?

Why would a society require students to salute their national leader? How does this regulation differ from practices that encourage students to salute their nation or pledge allegiance to their flag?

The memories of Elizabeth and other witnesses of the Third Reich can help teachers and students make distinctions between a democratic nation that encourages patriotism and tolerates dissent and a totalitarian society that insists upon total conformity and a demonstration of loyalty from all citizens. How would you distinguish between nationalism in a democratic society and nationalism in a totalitarian regime such as Nazi Germany? Can you make distinctions between patriotism and indoctrination?

In Gilbert's description of victims of Mauthausen, what are some of the common features among the groups marked for extermination?

Elizabeth often speaks to students in Facing History classes about her school days in Nazi Germany. She recommends that teachers show the film *Swastika* before her visit because the film shows the type of propaganda that was prevalent in Hitler's Germany. According to Elizabeth, images in films such as *Swastika* and in patriotic posters were particularly attractive to German people in the 1930s.

The reading "Childhood Memories" in the Resource Book provides supplementary details on Elizabeth's early years and her reactions to the Holocaust.

For information on ordering the film *Swastika* and borrowing samples of propaganda posters of the 1930s and 1940s, contact the Facing History Resource Center. Also available is a translated memorial book to Hitler with photographs illustrating the life of the Führer and his accomplishments: Germans obtained these photos by sending in empty cigarette boxes. In addition, the Resource Center has material on the techniques used by Nazi filmmakers such as Leni Riefenstahl and Hippler to popularize Adolf Hitler and his regime. See, for example, the episode "The Propaganda Battle" in Bill Moyers' documentary series *A Walk Through the Twentieth Century*.

A videotape of art teacher Barbara Traietti Halley teaching a lesson on examining and interpreting propaganda art is available at the Facing History Resource Center; lesson plan guides are also available.

See McKee's *Tomorrow the World* for a description of a girl who participated in a two-day youth rally in Weimar.

See the documentary *Force of Evil*, produced by WNEV-TV, Boston, which includes an interview of Elizabeth D. reflecting on her youth. A copy is available at the Facing History Resource Center.

For Further Reference

The following document is about the refusal of a daughter of Jehovah's Witnesses to give the Hitler salute. The document is a Judge's Letter in which a Nazi Minister of Justice (Otto Thierack) expresses his opinion on good and bad examples of sentencing during the Third Reich.

Refusal of the German Salute by a Child of School Age. Guardianship Court Judgment of 21 September 1940

An eleven-year-old girl has been noticed at school continually refusing to give the German salute. She gives her religious convictions as the reason and quotes several passages from the Bible. At school she shows a complete lack of interest in matters concerning the Führer.

The parents, who have another daughter of six, approve of this attitude and stubbornly refuse to influence the child in the contrary direction. They also refuse to give the German salute and refer to the biblical passage: 'Do nothing with a raised hand for this displeases the Lord.' They stick to this despite instructions from the court and from the headmaster of the school. The mother utterly refuses to speak to the child about it. The father is willing to do so but says the child must decide for herself. The parents show themselves to be opponents of the National Socialist state in other ways. They do not possess a swastika flag. They are excluded from the NSV because they had not joined in contributing although the father could afford it. Nevertheless they deny being opponents of the movement.

Because of their attitude the Youth Office has proposed the removal of both children from the care of their parents. The Guardianship Court has turned this down and has only ordered supervision, arguing in the judgement that it has not been proved that the parents are opponents of the National Socialist movement or have even fought against it; they simply do not 'regard the movement sympathetically and are not inclined to further it'. The judgement goes on to say: 'The parents are responsible for their personal attitude toward the National Socialist Movement only in so far as they break laws that relate to the movement.' The parents have to agree that the children must be brought up in the National Socialist spirit and that the school is bound to give this education. If the parents do not want to bring their children up in this spirit themselves or, from religious convictions, think it impossible for them to do so, they must be asked at least not to counteract the National Socialist education given by the school. Since the child is otherwise well brought up and the parents give the impression of having 'reliable characters' it may be assumed that they will make no further difficulties for the school in the future.

The Court of Appeal has revised the verdict of the Guardianship Court and removed the guardianship of both children from the parents because they are unsuitable to bring them up.

Comment by the Reich Minister of Justice:

The verdict of the judge of the Guardianship Court shows a misunderstanding of the principles of National Socialist youth education.

Those responsible for the education of German youth today are the parents, the school and the Hitler Youth (Law on the Hitler Youth of 1 December 1936). Working together, each in his own sphere, these fulfill the educational mission given to them by the community. The aim of the communal work of education is to educate youth physically, mentally and morally in the spirit of National Socialism for the service of the people and of the community. This aim can be achieved only through cooperation between parents, school and Hitler Youth. Every conflict and deviation in education endangers the common aim. Parents have been given a decisive role in education and a special responsibility. They are connected with the child by ties of blood. The child lives near them and continually watches his parents' habits and example. Education means guiding. Guiding means setting an example by their way of life. The child shapes his life according to his parents' example. What he hears and sees there, especially in early youth, he gradually adopts as a habit and a standard for his life. Therefore, the educational aim of the National Socialist State can be achieved only if parents are conscientious and responsible in thought and action and give the child a model example of how to behave in the communal life of our people. Part of the education of the German man or woman is the early conveying of respect and reverence for the symbols of the State and the movement. Here also the community expects active cooperation on the parents' part. Reserved neutrality here is just as damaging as combatting the National Socialist idea. Indifference towards education in patriotic citizenship, therefore, means a neglect by the parents of their duties and endangers the education of the child even if this is not immediately apparent.

. . .The danger for the child becomes apparent when the parents openly oppose education through the community. This was so here. Those who stubbornly refuse the German salute because of wrong doctrine, who exclude themselves for no reason from the socially constructive work of the NSV, purposely keep their children away from the Hitler Youth and are inaccessible to all advice, can no longer be said only to be "not sympathetically disposed" toward the movement or not to be further in it. Through their resistance they are fighting it and are its enemies. This is shown by their attitude and inclination.

The guardianship judge should therefore have deprived them of their guardianship with the simple explanation that parents who openly profess the ideas of the Jehovah's Witnesses are not suited for the education of their children in the National Socialist spirit.[69]

Excerpt 4: Krystyna (T-5)

This constant suspicion, suspense, this constant suspense. You are on the street, you [are] not safe. You are in school, you aren't safe. You go home again, and some good or bad news will await you at home.

Both Carl and Elizabeth (in Excerpts 2 and 3) offer insights into experiences of non-Jews in Germany who were attending school during the Third Reich. In this excerpt Krystyna, who grew up in Poland, speaks about her school experiences as a non-Jewish adolescent during the war.

One week before World War II broke out, Nazi Germany and the Soviet Union signed a Non-Aggression Pact agreeing to divide Poland into two parts. On September 1, 1939, Germans marched from the West into Poland, and on September 17th the Russian troops entered from the East.

Two million Polish Jews and twenty-two million Polish Christians came under Nazi control. Those portions of Poland which had been taken away from Germany following World War I (Danzig, West Prussia, Posen, and the eastern part of Upper Silesia) were reincorporated into the Reich in an area known as Wartheland that included the city of Lodz. The remaining portion of German-occupied Poland, which was not incorporated directly into the territory of the Reich, was known as the General Government and included the large urban areas of Warsaw, Lublin, and Cracow; Cracow became the capital of the puppet state, and Hans Frank, a Nazi legal expert who had belonged to the party since 1927, was appointed the Governor General.

Frank believed it was imperative to cleanse his capital of Jews as rapidly as possible. As he announced in a speech on April 12, 1940:

[I]f the authority of the National Socialist Reich is to be upheld, then it is unacceptable that representatives of the Reich should be obliged to meet Jews when they enter or leave the house, and are in this way liable to infection with epidemics. He [Frank] therefore intends to clear the city of Cracow of Jews, as far as at all possible, by November 1, 1940. There will be a major operation to move the Jews, on the grounds that it is absolutely intolerable that thousands upon thousands of Jews should go slinking around and occupy apartments in the city which the Fuehrer has granted the great honor of becoming the seat of a high Reich Authority . . . [70]

In the **Portraits** section, the testimonies of Nechama Tec, Sonia Weitz, and Rena Finder explain what the German occupation meant for Polish Jewish adolescents, discussing the suspension of formal schooling, separation of parents and children, and confinement in ghettos and concentration camps. Whatever opportunities these children had for education resulted from

228

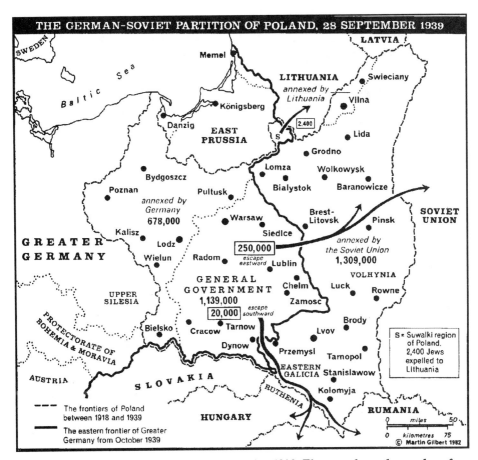

THE GERMAN-SOVIET PARTITION OF POLAND, 28 SEPTEMBER 1939

The German-Soviet partition of Poland, September 1939. The map shows the number of Jews living in the three principal divisions of Poland at the time of the German invasion. With the eastward extension of the frontiers of Greater Germany, nearly two million more Jews were brought under German rule: four times the number of Jews who had been living in Germany when Hitler came to power in January 1933.

attending clandestine schools or studying alone with available resources. These survivors were not able to resume formal education until the end of the war.

The excerpt from Krystyna's testimony describes the effect of the Nazi educational policies in her particular school in Warsaw. Krystyna explains how she and other Polish students managed to circumvent the restrictive educational policy: her teachers would "fail" their sixth graders so they would have to repeat the sixth grade before leaving elementary school. In the repeat year, teachers would cover junior high school material. Then groups of students transferred to the auxiliary trade schools, where they learned practical skills, such as sewing and hatmaking, to support the German war effort. Teachers in these schools often offered academic instruction, but the students sat at their machines and did not take notes in case German officials should make an unannounced visit. Also, to avoid detection, Krystyna's teachers did not use any textbooks and students were unable to read in preparation for classes. In such an educational setting, "we were always afraid," says Krystyna.

Before the war, fear was not part of Krystyna's life. She was born in Warsaw in 1928 and enjoyed a comfortable, middle-class childhood. She was not particularly aware of differences in religion and nationality among her friends, who were of diverse backgrounds. Her memory of a secure childhood in prewar Poland contrasts with those memories of Polish Jewish survivors who recall incidents of discriminatory behavior which marked them because they were Jewish.

The pleasant, secure environment ebbed as the war approached. Krystyna began speaking to her father about hatred among people; she was especially concerned about her friends, a set of twins, the children of a Polish Catholic father and a German Lutheran mother. One twin was raised Protestant while the other was raised Catholic, and by the time they were seven years old they engaged in bitter arguments about which twin was superior. Krystyna felt leery of Germans because adult friends warned her to be cautious of anyone with German blood. They might be pro-Nazi or pro-Hitler. This kind of talk, she recalls, began "all of a sudden," when she was eleven years old. When the war began, in September 1939, "all hell broke loose," she explains.

When they occupied Poland on September 1, 1939, the Nazis incorporated Warsaw into the administrative area of the General Government. They adopted a program for the destruction of Poland, beginning with the extinction of the intellectual and cultural life of the country. Shortly after establishing the capital of the General Government in Cracow, Governor General Hans Frank declared, "The Polish lands are to be changed into an intellectual desert." The educational directives denied Polish youth the right to university education. (However, due to the Nazi fears of epidemics, exceptions were made in educational policies for medical students.) Moreover, the Nazi educational regulations banned Polish language from elementary and secondary schools.

During the war, attendance in Polish elementary schools dropped to about half of what it had been in the prewar period. In Warsaw, where Krystyna was

230

attending school, there had been 380 elementary schools before the war; during the war only 175 elementary schools continued to operate. Trade schools offered the only education beyond the elementary level; Germans permitted these to remain open because they prepared Polish youth to serve wartime industries.

Krystyna remembers being constantly afraid of what might happen should Nazi authorities discover that she and her classmates were learning more than trade skills. Fear also dominated other aspects of her life, preventing her, for example, from helping Jews inside the Warsaw Ghetto. Once she saw a convoy of emaciated-looking Jewish teenagers. She wanted to offer them tomatoes and other fresh vegetables, but a voice within her kept warning her not to do anything foolish. If she were to help the Jewish children, she risked getting into trouble, and trouble was one thing Krystyna did not want. She had heard about people who were taken away for interrogation by the SS and never returned.

Krystyna and her mother were evacuated from Warsaw after the 63-day uprising in 1944. Along with thousands of other women and children, they were transported to Bergen–Belsen in October of that year. They remained there until liberation by Russian forces the following spring. For months afterward, mother and daughter searched displaced persons camps for missing relatives.

Commentary

Historically, Russians perceived Poles as their inferiors, a view that persisted after the Soviets came to power in 1917. Thus, in the fall of 1939 following the partitioning of Poland, the Soviet forces simply arrested those Polish officers captured in the area under their control; a year later, they murdered thousands of these officers and buried them in a mass grave in the Katyn Forest. Krystyna's father, an officer who had been called into active service when the war began, was one of the victims in this mass murder.

The Nazi administration in occupied Poland regarded the Poles as "subhumans." Historian Richard Lukas explains:

> [T]he Poles [from the Nazi perspective] were untermenschen (subhumans) who occupied a land which was part of the Lebensraum (living space) coveted by the superior German race. Thus the Poles were to be subjected to a program of extermination and enslavement. As Hitler made clear even before the German invasion of Poland, "The destruction of Poland is our primary task. The aim is not the arrival at a certain line but the annihilation

of living forces. . . . Be merciless! Be brutal! . . . It is necessary to proceed with maximum severity. . . . The war is to be a war of annihilation."[71]

Despite the effort of the Nazi authorities to extinguish Polish culture and destroy national unity, Lukas argues that the Nazi policies actually served to intensify Polish nationalistic sentiment.

Compensating for the enormous restriction on cultural activities, the Poles established a system of elementary and secondary schools in the annexed lands where the Germans had prohibited them. In the General Government, since the Germans allowed some elementary schools, special attention had to be given to establishing secret secondary schools. Various organizations, such as the Secret Organization of Teachers (Tajna Organizacja Nauczycielstwa), cooperated in this work, and by 1941 the Government Delegacy created a Department of Education and Culture to supervise educational affairs. Czeslaw Wycech, a quiet, unobtrusive academician, played a key role in the establishment of the Polish underground educational system. By 1942-1943, 5,252 teachers taught over 86,000 elementary school students, and over 5,600 teachers taught more than 48,000 secondary school students in the General Government. In the annexed lands, where the difficulties in establishing secret schools were even greater than in the General Government, 1,434 Polish teachers taught 18,713 elementary school students, and 205 teachers taught 11,671 secondary school students in 1942-1943.

The Germans were unaware that underground schooling was as extensive as it really was; in consequence, they did not give major attention to cracking down on it, especially during the latter part of the war. Nevertheless, the Germans arrested and executed a large number of Polish teachers; in the latter part of 1942, the Germans arrested 367 teachers, most of whom were sent to Auschwitz, where they perished. Until the Germans embarked upon the systematic murder of the Jews, there were by 1942 twenty primary and secondary schools in which 7,000 students were enrolled in the Warsaw Ghetto. Even university classes were held. Polish educators connected with the Secret Organization of Teachers also cooperated with Jewish educational officials.[72]

Krystyna herself did not witness the Warsaw Ghetto Uprising that erupted in the spring of 1943 and lasted for six weeks. She did hear an eyewitness account from her uncle who had been living across the street from the ghetto walls. (See the portrait of Helen K. in the **Portraits** section for a discussion of the Warsaw Ghetto Uprising.)

The Warsaw Uprising in the late summer and fall of 1944 represented the effort of Poles to rid the city of Germans. The surviving Jews of the Warsaw Ghetto joined the national uprising. The resistance leaders had expected the

Allied forces to assist them in their efforts but the anticipated assistance never arrived. Krystyna and other survivors of the uprising refer to the brutality of the German troops. One eyewitness of August 7, 1944, had the impression that the SS intended to kill everyone in Warsaw:

> When we passed No. 9 Gorczewska Street (a house which belonged to nuns), we were called into the house and ordered to carry out the corpses which were there. The courtyard was a dreadful sight. It was an execution place. Heaps of corpses were lying there; I think they must have been collecting there for some days, for some were already swollen and others quite freshly killed. There were bodies of men, women, and children, all shot through the backs of their heads. It is difficult to state exactly how many there were. There must have been several layers carelessly heaped up. The men were ordered to carry away the bodies—we women to bury them. We put them in anti-tank trenches and then filled these up. In this way we filled up a number of such trenches on Gorczewska Street. I had the impression that during the first days of the Rising everybody was killed.[73]

Using

How did educational opportunities for Jewish children in occupied Poland compare with those of their non-Jewish peers? See the excerpts of Nechama and Menachem and compare their experiences with those described by Krystyna. Also compare Krystyna's testimony with one of the following testimonies in the **Portraits** section: Nechama Tec, Rena Finder, or Sonia Weitz.

Why do you think the Governor General Hans Frank set out to make Poland an intellectual and cultural desert? What would be some major measures necessary for accomplishing this?

What were the new goals of education in German-occupied Poland?

Why do you think that the Nazi authorities in Poland were opposed to Polish Christian students studying languages and reading books?

Compare Krystyna's education with that of Elizabeth D. in Germany. How do you account for the different educational programs for non-Jews in Germany and Poland?

Excerpt 5: Walter K. (T-97)

I was the only Jew in my class and I was quite discriminated about. You know some boys spit on me and they told me "you dirty Jew" and things like that as a child.

In this excerpt Walter offers his testimony about public school life for German Jews during the Nazi era.

Walter lived in Peiskretscham, a town of 18,000 near Gleiwitz in Silesia. Walter's teacher, who belonged to the Nazi Party, beat him for no apparent reason. Walter recalls that he had no way to protest abuse and mistreatment. The principal could not help: unlike Walter's teacher, he was not a member of the Nazi Party. Walter's parents were unable to go to the police to register a complaint because the police were not interested in protecting Jews. Walter's classmates remained passive bystanders while their Jewish classmate suffered humiliation and mistreatment. In fact, throughout Walter's description of school in Peiskretscham, he does not mention any individual who risked helping him.

Walter was born in 1924. His father earned a comfortable living as an owner of a grocery store and was able to accumulate some savings despite the economic uncertainties of the 1930s.

From the beginning of the Nazi era, Walter and other members of his family experienced antisemitism. Walter was just beginning his public school education when the Nazis came to power. He was the only Jewish pupil in a class of fifty-five boys. His classmates singled him out as "the Jew" and stood by without protesting when instructors abused and insulted him. During extracurricular activities Walter often found himself the butt of jokes and pranks, and on one occasion he was told point blank that Jews were not permitted in the swimming pool. Walter's father and two uncles were arrested and detained at Buchenwald for three months. They were released only after the family provided proof that they had visas to enter Cuba and were planning for the entire family to leave Germany as soon as possible.

In 1939 Walter and his family, along with approximately 930 other passengers, boarded the SS *St. Louis*, bound for Havana, Cuba. Later, when Cuban and American authorities refused to allow the *St. Louis* to land, the passengers were forced to return to Europe, where Belgium, France, England, and Holland agreed to accept the refugees. Walter's family were assigned to go to France.

Most of Walter's family did not survive the war. After the German occupation of France, Walter's parents and sisters were arrested and probably deported to death camps. Walter never again heard from them. Only Walter and his older brother, Herbert, managed to avoid arrest by constantly shifting their hiding places in the French countryside. Some of their time was spent in a French school and during other periods they took part in French resistance activities.

Commentary

According to Richard Rubenstein and John Roth, the behavior of Walter's teacher was not unusual in the Nazi era, while the principal's lack of enthusiasm for Nazism was atypical of the era:

> German school teachers and university professors were not Hitler's adversaries. . . . Quite the opposite; the teaching profession proved one of the most reliable segments of the population as far as National Socialism was concerned. Throughout the Weimar era, Germany's educational establishment, continuing its long authoritarian tradition, remained unreconciled to democracy and nationalism. Once in power, the Nazis expunged dissenting instructors, but there were not many. On the other hand, at least two leading Nazis, the rabid antisemites Heinrich Himmler and Julius Streicher, had formerly been teachers. Eventually more than 30% of the top Nazi party leadership came from that background. Teachers, especially from elementary schools, were by far the largest professional group represented in the party. Altogether almost 97% of them belonged to the Nazi Teachers' Association, and more than 30% of that number were members of the Nazi party itself. From such instructors, German boys and girls learned what the Nazis wanted them to know. Hatred of Jews was central in that curriculum.[74]

The incident of the SS *St. Louis* illustrates the problems that occurred when German Jews sought asylum outside Germany in the late 1930s. The Cuban authorities had agreed to the immigration of German Jews. Nevertheless, when the ocean liner arrived in the Havana harbor, the Cuban government refused to allow the passengers to disembark even after representatives of the American Jewish community attempted to intervene on their behalf. The liner then headed for Miami. Here, too, the passengers were not permitted to disembark, and other harbors along the eastern seaboard of the United States followed suit. Finally the liner was forced to return to Europe, where four countries—Great Britain, France, Holland, and Belgium—agreed to take some of the passengers.

As it turned out, the asylum in western European states did not protect the refugees on the *St. Louis*. When the war broke out, German forces occupied

France, Holland, and Belgium and rounded up Jews. Many of the former passengers of the *St. Louis* were caught up in the roundups, including Walter's parents and sisters.

Using

Walter relates his memory of antisemitic incidents in his school in the 1930s. How does his story differ from Frank's memories?

"The Birthday Party" ("Preparing for Obedience," in the Resource Book) relates an event in which the authority of a teenager in the Hitler Youth transcended that of adults. Do you note any similarities between the patterns of authority in that story and the patterns described in Walter's excerpt?

The teacher whom Walter describes acted in one way while the principal acted in another. Do you think the principal jeopardized his position at school by not showing a total commitment to Nazi policies? What might have been the consequences if the Nazi authorities realized that the principal did not give his full loyalty to Nazi policies and behavior?

A large majority of the teaching profession was attracted to National Socialism and more than thirty percent were active in the teachers association affiliated with the Nazi Party. What factors in Nazism might have appealed to German teachers?

Before joining the Facing History staff as a Program Associate, high school teacher Joyce Kazanjian integrated selections from the montage "Childhood Memories" in her ten-week Facing History unit, which constituted the final segment of an American history survey course. During the opening weeks she examined the issues of society and the individual and antisemitism; between the third and fifth weeks she presented the rise of National Socialism, Nazi philosophy and policy; and in the sixth week she explored how German society became indoctrinated with Nazi ideology. The final weeks focused on the Holocaust and judgment at Nuremberg, as well as a study of the Armenian genocide. (See the complete outline of her course below.)

Kazanjian did not use the montage "Childhood Memories" until the middle weeks of the course. Nevertheless, dominant themes raised in the montage excerpts came up in the discussions of the relationship between society and the individual and prejudice that took place in the initial sessions.

As the students moved into the middle weeks of the course and considered what factors weakened the fabric of German democracy and facilitated Hitler's rise to power, the use of video testimonies deepened their understanding of what discriminatory legislation meant in the Third Reich. Having studied the long history of antisemitism in Europe during the first weeks of the course, they could empathize with Frank S. and Nechama Tec in "Childhood Memories," who relate the pain they encountered because they were Jews. The two excerpts of Rachel G., a Belgian Jewish child who hid in convents and Catholic homes during the war, sparked a discussion on the difficulty of suppressing one's true identity.

The class discussion of the excerpt of Walter K. most vividly illustrated the power of these testimonies with Kazanjian's students. Kazanjian prepared the class for viewing the excerpt with a series of questions about the contents of Walter's testimony: What are Walter's circumstances? How does he tell his story? Where could Walter have turned for help? What was the attitude of Walter's principal? How did Walter's testimony compare with that of Frank S.?

After hearing Walter recount the discrimination he as a Jew suffered from non-Jewish classmates and teachers in a Nazi school, Kazanjian's students discussed their thinking about racism.

One of the most interesting parts of the discussion occurred when Kazanjian asked students to compare the testimonies of Frank (Excerpt 1) and Walter. One student observed that Frank did not show as much emotion as Walter in recalling his childhood and reflected: "I don't think there is a lesser wrong. What happened to both of them; not one was worse than another." According to Kazanjian the sensitivity demonstrated in this comparison was indicative of what was taking place with all the students: they were beginning to put themselves in the situations of other people and look at issues from a variety of perspectives. "My students," says Kazanjian, "were moving beyond their self-centered views, and the more they broadened their outlook, the more they felt capable of taking action to change things rather than reacting to circumstances."

During the final weeks of the course when students met Holocaust survivor Rita Kesselman, they widened their perspectives on the Holocaust even further: they were able to compare Rita's experiences with those of Nechama Tec, Frank S., and Walter K.

Before using Facing History, Kazanjian and her colleagues had noticed among students a disturbing number of racist comments and derogatory remarks about non-white minorities. Because the school has an all-white population, Kazanjian thought that student intolerance derived in part from lack of exposure to people of other races and ethnic backgrounds. These excerpts exposed her students to Jewish and non-Jewish survivors from nations in western and eastern Europe and promoted discussion about racism.

For additional discussion on schooling in the Nazi era and attitudes among the teaching profession, see the video montage "Friedrich," designed to accompany reading the novel by that title, and the video montage "Childhood Experiences of German Jews."

The first half hour of the video montage "Flight from Destiny" chronicles the story of the SS *St. Louis*, using interviews of passengers who survived the war and representatives of the American Jewish agencies that tried to arrange for the disembarkation of the passengers. Walter K. and his brother both appear in "Flight from Destiny."

For the story of a young girl who, like Walter, survived the ill-fated voyage of the SS *St. Louis* and spent the war years in France, see "Judy's Story," in Eliach, ed., *I Too Had Dreams of a Bright Future*.

The feature film *Voyage of the Damned* (1974) traces the history of the 1939 journey of the SS *St. Louis* and its passengers.

Excerpt 6: Nechama Tec

> *I would go home and I would cry. I would ask my father how can they . . . hate the Jews so much, people that I like, how can they hate us so. We haven't done anything to them.*

In this excerpt, Nechama recalls what it was like to be a Jewish child in hiding among Polish Christians during the war. In particular, she remembers one sunny afternoon in 1943 or 1944 when she was speaking to a non-Jewish girl, Janka, whom she believed was a friend. Janka was repeating all the negative rumors and stereotypes she had heard about Jews. Nechama interrupted her, asking if she truly believed all these stories, and Janka retorted that all Jews were much too skillful to reveal their perfidy. Of course all the stories of Jews were true, she insisted, and Nechama was foolish to question them.

While these incidents were difficult for Nechama, she admits that she became more and more accustomed to such antisemitic remarks from the Christian world. As a defense, she began to identify with a Christian persona more than with her true Jewish identity.

Before the war Nechama had not been particularly concerned about her Jewish identity. She was born in Lublin, a large city in Poland, in 1931. Her city had a respected Jewish minority of 40,000, approximately twenty percent of the

238

Jews Marked Out for Death, 20 January 1942. At the Wannsee suburb of Berlin, German officials gathered on 20 January 1942 to discuss the final destruction of European Jewry. They also noted (see map) what they believed to be the precise number of Jews still to be killed. At the Wannsee Conference plans were made for what was called the "Final Solution," to be carried out by means of slave labour for all able-bodied Jews, the separation of men from women, and mass deportation.

SURVIVORS, AND THOSE WHO RETURNED, 1945

NORWAY
1,000

FINLAND
2,000

SWEDEN

BALTIC STATES
25,000

DENMARK
5,500

DANZIG
8,000

Memel

HOLLAND
20,000

WESTERN
SOVIET
UNION
300,000

BELGIUM
40,000

GERMANY
330,000

POLAND
225,000

LUXEMBOURG
1,000

CZECHOSLOVAKIA
44,000

AUSTRIA
7,000

HUNGARY
300,000

RUMANIA
430,000

FRANCE
200,000

SWITZ.

ITALY
35,000

YUGOSLAVIA
12,000

BULGARIA
50,000

SPAIN

Frontiers
of 1937

ALBANIA
200

GREECE
12,000

miles   250
kilometres   400

© Martin Gilbert 1982

7

161

In addition to the 300,000 survivors of the concentration camps, over a million and a half European Jews survived Hitler's efforts to destroy them. Some Jews everywhere, but particularly in France, Belgium, Holland, and Italy, survived because the Germans took longer to deport them than time finally allowed: the Allied landings on continental Europe coming while deportations were still in progress. Other Jews all over Europe escaped deportation altogether because they were sheltered by individual non-Jews who risked their own lives to save Jews.

total population. Nechama's father owned a large factory and the family lived in comfort. She remembers an elegant apartment, servants, and tutors. Nechama and her sister received an excellent education and learned to speak Polish much more fluently than their parents, who had not had the same educational advantages. Thinking back on the prewar era, Nechama admits that she and her sister were rather spoiled and took their comforts for granted.

When the war broke out, circumstances changed dramatically for Nechama's family, making her more aware of her Jewish identity. The family was forced to move into a small, cramped apartment in the Lublin Ghetto during the first year of the war. For brief periods, Nechama and her sister were separated from their parents and placed in Christian homes for protection. However, these separations did not work out, and life was becoming increasingly dangerous for Jews in Lublin.

In 1942 Nechama's father arranged to pay for his entire family to stay in the home of a Christian family in Kielce, a town hundreds of miles from Lublin, where they would not be recognized. In this situation, Nechama's parents remained "hidden" inside the apartment of the host family twenty-four hours a day because their "faulty" manner of speaking Polish would have immediately betrayed their Jewish identity. Nechama and her sister, who had blond hair and blue eyes and who had mastered the Polish language, "passed" as relatives of the host Polish family. They assumed Christian names, learned rituals and prayers of Catholicism, and memorized the genealogy of their new family. Daily they mingled with non-Jews in school and in their neighborhood; they remained the principal links between their parents and the outside world. In these circumstances, Nechama and her sister grew up "overnight." As their father observed, "Childhood is a luxury. Jewish children cannot afford it." Her father tried to help his daughters survive life in the Aryan world. He warned them not to be upset by the negative remarks made against Jews, explaining that people make such remarks out of ignorance and should not be blamed for their behavior.

It was during this same period that Nechama had the troubling conversation with her friend Janka that she recounts in the "Childhood Memories" excerpt. Nechama has never forgotten what it was like to hear someone she considered a friend malign Jews, and she often mentions this incident when she speaks to young people about the dangers of prejudice and stereotyping.

Nechama, her sister, and her parents all survived the war and returned to their native Lublin before deciding to leave Poland. Of the 40,000 Lublin Jews in prewar Poland, only 150 returned to the city at the close of the war. There were only three intact families: Nechama's was one of them. To compound the troubling nature of these statistics, Nechama and other members of her family were saddened by the reactions of the host family who had given them refuge for two years: they specifically asked not to be identified as having offered asylum to Jews, fearing reprisals from their neighbors.

Commentary

After the war, when Nechama and her family learned how unreceptive the inhabitants of Lublin were to their return, they emigrated to the United States. Nechama married, raised a family, and obtained her doctoral degree. Today she is a professor of sociology at the University of Connecticut.

For more than thirty years, Nechama did not speak of the war and tried to avoid thinking about it. Her research in sociology focused on questions of urban life. Then, in the 1970s, her memories began to stir. In time these memories became so powerful that she felt the need to write a memoir of her childhood. *Dry Tears* originally appeared in 1982 and is now widely used in classes where the Holocaust is studied. In working on her own story, Dr. Tec became interested in learning a more general context: How many Poles risked their safety to rescue Jews? What were the motivations of rescuers? What did Jews in hiding have to do to "pass" in the Christian world? Why did some Poles betray Jews while others went to considerable risk to save them? In order to answer these questions, Dr. Tec conducted a systematic study of Polish rescuers that appeared in her monograph *When Light Pierced the Darkness* in 1985.

Using

What did Nechama's father mean by saying, "Childhood is a luxury Jewish children cannot afford"?

Nechama's father said that prejudice comes from ignorance and that those who display it should be forgiven. What did he mean? How do you explain such ignorance when you consider that several high-ranking Nazi officials had doctorates in the arts and sciences? At what point do we forgive people for ignorance and at what point do we hold them responsible?

Nechama and her family were saved by a poor family that needed money for their services. What other motivations did non-Jews have for helping Jews and other minorities during the Holocaust?

Why did Nechama say it was a positive development for her when she became less sensitive to antisemitic remarks during the time when she and her sister were passing as non-Jews?

Recently, when Nechama spoke to a group of students about her experiences in Poland, she observed how important it was for contemporary youth to hear about the past:

> *History offers you a unique opportunity to enrich your personal life. When you hear about far away times and far away places, you temporarily identify with the characters you are hearing about and you take on their roles. This gives you an opportunity to add to your own experience and your own life. I hope to contribute to your experiences by telling you about my own life.*

In listening to Nechama, did you gain insights into what life was like in Poland during the war? What things did you learn from Nechama's personal testimony that you had not learned in reading some of the documents of the period?

The Facing History Resource Center has a class set of *Dry Tears* and copies of *When Light Pierced the Darkness*. In addition, there is a 35-minute video presentation by Nechama Tec and Ervin Staub, discussing motivations for helping and how the study of the Holocaust aids in research on altruism and prosocial behavior. This presentation is described in the proceedings of the Second Annual Facing History Conference "Making a Difference in the Shadow of History: Avenues to Participation," in Appendix 2.

One of the most painful passages in *Dry Tears* comes toward the end of the memoir when Dr. Tec recalls how the Homars, the Polish family from Kielce that rescued Nechama and her family, requested that no one know they helped Jews. This passage could be used for a discussion about the nature of antisemitism in Poland and why such feelings persisted even after the defeat of the Nazis. It should also be noted that a *pogrom* took place in Kielce in the summer of 1945. One hundred and twenty-five Jewish survivors returned to Kielce, Poland, where 19,000 Jews (one-third of the town's population) had lived before the war. Forty-three of these returning Jews were killed in the pogrom. (A pogrom is a popular demonstration against a minority group that is inspired by local or national leadership and is supported by the general population of an area. In contrast to the "Final Solution," which was tightly organized from the top leadership of the Third Reich, a pogrom tends to be more spontaneous so that the leadership does not have sufficient control to direct it.)

[After the liberation of their town] everything, indeed was changing too drastically and too fast. Even our relationship with the Homars had changed. They behaved toward us in a constrained, uneasy kind of way that made us feel uncomfortable and somewhat at a loss. Was it hard for them to accept us as free people, who were no longer dependent on them? We continued to regard them as our benefactors, acutely conscious that it was only thanks to them that we were alive.

At least a partial explanation soon emerged. One evening all of us, including Ziutka and Tadek, gathered around the table for tea and bread. The Homars were more tense than ever, and all of us were uncomfortable. For a while we engaged in small talk, although we all felt that eventually something else would have to be said. Finally Ziutka, the bluntest of them all, started out hesitantly: "Well . . ." Stammering and embarrassed, she continued, "we want to ask you. . ." And then, without looking at anyone, she finally came out with it. The Homars wanted us to leave Kielce as Poles, without revealing our true identity. They did not want anyone to know that they had helped a Jewish family to survive.

When Ziutka finished, we were stunned. There was a long silence. Not I, not my sister, not my mother could think of anything to say. In the end, my father, in an even but sadly quiet voice, agreed. He added that we were extremely grateful for what they had done for us, and that they ought to be proud of having saved our lives. His tone was flat, as if at last he was tired. The Homars' request may have been too much even for a strong man like him. We avoided looking at him and at one another.

Without commenting on what my father had said, Ziutka asked when we intended to leave. Clearly they wanted us to do so as soon as possible.

Perhaps, they were not actually sorry or ashamed about having saved us, but they undoubtedly felt that their friends and neighbors would not approve of what they had done. We had no reason to doubt that they were right. After all, they had to continue living among these people, and they had to be concerned about their own safety. All this was logical and reasonable enough. Why, then, were we so upset?

We were upset because they themselves failed to reassure us that they were glad we were alive and felt gratified by the part they played in our rescue. Expressions of such sentiments would have dispelled our doubts and lifted our spirits. Their failure to do so left us hurt, bewildered, and with lingering suspicions.[75]

Dry Tears

Excerpt 7: Rachel G. #1 (T-139)

My father took me. My mother was crying, crying so . . . and my father took me to the tramway. I remember my father crying like a baby in the middle of the street while he was taking me to those people . . . to strangers.

This excerpt from the testimony of Rachel, and the excerpt from the testimony of Zezette L. that follows, focus on the experiences of child survivors from Belgium, one of the western European countries occupied by the Nazis during the war years.

In this excerpt in "Childhood Memories," Rachel recounts the separation from her parents in the winter of 1942, when the Nazi administration in Belgium began the roundup and deportation of Belgian Jews. The landlady of the house in which eight-year old Rachel and her parents lived made arrangements with her nephew, who was a priest, to have the girl hidden. The separation was difficult and painful. On one occasion Rachel's father, a tailor, risked his life to visit his daughter. Rachel remembers that this visit occurred on her birthday, and her father brought a special gift—a new suit with a watch attached.

German forces invaded Belgium in the spring of 1940. By the following fall, the Nazis had established a military administration that enacted a series of racial laws over the next two years. In October 1940 the occupying force singled out Jews, requiring them to register with local authorities and dismissing them from the civil service and the legal profession. The Nazis simultaneously began the economic destruction of Belgian Jews. The following year, the military administration imposed a curfew and ordered all Jewish residents in Belgium relocated to the four cities of Antwerp, Brussels, Liege and Charleroi. In June 1942, Jews were required to wear the Yellow Star, and men (ages 16 to 60) and women (ages 16 to 40) were assigned to a Belgian quota for the first deportations. The security police established a transit camp for prospective deportees at Malines.

Rachel, born in Brussels in 1934, came from a native Belgian Jewish family. Before the war and during the first years of occupation, she continued to spend time with her non-Jewish friends. After Jews were required to wear the Yellow Star, she would try to remove hers while playing—she did not want to stand out, and she wanted to stay with the other little girls.

Belgian Jews faced their greatest threat during the period of deportations that began in western European countries in July 1942. The Jewish Council

245

assisted the military administration in ordering Jews to report to the forced labor camps. Those who defied the order faced immediate arrest and deportation.

Nevertheless, Jewish resistance organizations did what they could to slow these efforts. By warning the community of the impending roundups, resistance workers managed to save thousands of Belgian Jews, including almost 4,000 children.

Rachel recalls how her mother reacted to the rumors by going to the landlady of their apartment house and pleading: "They are taking away the children. All Rachel's little Jewish friends are going. Can you do something about my daughter? Can you take her and hide her somewhere?"

The landlady agreed to contact a relative who was a priest; he arranged for Rachel to hide as a Christian student in one of the convent schools. For the next three years, Rachel remembers living as a "Catholic little girl." She not only stayed with nuns in several convent schools, but also lived with a Catholic farming family as a foster child. What stands out in Rachel's memory is the confusion she felt about who she was or where she belonged. Repeatedly she was called upon to leave her convent and walk to a new hiding place. And she remembers that she had several different names during these years.

Commentary

The Nazi occupation of Belgium resembled that of other European countries, but there were several features that distinguished the Belgian experience. First, the Jewish population had a very high proportion of non-Belgians: historians estimate that at least ninety percent of the Jews living in Belgium on the eve of the war were not natives and spoke neither Flemish nor French. Second, neither the military administration nor the civil service carried out the antisemitic legislation with sufficient vigor to meet Nazi standards of efficiency. Of the 60,707 Jews living in Belgium in 1939, the authorities managed to register approximately 42,000 at the time of deportations in 1942-1943, and they estimated that an additional 10,000 were unregistered children. Finally, Belgium had one of the most organized and successful resistance organizations, the Comité des Juifs (CDJ). In contrast to the situation in Holland, where more than eighty percent of the Jewish population was eventually placed in transports, fifty-three percent of Belgian Jewry suffered this fate. The CDJ was successful, in part, because it had the cooperation and support of non-Jewish organizations, including the churches and child service organizations.

Helen Fein has pointed out the special efforts of the resistance organizations to save Jewish children.

> Its [the CDJ's] most impressive achievement was to save the lives of 3,000 of the estimated 4,000 Jewish children saved in Belgium. These children were placed in private homes and institutions, disguised as Aryan Belgians. They were recruited by special "assistants" from their mothers who were not informed of the children's whereabouts for fear that they would visit the children and expose them and their temporary guardians to reprisals. A circle of "godmothers" constituted the link between the home, the child, and the CDJ, representing the parents and guaranteeing the children's return to them. The CDJ was generously assisted by the official Belgian child-care organizations for public assistance and all the resources of the Catholic Church. Madame Yvonne Nevejen, Director General of l'Oeuvre Nationale de l'Enfance, arranged for the placement of Jewish children in the institutions and Cardinal de Roey authorized this action, explicitly proscribing efforts to convert them. The Cardinal also acted "to temper the pro-Nazi zeal of a certain number of people who called themselves believing Catholics, including the Burgomaster of Greater Antwerp."[76]

Using

What might have been some of the difficulties that Rachel had to deal with as she hid her identity as a Jew?

Why do you think the details of the birthday visit remain so vivid in Rachel's memory today?

Holocaust survivor and author Kati David observes that survivors who were children during the Holocaust rarely refer to the prevalence of bombs and wartime noises in recounting events of their early years. In listening to Rachel describe the first years of World War II, does she give any indication of serious concern about air raids and bombs threatening her community?

The documentary entitled *As If It Were Yesterday* contains interviews of men and women involved in rescue activity in Belgium. The documentary examines the motivations of those involved in rescue work and the risks they took to save Belgian Jews. *As If It Were Yesterday* is available at the Facing History Resource Center on half-inch VHS.

In putting together the documentary, the filmmakers came across a woman who had hidden Dori Katz as a young girl during the war years and informed Katz about their discovery. About five years ago, Katz went back to Belgium for a reunion with her rescuer.

The return to Belgium stirred Dori Katz's memories of her childhood. Over the last few years she had written several poems that refer to her childhood during the Holocaust. Compare her memories with those of Rachel. What are the similarities and differences in a way the poet Dori speaks of hiding as a child in Belgium with the way Rachel recounts her Belgian childhood in a video testimony?

Selections from the Poetry of Dori Katz, Child Survivor

Hiding
Hiding in other people's houses
First my mind must be absolutely calm
like water in a well,
of those back streets of childhood
unvisited for days but for the wind
moving a little dust from one tone to the next.
Then perhaps you might appear,
the four of you emerging in the street,
your faces ruddy from the unhampered wind. Now
you're in the house again, around the kitchen table;
father and son between wife and daughter, and me,
I'm squatting in a corner, crying, still
the wild child it will take months to tame.
It's very quiet in the room, you're praying
upset by my display of grief.
Slowly the child leaves her corner to join you in your meal.
This time no one will drive up to the door
at midnight to give warning,
this time no one will have to hide in the attic;
if questioned, I'll simply close my eyes and disappear.

Yes, my mind must be absolutely calm
to put myself back in your life
as the converted niece some dead friend gave you.
Remember the five of us kneeling in church, then strolling
through the town like any other family there?
The five of us working in the fields,
my job to sit under the cherry trees, banging a pot
to scare the blackbirds from the bough;
I scattered chicken feed and fetched the lambs.
After the Sunday meal, the father took me on his lap
to teach me Flemish songs and prayers.
And so it might have been, the little Jewish girl
you saved from damnation worse than Auschwitz
would grow up one of yours. Instead, at night,

I walked into my sleep like Bluebeard's wife
going to that forbidden room where dolls,
their stuffing coming out,
stared at me with faces like my mother's
and hanging by his hair, a man
turning into my father, burned and revolved.
Afterwards, I'd cry for hours
calling my name, my own banned, Yiddish name,
refusing the comfort of your crucifix.
Now when I try to find you, faceless figures turn their backs on me. A
smell of lard cooking
and of incense surfaces then retreats.
Unreconciled to my recurrent dream,
I can't imagine seeing you staring from streetcars
rattling uphill, or queuing up at banks
or waving from a boat going to America.
Since you won't budge, I am the one who must go back,
after so many years, to those deserted streets,
find your house, knock on the door and ask to be taken in.

The Story of Esther Gens

Esther Gens

Esther Gens, a Polish Jew who "passed" in the Christian world, can never forget the painful separation from her brothers. Before her parents had been forced to move to the ghetto, her mother located two farmers in the neighborhood: one farmer agreed to take care of Esther's twelve-year-old brother while the other agreed to take in Esther and her thirteeen-year-old brother. Soon thereafter, the farmer caring for Esther and her brother reported his wards to the Nazis and a Nazi arrived at the farm.

"I remember the farmer and soldier talking in whispers. The next thing I knew, we were going with the Nazi."

"By the mere random chance of my being female, blond, and blue-eyed, I had a good shot at avoiding detection [Esther continues]. To this day I still don't understand why, in some mysterious way, the soldier tried to save me. As we were walking along with the German soldier, he turned to me and said, 'Go back to the house.' After that I never saw my brothers again."

For the duration of the war years Esther "passed" with a number of Polish Christian families. She was never certain of her identity and had tremendous suspicions of the farmers who kept her in their homes. In one farmer's family she was treated as a Polish farmhand and sent to work as a shepherd.

"Being in a green meadow surrounded by bucolic beauty [she recalls], it seemed as if I were free. But I knew better. I knew what had happened to my brothers. There was the ever constant fear of being discovered, which is as keen as being discovered itself. I became proficient at being a chameleon in acting out the right role at the right time. The freedom which the sheep, the dogs, the birds enjoyed made me envious, because it had been denied to me."

Excerpt 8: Zezette L. (T-100)

> *I worked like hell to be as inconspicuous as possible [at Auschwitz]. . . . I think that probably I was trying to survive. . . . I was ripped apart from my parents and I'm sure I was traumatized. . . . I was probably completely traumatized.*

This excerpt deals with Zezette's memory of her two years in Auschwitz. Zezette was thirteen years old when she arrived at the camp in the spring of 1943; she was immediately separated from her parents. She remained at Auschwitz until the winter of 1944 and spent the closing months of the war at the women's concentration camp of Ravensbruck. As she remembers, she never opened her mouth while she was in the camps. She knew no one; she never encountered any sort of human kindness from inmates or guards. "I was dehumanized," she states.

The interviewer urges Zezette to remember stories similar to those of survivors who remember being helped as a child by others. However, Zezette's memory of Nazi extermination camps includes no recollections of individuals expressing care for others or of individuals singing and trying to carry on as if life was normal.

"What did you do in your day at Auschwitz?" continues the interviewer. Zezette mentions her memory of the roll call (*appel*), her arduous work carrying stones and later working in a munitions factory, and her time peeling potatoes as well as hours spent suffering from the discomfort of dysentery. What stands out most forcefully in this description of daily life at the camp is the total loneliness that the young teenager experienced. To this day Zezette finds it hard to convey to others what the camp was like and what her feelings about the experience were—and are—forty years after the Holocaust.

Born in Belgium in 1929, Zezette was eleven years old in the spring of 1940 when the Germans invaded and occupied her country. Her parents decided to go into hiding, placing their son with Trappist monks and their daughter with nuns in a convent school. Zezette found it exceedingly difficult to adjust to her Catholic identity. Literally overnight, she had been placed under the care of nuns and told to think of herself as a Catholic girl and practice the appropriate rituals. While Rachel G. (Excerpt 7) recalls how she acclimatized to life among the Christians and made friends, Zezette primarily recollects how miserable she felt having to live a life of deceit. Finally, one day while she was at confession, she blurted out that she was Jewish. The nuns decided that she should be baptized immediately so her true identity would be kept from the Nazi officials.

In April 1943, Zezette's period of "passing" as a Christian came to an end. It was Easter break at the school, and Zezette so missed her parents that she left the convent and went to visit them in hiding. Her parents decided to go on a fishing trip with their daughter. While this had been a normal family pastime in the prewar era, it was a dangerous one under the occupation, especially for Jews who were hiding.

"Obviously, we were followed and betrayed," explains Zezette. On the evening of Easter Sunday, after the trio returned from fishing, all three were seized and transported to Malines. From Malines the family was deported to Auschwitz. Zezette's mother was sent immediately to the gas chambers; her father, whom Zezette saw from a distance a few times at the camp, also died at Auschwitz. Zezette lived in the barracks of Auschwitz-Birkenau and worked in one of the munitions plants.

Commentary

The excerpt of Zezette is the only selection in "Childhood Memories" in which a survivor recalls adolescence in concentration camps. Auschwitz, the camp described below, is the place Zezette discusses in the excerpt. Toward the close of the war she was relocated to another camp, Ravensbruck, within Germany. (See the testimony of Renee Scott in **Portraits** for a description of Ravensbruck.)

The complex of concentration, labor, and death camps known as Auschwitz was located near the village of Auschwitz (called Oswiecim in Polish) in Upper Silesia, not far from Cracow.

The Nazis opened the main camp, known as Auschwitz I, on June 14, 1940, chiefly for political prisoners. However, after 1942 Jewish laborers were also housed there. Experimental gassings of Russian prisoners of war began in the cellars of some barracks in Auschwitz I, followed by the first cremations in a small crematory in the main camp. Another infamous landmark at Auschwitz I is the "Black Wall," against which thousands were shot.

Auschwitz II, known as Birkenau, opened toward the end of 1941 with barracks for 100,000 men and women. Adjacent to Birkenau, the killing center for Auschwitz, were four gas chamber and crematorium complexes where, between 1943 and 1944, the Nazis gassed between three and four million people, most of them Jews.

Auschwitz III, known as Buna-Monowitz, was a labor camp with factories for I.G. Farben and other German industrial firms. Here the prisoners, who were treated as slave laborers, worked until they literally dropped from exhaustion; no longer useful to the Nazi war machinery, they then were sent to the gas chambers at Birkenau.

Near the end of November 1944, Heinrich Himmler ordered the dismantling and destruction of the gas chambers and crematoria at Birkenau. In mid-January 1945, the Nazis began evacuating the remaining prisoners by forced death marches. Many thousands died from cold and hunger or were shot en route by the SS. Russian troops who liberated the camp a week later found about 5,000 prisoners, too ill even for the death march, whom the Germans had left behind. One of them was Primo Levi, author of *Survival in Auschwitz.* Two members of the forced death march were Elie Wiesel and his father. Sonia Weitz, whose story is included in **Portraits**, also went on the death march from Auschwitz.

It is estimated that as many as four million victims, Jewish and non-Jewish, died in the various Auschwitz camps.

Roman Mogilanski provides the following detailed description of living conditions for the prisoners at Auschwitz:

Between 700-1000 prisoners in the original camp lived in brick buildings meant to hold 400 prisoners. Sometimes as many as 1,200 people were confined to these barracks, which amounted to two square meters of space for each prisoner. Prisoners in the first transports slept on straw that had been spread on the floor. Later on, straw mattresses were placed in the barracks and two or three people slept on each mattress. About 200 prisoners slept in a room which, with difficulty, could accommodate only 40-50 people. Later, three-story bunk beds that took up nearly all the space in the room were introduced.

The conditions in Birkenau were even worse. The barracks, modeled after military field stables . . . were 40.76 meters long, 9.56 meters wide and 2.65 meters high. They were made from boards and had neither windows nor ceilings, covered only by thin roofing paper. The only furniture in the barracks were three-tiered bunk beds. Between 1,000-1,200 people were kept in barracks meant to hold only 300 prisoners. For each prisoner there were about .28 square meters of surface space and about .75 square meters of air space. The primitive stoves that ran along the length of the barracks were not able to warm them. There was no water, sanitary facilities, or even ventilation in these buildings and, instead of a floor, there was only packed-down clay. Another type of barracks was made from bricks; about 1,000 prisoners were kept in each of them and there were eight people in a single bunk.

The thin tunics and trousers given to the men and the thin dresses given to the women did not protect them from the cold. As the war progressed and there was a shortage of the striped prison uniforms, the prisoners were given civilian clothing taken from those who had been killed. The clothing was marked on the back with a stripe of red paint.

The prisoners received each day three meals that had a total calorie count well below that required by a person who is in a complete state of repose. In camp jargon, starving prisoners were called "muslims." A prisoner who was systematically underfed could live from three to six months, depending on the nature of his or her work. When the camp was liberated, the majority of the prisoners were in a bedridden state. They looked like skeletons covered by earth-colored skin. There were cases of swollen torsos with exuding fistulas and adults weighed an average of 30-35 kilograms, 50-70% below normal adult weight. A special legal-medical commission which examined 2,819 prisoners in February and March of 1945 attested that 2,189 of them were sick as a result of exhaustion and

hunger and that 223 had tuberculosis. Autopsies performed on 536 corpses indicated that in 474 cases, death had occurred from emaciation. Of the estimated 3,000 children born in the camp, 1,000 died of hunger and the rest were murdered. Only 180 children were liberated by the Soviet Army.
. . .

Prisoner slave labor in the camp was meant to bring about concrete economic results as well as to repress the prisoners. These two closely connected aspects had a decisive influence on the nature of work performed by the prisoners, on the working conditions and on the treatment of prisoners. Lacking machinery and technical equipment, the camp authorities massively exploited manpower in places where it would never have been used under normal conditions.

The prisoner's day began with reveille at 4:30 a.m. and often ended, depending on the distance of the work site, late in the evening. The work detachments left the camp to the music of the camp orchestra, which was made up of prisoners. The prisoners returned to the camp covered in blood and tired, carrying their dead comrades in stretchers, carts or on their backs. The dead bodies were laid down in order to be present for roll call (Appel) so that the number of prisoners tallied. The inhuman exploitation of the prisoners at Auschwitz led to countless number of deaths.[77]

Using

Several Holocaust scholars have explained the difficulty of using traditional language to explain the reality for victims of the ghettos and concentration camps in the Third Reich. Which words in Zezette's testimony seemed inadequate for describing what happened to her at Auschwitz?

Video testimonies offer certain forms of historical evidence that are not available in written and oral testimonies. Sometimes we learn something very different about the Holocaust by watching Zezette tell her story than we do by reading it. Discuss an aspect of the Holocaust found in Zezette's testimony that had not appeared in any of the written sources you have read.

Before she participated in this video interview, Zezette returned to Auschwitz to "bury her parents": this is a term Zezette uses to refer to her efforts to say a final good-bye to them. A few years later, through an advertisement in a Belgian newspaper, she was able to locate a non-Jewish friend from the convent school. At their reunion, the friend told Zezette that she and other students wondered what had become of Zezette after the Easter break of 1943.

Today Zezette speaks to students in classrooms about the danger of hate and about prejudice and discrimination. One eighth grade class was so moved by

Zezette L.

Zezette's personal visit that they prepared a collage of drawings that had been inspired by hearing her story.

Just as Zezette prompts students to reflect on the inherent dangers of racism and hatred with her personal visits to classrooms, the excerpt from her testimony in "Childhood Memories" leaves a powerful impression on students. Bill Miller, an eighth grade social studies teacher in Concord, Massachusetts, devoted an entire class period to Zezette's excerpt when he realized how much it helped students understand the gulf that separated their everyday normal existence from the abnormal world of *Lagers* (camps) in the Third Reich.

Miller and his colleagues teach an eight-week Facing History unit in their curriculum "The United States: A Search for Justice," which focuses on the question: What are the conditions that create a just society? The Concord team have found that Facing History fits in perfectly with the overall goals of their curriculum. It repeatedly prompts students to think about issues of justice: What measures did the Nazis use to remove rights from minorities? What opposition did Germans show to increasing restrictions on their freedom and the rights of due process? When did it become too late to stop the erosion of civil rights in Nazi Germany? What provisions exist in the American Constitution and Bill of Rights to protect minorities? What can Americans do to redress violations of these protections?

Aware that his students are particularly interested in learning about others in their age group, Miller decided to integrate excerpts from "Childhood Memories" throughout the eight weeks. For example, when he introduced the history of antisemitism early in the unit, he used the selection of Nechama Tec, recalling how she, a Jew, had to listen in silence while Polish girl friends made derogatory remarks about Jews. Later, while covering the chapters on Nazi education and philosophy, Miller used the excerpts of Frank S. and

Walter K. to stimulate thinking about the impact of humiliation and hatred in the classroom. Towards the final weeks when the class studied the Final Solution, the excerpts of Rachel G., Menachem S., and Zezette L. were presented to generate discussion on the effect that living in an unjust society has on individual choice.

From Miller's perspective, the class response to Zezette's testimony epitomized the value of these materials in classroom settings. As with all the excerpts, Miller prepared the students before meeting their video guest, asking them to tell about their favorite activities as thirteen-year-olds and speculate on the life of thirteen-year-olds in Nazi concentration camps. Then the students viewed the excerpt of Zezette telling about her adolescence in Auschwitz, and during discussion they began comparing her life to their own as thirteen-year-olds growing up in a free society. What most forcefully struck Miller's eighth graders was Zezette's description of her utter loneliness in the camp—she survived with no one and throughout her time in Auschwitz she remained silent, not communicating with anyone. "I can't imagine having no friends," exclaimed one of Miller's students. "I couldn't have done it. Friends are so important for me."

"It's all very complicated," another student remarked. "When we heard Rita Kesselman [a survivor who visited their classroom] speak to us, she mentioned how she survived with close friends from her town; Sonia Weitz, too, tells [in a reading in the Resource Book] of how she survived with her sister. But Zezette says she had no one."

For additional descriptions of Auschwitz and the administration of the camp, contact the Facing History Resource Center for a copy of a handout on Auschwitz Documents prepared to supplement material in the Auschwitz Exhibition "Auschwitz: Crime Against Mankind."

The Resource Center also has excerpts from the film *Liberation of Auschwitz*, which contains original Russian film coverage of Auschwitz at the time of liberation. This is graphic footage that illustrates the condition of prisoners as described in *The Ghetto Anthology*.

Also available at the Resource Center is a selection from the half-hour television program *Chronicle* on the career of Josef Mengele at Auschwitz; in the concluding segment journalist Mike Barnicle reflects on why it is still important forty years after the Holocaust to study Mengele's deeds at Auschwitz.

Rose Murra's video testimony, available at the Resource Center, includes a physical description of the camp as well as descriptions of work in Monowitz and modes of coping among female inmates.

Excerpt 9: Rachel G. #2 (T-139)

And one day nine months after the war was over. Nine months. I am sitting there in the classroom and this nun walks in, and without a word she just looked at me, and I just knew that my mother was right there.

This excerpt from Rachel G.'s testimony focuses on her postwar experiences. (In Excerpt 7 Rachel described her separation from her parents in Brussels in 1942.) At the close of the war Rachel was living with a Christian farmer and his wife. She loved them and felt as close to them as if they were her own parents. In fact, the foster family planned to adopt her: the law required that natural parents be given ten months to locate their children after the war before formal adoption proceedings could take place. In compliance with postwar regulations designed to help Jewish parents locate their children, Rachel returned to the original convent she entered when she first separated from her parents.

In the ninth months of waiting, Rachel began having dreams and premonitions that her mother had returned. Then, after two weeks of these dreams, Rachel's mother appeared at the convent to reclaim her daughter. Rachel learned that the very landlady who arranged for her rescue had turned her parents in to the Gestapo.

For a long time after the reunion Rachel distrusted her mother for having left her three years earlier. Moreover, Rachel had come to love the Catholic family who saved her. Still a child, she had no strong identification with her Jewish heritage. A considerable time elapsed before Rachel realized that her mother's action actually saved her by forcing her to go with the Christians before the deportations.

Commentary

Earl G. Harrison, appointed by President Truman in July 1945 to examine the situation of the displaced persons camps and the general conditions for victims of Nazism, prepared a report on his investigations. According to Harrison's report, one of the most noticeable factors was the delay in helping victims to reunite with the surviving members of their families.

> "Most of them [the victims] have been separated for three, four, or five years and they cannot understand why the liberators should not have undertaken immediately the organized effort to re-unite family groups." * [7887]

Further contributing to the discomfort and unhappiness of survivors were the shortages of food and clothing. Harrison wondered

> "how much longer many of these people, particularly those who have over such a long period felt persecution and near starvation, can survive on a diet composed principally of bread and coffee, irrespective of the calorie content. In many camps, the 2,000 calories included 1,250 calories of a black, wet and extremely unappetizing bread. I received the distinct impression and considerable substantiating information that large numbers of the German population—again principally in the rural areas—have a more varied and palatable diet than is the case with the displaced persons." [79]

Using

Marie Syrkin, an American educator who visited displaced persons camps at the end of the war and spoke with many survivors, describes some of the classes she witnessed with children who had survived the Holocaust:

> A Bible class was studying the life of Moses; they were reading the part where the infant Moses is left by his mother among the bulrushes. The teacher wanted to know if the mother was justified in abandoning her child to an unknown woman, the Egyptian princess. Was that how a mother would act? This was no problem for the children. They had to make an effort of the mind and imagination beyond their years in order to produce replies. Of course, agreed the children, that's how a real mother would act.
>
> In another class Jewish holidays were being studied. Many of the children had forgotten their religious training or had been too young to receive any when the deportations began. The teacher was explaining the significance of the prayer Kol Nidre, in which Marranos, secret Jews who accepted Christianity in fear of the Inquisition, pray for forgiveness for the false vows they must take. Here, too, the children had no lack of parallels to offer. Had not their parents done the same thing if they lived on "Aryan" papers? [80]

From what Rachel says about her postwar thoughts and reactions, how do you think she would have responded to such classes?

Why do you think that Rachel responded as she did to the reunion with her mother? What were some of the readjustments that Rachel had to make at the close of the war?

Dori Katz reflects on her thoughts in the immediate postwar era in her poem "Photographs." Compare how she remembers her relationship with her mother at this time with Rachel's memory of the reunion with her mother in 1946.

Photographs
By now I'm glad you've kept that photo
that's taken after the holocaust
in a professional studio,
in Belgium, to show that we've been saved.
You are wearing heavy high heel shoes;
your nylons washed and mended to last
make your legs gleam; your hair is banded
on your forehead for that forties look.
Also dolled up, I stand on a chair
to be your height so that we hold hands,
arms crossed, like skaters. A curtain hangs
behind us, ending the war drama,
showing the tragedy is over.
We look like two survivors, smiling
very proudly at deserved applause.

The picture snapped, I climb down my chair,
you take your nylons off and wrap them
and we're back in nineteen forty–six.
War's over. I come out of hiding.
Glad to have me back, you must now teach
me I'm nobody else's daughter.
Unconverted, I still cross myself
as I hide from you under the stairs,
and you must break the imagined spell
again. Eventually we will speak
each other's language; I'll learn Flemish
while you pick up a few French words
but when alone, we talk in Yiddish.

Six years later, we cross the ocean
as immigrants, fingerprinted, sworn,
photographed, questioned, rephotographed,
but here's a picture that wasn't snapped;
you sewing in airless factories,

stacks of flimsy blouses at your feet,
trying to finish them before they,
or you fall apart; nickel a piece.
You, being charged five bucks for a bag
of apples, then riding the streetcar
for hours, forgetting the way back.
Me sitting in front of a mirror
watching myself speaking English words,
trying to be like everybody else,
inconspicuously American.

Today you live West with changing friends
and a man who shares your discontent.
Almost as though we traded places,
I keep driving myself further East,
looking for something to settle on.
Perhaps, we're not worlds apart but still
at that starting point in the photograph, featured on your buffet. In it,
you see the bright ghost of your beauty
and the child you thought would fill your life
caught in their breakable promises.
I see the same child holding your hand
as though it were a favorite new toy someone is bound to
confiscate. Too old
not to confront such disappearance
now but still needing to play it safe,
whenever I visit we get snapped
together, coming out slightly blurred.

The Resource Book summarizes the variety of responses in different nations to the Holocaust.

The rescue efforts for children in France that might be compared with those in Belgium are discussed in Klarsfeld, ed., *Les Enfants d'Izieu: Une tragedie juive*; and in Hallie, *Lest Innocent Blood Be Shed*.

For additional discussion of the postwar readjustments of children, see Marion Pritchard's video testimony (T-754) and the video testimonies of Steven and Marion Hess (T-542, T-543, and T-44) at the Fortunoff Video Archive for Holocaust Testimonies.

Excerpt 10: Paul D. (T-48)

My first memory of the horror of deportation was this. . . . We [my family and I] went into hiding and I remember we were in the attic of a gentile friend of the family. And I saw through a little crack in a window Jews being herded towards the railroad station. . . . [After the roundup I went out and looked in the home of the Shochet of Hummene.] Somehow then I realized that this man was taken away.

The two segments from Paul's testimony comprising this excerpt describe how Paul has tried to preserve the memory of his childhood culture in eastern Europe and transmit it to the next generation. In the first segment, Paul speaks of his visit to the home of the *shochet* (the butcher who follows the correct ritual for the preparation of kosher meat) and his realization that this important figure of the Jewish community had disappeared. In the second segment Paul describes why, several years ago when he was laid up with a back injury, he felt the need to speak to his children about the Shochet of Hummene. He called his son and daughter into his bedroom and related the story of going to the home of the *shochet* and learning of his disappearance. Paul's children promised they would remember the story and would pass it on to their own children.

Born in Moldava, Czechoslovakia, Paul grew up in an Orthodox Jewish environment. Moldava was the hometown of his paternal grandparents who were Orthodox Jews, and the family observed all the appropriate rituals with the other Jewish families in the town.

During the late 1930s, while Hitler was negotiating with the Allied powers to redraw the map of Europe and preparing for war, major changes took place in Paul's family life. In 1938 Paul's father died. Soon thereafter, Paul's mother decided to move her three-year-old son to her own home town of Hummene in Slovakia. Here she took a second husband, a good man who was devoted to Paul and provided him with a dog and toys. As in Moldava, Paul's life in Hummene was steeped in traditional Jewish culture.

Although Slovakia had become a German satellite in 1939, local officials did not exercise anti-Jewish legislation stringently in the first years of the war. Paul and his parents were fortunate enough to have the same protection as converted Jews in these years. Nevertheless, by 1941 the exemptions for converted Jews in Slovakia no longer held. All Jews were being identified, rounded up and deported. While several of Paul's close relatives were deported to Lublin, Paul and his parents secured false papers and went into hiding with gentile friends.

Paul spent the remainder of the war moving from place to place in order to avoid arrest and deportation. When circumstances in Slovakia became particularly threatening for Jews in 1942, Paul's parents sent him to live with his grandparents in Hungary where roundups had not yet begun. After the roundup of Hungarian Jews commenced in May 1944, Paul rejoined his parents in Slovakia and hid in the forests and remote villages in the Carpathian Mountains before liberation by the Russians in the early spring of 1945.

One of Paul's most vivid boyhood memories is of the early period of deportations from Slovakia. One day after a roundup, Paul and several of his Jewish friends who were also hiding with gentile families went to see the home of the Shochet of Hummene, who customarily distributed colored tickets from little books to his customers. On the day Paul and his friends went to the *shochet*'s home, Paul realized that the *shochet* had vanished: all that remained were tickets from his books that were scattered on the floor.

Commentary

Lucy Dawidowicz emphasizes how the Holocaust destroyed Jewish culture in European civilization:

> The effect of the murder of 6 million Jews is still to be evaluated. From the Jewish point of view, we know one thing now for certain. The immensity of the Jewish losses destroyed the biological basis for the continued communal existence of Jews in Europe. Every country and people ravaged by the war and by the German occupation eventually returned to a normal existence. All the nations, the victims now become victors, the aggressors now defeated, once again assumed their positions in the political order. . . . But the annihilation of 6 million European Jews brought an end with irrevocable finality to the thousand-year-old culture and civilization of Ashkenazic Jewry, destroying the continuity of Jewish history. This is the special Jewish sorrow. This is why the surviving Jews grieve, mourning the loss of their past and the imperilment of their future.[81]

The authors of *Remnants: The Last Jews of Poland* interviewed Mr. Datner, a Polish Jew, about Polish-Jewish relations and the legacy of the Holocaust for Polish Jewry. According to Datner, contemporary economic conditions in addition to long-standing social attitudes among Poles interfere with efforts to preserve the heritage of Polish Jewry in Poland. His main hope lies in the fact that American Jewry will carry on the traditions and memory of east European Jewry:

Question: "And what is happening with the architectural monuments?"

Answer: "Some of the surviving synagogues have been restored. They are no longer places of worship, however, because there is no one left who could pray in them. Some of the monuments are deteriorating, falling down. Even here some work is being done, but it demands billions of zloty. And now we are not talking about intentions but about capabilities. Poland is in a severe economic crisis. It is a poor country. There is not even enough money to save Wawel Castle, which is the most valuable national monument that the Poles have. So there is no thought of funding for other similar goals."

Question: "And cemeteries? There are more than four hundred fifty of them in Poland and most of them are in disastrous shape."

Answer: "This is a very painful problem. The Germans destroyed most of the cemeteries, either demolishing them on the spot or ordering that the stones be used for paving the streets. Jews themselves often had to do this. After the war, therefore, we found our cemeteries in very poor shape. Only a few places, like the Remu Cemetery could be put in order. Afterward, the Jews left, and the cemeteries were completely abandoned. They are formally under the management of the Congregation. But how can we, a few old people, go about caring for several hundred cemeteries scattered all over the country? So they go on collapsing."

Question: "It is thought, particularly abroad, that Poles deliberately destroy Jewish cemeteries."

Answer: "They are a no man's land. Sheep and cows graze there, the local drunks go there to imbibe, and someone occasionally breaks a tombstone. But these are outbreaks of hooliganism rather than symptoms of a dislike for Jews."

Question: "And digging up graves to look for valuables?"

Answer: "There are cemetery hyenas everywhere, and they usually gorge themselves in unguarded places."

Question: "For a couple of years, a Social Committee for the Protection of Jewish Cemeteries has been active in Poland."

Answer: "People, especially the young, are trying to do something, and I praise them for that. Except that this is a job for thousands, and it demands enormous funding that is not there."

Question: "Mr. Datner, during my conversations with Polish Jews one issue always surfaces: fear. It is imbedded, more or less concealed, in everyone, regardless of age, background, or present circumstances."

Answer: "In this matter I cannot link myself with my brethren. There is no fear in me. Perhaps that is because I am already old. The fact that I will soon have to take my leave is a source of peace for me."

Question: "How do you see the future of Polish Jews? Is there any future at all?"

Answer: "Polish Jews give the impression of a group that is becoming extinct. But after all, our people have been dying for two thousand years and somehow they have not died out. Of course, this community in Poland has been reduced. But it can survive. New, young people came to us not long ago. It seemed that they had fallen away from the Jewish tree, and yet they have returned. Three months ago I experienced great joy—there was a *Bar Mitzvah*. So, perhaps, there will be something, someone left, when we are gone. . . . And besides, I am generally an optimist. Take a look around: the Polish Jews were cut down to the stump, but the powerful Jewry of America has grown. Now there are six million of them—as many as were murdered in Europe. The state of Israel was established, and new generations of Jews have grown up there. Yes, even if some branches are cut off, and if others wither and fall, the Jewish people exist and will exist."[82]

An indication that Mr. Datner's optimism is warranted is found in the story of YIVO. YIVO, an institution dedicated to the preservation of Yiddish culture, originated in Vilna, Poland in 1925. In 1941, after the Germans occupied Vilna, YIVO was used as an office for collecting Jewish treasures from eastern Europe to be sent back to Germany. Later, after the war, many of the YIVO books and archives were found in the American zone of Germany and were eventually returned to YIVO in New York City. YIVO had been centered in New York during the war years because the founder and librarian, who had been in western Europe when the Germans commandeered YIVO in Vilna, settled in New York City during the war and created an American office with no documents, no staff, no library, and no archives. Today YIVO is thriving as a center for the study of Yiddish culture and language: American Jews who support the institution are not solely interested in preserving the memory of what was destroyed in the Holocaust.

Forty-five years after its reincarnation in the United States . . . the institute appears to represent a social and cultural bridge that spans the gulf created by the Holocaust and several decades of Jewish assimilation in this country. . . . More and more, they [young American Jews] want to know where they come from, and their interest expands from there to culture, politics, and history. And sometimes the unsophisticated, information-hungry younger person is so intense that he or she becomes, despite the differences in age and in background, one of the "old timers."[83]

Using

Why do you think that Paul decided to tell his own children about the Shochet of Hummene? Why do you think that the memory of the *shochet* remains so strong for Paul?

Excerpt 11: Menachem S. (T-152)

I was like 70 years old. I was a real old man. I was short but I was old. And . . . [I felt] the whole responsibility of the whole world for myself. I knew that . . . what I have to finally rely upon is myself.

"Childhood Memories" includes two segments from the testimony of Menachem S. In the first, Menachem describes the scene in the labor camp at Plaszow, a suburb of Cracow, when his parents sent him away. He was only five years old. In the second excerpt, he recalls an incident in his adult life that reflects the permanent impact of the Holocaust experience: after the birth of his first daughter he went on a shopping spree, buying items such as electric trains and other toys that were inappropriate for an infant. When his wife asked why he had bought those things, he answered that the child needed toys. Upon further reflection, he realized that he was trying to recapture his own nonexistent childhood.

It is not surprising that as an adult, Menachem felt he had lost much of his own childhood. In fact, Menachem's infancy was the most stable period of his early life. He was born in 1938 into a prominent Jewish family of Cracow, one of Poland's largest cities, where the Jewish community dated back to the fourteenth century. In the 1930s, there were 60,000 Jews in a total population of 259,000; in 1939, an additional 20,000 Jews sought refuge in Cracow after their expulsion from Austria, Silesia and other Nazi occupied areas. In the prewar years, as restrictions on Jews intensified, Menachem's family had the resources to emigrate. But his grandfather, a wealthy gem merchant and community leader, would not hear of leaving his native city where the family had lived for generations.

Menachem was only eighteen months old when the Germans invaded Poland; he was seven when the war ended. During those years, the conquering German forces established Cracow as the seat for the Nazi-administered General Government. This encompassed the regions of central Poland that had not been directly incorporated into the German Reich.

Hans Frank, the Governor General of this puppet state, was particularly eager to remove all Jews from Cracow as soon as possible. According to Frank, the German generals and Nazi officials stationed in the city "should not have to breathe the same air as Jews and expose themselves to contagious diseases." Between the spring of 1940 and March 1941, the Nazis expelled more than 35,000 Jews from their homes and sent many of them to labor camps. Thus there were only about 18,000 Jews left to fill the Cracow Ghetto, established in the fall of 1941.

Menachem and his parents were among that number. His earliest memory of life in the ghetto was when he was four years old and developed an ear infection. His father risked taking him to a doctor just as the curfew hours were ending. A soldier caught them, threatening to shoot them for failing to observe the curfew. Fortunately, Menachem's father managed to convince the soldier that the curfew had ended, and father and son were released with a stern warning to observe restrictions in the future.

Another of Menachem's memories concerns the transfer of his family to the labor camp of Plaszow. This was "like moving into a different planet," Menachem recalls. Although his uncles had the good fortune to work for Oskar Schindler, a factory owner who protected his workers against the worst excesses of the SS guards and even provided extra food rations, Menachem witnessed terrible suffering among his parents and their friends.

Menachem's parents decided that the only way to save their son was to smuggle him out of the camp, a complicated and dangerous undertaking. After they devised elaborate schemes for a groom who cared for SS horses to escort Menachem out of the camp, they had to abort the plans. Finally Menachem's parents managed to bribe one of the guards to help their son escape. Menachem's mother tied an old scarf around her son's head and gave him an address of a local brothel. As she pushed him away to leave with the guard, she promised that Menachem would see both his parents after the war, pressing into his hand her high school identification card containing her photograph. This, she said, would help Menachem recognize her when they met again.

The young boy fended for himself in the streets of Cracow. He spent the first three months in the brothel until police raided the establishment. Left to roam in the city streets, he took up with gangs of orphans and survived by stealing and begging. During the winter of 1943, a Polish woman took him into her home: she was so used to seeing children in the streets during the war years that she did not even bother to ask her ward about his background.

As the police intensified searches for stray Jewish children, the woman with whom he stayed in Cracow sent him to her sister in the country. In this rural setting Menachem found refuge—and a bit of security—with a street sweeper and his wife.

After the war Menachem was reunited with his parents and emigrated to Israel where he attended elementary and high school. Eventually he married and began raising his own family. In the immediate postwar years, he had a very difficult time adjusting to life with his parents. Like Rachel, the girl who had survived with Catholic rescuers in Belgium, he was confused by his reunion with his parents. He felt as though they had deserted him by sending him away into the streets of Cracow. He remembers being particularly uneasy when he saw his parents: his father, a healthy six-foot, two-inch man before the war, had teeth hanging loosely from his jaw and weighed 110 pounds or less at liberation; his mother was similarly emaciated and no longer bore the slightest resemblance to the photo in her high school identification card. For some time, Menachem says, "I used to address them by calling them Mr. and Mrs. . . . . I had to become a child again, which I resented. I just couldn't."

Before his family settled in Israel in 1950, Menachem had recurrent nightmares, and he felt utterly helpless. Once in Israel, the nightmares disappeared until the proceedings of the Eichmann Trial, in 1961, revived the memories of his childhood.

Commentary

The Cracow Ghetto was created by the decree of the governor of the district, Otto Waechter, on March 3, 1941, and was liquidated on March 13-14, 1943.

A wall surrounded the ghetto to isolate the Jews from the rest of the population. The remaining Jewish population of Cracow, approximately 16,000 people, were forced into the ghetto area upon its creation. During the fall of 1941 the Nazis relocated Jews from the countryside surrounding Cracow to the ghetto, increasing the Jewish population to about 24,000. In the first months the ghetto inhabitants tried to carry on normal lives, establishing pharmacies, a home for the elderly, an orphanage and workshops for artisans. Three synagogues were allowed to function.

It was extremely difficult for inhabitants of the ghetto to make contact with people on the outside. Sentries stood at three gates, and no person had the right to enter—or exit—without permission. Guards searched anyone who entered the ghetto. If they found anything, they took it away. The German police kept order in the ghetto and also created a Jewish police force. The SS created terror. They attacked passersby, beating and kicking them. Searches took place daily. Then, on June 1, 1942, the deportation actions began.

In the first deportation and the two that followed (on June 4 and June 8), the Nazis removed approximately 7,000 people to the Belzec annihilation center and murdered 150 more. Soon after, they reduced the boundaries of the ghetto territory. On October 28, 1942, 7,000 more people were deported to death camps and about 600 murdered on the spot, mainly the sick, crippled, and elderly. The Nazis chose that same day to victimize the people in charge of the orphanage. Once again they narrowed the ghetto territory, this time to half its former size.

On December 6, 1942, the Nazi administration divided the ghetto into two parts, part A for those who could work and part B for those who could not. They also established a *Kinderheim* (home for children) for children under fourteen.

The final liquidation of the Jewish quarter began on March 13, 1943. Police formations surrounded the ghetto. All the inhabitants of part A were gathered at Zgota Square and transported to the labor camp at Plaszow, where a few hundred were murdered on the spot. The liquidation of part B took place on March 14. The patrols searched each house, driving people into Zgota Square or simply killing them. At Zgota Square, Nazi soldiers either shot people or herded them to the gate at Wit Stowosz Street and shot them there. They shot the older children from the *Kinderheim* and loaded the younger ones onto trucks in baskets. They also killed everyone in the hospitals: the sick, doctors, and nurses. Then they selected about 150 people at Zgota Square to remain behind and clean up the ghetto after the liquidation, reducing this number by half when they shot seventy-five of them. All told, on March 13 and 14, the Nazis murdered an indefinite number of Jews, and transferred 3,000 to labor camps in Plaszow and 2,000 to Auschwitz.

Plaszow was a suburb of Cracow. The Nazi administration turned it into a large concentration camp complex, expelling the remaining Jews of the Cracow Ghetto there and to other camps on March 13-14, 1943. The civilian populace in the area around Plaszow also worked in the many factories of the camp along with the Jewish prisoners.

Amon Goeth, the Commandant of Plaszow, was notorious for sadistic behavior, especially towards children in the camp. Survivor Jakob Stendig provides the following description of Goeth's behavior. (His spelling of Goeth is Gett.)

We are already accustomed to death; it is an everyday occurrence with us. The best and noblest among us are seized suddenly and at the least provocation. It might be for taking a breathing spell, for leaning on one's shovel or for a moment's rest on the dumpcart containing a tombstone, which one trundles with superhuman effort. Or it might be for a "perspiring face," an offense for which Gett had once passed judgment on two young Jews who were standing in the line, ready to go to their work detail. During the roll call, Gett commanded them to step forward, whereupon he shot them dead in the presence of thousands of inmates of the camp.

Once a sixteen-year-old lad, named Haubenstock, hummed under his breath, in all likelihood unconsciously, the melody known as *"Tchubchik."* Someone overheard it and, assuming it to be a communist tune, denounced the boy to the authorities as a communist.

[The Gestapo was ordered to execute the boy, but the executioner failed to carry out the task correctly.] I stood at some distance from the execution, and could not observe the face of the victim. But even if I had found myself close enough, I could not possibly have brought myself to gaze into those glassy eyes that desperately searched for some sign of hope. The boy dropped into the container, still alive. Gett called down curses on the head of the executioner; and the latter hurriedly extricated the boy and proceeded to fasten the noose on him again. The victim pleaded with Gett for mercy, but the officer commanded that the "job be disposed of." This time the task was successful and the body remained dangling in the air. . . .

And once, at twilight, a group consisting of sixty young men and women returned to the barracks from the work camp known as *Banarka*, lugging provisions for the other inmates of the barracks in their knapsacks. They were detained and inspected by the Gestapo, one of whom, named Will, reported to Gett that the inspection had yielded positive results. Whereupon Gett ordered that the entire group be "liquidated." A detachment of Blackshirts then surrounded the sixty unfortunates and marched them, five abreast, to the hill known as *Hoiawaa Gurka* where they were all put to death.[84]

After the war Goeth was condemned to death by a Polish tribunal and executed on September 13, 1946.

See the testimonies of Sonia Weitz and Rena Finder in **Portraits** for descriptions of teenagers' experiences in Plaszow. Unlike the young boy Menachem, Sonia and Rena were old enough to work in the camp. Also relevant is the documentary film "Wallenberg and Schindler" that includes a fifteen-minute segment describing Schindler's efforts to help Jewish workers in his factories.

Using

What did Menachem mean by the statement: "I was like seventy years old. I was a little old man. I was short, but I was old. And [I felt] . . . the whole responsibility of the whole world for myself"?

Compare the circumstances of Menachem's rescue with the experiences Rachel and Nechama had with Christian helpers.

Survivors of the Holocaust and a number of scholars in Holocaust studies observe that survival was largely a matter of luck—there was no specific way to guarantee that one would survive. In Menachem's story, what indications are there that luck was a critical factor in his particular situation? Also, point out what factors in Menachem's survival were due to careful planning on the part of his parents.

The following eyewitness testimony is offered by a woman who was a child in the Cracow Ghetto and Plaszow. Here she describes her experiences in Plaszow. Compare her experience as an child in a labor camp with Menachem's experiences. How do the observations in this testimony add to what you learned from Menachem?

> The Cracow Ghetto was liquidated at the start of 1943. Most of the people still left inside the ghetto were taken to the death camps. . . . The 100 Jews who worked at the factory—including my parents and me—were taken to Plaszow. There, my mother and I were put in the women's camp and my father was separated from us along with the men. The 100 of us were taken to work at the factory from Plaszow just like we'd been taken from the Cracow Ghetto. After two months in Plaszow, I was no longer allowed to work at the factory because the Germans said my strength was failing and I could no longer do the work right. They had me work at the brush factory in Plaszow for the time. I could no longer see my parents, either, because the 100 Jews who worked at the factory were locked up inside and never let out—they were no longer part of Plaszow as they had been till now. I heard that this happened because the Poles and Germans of Plaszow protested against the Jews appearing through "their" streets.

> *Selektsyes* [selections] took place all the time now, and the people were sent either to other labor camps or to Auschwitz. The most tragic selection was the one in August 1943. Children, sick people, and the aged were hunted down, herded together, and packed off to Auschwitz.

> There was a children's home in Plaszow where the workers left their children for the day. The children of the *Judischer Ordungsdienst*. I was put inside this house with many other children while the big selection I just mentioned was going on.

The head of the Jewish police in Plaszow had been a suspected informer, but said he'd only been a milkman, in Cracow. His name was Chilewicz. He knew I was going by a false birth certificate, that I was still a child. His wife was the head inmate of the women's camp. Soon, during an *Appel*, Chilewicz's wife took me out of line and sent me to the children's home where all the other children were being gathered for deportation. She said I was also a child and belonged with them.

There were about 500 or 600 of us inside the children's home. The building was sealed behind barbed wire and guarded by Gestapo agents and not the sentries of the *Ordungsdienst*. I spent only one night inside this children's home. The following morning, they started loading the children into trucks headed for Auschwitz. I felt sure they were leading us away to die and I decided to escape. As they were pushing me toward a truck with the other children, a German guard stopped a moment to light his cigarette. He stood spread-eagled. In a second, me and three other children—a boy and two girls—dropped out of line and, running low to the ground, we shot through the German's spread long legs. We broke for the latrine. The German whirled around and fired but he didn't hit anyone because we dropped to the ground as soon as we heard the first of his many shots. He couldn't come after us because he was afraid if he left the other children, they'd break away, too.

The camp latrine, in which the three children and I hid, was exposed. As we stood there, we could be seen from all sides and we were afraid they'd spot us. So I quickly ripped out one of the boards covering the pit and jumped right into the hole, into all the excrement. The children jumped down after me. The last child dragged down the board I had ripped out with him, and this saved us. The latrine ditch was very deep because they dug the waste out ever few days. We edged the board in between two walls of the pit and sat over the feces on it for six long hours, not knowing what to do or how to get out. . . .

The Jewish women [in the camp] finally heard our screams and knocking, they yanked the boards out of the floor and pulled us up. . . . There were now no other children left in the camp—we were the last four Jewish children in Plaszow.

The women brought us inside their barracks and hid us in the top bunks. We were separated—each one of us to a different barrack. The women got one of the Jewish doctors in the camp to come see us and he gave us shots against cholera—this was all done secretly, of course, We were hidden inside the four separate barracks for a week. The women took very good care of us and brought us food. Finally, the head of the women's camp— Chilewicz's wife—found out about us and informed the camp commandant, Goeth. This German said to her that if we four children had the guts to jump into the waste to save ourselves, then we should be spared and not deported like the other children. This is how we were able to remain in the camp legally. We were the only children there and were really well taken care of—this was because the thousands of Jewish women who lost their children to the death camps treated us like their own.

My mother no longer believed I was alive—she again thought I'd been taken away with the other children when they cleared out the children's home. . . . When my mother heard I'd survived, she went straight to the factory supervisor and begged him to let me come to her. . . . The supervisor was a German, Captain Fischer—a decent man. This German gave in to my mother's pleas and went to the Plaszow Gestapo chief himself to take out a permit that would let me work in the factory with my mother. . . . My mother had no idea this would happen. . . . But Captain Fischer and his aide were kind—it's because of them that I'm alive. . . . From then on, I stayed at the plant with my mother and the others—we worked together past the summer of 1943.[85]

For other accounts of conditions in the Cracow Ghetto and at the labor camp of Plaszow, see the descriptions of Sonia Weitz and Rena Finder in **Portraits**.

Montages

1. Wiesel, *Night*, p. 109.
2. Aarvik, "The Nobel Peace Prize, 1986," pp. 4-5.
3. Wiesel, "Wiesel's Speech at Nobel Ceremony," pp. 6-7.
4. Wiesel, *Night*, p. 5.
5. Fein, *Accounting for Genocide*, p. 316.
6. For additional details on immigration and the numbers of German Jews who left during the Third Reich, see the commentary for the video montage "Childhood Experiences of German Jews."
7. Wiesel, *Night*, p. 37. "Achtung! Todesgefahr!" ("Warning: Danger of Death") is a sign found on fences at Auschwitz today, a frightening reminder of the days that Wiesel describes. Beneath the words is a skull and crossbones covered with a black "X".
8. Marrus, *The Holocaust in History*, p. 135.
9. As quoted in Gilbert, *The Holocaust*, pp. 575-576.
10. Marrus, *The Holocaust in History*, pp. 27, 39.
11. Mermelstein, *By Bread Alone*, pp. 142, 146.
12. Ota Kraus & Erich Kulka, *The Death Factory: Document on Auschwitz*, tr. Stephen Jolly (Oxford: Pergamon Press, 1966), as quoted in Des Pres, *The Survivor*, p. 141.
13. Wiesel, *Night*, p. 95.
14. Levi, *Survival in Auschwitz*, pp. 112-113.
15. Mogilanski, *The Ghetto Anthology*, p. 206.
16. As quoted in Des Pres, *The Survivor*, p. 165.
17. Wander, *The Seventh Well*, pp. 33-35.
18. Delbo, *None of Us Will Return*, p. 82.
19. Levi, *The Drowned and the Saved*, pp. 89-90.
20. Wyzanski, "Vignettes of My Years as Youth Aliyah Chairman," p. 4.
21. Eisenberg, ed. *Witness to the Holocaust*, p. 116.
22. Schleunes, *The Twisted Road to Auschwitz*, p. 145.
23. As quoted in Eisenberg, ed., *Witness to the Holocaust*, pp. 74-76.
24. Gilbert, *The Holocaust*, p. 54
25. These photographs appear in the catalogue for the exhibition *Anne Frank in the World 1929-1945*, Anne Frank Museum, Amsterdam; see pp. 32-34 and 45-48. The catalogue is available at the Facing History Resource Center.
26. Arad, Gutman, & Margaliot, eds., *Documents on the Holocaust*, pp. 95-98.
27. Catalogue for the exhibition *The Jews in Germany Under Prussian Rule*.
28. Catalogue for the exhibition *The Jews in Germany Under Prussian Rule*.
29. P. 32.

30. As quoted in Mosse, ed., *Nazi Culture*, pp. 271-272.

31. See Hoffmann, *German Resistance to Hitler*, pp. 109-111.

32. Shirer, *20th Century Journey*, pp. 119-120.

33. Hilberg, *The Destruction of the European Jews*, p. 177.

34. As cited in Noakes & Pridham, eds., *Documents on Nazism*, p. 357.

35. Hilberg, *The Destruction of the European Jews*, p. 166.

36. Uhlman, *Reunion*, pp. 101-103.

37. Richter, *Friedrich*, p. 72.

38. Richter, *Friedrich*, p. 73.

39. Catalogue for the exhibition *The Jews in Germany Under Prussian Rule*.

40. Levin, *The Holocaust*, p. 62.

41. Gilbert, *The Holocaust*, p. 47.

42. Schleunes, *The Twisted Road to Auschwitz*, p. 187.

43. As quoted in Engelmann, *In Hitler's Germany*, p. 127.

44. As quoted in Engelmann, *In Hitler's Germany*, pp. 127-129.

45. Levin, *The Holocaust*, p. 81.

46. Hilberg, *The Destruction of the European Jews*, Vol. 1, p. 171.

47. Conot, *Justice at Nuremberg*, pp. 384-385.

48. As quoted in Harris, *Tyranny on Trial*, p. 284.

49. As quoted in Harris, *Tyranny on Trial*, pp. 284-285.

50. Hilberg, *The Destruction of the European Jews*, Vol. 3, p. 1155.

51. Lipstadt, *Beyond Belief*, p. 119.

52. Marrus, *The Unwanted*, p. 177.

53. Feingold, *Politics of Rescue*, p. 15.

54. Morse, *While Six Million Died*, p. 280.

55. See *Facing History and Ourselves: Holocaust and Human Behavior*, pp. 282-284.

56. Dinnerstein, *America and the Survivors of the Holocaust*, p. 3.

57. Tec, *When Light Pierced the Darkness*, p. 22.

58. Goleman, "Is Altruism Inherited?", p. 66.

59. Sauvage, "A Most Persistent Haven: Le Chambon-sur-Lignon," p. 35.

60. For further information on the research on twins from Auschwitz, contact: Eva Kor, 24 W. Lawrin Boulevard, Terre Haute, IN 47803; and Nancy L. Segal, Department of Psychology, University of Minnesota, Minneapolis, MN 55455.

61. As quoted in Mosse, ed., *Nazi Culture*, pp. 80-81.

62. As quoted in Eisenberg, ed., *Witness to the Holocaust*, p. 125.

63. As quoted in Eisenberg, ed., *Witness to the Holocaust*, p. 127. For details on the World Movement for the Care of German Children, including additional reminiscences of men and women rescued by the organization, see also pp. 122-126.

64. Harris, *Tyranny on Trial*, pp. 286-287.

65. Mosse, ed., *Nazi Culture*, p. 64.

66. Hitler, *Mein Kampf*, as quoted in The Schools Council, *Nazi Education*, p. 5.

67. As cited in Distel & Jakusch, eds., *Concentration Camp Dachau 1933-1945*, p. 62.

68. Gilbert, *The Holocaust*, p. 807.

69. As quoted in Noakes & Pridham, eds., *Documents on Nazism 1919-1945*, pp. 277-279.

70. Arad, Gutman, & Margaliot, *Documents on the Holocaust*, pp. 197-198.

71. Lukas, *The Forgotten Genocide*, p. 4.

72. Lukas, *The Forgotten Genocide*, pp. 103-104.

73. Lukas, *The Forgotten Genocide*, pp. 202-203.

74. Rubenstein & Roth, eds., *Approaches to the Holocaust*, pp. 235-236.

75. Tec, *Dry Tears*, pp. 213-214.

76. Fein, *Accounting for Genocide*, p. 157.

77. Mogilanski, *The Ghetto Anthology*, pp. 205-208.

78. As quoted in Dinnerstein, *America and the Survivors of the Holocaust*, p. 40.

79. As quoted in Dinnerstein, *America and the Survivors of the Holocaust*, p. 41.

80. Syrkin, p. 22.

81. Dawidowicz, p. xvi.

82. Niezabitowska & Tomaszewski, *Remnants: The Last Jews of Poland*, pp. 258-260.

83. As quoted in Barmash, "The YIVO Story," p. 28.

84. Stendig, "Execution in Plaszow," pp. 250-252.

85. Trunk, ed., *Jewish Responses to Nazi Persecution*, testimony 13, pp. 117-119.

Scholars Reflect on Holocaust Video Testimonies

This section includes essays from specialists in the fields of history, literature, library science, and museum studies who have had experience using testimonies in Holocaust education. Included in the section are five essays by Lawrence Langer, consultant to Facing History, which reflect the collective thinking of the Facing History program staff and Dr. Langer, who met regularly to discuss the potential use and abuse of video testimonies in Holocaust education.

Six major observations made during these sessions receive special attention in Langer's essays and are also touched on, individually or severally, in the other essays in the section. These observations provide a framework in which to view the video testimonies.

(1) The video testimonies of Holocaust survivors supplement what we learn from written sources such as memoirs, memorial books, governmental records, and trial transcripts.

(2) The video testimonies enable us to look at the Holocaust from a multidisciplinary perspective, since the witnesses touch on geography, sociology, psychology, economic history, politics, art, and literature in their accounts.

(3) The video testimonies allow us to respond to the variety of responses of the victims to the policies of the Third Reich; we cannot generalize about survivors' experiences since each survivor has a unique story.

(4) The video testimonies raise a number of questions about memory, which in turn make the viewer reconsider what is historical evidence: how accurate can an account be after thirty or forty years? How does the viewer deal with discrepancies within the testimony? How selective is the witness's memory?

(5) The video testimonies primarily offer insights into the history of the Holocaust from the point of view of the victim; perpetrators are not likely to testify on videotape about their experiences.

(6) The video testimonies often lack information on the more general historical framework of the Third Reich since the witnesses convey their own personal experience.

The Importance of Survivor Testimony

Nora Levin

Nora Levin, author of The Holocaust: The Destruction of European Jewry *and Associate Professor of Modern Jewish History and Director of the Holocaust Archive at Gratz College, Philadelphia, spoke on a panel with Martin Gilbert in 1987 at a symposium sponsored by the Anti Defamation League of B'nai B'rith. She reinforced Gilbert's views on the value of oral testimony and reminded scholars of the existence of contemporary victims' testimony in addition to postwar accounts. She also emphasized the role that Holocaust testimonies play in the preservation of memory of traditional Jewish culture in European society.*

The recent publication of Martin Gilbert's book *The Holocaust: A History of the Jews of Europe During the Second World War* has done much to move the focus of Holocaust research to the survivor, or more precisely, to return to that focus. Continuously and unsparingly, Dr. Gilbert keeps himself and the reader locked into the suffering of the victims as they face death in all of the hideous ways devised by the Nazis. It is he who has given many thousands the posthumous burial and humanity they were denied by the Nazis. Each is named and snatched out of the anonymity that survivors and, indeed, Jews throughout history have not been able to bear—an unknown gravesite for the dead.

Dr. Gilbert's insistent focus on the victim, who is after all the very center of Holocaust history, recalls to mind a similar focus of the very distinguished Holocaust historian, Dr. Philip Friedman, himself a victim, who somehow was able to transcend his own suffering and loss of family to Holocaust history. While the war was still raging in the fall of 1944, Dr. Friedman founded the Jewish Historical Commissions in Lublin and Lodz. He also gathered first-hand data from the surviving victims inside the displaced persons camps of the liberated zones and wrote the first monograph on Auschwitz in 1946. Many other works followed. He saw the earliest studies and accounts by survivors and witnesses and judged them critically, as a disciplined historian. He also predicted accounts from partisan or particular points of view—Zionist, Bundist, Communist, religious—and, as they appeared, was likewise critical. He died in 1960 and so, regrettably, could not critique the important works of the past twenty-five years, or, more important, make additional important contributions himself. However, we still profit from the works that he left and from many of his ideas regarding Holocaust research, including the admonition to write Holocaust history "from the inside."

In 1957, in a lecture in Jerusalem, Friedman also envisioned works that would concentrate on the Jewish life that continued under and despite the persecution, terror, and mass murder. His challenge was rooted in his own powerful sense of the ongoingness of Jewish history, a mighty flow which not even the Catastrophe stopped. His hope was that there would be a radically new kind of Holocaust history "in which the central role is to be communal existence with all the manifold and numerous aspects involved." In reflecting on this concept, I believe that we already have many studies that reveal the desperate efforts to keep community bonds and traditions, both religious and secular, maintained, even as communities were being extinguished. We see these efforts in the underground cultural life of the ghettos, the house committees, the classes for children, the secret work of the archivists in Lodz and Vilna, the remarkable Ringelblum Archives, the bonding in the Zionist and socialist youth movements and resistance cells, the struggles of the Jewish Councils to hold on to shreds of the old Kehillah and *kultesgemeinde* [Jewish religious communal body] functions and responsibilities in a nihilist universe.

The Warsaw Diary of Adam Czerniakow, I believe, is one of the most powerful documents of this kind in all of Holocaust literature. We have other evidence of desperate efforts by many Jews to keep fragments of communities, sub-communities, and group traditions from destruction, to prevent, at the extremes of risk and fear, a complete sundering from the past. These efforts, as we know, were doomed, but they reveal the tenacity of the hold of the old communal patterns and a dread of total dissolution. This does not mean a mythical Jewish unity, of course, which we have never had—but bonds within sub-groups that constituted Jewish communal existence before the war, an existence that was characterized often by conflict.

The drive to salvage records, community histories, photographs, libraries, and memorabilia attests to the fear and dread of a rupture, a shattering of the ties to the past. And the urgent need to write, to describe what could not be described, was to bind past to the future, to bear witness to what could not be borne.

Facing death, victims felt the importance of saving some shred of their experiences from obliteration, knowing that the Jewish future—if there would be any—would depend on a valid transmission of the past. There are many examples of this. The historian Yitzchak Schipper told Alexander Donat in

Auschwitz that "everything depends on who transmits our testament to future generations." In the memorial book for Tarnow, we come to know the comrades who worked with Schipper in the kitchen in Maidanek. They realized what was at stake in trying to save him so as to provide this transmission, but he perished.

To speak of Schipper immediately calls to mind the names of other Polish Jewish historians—Meyer Balaban and Emmanuel Ringelblum, who also perished—and they call to mind the name of Simon Dubnow, the historian of Polish and Russian Jewish history. All perished, but their works have not, and their works form part of the large historic Jewish communal experience—a legacy for new generations to study and ponder.

We still struggle to pierce the reality of Planet Auschwitz, to overcome the abyss that separates the victims from the rest of us who were not there. But not language, not film, not the utmost stretching of literary or visual gifts can ever achieve this. We continue nevertheless.

Of surpassing importance, I believe, are the massive collections of survivor testimony, still largely unopened and unexamined. The obsession to save everything we have of survivor testimony and collect even more seems not to abate. Each interview is wholly unique and taps new valuable material of historic, social, and psychological value. Those researchers who are using these oral history archives are continuing to deepen and expand not only our factual knowledge but also our appreciation of the abyss. Those who interview survivors come to realize that the experiences simply cannot be conveyed in ordinary language. The groping for words, the painful silences, disjointed narrative, random details, and fragmented images defy ordinary—even extraordinary—language. In our interviewing we are outside of chronological time. The survivor is actually back in the ghetto, fighting hunger, or watching a dear one being snatched away, or living through a selection, or watching a beating in camp barracks, in a trance-like state, alone with his unsharable horror and harrowing memory. He has lost us and the so-called "real world."

This foreknowledge that what was experienced can never be shared or conveyed often leads a survivor to decide not to try to speak, even or especially to one's children. However, the movement of survivor gatherings increased popular awareness of the Holocaust, and the sense that it soon will be too late has encouraged survivors increasingly to break the silence. There is inevitable pain, but also, I find, a quality of healing in bringing out part of the buried past, of overcoming some of the remembered helplessness in speaking about it and in partly mastering the past this way. The interview with a nonjudgmental listener also helps to recover the personhood, the individual human being whose identity was wiped out.

Sometimes the children themselves find the right moment to break open the seals. At this very time, I know two young women, second-generation children who are now able to speak to hitherto silent mothers: one who lived in Germany; another who was in Transnistria, whose daughter only now has been able to read about the camp and whose mother has written a journal which neither she nor her daughter has been able to open until now. The experiences of survivors tell us much about the breakdown of all coping mechanisms, the destruction of selfness—what Primo Levi calls "the demolition of man"—an evocation of a world for which we have no words, human experiences which do not fall within the ordinary framework of historic research, but which every researcher in Holocaust history must be keenly aware of. Such experiences are as much source material as the more conventional documents. When we move down to the terms of conventional language, and think of organizing this huge sea of survivor testimony, we realize that we are only in the primitive first stages of classifying taped and transcribed material and putting it into library catalog systems and computer data bases for access. I believe that wholly new dimensions of Holocaust history, wholly new approaches and techniques, will become possible as the archival centers organize the material and create inter-archival center networks. We at Gratz have been in touch with the Video Archive for Holocaust Testimonies at Yale and the Center for Holocaust Studies in Brooklyn (which is directed by Dr. Yaffa Eliach), to look into the possibilities of standardizing categories for abstracts and access terms.

Meanwhile, individual centers have been working on special projects that contribute to Holocaust history. The Center for Holocaust Studies has produced the valuable *Hasidic Tales* and a work on the liberation of the camps. We at Gratz are collecting material on the French concentration camps to which refugee Jews, including children, were confined—camps organized and maintained by the French in 1939-1940, before the German occupation. We also are making special efforts to interview Soviet Jews who survived the war—a part of Holocaust history about which we would like to know much more than we do. We also are publishing an anthology of testimony of survivors who were adolescents during the war, whose experiences coincided with their vital growing years from childhood to adulthood. Some were caught as children, putting them into this framework as young teenagers. Others were older teens with more life experience. These years took them into their early adulthood, followed many times after the war by immediate marriage and new families. What is valuable in these accounts is the interweaving of coping skills in order to survive, of denial and risk-taking, of mastery over feelings of vulnerability, of developmental tasks of adolescence aborted, crippled, speeded up, or delayed.

We also have, as part of the burden of Holocaust history and the history of Jewish communities in Europe, documentation in the memorial books—*yisker* books—which are in the tradition of Jewish communal existence. Mr. S. Schneiderman, the Yiddish journalist, estimates that more than one thousand memorial books have been published in Tel Aviv, New York, Buenos Aires and Paris, the latest one for a 600-year-old Jewish community in Breziv, in southwest Galicia, Poland. The first of these was a memorial book of Lodz, which appeared in 1943. A unique volume was published in a displaced persons camp in Munich in 1947, in memory of the destroyed community of Sherpts, written in Yiddish but in Latin letters. Many thousands of writers and editors have participated in the creation of these books, and they vary in quality, but they represent an astonishingly rich resource which until now very few professional historians have used. The books contain pre-Holocaust histories of towns and cities, including economic, cultural, and religious life, political conflicts, prominent personalities, and folklore. For the Holocaust period, there are details of physical and spiritual resistance, as well as details of the destruction of the towns and lists of names of townspeople who perished. Here we have, then, as we do in Dr. Gilbert's book, the victims— communities and individuals—rescued from anonymous ashes and bone and given their human due.

Soon after the war, memorial books became a major project of *landsmanshaften*—mutual aid and fraternal societies of pre-war emigrants and survivors from the same town. In addition to relief help for the needy and funeral benefits, the *landsleut* [countrymen] began to search everywhere for survivors from their town, and for ways to commemorate the dead in local cemeteries. Often widely dispersed, they have come together on the anniversary of their town's liquidation by the Nazis, or some other commemorative occasion.

Jack Kugelmass and Jonathan Boyarin have recently translated and edited excerpts from seventy-three of these memorial books in a volume called *From a Ruined Garden* (which includes a geographical index and bibliography by Zachary Baker), thus opening up very rich sources, enabling us to have a taste of what can be found.

The memorial books are a genuinely communal response to the Holocaust, a way of binding and bonding the living with the dead, the *landsleut* of the pre-war and Holocaust years, and the generations of the Holocaust with those of us who want to remember them. I myself have witnessed the compelling need to search for these connective strands across the abyss. A few years ago, in Philadelphia, I helped Shimon Kipnis and a small group of Soviet Jewish newcomers and Yiddish-speaking American Jews from Russia collect the names of 2,000 Jews whose relatives had been murdered at Babi Yar. Letters streamed in from every part of the world, as far away as New Zealand, letters written by hand, containing precious family photographs and details about the lives of the dead, beseeching us to reproduce everything in a *yisker* book so that the dead might be rescued from oblivion.

The Jewish historian Yosef Yerushalmi has written a provocative book called *Zakhor* which has displeased some historians, but which says something profoundly significant about the importance of memory of the past as a central component of the Jewish past. He makes a distinction between memory and historiography and argues that the Jewish historian has had only a restricted role in the preservation of Jewish memory, that ritual and liturgy have played the crucial role in the past. Who can heal what Yerushalmi calls the disruption of Jewish memory? Who can help heal the wounds inflicted upon Jewish life? He finds historians, including himself, unequal to the task because of the immensity of the burden. The historian, Yerushalmi believes, characteristically, is not a restorer of Jewish memory, nor does he come to replenish the gaps in memory. In Yerushalmi's words,

> He constantly challenges even those memories that have survived intact. No subject is potentially unworthy of his interest, no document, no artifact, beneath his interest. . . . all features which cut across the grain of collective memory which is drastically selective. Certain memories live on; the rest are winnowed out, repressed, or simply discarded by a process of natural selection which the historian, uninvited, disturbs and reverses. The question remains whether, as a result, some genuine catharsis or reintegration is foreseeable.

It is a very troubling question, I believe, which we continue to grapple with.

To remember, in Jewish tradition, has been a holy obligation—perhaps never in our history as powerful a force as we feel it now in trying to find appropriate rituals, prayers for, and monuments to the Holocaust dead. Some of these efforts are undoubtedly in poor taste, too unrestrained, and inappropriate. But these are tangible symbols of the need to remember, to bond with the dead, to add to the threads over the abyss. Such efforts are healing. They serve memory. They allow survivors to mourn as they must do, and momentarily create a community of survivors and the rest of us who were spared.

In the field of Holocaust history, it seems to me, there are possibilities for binding up the separation of historian and memory keeper, even to advance the healing process—to mourn and record, to feel pain and remember, to examine documents, to bond with survivors and take strength from their recovery from the world that destroyed man—to reform and reconstitute images and realities of self and community.

The Holocaust Archive at Gratz College primarily houses audiotaped testimonies of Holocaust survivors. Transcripts of many of these tapes are available from Gratz College.

Transforming Oral History: From Tape to Document

Brana Gurewitsch

Brana Gurewitsch, librarian and archivist at the Center for Holocaust Studies in Brooklyn, New York, describes the process developed at her center for verifying the historical accuracy of oral testimonies given by Holocaust survivors.

"Don't ask me dates" is the title of a poem written by a survivor interviewed by the Center for Holocaust Studies several years ago. The apparent conflict between this survivor's impulse to describe and the historian's need to quantify, however, is neither absolute nor inevitable. Within the unique nature of Holocaust oral history lies a special blend of reality and unreality, of the factual and unbelievable.

For over forty years, writers have been struggling against the inadequacy of language to describe the Holocaust. Elie Wiesel said, "I prefer to take my place on the side of Job, who chose questions and not answers, silence and not speeches."[1]

Yet the result of silence is forgetting. To be silent is to consign to oblivion a cataclysmic event and an entire generation. And just as Elie Wiesel has not been silent, the same overwhelming need to tell the story has gripped thousands of survivors, who have either written their memoirs or participated in various oral history projects which record their memories in systematic fashion.

By definition, oral history seeks to identify gaps in the written historical record, locate the eyewitnesses whose personal testimony relates to those gaps, and by means of a tape recorder, attempt to fill these gaps systematically, using the criteria and methods of the historian.

The unique challenge of Holocaust oral history is that these criteria and methods may seem incompatible with verbal expression of Holocaust experiences. No taped interview, regardless of length, can record all of what the survivor may want to express. Neither can the most extensive written memoir. The carefully constructed interview can, however, capture subtle nuances of meaning in the interviewee's voice and gestures.

The need to pursue additional information may well be questioned by those familiar with the voluminous written documentation already available on the Holocaust. The military, civil, and economic records of the period are indeed of primary importance, and no serious historical inquiry will proceed without them. However, these records, produced with specific political and ideological goals, leave gaps which can now be filled only by oral history. The Nazi ideology of the Jew as *Untermensch* [sub-human] does not portray Jews reacting and responding to the events which overtook them. Indeed, the Nazi-Deutsche language of euphemism and subterfuge was deliberately designed to disguise what was really happening, rather than to record events objectively for the future. With "resettlement" meaning deportation to death camps and "evacuation" referring to death marches, it is clear that while Nazi records may be useful, they fail to completely describe what was happening. Allied records, too, are not always accurate reflections of reality. With uniquely "blind" objectivity, American records do not list Jews among those liberated from concentration camps, for in the United States, Judaism is defined as a religious grouping, not a nationality. Similarly, because concentration camps were not military objectives, the records of their liberation are extremely scanty in American military reports, where they appear at all. The effect of these omissions is to erase the Jewish survivor from the records of the American occupation, an absurdly painful situation which was not rectified until August 1945, after the Harrison Report made it clear that the American policy of not identifying Jews was counterproductive if not scandalous.[2]

These, and other gaps in existing written documentation, were recognized by Professor Yaffa Eliach in the early 1970s, and a systematic oral history project was begun which sought out eyewitnesses whose testimony would add information and broaden the historian's perspective. Several groups of eyewitnesses were identified whose recorded interviews would indeed begin to fill these gaps. The testimonies of Hasidic and religiously observant Jews add a dimension not previously explored: the reactions and responses of Jews as Jews to a situation in which choices were not viable, to circumstances which left the Jews with no options, where all avenues of escape were blocked. The testimonies of American and other Allied liberators add the perspectives of the bystander and the response of young people brought up in a democratic society to the excesses and extremes of Nazi fascism. The experiences of the Greek Jews, of Sephardic background, are another previously unexplored dimension of the Holocaust, demonstrating the similarities and differences with which Jews of various cultural backgrounds responded to persecution. Finally, the experiences of people who were children during the Holocaust, ignored by those who mistrust the testimony of eyewitnesses too young to properly evaluate what was happening, have yielded a treasure house of material about the Jewish family, Jewish values, Jewish education, and community responses.

In addition to identifying particular groups of eyewitnesses whose testimony needed to be recorded, Professor Eliach also pioneered the systematic process of verification of the testimony, by which raw interviews are transformed into reliable documentation. By training interviewers to include historical data in their interviews, and by subjecting the interviews to a rigorous process of historical verification, the Center for Holocaust Studies with the guidance of Professor Eliach has succeeded in creating a valuable, reliable resource in its growing collection of more than 2,000 recorded interviews.

This process begins with the training of interviewers. Interviewers must see themselves primarily as historians searching for additional information. The primary requisite is, therefore, knowledgeability of the subject matter, rather than simple good will or a sympathetic nature. Although the sympathy must be present, it is the interviewer's knowledge of the material which will determine the value of the interview and even the response of the interviewee. The interviewer who is well informed, having asked certain key questions in advance and having prepared thoroughly for the interview, will gain the confidence of the interviewee. Knowledgeability helps to overcome the interviewee's doubts about adequately describing what happened. If the interviewer demonstrates knowledge of specific facts and events, the interviewee will feel less "alone" with the material.

The interviewer never loses sight of the need to insert the verifiable markers of the time, geography and names into the interview. Interviewees who insist that they do not remember dates can often be assisted in locating an event in time if the concept is expanded beyond the secular calendar (a birthday, anniversary, etc.). "Jewish time" relates to the Jewish, lunar calendar which could be and was calculated, even in Auschwitz, by the rising of the new moon each month. The seasons of the year are another aspect of time which are universal. Using these guidelines the testimony of a very young child, who remembered that the Germans first took action against his town in summer (because it was hot and he wore short pants and sandals) and on a Friday (because the Jews all went to the synagogue that evening) could be verified. It was indeed on Friday, July 5, 1941 that the Germans executed the Jewish leadership of that child's small town of Herz, Rumania, among them his father, the Rabbi.[3]

The geographic markers are equally important, and the careful interviewer will make sure that the location of each event is clear, adding such landmarks as rivers, mountain ranges, or nearby larger towns or cities for more precise identification. Finally, it is essential to know who the participants were, and to name them wherever possible. The sympathetic interviewer will often be able to overcome the reluctance of the interviewee to name individuals described negatively, and conversely, the interviewee may see the interview as a "living memorial" to an individual whose name and deeds would otherwise be forgotten.

Verification involves using standard reference works to clarify and standardize spellings and the sequence of events. A variety of reference works must often be used, in various languages, to take note of changes in spellings of places, names, or the Yiddish variants often used by interviewees. The need for researchers with language skills is paramount. The sequence of events can be verified from historical studies relating to particular areas, from German documents, U.S. Army documents, and other oral histories relating to the same events. Other useful sources are yiskor books (memorial books) published in memory of specific Jewish communities, which often have extensive articles relating to specific events of prominent personalities.

In order to verify events or descriptions from other oral histories, a useful cataloguing system has been established at the Center for Holocaust Studies, which reflects not only locations and names, but both broadly and narrowly defined subject areas. At the Center for Holocaust Studies, each interview is abstracted and catalogued under several cross-referenced categories. This subject cataloguing provides the researcher with immediate access information from the verified oral histories in the Center's collection.

When a transcript is prepared, the verified place names, names of people, and subject titles are assembled alphabetically into an index keyed to page numbers, thus facilitating the researcher's access to specific episodes in the interview. When doubts are raised by the researcher about the clarity of the testimony or about testimony which seems to contradict other, documented sources, these comments are entered into the file or inserted as footnotes in the transcript. Any restrictions which the interviewee may have placed on the interview are carefully observed.

Uncorroborated, unverified taped memoirs are not real history. They may be of interest within a family, as folklore, or as "human interest stories." But people have been transmitting their history in oral form from time immemorial. Over the course of centuries, tradition has exercised its judgment and decided what is history and what is myth. With the assistance of twentieth century technology, we can systematically capture oral memoirs, subject them to the most rigorous scrutiny and deliberately add them to our fund of reliable history. In the case of Holocaust history, to do this is to rescue the memories of the martyrs and the heroes, and to retrieve from memory a chapter which we must begin to assimilate if we want to move civilization forward.

Perspectives on Oral History by the Historian Martin Gilbert

Mary Johnson

In April 1988 Facing History and Ourselves invited Martin Gilbert to speak on "The Search for the Evidence of the Holocaust." He ilustrates his arguments with passages from his recent study The Holocaust: The Destruction of European Jewry During World War II. *This summary of the major themes pertaining to testimony in Gilbert's lecture was written by Mary Johnson.*

"It has become fashionable among historians," remarked Martin Gilbert at a recent lecture on Holocaust scholarship, "to dismiss oral testimonies as inadequate, unverifiable evidence for historical research." Objecting to this anti-oral history trend, Gilbert argued that it is not the nature of evidence from oral testimonies that should receive such strong criticism. If historians were properly trained to analyze and interpret survivor testimonies, oral history could yield valuable insights and enhance information gleaned from written contemporary records. Oral testimonies could help historians enter into fuller understanding of the victim's experience in Nazi Germany than is possible with the more traditional tools of historical research—public documents, private correspondence, and statistics. In his comprehensive study of the Holocaust from the victims' point of view, Gilbert estimates that between forty and fifty pages draw heavily from evidence in oral testimonies; at times, long quotations are used from transcripts. "These add a certain flavor and texture," Gilbert explains, which bring one closer to this history.

Gilbert pinpoints three features of oral testimonies that have made them valuable tools for his research: accumulation of detail; cross referencing; and documentation of events not documented in contemporary evidence.

Oral testimonies allow for an accumulation of detail about an event. Different survivors describing the same event might elucidate different aspects of the event as they bear witness. By listening to their different voices, the historian gains a richer understanding of the event in question.

Oral testimonies also allow for cross-referencing. For example, many accounts tell of the hanging of Rosa Robota, involved in the plot to blow up the crematoria at Auschwitz. Studying the diverse interpretations of the execution, the historian has an opportunity to check for contradictions and inaccuracies in memory. Moreover, the historian has a chance to study how an event such as this had a varying impact on the witnesses.

Another important feature of oral testimonies is that at times they provide the only evidence of an event since no contemporary evidence of the event has surfaced.

The testimony of Rudolf Reder, one of the two survivors of Belzec concentration camp, is a case of how oral testimony affords insights into something for which no evidence exists in contemporary accounts. Reder, who settled in Canada after the war and died recently, was not a meticulous recorder, but he does allow us to know something about the punishment procedures in the killing center. Gilbert reads Reder's description of a boy who got off one of the transports asking, "Does anyone ever escape from here?" The boy was hanged; since he was strong, he was still alive after three days. The Nazis completed the job by stuffing sand down the boy's throat with sticks until he died.

The second survivor of Belzec, Chaim Hirschman, left his testimony through the voice of a third party. He had begun his testimony on March 19, 1946 before the Lublin Commission. Since he had not completed testifying on this day, he returned home with plans to return the following day and resume his testimony. As he was going home, he was murdered. His second wife, Pola, whom he had married shortly after the war, asked to testify in Chaim's place, since he had told her about Belzec. While this is third party evidence, Gilbert explained that Pola had heard of the camp so soon after the war that she was able to preserve details that would otherwise be lost with the death of her husband.

Postwar accounts of the *Einsatzgruppen* [Nazi mobile killing units] actions are also important because so little contemporary evidence survives. According to Gilbert, the testimony of Rivka Yosselevich at the Eichmann trial in 1961 is truly remarkable. She was a simple woman, Gilbert explains, but the event was such that her description comes across as almost poetic.

Testimonies such as those of Rivka Yosselevich and Kurt Gerstein have led Gilbert to believe that historians ignore oral testimonies of Holocaust survivors at their own peril: these rich resources supplement existing documents and at times fill gaps in historical knowledge. Above all, Gilbert has found that oral testimonies from the Holocaust enrich our knowledge of the victims' experiences in ghettos and concentration camps even though we can never truly understand the full dimensions of their experience in the "other world."

See Martin Gilbert's "The Search for the Evidence of the Holocaust" in **Resources** *for a more comprehensive discussion of various forms of historical evidence including the use of oral testimony.*
A videotaped presentation of Martin Gilbert's presentation is available at the Facing History Resource Center.

Preliminary Reflections on Using Videotaped Interviews in Holocaust Education

Lawrence Langer

One startling discovery emerging from the viewing of the Fortunoff Video Archive tapes is the impossibility of drafting a profile of a prototypical survivor or survival experience. Although it might be an exaggeration to call every experience unique, it is clear that each one is different. Even when witnesses have been in the same labor, concentration, or death camp, the details of recollection are modified by so many distinct factors—memory, personality, extent of loss, duration of imprisonment, health, moral attitude, depth of spiritual commitment—that no unified view emerges from the testimony. Anyone who believes that survivor ordeals were similar will be disappointed by these tapes, which confirm exactly the opposite: the separate value of each survivor narrative.

An initial challenge we have encountered is the difficulty of entering into the world of the witness, whose living presence on the screen establishes a personal confrontation that written memoirs only occasionally achieve. Here the face and voice of the survivor rivet the audience's attention to the unfolding story, whose details are so radically unlike the knowledge and experience we bring to the encounter. One needs to study these tapes as one reads a book, before attempting to teach it. But the task is especially weighty, since the pleasure and entertainment that often accompany the reading and teaching of history or literature are totally absent from viewing these testimonies. And for this vacuum, all viewers, whether educators or students or the general public, need to be prepared.

One way of doing this is to reflect collectively on another of our preliminary findings, the noticeable differences between written and oral survivor testimony. If confirmed, these differences may turn out to be profoundly significant, for our understanding to date has been based primarily on published memoirs and interpretations of these memoirs. The literary memoir is a written document, governed by considerations of style, narrative, and often chronological continuity; conceptions of character that may be influenced if not determined by literary precedents, particularly ideas of heroes, heroines, and villains; and finally, a controlling moral vision, which suggests that certain kinds of behavior generate specific consequences: together is better than alone, cooperation better than self-concern, and most of all, perhaps, a theme repeated in memoir after memoir, that the human spirit is a crucial factor in the challenge to physical survival in the camps.

Deromanticizing Experience

One surprising preliminary revelation of these tapes is the virtually unanimous determination of the witness to deromanticize his or her experience. Indeed, the words "hero" and "heroic" have never been mentioned on the tapes we have seen thus far—except by the interviewers. Although many witnesses testify to their will to survive, they freely admit the vulnerability of this "will," which was not an heroic resolve but an effort to keep alive. Many confess that the desire to die alternated with the will to live, the one in the forefront depending on the circumstances at the moment. The same woman who tells of staying in her bunk refusing to eat the meager rations supplied her speaks forcefully of her resolution at other times not to die because that was exactly what the Germans wanted. Literature teaches us that heroic behavior harmonizes contradictory inclinations into a unified vision of reality, which in turn provides a sturdy basis for dignified conduct. The testimony on these tapes offers no apology for the inability to unite contradictory attitudes. The unpredictable nature of so much of the survivor experience eliminated the possibility of total or even primary control over one's future. One did what one could and hoped for the best, knowing that nonetheless the worst might gain the victory.

We are now discussing how these distinctions might be used to advantage in educational situations. The subject in print or on tape is identical: the Holocaust. But the oral witness, limited to one or two hours of testimony (unlike the author, who can stop writing, reflect, reconstruct, consult other individuals, revise), usually must draw on spontaneous (though sometimes premeditated) recollection; is not bound by chronology, but can leap forward or backward in time in the narrative without worrying about disrupting continuity; and—perhaps most important—is involved in his or her own story in a way that is immediately and visibly evident. There are moments when we can see the narrative literally overtaking the narrator, as the eyes turn inward away from the camera, and he or she is in communion with a reality in whose presence we are guests rather than participants. One overwhelming quality of such video testimony is its intensity, its captivating emotional power, its frequently ruthless honesty, its almost instant fascination. Anyone who has tried to involve students of any age in a written text will appreciate the advantage of such instantaneous appeal in a learning situation.

The effect of such appeal on an audience, of course, is equally important, and that is why preparation is necessary for everyone included in the encounter. The vacuum left by the absence of pleasure and entertainment is abundantly filled by pain, a pain that grips us despite attempts to remain detached and objective. As viewers of videotaped testimonies, we have to tune our ears to the dissonant voices of the witnesses, not to the harmonies of our own expectations. Everyone concerned with these tapes brings to the encounter his or her own agenda. We have found that a vital first step is developing the ability to suspend that agenda temporarily and to submit to the visible and audible realities on the tapes, however disconcerting or threatening or contradictory they may be. Although the narratives are frequently depressing, rarely uplifting, we cannot permit our emotional reactions to define or categorize our response. We do not yet know, of course, what that viewing experience will be like for the diverse audiences Facing History is concerned with: educators, students, clergy, adult education groups, community organizations. But we do know from our own experience how essential (and difficult) it is to surrender to the content of the testimonies with minds cleared of the accumulated myths resulting from years of exposure to Holocaust studies.

Surrendering Myths

One of these myths is that there is a particular mode of behavior that promotes or ensures survival under the extreme conditions of the concentration camps. There is no evidence from these accounts that such prototypical forms of conduct existed. We must be prepared to accept the unpleasant possibility that chaos did not necessarily breed order and that dehumanization did not gradually crystallize into redeeming visions of the human. The witnesses, with few exceptions, are simply not asking us to see suffering as a spiritually transfiguring experience. They almost never mention the romantic behavior that our contact with imaginative literature has nurtured in us. Solzhenitsyn's Nerzhin from *The First Circle* and Camus's Dr. Rieux from *The Plague* do not appear on these tapes. The witnesses here are uniformly modest about their "achievements" in surviving and resist all attempts to make their ordeal seem heroic. That impulse seems to come from us, not them.

It may seem unrealistic to expect audiences to suspend anticipation when confronting witness testimony, but the inability to do so can lead to some curious results, as occurred with the interviewers in some of these tapes. At the end of one tape, for example, the interviewer cannot resist admiring what

293

she calls the witness's "pluck" in managing to survive her camp ordeals. "No, dear," the survivor disagrees, rejecting pluck and substituting luck, only to revise even this with the insistence that it was "stupidity" that enabled her to survive. But she is not permitted to elaborate on her meaning, since the interviewer clings to her notion of pluck, while the cameraman interjects his own enthusiasm with the exclamation, "You had guts, lady!" and the tape ends with this verbal tug of war, reflecting not "ultimate truth" but the interpretations of the participants, which in turn depend on the kind of vision of reality each needs to preserve the harmony of his or her own life. Unless we remain open to the possibility that "stupidity," with all of its implications, may indeed be one reason for survival, we will miss a vital dimension of these testimonies.

The Problem of Accuracy

A second challenge has to do not with us but with the witness, and that is the challenge of memory, or accuracy. Our response to witness testimony (as to all autobiography) is an act of faith. The narrator, we assume, does not invent but reconstructs. Thirty or forty years later, however, memory can be imperfect, and witnesses make mistakes. Some of them are inconsequential details, like having the wrong year for deportation; others are more significant, like suggesting that there were gas chambers in camps where we know there were none. But some errors are major and might seriously mislead audiences. For example, a crucial error occurs in the testimony of a woman who worked in the crematorium area of Auschwitz-Birkenau. She reports vividly of the day in October 1944 when she saw the gates of the area burst open and the men rush forth in an escape attempt, when suddenly simultaneously all four of the crematoria blew up. In fact, only one crematorium exploded and a second was slightly damaged, while the other two remained intact and continued to function until Himmler ordered them dismantled more than a month later, as Soviet troops approached the camp.

How shall we address this problem? One feels uncomfortable leaving such mistakes unacknowledged, since by doing so we are hardly performing a service for the current student or future researcher, who may not be aware of the real facts. Certainly if we use these tapes with students, we cannot expect them to be so thoroughly informed. Interrupting a witness in the midst of a narrative to point out the error could prove intrusive, not to say embarrassing, and might well destroy the rapport necessary for the uninterrupted flow of memory. Perhaps videotaped testimony should be annotated; perhaps we should conclude that historical accuracy is not of primary importance for this particular medium. The problem is not insoluble, but it exists, and we need eventually to confront it.

But for instructional purposes, especially at a time when revisionists allege the exaggerations and distortions of Holocaust testimony, these discrepancies are a humbling revelation. One of the recurrent themes in these tapes is human fallibility, the differences between our images of what we may become and what in fact circumstances frequently impose on us. One of the most surprising moments appears when a survivor speaks of the "foolish act" of resistance. Challenged, he explains; his memory is clear. The Germans in his town posted an edict, listing the names of ten of his townsmen; for any German attacked or injured, those specific ten men would be shot. Later, he continues, in the labor camp where he was sent, the Germans announced that for each attempt to escape or damage equipment, fifteen coworkers would summarily be executed. So sabotage, he concluded, was suicidal. And successful escape, he might have added, was murder. "You had to help your fellow man," he says, by which paradoxically, he means "Submit." And in his furrowed brow as he speaks, one can discern the pain of his remembered humiliation at having to behave according to these principles. Reformulated reality, like errors of memory, may have less to do with distortion than with the efforts of the surprised sensibility to cope with extraordinary facts and find a place for them in some moral scheme in the present. These efforts reveal the fragile society from which the survivor emerges and challenge audiences to wrestle with the unfamiliar features.

This becomes especially evident when we consider the role of the interviewers in these tapes. They are one link between the speaker and the audience, whose members cannot address the tape but must only listen. In this sense, the interviewer is a surrogate for the audience; hence one entry for the student into the survivor's reality is to study carefully the encounter between survivor and interviewer. Will members of an audience grow more conscious of their own agendas by recognizing the interviewer's? This is a supposition we may want to test. We study these videotapes not only to learn about the survivor experience but also to learn about the challenge of videotaping accounts of survivor experience. These range from the witness who breaks down in the midst of her account to appeal: "I came here hoping to find help; I do not know what to do anymore," to the interviewers, who often are visibly moved.

The interviewer reaction warns us about a situation we may encounter with audiences. Anyone proposing to use these tapes with audiences must be aware of the threat they represent to one's emotional integrity. The spectacle of overwhelming human misery, even in retrospect and insulated by language, is not easy to deal with. Interviewers and viewers alike seek ways of protecting themselves (as indeed, often, do the witnesses). These videotapes compound the problems of anyone preparing Holocaust curriculum: How to help viewers react in ways that will not be destructive. How to ask or formulate questions that will be illuminating rather than evasive without in any way injuring the dignity of the survivor or denying or retreating from what he or she is saying. How to retain contact between our own orbit of reality and what seems to be the witness's intersecting orbit of unreality.

Developing Engaged Empathy

How do we develop what we might call an "engaged empathy" with the witness or survivor? He or she comes from a world of "there," and we dwell in a world of "here," and these tapes are valuable insofar as they help us build a bridge across the intervening abyss. As the interest grows around the country in disseminating videotaped survivor or witness accounts, we need to recognize the liability of showing them to audiences who are merely curious or well-intentioned or enthusiastic but not informed—or prepared. That, indeed, is one of the major commitments of Facing History and Ourselves: to create historically- and emotionally-informed audiences. Prepared to hear details they will be unable to believe. Minimally aware of the vocabulary so many testifiers use as if the words had been absorbed into English: *Appel* (roll call), *Lager* (camp), *Haftling* (prisoner), *Kapo* (prisoner unit-leader), and so forth. Numerous times in these tapes a witness will lean forward to inquire of the interviewer, "Do you understand what I am trying to tell you?" That the question remains suspended forty years after the event indicates how much we still have to learn.

Although these videotapes contain much information supplementing what we already know about matters of perennial concern like survival and resistance, one of their most promising features is how few stereotypical responses they include to issues of faith, moral dignity, and spiritual defiance. One is surprised by how seldom a witness evokes these traditional values of a civilized world. Total oppression by force, combined with fear and a sense of utter helplessness, sometimes played bizarre variations on traditional reverence for the human in the world of the camps. If we are disappointed by how rarely narratives of heroic gestures appear in these tapes, we should consider the distress of the survivor across whose face a look of despair slowly spreads at the humiliating recollection of his reaction, deceived by the enemy and his own innocence into not recognizing the fatal significance of that crucial moment when he was sent to the right and the rest of his family to the left and their death.

For a videotaped presentation of Lawrence Langer discussing the uses of video testimonies in studying the Holocaust, see his "Imagining the Unimaginable" in Appendix 1.

The Act of Recall: A Variety of Voices

Lawrence Langer

A man's face appears before us, in communion with himself, barely aware of the video camera that is recording his testimony. He tells of the evacuation of Blechhamer work camp in the bitter winter of 1944 as the Russians approached—not as bad as Auschwitz, but bad enough. They walk for hours that seem like days: finally they stop for the night. He tells of lying on a floor next to another prisoner, an older man, who is ill. They are brought a small bread ration, the first food all day. And the witness, still in dialogue with his memory more than with us, whispers: "I waited for him to die, so that I could eat his bread myself." An artless, unhappy confession, reviving a moment nearly forty years in the past, but as fresh in his memory now as if it had happened yesterday.

Clearly one of the most painful ordeals for the survivor who consents to such recorded testimony is the reawakening of what we might call the humiliated imagination. "How can I tell these things to my children?" asks this particular witness, who can scarcely tell them to himself. "Why should I hurt them with stories of how they [the Nazis] hurt me?" And his question is unanswerable; of course, he shouldn't—he is unable to. Yet if we are to understand the extraordinary demands made by the Holocaust on man's moral nature, we must have such honest testimony, and the impersonal camera plays a vital role in encouraging its expression. A member of a large family himself, all but two of whom were murdered, this survivor recalls the brother who was in Blechhamer with him. He tries to explain, still as much to himself as to us, what a human being is like when he is so weakened by hunger that he can barely drag his feet along. When you are struggling to survive, he says, and just stay alive a while longer, nothing else matters. So when his brother, who is walking beside him, complains that he cannot go on, and asks for help, the witness can do nothing; he can scarcely support himself. Then the Germans take his brother out of line and shoot him. "Today," the witness says, signs of the humiliated imagination imprinted on his face, "I ask myself whether I could have done anything. I should have been able to do something." Obviously, behavior that seemed inevitable then appears insufficient now. No bridge crosses the gulf between two alien ethical moments, between the principle of brotherhood as we define it in our leisured security and the counterclaims of survival and mutuality in the uncertain moral terrain of the Nazi system of dehumanization. And the humiliated imagination is left hovering over this abyss, wondering whether the deficiency lies in oneself, struggling to live with the unreconciled challenge.

Another voice from these videotapes succinctly expresses the dilemma, one of the cruelest legacies of the Nazi violation of human feelings: today, he insists, "the memory of what we were unable to do is worse than the recollection of what they did to us." Not all might agree, but the point is forcefully made by the formulation itself. Returning to Auschwitz recently to commemorate the fortieth anniversary of the camp's liberation, Elie Wiesel responded to an interviewer's question about why the Jews didn't do more to protect themselves with the reply that Auschwitz was a universe with rules of its own. Since those rules often contradicted the principles of behavior that nurture us and those we seek to educate, these tapes, and narratives like the one I have cited, are invaluable for conveying to the uninitiated certain unhappy truths about the survivor ordeal with an immediacy that we can share in no other way.

But not all such truths are unhappy. If the humiliated imagination is despondent at the memory of a will paralyzed without consent, there also exist in these tapes instructive examples of the gratified imagination (the other side of the coin, as it were), instant decisions having nothing to do with heroic gestures that saved lives when reflection, passivity, or procrastination would have doomed them. I think of the French soldier, captured during the German invasion of France in 1940, who is sent with several hundred other military men to a prisoner-of-war camp deep inside Germany. Some months later, a detachment of SS appear one day and at roll call ask all Jewish soldiers to step forward. All do—with the exception of the witness testifying on this tape. He says that some of his Jewish friends nod at him as if to ask "Why are you holding back? Didn't you hear the order?" But he persists, determined to ignore the command. Satisfied with the number they have procured, the SS march off with their victims. The survivor says he never saw them again. He himself later escapes, makes his way to southern France, and joins the underground. What motivated him not to step forward? He can hardly say himself, but he knows that instant decision is responsible for his being here to tell his story today.

A mind wary of threat perhaps stocks itself with potential strategies: is this one of the crucial lessons of these testimonies? Sometimes they work; sometimes they don't. A husband and a wife testifying together, both physicians from Lvov, tell how they falsified their papers, changed their names, and passed as Polish non-Jewish doctors during the Nazi occupation. But one day the local Underground, not known for their sympathy to Jews posing as Christians, arrange to send one of their members for a consultation: a recent graduate from Lvov medical school himself. They are terrified: how does one prepare for such an encounter? What if he recognizes them as former Jewish classmates? Will he denounce them? He arrives, knocks on the door; it opens—and they instantly recognize each other! But he is more alarmed than they, for he too is Jewish, posing in the Underground group as a non-Jew, with forged papers! In this instance, strategy was not necessary; coincidence intervened.

But later this husband and wife are not so lucky. They are trained by the Polish Institute of Health as experts in lice extermination—his very word, uttered without a trace of irony—and they are dispatched to Warsaw to help control a typhus epidemic. At the train station a Polish policeman comes up to him and says "You look Jewish," and takes them both to the police station across the street. They inspect his wife's papers, which are falsified in several places, and declare them authentic; they examine his, and refuse to believe he is not Jewish. So they take him into the next room for the "ultimate" test: he drops his trousers, and is quickly identified as a Jew. The Polish policeman announces that he is taking him to Gestapo headquarters.

What options are available to the victim at this moment? Had fear paralyzed him, his doom would have been swift and certain: the Germans did not know the meaning of mercy. So his instant decision is to start swearing at the Polish police officials, reminding them that the battle of Stalingrad had recently been lost, that bastards like them would certainly receive retribution after the Russians arrived, that he was in Warsaw to protect them against typhus and they were turning him over to their common enemy—at which point his wife says "Give him your watch," and he slides off his watch and thrusts it into the official's hand. The official says one word—"Go." And their lives are saved.

The witness, as well he might, exhibits great satisfaction at his successful maneuver, which preserved his own life and probably his wife's. He attributes the favorable results of his refusal to accept a *fait accompli*. But we know that no general principle of survival behavior can be deduced from his action: in the presence of a Gestapo official, his strategy would have failed. A year earlier, before the battle of Stalingrad, it might have failed too. Was it greed, fear for his own future well-being, or grudging respect for the victim's determination not to appear craven that motivated the policeman to release him? So many variables impinge on the situation that it defies exact analysis. Yet it confirms the value of instant decision rather than hesitation at crucial moments like these where options are possible.

These videotaped interviews illuminate with stunning clarity the meaning and vital importance of that expression, "where options are possible." Later generations will add to the importance of locale the equally significant temporal complement of "when options are possible." Understanding victim behavior requires a clear perception of the role time and place played in responses to potential atrocity. Expecting the weak and starving witness from our first example to draw on "instant decision" is as foolish and uncharitable as wondering why the Jewish doctor posing as a Christian does not manifest the "humiliated imagination" during his narrative. They come from two worlds of experience: only we the audience can encompass both.

But no conclusion is conclusive, as anyone who has viewed one hundred of these videotaped testimonies will verify. Asked at the end of their presentation what they remember most from their ordeal, the husband-and-wife medical team answer differently: "My memory is filled with four years of fear," the wife immediately replies. And almost simultaneously, her husband insists: "I have no memory of fear. Only defiance—and always being ready for what may happen!" The humiliated imagination confronts the voice of instant decision, and we must be wise and compassionate enough to appreciate the need and the reasons for both. And shrewd enough to realize that for the survivor the painful act of recall involves judgment as well as memory, self-justification as well as truth.

300

Making Distinctions: The Ultimate Challenge

Lawrence Langer

"We were always afraid," says a Jewish survivor who was thirteen at the time of the Warsaw ghetto, of which she is speaking.

They never knew when the Germans would make an incursion into the ghetto and round up a group for deportation. So they lived in constant fear for their lives. "We were always afraid," says another witness, also thirteen at the time, whose testimony is also recorded on one of the tapes in the Video Archive for Holocaust Testimonies at Yale University. But the second witness is a young Polish non-Jewish girl, and the fear and danger she is speaking of, though entirely real, are of another order. These two testimonies remind us of the absurdity of undertaking studies in comparative suffering. They also confirm, however, the need for making distinctions, if we are ever to understand the meaning and significance of the Holocaust experience for those who were its victims and for those caught in the web of Nazi oppression without being subject to genocide.

The perspective of the speaker is of primary importance, since it shapes the response of the uninitiated learner. The non-Jewish Polish girl is describing the illegal high school she attended in Warsaw, where presumably she was studying a trade but actually was receiving forbidden instruction in regular high school subjects.

Periodically, without warning, the Germans visited or raided these schools. Each classroom was wired with a buzzer to warn the teacher that an "inspection" was coming; promptly each student would turn to a sewing machine pretending that she was receiving instruction in making underwear. So they were in constant suspense, for discovery by the Germans meant punishment (though certainly not death in gas chambers).

Much is to be learned, therefore, as we listen to the voices of non-Jewish witnesses, about kinds of fear, kinds of suffering, and kinds of victimhood. We discover the imaginative energy required to move beyond one's personal ordeal of deprivation, and we see how difficult it is to make that leap, when one's own experience of the "worst" seems incomparable.

"They expect the worst," writes Auschwitz survivor Charlotte Delbo in *None of Us Will Return* of unsuspecting new arrivals at the deathcamp. "They do not expect the unthinkable."

301

But for the young non-Jewish Polish girl in the illegal high school, whose father apparently was a victim of the Katyn forest massacre, who saw several hundred Polish hostages executed in the streets in retaliation for the Polish Underground's assassination of a German officer, the worst is the unthinkable. And we cannot dispute her point of view, nor fail to sympathize with her memory of ruin.

Yet the complexities of these taped narratives compel us to discriminate, while retaining a sensitivity to the ordeal of everyone who suffered pain and loss.

"We were always hungry," recalls another witness, only a child during the German occupation of the Soviet Union, where he was born and where his family had to work in a forced labor camp. They did the best they could, but they never had enough to eat. Only occasionally could his father come up with a chicken, he remembers—stark evidence of one kind of minimal diet, but positive luxury when juxtaposed with the testimony of a woman who tells of watching a camp inmate steal food from her own daughter, or of another painfully revealing how she stole a piece of bread and margarine from the woman sleeping next to her on a bunk in Auschwitz.

"I felt bad all the next day," she says, "but I was so hungry. So this wasn't good and that wasn't good; what choice did you have?"

The situation is summed up by a Jewish character trying to describe hunger to the non-Jewish narrator of one of Tadeusz Borowski's Auschwitz stories: "Real hunger is when one man regards another man as something to eat. I have been hungry like that, you see."

To our stunned silence the partial though inadequate response might be Primo Levi's explanation in *Survival in Auschwitz: "Just as our hunger is not that feeling of missing a meal, so our way of being cold has need of a new word."*

The need for new words becomes thunderously clear from the testimony of another non-Jewish survivor, who with perfect innocence fails to recognize the transparent transference of language which is taking place as he describes the persecutions he suffered during the war.

While his father was away in the army, the family home in Vienna was bombed, so the authorities sent him and his mother to live in a small village near Salzburg for the duration of the war.

As city people, he complains, "We were never accepted" there. He says that as a child he just could not understand why people rejected him. "Why did I look like a Martian to them?" he complains. "Why did they think I was wearing funny clothes?"

The self as victim obviously wears many guises, or disguises, and the failure or refusal to make distinctions teaches us something about the ease of confusing anguishes.

This particular witness remembers his father's appearance after he escaped from Russian captivity and walked a thousand miles westward across Czechoslovakia back into Austria. "My father, of course," he matter-of-factly observes, "was a physically and spiritually broken man when he got home. He was down to 110 or 105 pounds."

What is happening here (and the reader may interpret it as he or she will—the explanations are not simple) is an appropriation of the "imagery" of the Holocaust survivor to another kind of suffering.

"Well, it's not like being stuck in a camp," this witness admits; "but it was bad. Sometimes it's easier to deal with bad certainties than huge uncertainties, because you have no way to plan."

Now what is meant by "bad certainties"—the fate of the Jews in the death camps? And "huge uncertainties"—his family's future, the father somewhere in Russia, the rest of them relocated in a village alien to the urban culture they were accustomed to?

Half-jokingly, this witness refers to himself as one of the first displaced persons in Austria, an unmistakable if unconscious adaptation of the language of Holocaust experience to the disruption of domestic tranquility.

Clearly, the differences between "bad certainties" and "huge uncertainties" still need to be explored and defined.

What I have called the humiliated imagination afflicts witnesses on virtually all of these tapes, as they wrestle today with their failure or inability to see clearly then and to have found a way of acting that would satisfy their vision now of how they should have behaved.

A long and often profound interview is with a non-Jewish Polish man, merely fourteen when the war broke out, who was recruited by the Polish Underground as a messenger and then trained as a transmitter to send radio messages to England during the war.

The job was fraught with unrelieved danger, since the Germans were searching for illegal transmitters around the clock. Although one of his responsibilities was to send information about events in the Warsaw Ghetto and the death camps, including eyewitness testimony from two escapees from Maidanek (which may have been the first "hard" evidence about the gassings to reach the free world), this witness frankly admits rather apologetically that they didn't understand at the time what the Jews were trying to say.

"It just didn't occur to us that it was urgent and something great had to be done," he confesses, reflecting the attitude of political leaders around the world. "We were thinking of other things ourselves."

The honest testimony of this witness—and certainly he does not speak with pride—reveals something about the mindset of millions during this period.

He didn't analyze the moral implications of what was happening to the Jews, he says, because other matters were more urgent. He had only fifteen minutes to get his messages through, then had to move on, since he was always hunted.

"It was routine work for me. My only obligation was to transmit the messages that were given to me."

It is easy enough to condemn this as a bureaucratic insensitivity to the agony of strangers, or even a thinly veiled antisemitism. But I think it is neither. It is the recognizable voice of a generation and a century that has lived through repeated physical crises but has never been trained to view them or adjust to them with the moral urgency they demand.

Historians may some day record this as a crucial distinction of our era: our complacent (or suppressive) ability to endure actual and threatened crises without acknowledging their impact on the moral reality of our lives. Misconceptions, distortions, and evasions abound (one thinks immediately of the nuclear situation) because they are easier to cope with than the possible atrocities they conceal.

The education of our Polish Underground member illustrates the dilemma. He concedes that at the time he envied the Jews in the camps because, as he puts it, they could hold hands. They were together. They could face their fate even if they were killed with each other. (Here we see how "killed," like "hunger," requires a "new word" if it is to be properly understood.)

While the Jews were there, he continues, they could sleep "on time." They could get up on time. He himself, on the other hand, was alone, hunted, always afraid of being shot and just left in a ditch and no one would ever know what had happened to him.

There were victims and victims under Nazi domination, each overwrought by his or her own sense of personal danger. This truism may help to explain the failure of imagination that prevented so many from recognizing the impending doom of the Jews.

Today, this witness confesses, "I understand that they were alone in a block, and that the moral vacuum they had to face was worse than what I had to face, but I didn't understand that at the time."

After the war, the truths of the death camp ordeal had penetrated his consciousness, and he is open in his admission of the shift in his perception.

Indeed, his present lucidity illuminates his remembered account of what it was like to live as a human being under perpetual stress, and his illustrations help us to distinguish between life in crisis as an Underground fighter outside the death camps, and as a helpless victim within. Outside, he says, you operate on two levels of response—a normal level and a level of tension.

During the city of Warsaw uprising in August 1944 he was going from home to home with a friend in search of German soldiers, when suddenly his friend moved around a corner, was shot, and fell down dead.

He darted around the corner himself, raked his machine gun back and forth, and he says, "I killed all four of them." "Then," he adds, "you suddenly go back to normal, and you realize your friend is dead, and you've killed four other people, and you feel bad, but you didn't have time to think about it when you were doing it."

During those tense moments, he explains, "you mobilize yourself on your survival instincts, and after it's over, you come back. You need someone to hold you because you are in very bad shape."

Much more needs to be said about the difference between two relentlessly painful ordeals: "coming back" from the tense context of killing as this member of the Underground describes it, and "coming back" from the tense context of a nearly successful program of genocide.

The inclusive vision of this witness culminates in an observation that poses the most problematic challenge of the Holocaust: "The tragedy of my life is that I cannot convey my experience to another person and make him better through my experience."

In this brief discussion of distinctions, let me end with a most difficult distinction that faces all educators trying to teach about this event: although the Holocaust is not essentially a morally instructive experience, in the sense that knowing about it improves our humanity, and perhaps not even a "tragedy," if by that word we mean to imply learning through suffering, we must study it nonetheless for an adequate understanding of those much-abused terms on whose proper appreciation in our time and *in* time the future security of our universe may depend—suffering and humanity.

The Missing Voices of the Killers: What Could They Tell Us?

Lawrence Langer

"If you hate," says one Jewish witness who survived the Holocaust, "you kill with passion. They killed us without even caring." Among the hundreds of recorded testimonies in the Fortunoff Video Archive for Holocaust Testimonies, as far as I know, there are no voices of the killers. We must reconstruct the personalities and motives of the killers from the scant information provided by their surviving victims, from the records of the Nuremberg War Crimes Trials, from transcripts of the Eichmann trial interrogations, from the "autobiography" that Rudolf Hoess, Commandant at Auschwitz, wrote before his execution, from scattered interviews with Auschwitz guards now serving life sentences in Germany, and from secretly filmed interviews with former concentration camp guards and other Nazi officials in Claude Lanzmann's film *Shoah*.

But even with this information, what do we have? How far have they led us along the path of understanding how some human beings could have murdered so many millions of others "without even caring"? The truth is that despite all our sources and resources, this question still haunts and perplexes us. It continues to do so because the killers who speak up, grudgingly or boastfully, do not tell us what we want to know. Why should they? They hedge, evade, distort, suffer lapses of memory, engage in self-pity, shift blame, claim ignorance, or simply lie. The lie was normally the first line of defense. I remember attending the trial of SS General Karl Wolff, Himmler's liaison to Hitler, in Munich in 1964 and hearing the youthful prosecutor ask the elderly Wolff whether he had ever visited the Warsaw ghetto. (One of the charges against Wolff was that he had arranged rail transportation to the ghetto for Jews who were then sent to their death in Treblinka.) Wolff's prompt reply was "No." The young attorney then read an entry from a diary kept by a military official on duty in Warsaw, announcing the arrival in the

306

ghetto of Reichsführer SS Himmler and SS General Karl Wolff, giving specific time and date of arrival. Confronted by this documentary evidence, Wolff searched his memory and admitted that he might have been to the ghetto once. Asked why he hadn't said so in the first place, Wolff replied: "Ich bin ein alter Mann"—"Your honor, I'm an old man, and I can't remember everything." The presiding judge leaned forward, pointed at Wolff, and observed: "Herr Witness, If *I* had ever visited the Warsaw ghetto, I would *never* have forgotten it." The observation was superfluous, since obviously Wolff had not forgotten either, but it underlines the ease with which the accused denied incrimination until confronted with incontrovertible proof.

Perhaps we should not expect otherwise in a court of law. Even when war crimes are the issue, we should expect the accused to maintain his innocence. What then are we to make of the "secret" interview in *Shoah* which Claude Lanzmann conducted with Franz Suchomel, former Treblinka guard, whom Lanzmann assured (himself lying now) that he would neither record nor videotape his testimony? (He did both with concealed equipment.) Believing that he is engaged in a private conversation, Suchomel says that his first impression of Treblinka was "catastrophic." They had not been told, he adds, "how and what . . . that people were being killed there. They hadn't told us." "You didn't know?" Lanzmann asks. "No! Suchomel replies. "Incredible!" is Lanzmann's rejoinder. "But true," insists Suchomel. "I didn't want to go."

The newly arrived camp guards, including Suchomel, are taken on a tour of the camp: "Just as we went by, they were opening the gas-chamber doors, and people fell out like potatoes. Naturally, that horrified and appalled us. We went back and sat down on our suitcases and cried like old women." For someone appalled by the spectacle of Jews tumbling from the gas chamber like potatoes (a singularly inept image), Suchomel offers some of the most excruciatingly graphic descriptions in the entire film of the killing process and the disposal of bodies. Indeed, he seems to take a bizarre pride in his role as one of the few remaining authorities on the history of the death camp Treblinka. He is almost pedagogical in his vivid description of Treblinka as "a primitive but efficient production line of death." Somehow, he has detached his own person from the event, and it simply never seems to occur to him that he shares some responsibility and blame for the mass murder he depicts.

Unable to argue that he was never in Treblinka, or that he has forgotten what happened there, Suchomel adopts a strategy common to Eichmann and other functionaries who were directly involved in the killing of Jews. They never view themselves as agents, but only as instruments, obeying orders initiated elsewhere. Hence Suchomel can even fabricate a strange camraderie between the camp guards and the several hundred Jews of the work detail in Treblinka, who were not sent directly to their death. When the deportations slackened temporarily early in 1943, those Jews stopped believing that they would survive. The guards, says Suchomel, offered support: "We kept on insisting 'You're going to live!' We almost believed it ourselves. If you lie enough, you believe your own lies. Yes. But they replied to me: 'No, chief, we're just reprieved corpses.'"

So we are invited to believe in the spectacle of SS men arriving in Treblinka but not knowing where they are; of SS men seeing their first Jewish corpses and crying like old women; of SS men bolstering the faltering courage of discouraged Jews, although their freely-given oath is to support the program to make Germany and Europe free of Jews. "If you lie enough, you believe your own lies. Yes."

To be sure, we gain some valuable descriptive information from Suchomel about a death camp that no longer exists. But apparently human beings like himself were transformed into mere cogs in what he calls "the efficient production line of death" at Treblinka. No shred of introspective self-analysis, of what it means to have been a living and active participant in the destruction of European Jewry, emerges from his testimony. The human value of his words is diluted, virtually extinguished, by the ease with which he adopts a self-exonerating attitude. He simply does not see himself as a villain.

How else are we to explain the insistence of so many Nazi functionaries after the war, including Eichmann himself, that they never hated Jews? By dispensing an image of Jewish inferiority as if they were selling the idea for a new product, the Nazis predisposed an entire population, as well as the much smaller band of perpetrators, to an attitude toward the potential victims that was divorced from the usual emotional sources of virulent hatred. Paradoxical as it may sound, they dispensed what we may call a dispassionate antisemitism which enabled the individual to achieve a divorce between demeaning hatred and sheer political hygiene, the practical reality that if a nation were to be pure, it must be purged of its "diseased" elements.

Dispassionate antisemitism encouraged a healthy schizophrenia, which allowed men like Suchomel and Eichmann to distinguish untraumatically between their own human selves and their less-than-human victims. Therefore, when they comment on their roles during the war, they do not speak of a collapse of their private moral systems. Asked after the war whether he thought the Jews were guilty of anything, Rudolf Hoess,

Commandant at Auschwitz, replied that the question was unrealistic: he "had never really wasted much thought on it." When he finished building the gas chambers and crematoria of Auschwitz, Hoess rejected the carbon monoxide used for killing at Treblinka for the swifter and deadlier insecticide hydrogen cyanide (Zyklon B), and boasted that his installations had a capacity ten times greater than those of Treblinka. Disposing of bodies became for him a problem in "fuel technology." But the disguised vocabulary for mass murder was not a demonic subterfuge; rather, it represented the smug satisfaction of a man who until his execution in 1947 could not see himself as a monster, but only as a superior methodologist. From the commandant at Auschwitz to the simplest clerk in the railway ministry who arranged timetables for transports, Nazi antisemitism expertly transformed accomplices to mass murder into well-trained methodologists, doing a job as well as they could. And that is how they conveniently perceived themselves.

Because of this, even when we fill in the missing voices of the murderers who do not appear on our videotaped testimonies, we remain perplexed and discontent. They offer us far less than we desire. Their transparent evasions do not compare with the anguished searching of memory we get from authentic survivors of the Holocaust, who confront their own limitations with a courage and honesty that the Suchomels and Eichmanns lack the imagination to understand. When Lanzmann in *Shoah* asks Franz Grassler, deputy to the Nazi commissioner of the Warsaw ghetto during the war, what he remembers of "those days," he replies like Karl Wolff: "Not much. I recall more clearly my prewar mountaineering trips than the entire war period and those days in Warsaw." One is left gasping with disbelief at Grassler's bold-faced insistence that the "German administration was never informed of what would happen to the Jews." He is the only former Nazi in the film not to insist on an unfilmed interview, or to exact a promise that his name would not be used. He is untroubled and unashamed, has no recriminations, suffers no remorse, and makes perhaps only one unreservedly true statement in his entire conversation with Lanzmann: "Mr. Lanzmann, this is getting us nowhere." And I am afraid that much the same would have to be said of most of the testimony from the "missing voices" of the perpetrators, were they available to us for study.

We would like to understand better the evil that was Nazism, and the mental process of the men who willingly and eagerly undertook the extermination of European Jewry. But one cannot explore or illuminate the demonic in men who were not demons. We only expose the ordinary. And the efficient. And the indifferent. And the cruel. We expose the effects, which were murderous, and still wrestle with the "causes," all of which, no matter how scrupulously scrutinized, continue to seem insufficient. If there is little honor among thieves, there is even less, as a skeptical Claude Lanzmann discovered, among mass murderers—a designation which none of the "missing voices" among the killers has ever accepted for its accuracy. Listening to Franz Suchomel sing the worksong of the doomed Jews in Treblinka—twice!—as if he were chanting some popular boy scout anthem, makes one wonder what kind of human creature we are confronted with. He boasts that not many people know the words to that song anymore, as if his contribution to historical research makes him an invaluable instrument in the efforts to recover the "facts" of that place called Treblinka. *Why* so few people recall the words today, and his connection to the reason why, never seems to occur to him. Like his superiors in the dock at Nuremberg, after having been stripped of their power, he appears pathetic. All the "missing voices," deprived of power, speak in evasive whispers, or not at all. For that reason, we applaud all the more the persistence of interviewers and witnesses whose testimonies are recorded in the Fortunoff Video Archives. Their voices *break* the silence, giving us access to murderous deeds that future generations of students will examine, even though the murderers refuse to do so themselves.

Interpreting Oral and Written Holocaust Texts

Lawrence Langer

After having spent twenty years reading and interpreting the implications of innumerable survivor memoirs, including exceptional literary achievements like Elie Wiesel's *Night* and Primo Levi's *Survival in Auschwitz*, to say nothing of dozens of plays, poems, and novels on this grim subject, one approaches the viewing of videotaped survivor testimonies with a certain perplexity and trepidation. The experienced reader and critic come equipped with tools of the profession, as it were, prepared to confront questions of style, continuity, character, authenticity, tragic vision, moral conflict, and spiritual growth. But what critical "tools" are available to the *viewer* of this unfamiliar form of "testimony," and how does viewing differ from the familiar challenge of reading a written text? Is there such a phenomenon as an oral "text," which invites us to do more than simply sit as passive audience to watch and listen, shuddering at the unfolding horrors in the narrative without apparent structure and often without chronological sequence, dredged up from memory by a prodding interviewer and the witness's own voluntary determination to find a vocabulary for his or her ordeal? The vast majority of Holocaust survivors are not writers, even amateur ones, so the videotaped interview is the only chance they have to move from invisible silence to visible expression. But just as a written text is "meaningless" without responsible readers, so oral testimony gains validity from viewer response, from the search for a principle of organization concealed in the narrative that even the witness may not be conscious of. Looking at these videotaped testimonies, in other words—and I now have seen more than 150 of them—gradually imposes on one the need as well as the responsibility to become an active participant in the narrative process even though one was not present at the original interview. In the beginning, I was convinced that these testimonies represented spontaneous narratives, unmediated by devices analogous to but not identical with ones we find in self-conscious literary texts. Now I am not so sure, and I would like to offer some illustrations why.

Consider the testimony of Sidney L., born in 1927 in a small town in Poland. His first piece of information is that he was one of nine children—not an extraordinary detail, since many survivors begin with a recital of their family situation. But as the narrative of more than two hours proceeds, this seemingly innocuous fact turns out to be a key to its internal structure. The testimony is virtually uninterrupted by questions; it seems to be a simple recounting of how Sidney L. survived. And on its most obvious level, it is. But its counter flow, its alter ego, as it were, is the rehabilitation through memory of the family that has vanished.

This explains the first hour of the interview, a patient recital of Sidney L.'s family experience in pre-war days, including a description of his grandparents' house and the visits there. At first, one wonders why he alludes so often to the difference in age between himself and his three older sisters, his two older brothers, his younger siblings, including a "kid" sister. It is as if he needs to establish a separate identity for each one of them. The reason becomes clearer with the outbreak of war, which abruptly and violently and permanently alters the family's destiny. Two or three days after the Nazi invasion of Poland, still early in September 1939, his father sends him to buy some tobacco, and when he returns home about ten minutes later, he finds that a stray Nazi bomb has left a crater where his house once stood. He arrives in time to find some men digging out his mother's body. The bodies of three sisters and two brothers soon follow. His father and youngest sister are wounded, but survive. His married brother, not living at home, is safe; another brother is uninjured. And himself.

So by his count, five remain. Although other details intervene, the next episode he recalls vividly is returning home one day to see two Gestapo men leading his father and married brother (who lived nearby) into a courtyard, where they are put against a wall and shot. The rest of his narrative recounts his existence until "liberation," but one main focus is on the fate of his younger sister, whose whereabouts he can trace until early 1943, when she is deported somewhere and disappears without a trace, never to be heard from again. He and his brother remain, and both pass through various labor camps, though the subterranean theme of his narrative is that part of himself vanishes with the death of each sibling, part of his sense of family, community, control over his future. For this reason, his brother plays an increasingly crucial role in his story. Though separated for long intervals, they are reunited in Bergen-Belsen in 1944, when they find themselves to be in adjacent compounds of the camp.

At this point, he tells us, he had a "vision" that they were both going to survive, an instinctive conviction that their reunion had a special meaning for the future. He enters into a kind of dialogue with himself, revealing the process whereby the imagination manufactures the idea of "fate" to protect itself from the ravages of random circumstance. He returns in desperation to what we might call the predictive spirit, that capacity in us which, notwithstanding the counter-momentum of experience, tries to impose a meaningful sequence on the details of one's life. If it turns out so, if the reunion with his brother did indeed foretell survival for both of them, he will have retrospective proof of his intuition.

But it doesn't turn out that way, and this provides him with the melancholy coda to his narrative. While he is in the infirmary at Bergen-Belsen, his brother is taken away to another labor camp: "I never saw him again." In the closing moment of his narrative, Sidney L. tries to express how this disappointment undermined his sense of continuity in life: "There were certain things that I believed—" Here he gestures with his fist, as if in resistance to a contrary universe, though he knows that the gesture is futile. "—and it didn't turn out to be. I was *positive* that I was going to live with my brother till the end of the war." He even uses the word "predestined," but only to expose how its value has been exhausted by his experience of the Holocaust. We are present at the birth of a point of view when the interviewer asks Sidney L.,

"Do you think it was your ability to hold onto that idea [that he and his brother were "predestined" to survive] that got you through to the end?"

The question invites simplified closure and reassuring conclusions, but the witness, drained by the implications of his own narrative, resists the temptation implicit in the question. "I don't know," he replies. "In all these things that happened—I played a very small part in everything that happened. There were very few things that I initiated, or planned out on this. This is how it happened: it took me from here and put me there . . . it was not my plan; it was not my doing." He defines his moral situation—or the moral paralysis of his situation—when he says: "I was never given a choice; I was never asked 'Do you want to do such and such?'"

Thus his narrative emerges not as a story of survival, but of deprival— deprival of his personal will, and of the members of his family. What he calls the power of "It" whittles away at his family until no one is left but himself, and only at the end do we realize that all along, while he has ostensibly been telling us how he managed to survive (the interviewer's question confirms our sense that this has been the substance of his story), the essence of his testimony has been the fate of those in his family who did not survive. His conviction that he and his brother at least were predestined to live is a last attempt to rescue from the ordeal of destruction some confidence in the experience of life; and when this fails, we as audience experience an existence defined not by its own survival, but by the death of others. It is a revelation filled with the vitality of its insight—and the gloom of its finality.

It is also a revelation, repeated again and again in these testimonies, of the crucial importance of continuous viewer complicity in the narrative process. A written narrative is finished when we begin to read it, its opening, middle, and end already established between the covers of a book. But oral testimony steers a less certain course, like a fragile craft veering through turbulent waters without knowing where the safe harbor lies—or whether it even exists.

My other illustrative testimony offers dramatic evidence of the difference between two forms of presentation, since the witness herself has written what she calls a historical novel about her experience of the Holocaust.

Barbara T. draws on her memory of that experience as well as on the book she has written about it. Since she uses both in her oral narrative, we have a chance to respond to each, and to observe the sharp disjunction between her oral testimony and the reading about her ordeal that she interjects into her account. Asked by the interviewer to describe her arrival at Auschwitz, she begins:

313

It was night, but it was light because there were powerful searchlights in the square. The air stank. Some people in the cars had died of thirst, of hunger, of madness. I felt a tremendous thirst. We had no water. And as the doors opened, I breathed in air as if it would be water, and I choked. It stank. And eventually we saw these strange looking creatures, striped pajamas, who got us into a marching line. . . .

Then an odd thing happens. The witness pauses, half mesmerized by her own narrative, as if returning from another place, and apologizes for her "absence": "I'm sorry, OK, I. . . I . . . forgive me . . . all right . . . I'm going to . . . I kind of was back there." Intensely aware of the exclusive *and* inclusive privacy of that moment, which she inhabits simultaneously alone and in the presence of a large potential audience (and the complicit viewer will be as aware as she of this complex interaction), she tries to resume her narrative, and succeeds—but only for a few moments: "Inmates whipped us out of the cattle cars, and they got us into rows of five."

At this point the interviewer, recognizing the strain, asks "Do you want to talk about that?" and Barbara T. replies: "Yes. I think so. I would like to read it. It's easier." She then reaches for her book, opens it to the appropriate page, and begins to read on camera:

We are dragged out of cattle cars, vomited into an impenetrable black night. Suddenly torches brighten up a black sky and I clearly see the night; it engulfs a square drenched in searing brilliance by powerful floodlights.

She hesitates an instant, skips a paragraph, and resumes:

Then screams knife the air and I cover my ears with my hands. Torches keep licking the sky like rainbows, and I quickly close my eyes but I still see the flames through my closed lids and the screams slash through my hands, into my ears, then a horrible stench hits my nostrils, I gasp for air but I choke. I am terrified. I don't know what to do.

Certainly the written passage is effective. But it is also transparently literary, alien to the verbal rhythms of the oral narrative. Of the dozens of testimonies I have viewed about arrival at Auschwitz, not one has mentioned being "vomited into an impenetrable black night." If we compare this self-conscious striving for stylistic impact with Barbara T.'s spoken testimony—"Inmates whipped us out of the cattle cars"—we cannot (or at least *I* cannot) escape the uncomfortable feeling that the book's idiom is intrusive on and distracting from the more spontaneous flow of the oral narrative. One gets the impression that the witness herself senses the disparity of tones, since she quietly puts the book down and never picks it up again.

Literature prods the imagination in a way that speech does not, striving for analogies to initiate the reader into the particularities of its world. Holocaust literature faces a special challenge, since it must give most readers access to a totally unfamiliar world. When flashlights and searchlights at Auschwitz lick the sky like "flaming rainbows," the reader is invited to use the simile as a ticket of entry to the bizarre landscape of a death camp. The singular inappropriateness of this image of natural beauty, good luck, and happiness to illuminate arriving at Auschwitz underlines the difficulty of finding an imaginative vocabulary for such an incomparable atrocity. Indeed, this fortuitous juxtaposition of literary and oral versions of the same moment of survivor experience raises some vital questions about interpreting survivor testimony that until now few commentators have sought to confront.

When the witness in an oral testimony leans forward toward the camera, apparently addressing the interviewer(s), but also speaking to the potential audience of the future (and this happens frequently in the tapes), asking: "Do you understand what I'm trying to tell you?"—that witness confirms the vast imaginative space separating his or her ordeal from our capacity to comprehend it. Written memoirs, by the very strategies available to the author—style, analogy, chronology, imagery, dialogue, a coherently organized and developed moral vision—strive to narrow this space, easing us into their unfamiliar world through recognizable literary devices. The impulse to portray reality when we write about it seems irresistible. Describing the SS man who greeted her mother and her on the ramp at Auschwitz, Barbara T. writes: "His pale blue eyes dart from side to side like a metronome," and once again one has the uncomfortable feeling of the literary transforming the real in a way that obscures even as it discloses. Yet until now we have depended almost entirely on written accounts of the death camp experience to gain insight into the nature of atrocity.

For the moment, I will argue no more than that videotaped testimonies provide the student of the Holocaust with an unexplored archive of "texts" that solicit from us original forms of interpretation. Reading a book that tries to carry us "back there" is an order of experience entirely different from witnessing someone like Barbara T. vanishing from contact with us even as she speaks, momentarily returning to the world she is trying to evoke instead of recreating it for us in the present. Her presence before us dramatically illustrates a merging of the time senses (so often revealed by witnesses in oral testimonies) that is virtually impossible to capture in the pages of a book. Yet this is one of the seminal responses of survivors to the Holocaust ordeal. A different kind of "continuity" seems to establish itself in many of these testimonies, one alien to the chronological sequence that governs most written memoirs.

Much work remains to be done in the new field of interpreting oral testimonies. Just as generations of commentators have investigated how readers "read" a written text, so we must begin to ask how viewers "view" a videotaped testimony. To be sure, not all testimonies are equally valuable for the student of the Holocaust, any more than are all novels, memoirs, or historical studies. Nevertheless, the patient viewer encounters enough unprecedented challenges to imaginative participation in the ordeal of memory before one's eyes on these tapes to convince me that they now form an indispensable untapped creative source for our understanding of the Holocaust experience.

Beyond Judgment

Primo Levi
translated by Raymond Rosenthal

Primo Levi helps us understand some of the difficulties involved in making the leap from the world of "normalcy" into the "other world" of the Holocaust. In pointing out the complexities of entering the abnormal world of concentration camps, Levi addresses the questions most frequently posed by students and teachers studying the Third Reich: Why didn't the victims escape? Why didn't they rebel? Why didn't they avoid capture beforehand?

Those who experienced imprisonment (and, more generally, all who have gone through harsh experiences) are divided into two distinct categories, with rare intermediate shadings: those who remain silent and those who speak. Both have valid reasons: those who remain silent who feel more deeply that sense of malaise which I for simplicity's sake call "shame," those who did not feel at peace with themselves, or whose wounds still burn. The others speak, and often speak a lot, obeying different impulses. They speak because, at varied levels of consciousness, they perceive in their (even though by now distant) imprisonment the center of their life, the event that for good or evil has marked their entire existence. They speak because they know they are witnesses in a trial of planetary and epochal dimensions. They speak because (as a Yiddish saying goes) "troubles overcome are good to tell." Francesca tells Dante that there is "no greater sorrow/than to recall happy times/ in misery," but the contrary is also true, as all those who have returned know: it is good to sit surrounded by warmth, before food and wine, and remind oneself and others of the fatigue, the cold and hunger. It is in this manner that Ulysses immediately yields to the urgent need to tell his story, before the table laden with food, at the court of the king of the Phaeacians. They speak, perhaps even exaggerating, as "bragging soldiers," describing fear and courage, ruses, injuries, defeats and some victories, and by so doing they differentiate themselves from the "others," consolidate their identity by belonging to a corporation, and feel their prestige increased.

But they speak, in fact (I can use the first person plural: I am not one of the taciturn) we speak also because we are invited to do so. Years ago, Norberto Bobbio wrote that the Nazi extermination camps were "not one of the events, but the monstrous, perhaps unrepeatable event of human history." The others, the listeners, friends, children, readers, or even strangers, sense this, beyond their indignation and commiseration; they understand the uniqueness of our experience, or at least make an effort to understand it. So they urge us to speak and ask us questions, at times embarrassing us: it is not always easy to answer certain whys. We are neither historians nor philosophers but witnesses, and anyway, who can say that the history of human events obeys rigorous logic, patterns. One cannot say that each turn follows from a single why: simplifications are proper only for textbooks; the whys can be many, entangled with one another or unknowable, if not actually nonexistent. No historian or epistemologist has yet proven that human history is a deterministic process.

Among the questions that are put to us, one is never absent; indeed, as the years go by, it is formulated with ever increasing persistence, and with an ever less hidden accent of accusation. More than a single question, it is a family of questions. Why did you not not escape? Why did you not rebel? Why did you not avoid capture "beforehand"? Precisely because of their inevitability, and their increase in time, these questions deserve attention.

The first comment on these questions, and their first interpretation, are optimistic. There exist countries in which freedom was never known, because the need man naturally feels for it comes after other much more pressing needs: to resist cold, hunger, illnesses, parasites, animal and human aggressions. But in countries in which the elementary needs are satisfied, today's young people experience freedom as a good that one must in no case renounce: one cannot do without it, it is a natural and obvious right, and furthermore, it is gratuitous, like health and the air one breathes. The times and places where this congenital right is denied are perceived as distant, foreign, and strange. Therefore, for them the idea of imprisonment is firmly linked to the idea of flight or revolt. The prisoner's condition is perceived as illegitimate, abnormal: in short, as a disease which must be healed by escape or rebellion. In any case, the concept of escape as a moral obligation has strong roots; according to the military code of many countries, the prisoner of war is under an obligation to free himself at all costs, to resume his place as a combatant, and according to the Hague Convention, the attempt to escape must not be punished. In the common consciousness, escape cleanses and wipes out the shame of imprisonment.

Let it be said in passing: in Stalin's Soviet Union the practice, if not the law, was different and much more dramatic. For the repatriated Soviet prisoner of war there was neither healing nor redemption. If he managed to escape and rejoin the fighting army he was considered irremediably guilty; he should have died instead of surrendering, and besides having been (perhaps only for a few hours) in the hands of the enemy, he was automatically suspected of collusion. On their incautious return home, many military personnel who had been captured by the Germans, dragged into occupied territory, and who managed to escape and join the Partisan bands active against the Germans in Italy, France, or even behind the Russian lines were deported to Siberia or even killed. In wartime Japan as well, the soldier who surrendered was regarded with great contempt: hence the extremely harsh treatment inflicted upon Allied military personnel taken prisoner by the Japanese. They were not only enemies, they were also cowardly enemies, degraded by having surrendered.

More: the concept of escape as a moral duty and the obligatory consequence of captivity are constantly reinforced by romantic (*The Count of Monte Cristo*) and popular literature (remember the extraordinary success of the memoirs of Papillon). In the universe of the cinema the unjustly (or even justly) incarcerated hero is always a positive character, always tries to escape, even under the least credible circumstances, and the attempt is invariably crowned by success. Among the thousand films buried in oblivion, *I Am an Escaped Convict* and *Hurricane* remain in our memory. The typical prisoner is seen as a man of integrity, in full possession of his physical and moral vigor, who, with the strength that is born of despair and ingenuity sharpened by necessity, flings himself against all barriers and overcomes or shatters them.

Now, this schematic image of prison and escape bears little resemblance to the situation in the concentration camps. Using this term in its broadest sense (that it, besides the extermination camps whose names are universally known, includes also the many camps of military prisoners and internees), there existed in Germany several million foreigners in a condition of slavery, overworked, despised, undernourished, badly clothed, and badly cared for, cut off from all contact with their native land. They were not "typical prisoners," they did not have integrity, on the contrary they were demoralized and depleted. An exception should be made for the Allied prisoners of war (American and those belonging to the British Commonwealth), who received foodstuffs and clothing through the International Red Cross, had good military training, strong motivations, and a firm esprit de corps, and had preserved a solid enough internal hierarchy. With a few exceptions, they could trust one another. They also knew that, should they be recaptured, they would be treated in accordance with international conventions. In fact, they attempted many escapes, some successfully.

For everyone else, the pariahs of the Nazi universe (among whom must be included gypsies and Soviet prisoners, both military and civilian, who racially were considered not much superior to the Jews), the situation was quite different. For them escape was quite different and extremely dangerous; besides being demoralized, they had been weakened by hunger and maltreatment; they were and knew they were considered worth less than beasts of burden. Their heads were shaved, their filthy clothes were immediately recognizable, their wooden clogs made a swift and silent step impossible. If they were foreigners, they had neither acquaintances nor places of refuge in the surrounding region; if they were German, they knew they were under careful surveillance and included in the files of the sharp-eyed secret police, and that very few among their countrymen would risk freedom or life to shelter them.

The particular (but numerically imposing) case of the Jews was the most tragic. Even admitting that they managed to get across the barbed wire barrier and the electrified grill, elude the patrols, the surveillance of the sentinels armed with machine guns in the guard towers, the dogs trained for manhunts: In what direction could they flee? To whom could they turn for shelter? They were outside the world, men and women made of air. They no longer had a country (they had been deprived of their original citizenship or a home, confiscated for the benefit of citizens in good standing). But for a few exceptions, they no longer had a family or if some relative of theirs was still alive they did not know where to find him or where to write to him without putting the police on his tracks. Goebbels' and Streicher's anti-Semitic propaganda had borne fruit: the great majority of Germans, young people in particular, hated Jews, despised them, and considered them the enemies of the people: the rest, with very few heroic exceptions, abstained from any form of help out of fear of the Gestapo. Whoever sheltered or even simply assisted a Jew risked terrifying punishment. In this regard it is only right to remember that a few thousand Jews survived through the entire Hitlerian period, hidden in Germany and Poland in convents, cellars, and attics by citizens who were courageous, compassionate, and above all sufficiently intelligent to observe for years the strictest discretion.

What's more, in all the *Lagers* the flight of even a single prisoner was considered the most grievous fault on the part of all surveillance personnel, beginning with the functionary-prisoners and ending with the camp commander, who risked discharge. In Nazi logic, this was an intolerable event: the escape of a slave, especially a slave belonging to races "of inferior biological value," seemed to be charged with symbolic value, representing a victory by one who is defeated by definition, a shattering of the myth. Also, more realistically, it was an objective damage since every prisoner had seen things that the world must not know. Consequently, when a prisoner was absent or did not respond at roll call (a not very rare event: often it was simply a matter of a mistake in counting, or a prisoner who had fainted from exhaustion) apocalypse was unleashed. The entire camp was put in a state of alarm. Besides the SS in charge of surveillance, Gestapo patrols intervened; the *Lager* and its work sites, farmhouses, and houses in the camp's environs were searched. The camp commander arbitrarily ordered emergency measures. The co–nationals or known friends or pallet neighbors of the fugitive were interrogated under torture and then killed.

In fact, an escape was a difficult undertaking, and it was unlikely that the fugitive had no accomplices or that his preparations had not been noticed. His hut companions, or at times all the prisoners in the camp, were made to stand in the roll call clearing without any time limit, even for days, under snow, rain, or the hot sun, until the fugitive was found, alive or dead. If he was tracked down and captured alive, he was invariably punished with death by public hanging, but this hanging was preceded by a ceremony that varied from time to time but was always of an unheard-of ferocity, an occasion for the imaginative cruelty of the SS to run amok.

To illustrate how desperate an undertaking an escape was, but not only with this purpose in mind, I will here recall the exploit of Mala Zimetbaum. In fact,

I would like the memory of it to survive. Mala's escape from the women's *Lager* at Auschwitz-Birkenau has been told by several persons, but the details jibe. Mala was a young Polish Jewess who was captured in Belgium and spoke many languages fluently, therefore in Birkenau she acted as an interpreter and messenger and as such enjoyed a certain freedom of movement. She was generous and courageous; she had helped many of her companions and was loved by all of them. In the summer of 1944 she decided to escape with Edek, a Polish political prisoner. She not only wanted to reconquer her own freedom: she was also planning to document the daily massacre at Birkenau. They were able to corrupt an SS and procure two uniforms. They left in disguise and got as far as the Slovak border, where they were stopped by the customs agents, who suspected they were dealing with two deserters and handed them over to the police. They were immediately recognized and taken back to Birkenau. Edek was hanged right away but refused to wait for his sentence to be read in obedience to the strict local ritual: he slipped his head into the noose and let himself drop from the stool.

Mala had also resolved to die her own death. While she was waiting in a cell to be interrogated, a companion was able to approach her and asked her, "How are things, Mala?" She answered, "Things are always fine with me." She had managed to conceal a razor blade on her body. At the foot of the gallows, she cut the artery of one of her wrists, the SS who acted as executioners tried to snatch the blade from her and Mala, under the eyes of all the women in the camp, slapped his face with her blooded hand. Enraged, other guards immediately came running: a prisoner, a Jewess, a woman, had dared defy them! They trampled her to death; she expired, fortunately for her, on the cart taking her to the crematorium.

This was not "useless violence." It was normal for new prisoners to think of escaping, unaware of these refined and tested techniques; it was extremely rare for such a thought to occur to older prisoners. In fact it was common for escape preparations to be denounced by the members of the "gray zone" or by third parties, afraid of the reprisals I have described.

I remember with a smile the adventure I had several years ago in a fifth-grade classroom, where I had been invited to comment on my book [*Survival in Auschwitz: The Nazi Assault on Humanity*] and to answer the pupils' questions. An alert-looking little boy apparently at the head of the class, asked me the obligatory question: "But how come you didn't escape?" I briefly explained to him what I have written here. Not quite convinced, he asked me to draw a sketch of the camp on the blackboard indicating the locations of the watch towers, the gates, the barbed wire, and the power station. I did my best, watched by thirty pairs of intent eyes. My interlocutor studied the drawings for a few instants, asked me for a few further clarifications, then he presented to me the plan he had worked out: here, at night cut the throat of the sentinel; then, put on his clothes: immediately after this, run over there to the power station and cut off the electricity, so the search lights would go out and the high tension fence would be deactivated; after that I could leave without any trouble. He added seriously: "If it should happen to you again, do as I told you. You'll see that you'll be able to do it."

Within its limits, it seems to me that this episode illustrates quite well the gap that exists and grows wider every year between things as they were "down there" and things as they are represented by the current imagination fed by books, films, and myths that only approximate the reality. It slides fatally toward simplification and stereotype, a trend against which I would like here to erect a dike. At the same time, however, I would like to point out that this phenomenon is not confined to the perception of the near past and historical tragedies; it is much more general, it is part of our difficulty or inability to perceive the experience of others, which is all the more pronounced the more distant these experiences are from ours in time, space, or quality. We are prone to assimilate them to "related" ones, as if the hunger in Auschwitz were the same as that of someone who has skipped a meal, or as if escape from Treblinka were similar to an escape from any ordinary jail. It is the task of the historian to bridge this gap, which widens as we get farther away from the events under examination.

With equal frequency, and an even harsher accusatory tone, we are asked: "Why didn't you rebel?" This question is quantitatively different from the preceding one but similar in nature, and it too is based on a stereotype. It is advisable to answer it in two parts.

In the first place, it is not true that no rebellion ever took place in a *Lager*. The rebellions of Treblinka, Sobibor, and Birkenau have been described many times, with an abundance of details; others took place in minor camps. These were exploits of extreme audacity worthy of the deepest respect, but not one of them ended in victory, if by victory one means the liberation of the camp. It would have been senseless to aim at such a goal: the excessive power of the guarding troops was such as to cause its failure within minutes, since the insurgents were practically unarmed. Their actual aim was to damage or destroy the death installations and permit the escape of the small nucleus of insurgents, something which at times (for example, in Treblinka, even though only in part) succeeded. However, there was never the thought of a mass escape: that would have been an insane undertaking. What sense, what use would it have been to open the gates for thousands of individuals barely able to drag themselves around, and for others who would not have known where, in an enemy country, to look for refuge?

Nevertheless, there were insurrections; they were prepared with intelligence and incredible courage by resolute, still physically able minorities. They cost a fearful price in human lives and the collective sufferings inflicted in reprisal but served and still serve to prove that it is false to say that the prisoners of the German *Lagers* [camps] never tried to rebel. In the intentions of the insurgents they were supposed to achieve another, more concrete result: to bring the terrifying secret of the massacre to the attention of the free world. Indeed, those few whose enterprise was successful, and who after many more depleting vicissitudes had access to the organs of information, did speak. But they were almost never listened to or believed. Uncomfortable truths travel with difficulty.

In the second place, like the nexus imprisonment-flight, the nexus oppression-rebellion is also a stereotype. I don't mean to say that it is never valid. The history of rebellions, that is, of insurgencies or revolts from below by the "many oppressed" against the few powerful, is as old as the history of humanity and just as varied and tragic. There were a few victorious rebellions, many were defeated, innumerable others were stifled at the start, so early as not to have left any trace in the chronicles. The variables at play are many: the numerical, military and idealistic strength of the rebels and those of the challenged authority as well, the respective internal cohesions or splits, the external assistance available to one or the other, the ability, charisma, or demonic power of the leaders, and luck. Yet, in every case, one can see that it is never the most oppressed individuals who stand at the head of movements: usually, in fact, revolutions are led by bold, open-minded leaders who throw themselves into the fray out of generosity (or perhaps ambition), even though they personally could have a secure and tranquil, perhaps even privileged life. The image so often repeated in monuments of the slave who breaks his heavy chain is rhetorical; his chains are broken by comrades whose shackles are lighter and looser.

The fact is not surprising. A leader must be efficient: he must possess moral and physical strength and oppression, if pushed beyond a certain very low level, deteriorates both. To arouse anger and indignation, which are the motor forces of all true rebellions (to be clear about it, those from below: certainly not the Putsches or "palace revolts"), oppression must certainly exist, but it must be of modest proportions, or enforced inefficiently.

In the *Lagers* oppression was of extreme proportions and enforced with the renowned and in other fields praiseworthy German efficiency. The typical prisoner, the one who represented the camp's core, was at the limits of depletion: hungry, weakened, covered with sores (especially on the feet: he was an "impeded" man in the original sense of the word—not an unimportant detail!), and therefore profoundly downcast. He was a rag of a man, and, as Marx already knew, revolutions are not made with rags in the real world but only in the world of literary and cinematic rhetoric. All revolutions, those which have changed the direction of world history and those miniscule ones which we are dealing with here, have been led by persons who knew oppression well, but not on their own skin. The Birkenau revolt, which I have already mentioned, was unleashed by the special *Kommando* [unit] attached to the crematoria: these were desperate, exasperated men but well fed, clothed, and shod. The revolt in the Warsaw ghetto was an enterprise worthy of the most reverent admiration. It was the first European "resistance" and the only one conducted without the slightest hope of victory or salvation, but it was the work of a political elite which, rightly, had reserved for itself a number of basic privileges in order to preserve its strength.

I come now to the third variant of the question: Why didn't you run away "before"? Before the borders were closed? Before the trap snapped shut? Here too I must point out that many persons threatened by Nazism and fascism did leave "before." These were political exiles, or intellectuals disliked by the two regimes: thousands of names, many obscure, some illustrious, such as Togliatti, Nenni, Saragat, Salvemini, Fermi, Emilioi Sergre, Lise Meitner, Arnald Momigliano, Thomas and Heinrich Mann, Arnold and Stefan Zweig, Brecht, and many others. Not all of them returned, and it was a hemorrhage that bled Europe irremediably. Their emigration (to England, to the United States, South America, and the Soviet Union, but also to Belgium, Holland, France, where the Nazi tide was to catch up with them a few years later: they were, as are we all, blind to the future) was neither flight nor desertion but a natural joining up with potential or real allies, in citadels from which they could resume their struggle and their creative activity.

Nevertheless, it is still true that the greater part of the threatened families (the Jews, above all) remained in Italy and Germany. To ask oneself and us why is once again the sign of a stereotyped and anachronistic conception of history, more simply put, of a widesperad ignorance and forgetfulness, which tends to increase as the events recede further into the past. The Europe of the period

1930-1940 was not today's Europe. To emigrate is always painful; at that time it was also more difficult and more costly than it is now. To emigrate one needed not only a lot of money but also a "bridgehead" in the country of destination: relatives or friends willing to offer sponsorship and/or hospitality. Many Italians, peasants above all, had emigrated during the previous decades, but they were driven by poverty and hunger and had a bridgehead, or thought they did. Often they were invited and well received because locally there was a scant supply of manual laborers. Nevertheless, for them and their families leaving their "fatherland" was also a traumatic decision.

But the Europe of the 1930s was very different indeed. Although industrialized, it was still profoundly agricultural, or permanently urbanized. "Abroad" for the great majority of the population was a remote and vague landscape, mainly for the middle class, less pressed by necessity. Confronted by the Hitlerian menace, the majority of indigenous Jews in Italy, France, Poland, and Germany itself chose to remain in what they felt was their *part* for reasons that to a great extent they held in common, albeit with different nuances from place to place.

Common to all were the organizational difficulties of emigrating. Those were times of grave international tension: the frontiers of Europe, today almost nonexistent, were practically closed, and England and the Americas had extremely reduced immigration quotas. Yet greater than this difficulty was another of an inner, psychological nature. This village or town or region or nation is mine, I was born here, my ancestors are buried here. I speak its language, have adopted its customs and culture; and to this culture I may even have contributed. I paid its tributes, observed its laws. I fought its battles, not caring whether they were just or unjust. I risked my life for its borders, some of my friends or relations lie in the war cemeteries, I myself, in deference to the current rhetoric, have declared myself willing to die for the *part*. I do not want to nor can I leave it: if I die I will die "in part"; that will be my way of dying "for the part."

Obviously this sedentary and domestic rather than actively patriotic morality would not have stood up if European Judaism could have foreseen the future. It isn't that the premonitory symptoms of the slaughter were lacking: from his very first books and speeches Hitler had spoken clearly. The Jews (not only the German Jews) were the parasites of humanity and must be eliminated as noxious insects are eliminated. But disquieting deductions have a difficult life: until the last moment, until the incursion of the Nazi (and Fascist) dervishes from house to house, one found a way to deny the signals, ignore the danger, manufacture those convenient truths of which I spoke earlier.

This happened to a greater extent in Germany than in Italy. The German Jews were almost all bourgeois and they were German. Like their "Aryan" quasicompatriots they loved law and order, and not only did they not foresee but they were organically incapable of conceiving of a terrorism directed by the state, even when it was already all around them. There is a famous, extremely dense verse by Christian Morgenstern, a bizarre Bavarian poet (not Jewish, despite his surname), which is quite apposite here, even though it was written in 1910, in the clear, upright, and law-abiding Germany described by J.K. Jerome in *Three Men on the Bummel*. A verse so German and so pregnant that it has become a proverb and cannot be translated except by a clumsy paraphrase: "Nicht sein kann, was nicht sein darf" ("What may not be cannot be").

This is the seal of a small emblematic power: Palmstrom, an extremely lawabiding German citizen, is hit by a car in a street where traffic is forbidden. He gets up bruised and battered and thinks about it. If traffic is forbidden, vehicles may not circulate, that is, they do not circulate. Ergo he cannot have been hit: it is "an impossible reality," an "Unmogliche Tatsache" (this is the title of the poem). He must have only dreamed it because, indeed, "things whose existence is not morally permissible cannot exist."

One must beware of hindsight and stereotypes. More generally one must beware of the error that consists in judging distant epochs and places with the yardstick that prevails in the here and now, an error all the more difficult to avoid as the distance in space and time increases. This is the reason why, for us who are not specialists, comprehending biblical and Homeric texts or even the Greek and Latin classics is so arduous an undertaking. Many Europeans of that time—and not only Europeans and not only of that time—behaved and still behave like Palmstrom, denying the existence of things that ought not to exist. According to common sense, which Manzoni shrewdly distinguished from "good sense," man when threatened provides, resists, or flees, but the threats of those days which today seem evident were at that time obfuscated by willed incredulity, mental blocks, generously exchanged and self-catalyzing consolatory truths.

Here rises the obligatory question, a counter-question: How securely do we live, we men of the century's and millenium's end? And, more specifically, we Europeans? We have been told, and there's no reason to doubt it, that for every human being on the planet a quantity of nuclear explosive is stored equal to three or four tons of TNT. If even only 1 percent of it were used there

326

would immediately be tens of millions dead, and frightening genetic damage to the entire human species, indeed to all life on earth, with the exception perhaps of the insects. Besides, it is at least probable that a third world war, even conventional, even partial, would be fought on our territory between the Atlantic and the Urals, between the Mediterranean and the Arctic. The threat is different from that of the 1930s: less close but vaster; linked, in the opinion of some, to a demonism of history, new, still indecipherable, but not linked (until now) to human demonism. It is aimed at everyone, and therefore especially "useless."

So then? Are today's fears more or less founded than the fears of that time? When it comes to the future, we are just as blind as our fathers. Swiss and Swedes have their antinuclear shelters, but what will they find when they come out into the open? There are Polynesia, New Zealand, Tierra del Fuego, the Antarctic: perhaps they will remain unharmed. Obtaining a passport and entry visas is much easier than it was then, so why aren't we going? Why aren't we leaving our country? Why aren't we fleeing "before"?

"Beyond Judgment" is drawn from Primo Levi's book The Drowned and the Saved. *This book, as well as Levi's earlier works, are available at the Facing History Resource Center. Also available are several articles about Levi's post-Holocaust career as a scientist and author.*

1. Wiesel, *Legends of Our Time*, p. 181.

2. In June 1945 Earl G. Harrison, a Princeton law professor, was sent by President Truman to visit the displaced persons camps and report his findings directly to him. Harrison's report, released in September 1945, recognized that because of the special nature of the persecution suffered by the Jews, American policies were in effect discriminating against them. He proposed changes to alleviate the deprivation in the displaced persons camps, and suggested that 100,000 Jews be allowed to go to Palestine. Oral History of Rabbi Judah Nadich (RG 387, Center for Holocaust Studies, 1978).

3. Oral History of Mayer Moskowitz (RG 118, Center for Holocaust Studies, 1974) and Fischer, *Transnistria, The Forgotten Cemetery*, p. 35.

Appendix 1: Resource Speakers

Videotapes of scholars and educators who take part in Facing History workshops and institutes shed light on the most recent research in Holocaust studies and suggest areas to examine for better comprehension of the Holocaust and its lessons for contemporary society. The summaries of the resource speaker video presentations are keyed to chapters of the Resource Book.

"An Overview of Facing History and Ourselves" (Margot Stern Strom) outlines the main goals of the program.

"The Teaching of Contempt" (Eva Fleischner) examines the origins and perpetuation of antisemitism.

"Confronting the Complicity of Churches in the Third Reich" (Fr. Robert Bullock) discusses the Christian roots of antisemitism and contemporary efforts to counteract this trend.

"Investigating Anti-Jewish Attitudes in the Christian Scriptures" (Rev. Spencer Parsons) traces the stereotypes against Jews in early Christian tradition and their continuity through two thousand years of Christianity.

"The Weimar Era, 1919-1933" (Sol Gittleman) outlines the dominant intellectual and cultural forces that undermined confidence in Weimar and contributed to the rise of Nazism.

"The Rise of Nazism" (Henry Friedlander) examines the components of National Socialist ideology that attracted a popular following in the 1920s and 1930s.

"The World of Anne Frank: Historical Background" (Paul Bookbinder) looks at political and social factors that contributed to the weakening of Weimar and the rise of National Socialism.

"1941: Turning Point in World War II" (Steve Cohen) explores, in a classroom discussion, events occurring in 1941 that played a major role in the final outcome of World War II.

"Women in the Resistance and in the Holocaust" (Vera Laska) examines the roles women played in resistance activities and their conditions in concentration camps.

"Forms of Mass Slaughter in Human History" (Eric Goldhagen) places the policy of Nazi Germany in the context of the long historical tradition of mass slaughter.

"Imagining the Unimaginable" (Lawrence Langer) raises the question of how European Jews could anticipate an unprecedented policy of extermination.

"The Armenian Genocide" (Richard Hovannisian) considers what can happen when the world fails to acknowledge a genocide has occurred.

"The Stages of the Final Solution" (Henry Friedlander) traces the evolution of Nazi policy between 1933 and 1942.

"Confronting the Holocaust" (Franklin Littel) raises questions about the response of American religious leaders and academics to news of Nazi persecution of minorities.

"The Search for the Evidence of the Holocaust" (Martin Gilbert) describes the various forms of written and oral evidence that historians can use in studying the Holocaust.

"Witnesses to the Holocaust" (Henry Feingold) discusses the failure of the U.S. State Department and American Jewish leaders to respond decisively to news of the Holocaust.

"The Politics of Remembrance" (Raul Hilberg) traces the response of Allied powers, the United States in particular, to information on the Holocaust in the postwar era.

"The Belarus Secret" (John Loftus) examines how former Nazis entered the United States and why there was little effort to deport them before the late 1970s.

"Anne Frank's Legacy" (Liv Ullmann) discusses the meaning and significance of Anne Frank's phrase, "In spite of everything I still believe that people are really good at heart."

"Lessons to be Learned From Studying the Holocaust and the Nuremberg Trials" (Bill Moyers) discusses the importance of distinguishing fiction from reality in an examination of the Third Reich.

"Social Responsibility of the Artist" (Sybil Milton) describes the official art of the Third Reich and the modes of protest from artists before and during World War II.

"Degenerate Art in the Third Reich" (David Joselit) examines the lives and works of artists who opposed the artistic dictates of National Socialism.

"Helping Students Interpret Propaganda Art" (Barbara Halley) demonstrates, in a classroom setting, the application of description, analysis, and interpretation skills to the study of art forms used as propaganda.

"Adolf Eichmann: Nazi Bureaucrat or Slavemaster?" (Paul Bookbinder) examines the career of Eichmann and the impact of the Eichmann Trial on public opinion about the Holocaust.

An Overview of Facing History and Ourselves

Facing History was originally developed in 1976 with U.S. Department of Education funds for improving secondary education. Since then it has evolved into a nonprofit organization providing educators with services and resources for examining the history of the Holocaust, genocide, racism, and issues related to adolescent and adult development. The Facing History program is used in public and private schools, colleges and universities, technical vocational schools, and adult education programs throughout the United States and abroad.

The program reaches nearly half a million students each year in forty-six states and Canada. Teacher training teams and regional coordinators across the country supplement the core staff and extend its ability to provide ongoing support to local sites. Since 1981, the U.S. Department of Education has recommended Facing History and Ourselves as an exemplary model teacher training program, worthy of replication throughout the country.

Facing History offers an extensive process for strengthening school curricula and fostering teacher growth and adult development that includes intensive introductory and follow-up workshops, technical assistance, institutes, and resources from the Facing History publication and film library. The Facing History and Ourselves National Foundation operates a Resource Center in Brookline, Massachusetts, through which educators across the country have access to materials, films, books, and speakers for their classrooms. These services and materials are made available in an atmosphere conducive to sharing ideas, experiences, and advice, and are replicated in sites across the country for teachers from a variety of educational settings with student populations of various social, economic, ethnic, and racial backgrounds. The

Facing History staff provides teachers with ongoing training and counseling to support the implementation of the program in their classrooms. Adult education and related community activities also are unique and essential elements of the program.

Teaching methods employ films, readings, class discussion, guest speakers, and student journals which promote reflection and analysis. The program is interdisciplinary and can be used to enhance existing courses or as a self-contained unit. Basic skills of reading, writing, comprehension, and critical thinking are strengthened as classes investigate the complexities of an historical era that embodies meaning and relevance for responsible citizenship.

Facing History's model program, "The Holocaust and Human Behavior," is part of an overall process, an approach to education that uses history to explore complex issues that affect our society today. The program challenges teachers and students alike to apply critically the lessons of this century's formative experience to their own social environment. This study of the Holocaust takes a close look at the social systems, psychology, economics, and value structure within which it occurred and explores the ethical issues of acquiescence, denial, dehumanization, violence, and the role of individual responsibility in order to illuminate opportunities for effecting change.

Facing History teaches these lessons to children when it counts most—when they are young and forming values which they will hold for the rest of their lives. It teaches these lessons in school classrooms, the only place where people of all races, religions, and backgrounds must come together.

Facing History speaks to educators who want to think about teaching the Holocaust and the preconditions which increase the capability of governments to commit genocide. Workshops for educators explore clear examples of abuse of power, individual rights and freedoms, and unthinking obedience by tracing the roots of prejudice and discrimination, first individually and in the present day and then in history. The focus is on the collapse of democracy and the rise of Nazi totalitarianism. Workshop participants investigate the range of responses by individuals, groups and nations and explore a history that was not inevitable. They examine the genocide of the Armenian people, just decades before the rise of the Nazis, and confront the power of avoidance and denial. Finally, they think about prevention and the avenues of participation that can be used to try and make a difference in the future.

Facing History is a profound educational experience. Students learn a great deal of historical content. In the process, they develop insights into the meaning of morality, law, citizenship, and human behavior. They draw comparisons and parallels to past and contemporary events when appropriate. They explore the root causes of hate and ways to combat prejudice. And most important, students discuss the responsibilities of the individual in society, the need to think, and the need to make independent moral judgments.

Facing History takes seriously the need for mutual respect among all educators in a school community. Principals, counselors, librarians, and teachers from all departments join together in content workshops that confront the stereotyping, labeling and negative peer pressure that pollute a school climate. They explore how educators can teach about and reinforce tolerance, show an appreciation of diversity, and relay a concern for others that underlies a positive healthy school culture.

Teachers find that the Facing History and Ourselves curriculum revitalizes their teaching and builds their repertoire of such skills as leading discussion, framing questions, probing for evidence, and provoking analysis. They welcome the opportunity to meet with scholars and attend seminars where they study content and pedagogy and have the opportunity to enhance their own professional development.

Services

Introductory Presentations

One or two hour sessions are conducted in schools or communities by a member of the Facing History staff. Presentation will include an overview of the organization and the program, as well as responses of Facing History students, parents, and educators.

Workshops

One, two or three days sessions scheduled at the Facing History Resource Center, or in requesting communities or schools, that will provide an in-depth introduction to the Facing History program. These workshops give participants the opportunity to explore and understand Facing History's rationale, content, methodology, and materials.

Institutes

Intensive four or five day programs prepare educators, from across the United States and abroad to implement Facing History into the curriculum of a particular classroom, school, and/or community. Facing History staff and resource speakers introduce the latest scholarships, explain methodology and assist with plans for implementation. Annual follow up workshops and advanced institutes are held to provide ongoing support to teachers using the program.

Adult Education

Usually organized in cooperation with a community organization or interfaith clergy group, this is a Facing History and Ourselves course designed specifically for adults. The length of the course is flexible, although it generally meets once a week for eight weeks and is open to all. Many of the adult students are parents of young people who have experienced a Facing History program in their classrooms.

In-Service Teacher Training

This seminar is designed for educators in a school or a community. The number of sessions is flexible and the course is generally conducted after school during hours designated for staff development.

Resource Center

The Facing History and Ourselves National Foundation operates a Resource Library in Brookline, Massachusetts. Here, teachers have access to a wide variety of books, periodicals, films and resource speakers to supplement and enrich Facing History classes. Our program associates work with individual classroom teachers to ensure that selected materials tailor the program to specific needs and concerns of a school and community. These services and materials are made available in an atmosphere conducive to sharing ideas, experiences, and advice. Teachers from a variety of educational settings with student populations representing various social, economic, ethnic, and racial backgrounds receive ongoing training and counseling to support the implementation of the curriculum into their classrooms.

The Teaching of Contempt

Eva Fleischner

Supplements "Antisemitism, A Case Study in Prejudice," in the Resource Book.

Eva Fleischner, Professor of Religion at Montclair State College (New Jersey), edited the anthology *Auschwitz—Beginning of a New Era: Reflections on the Holocaust.* This book is based on papers presented at the 1974

International Conference on the Holocaust held at the Cathedral of St. John the Divine in New York City. In her presentation, Dr. Fleischner reviews the dominant themes in the anthology and clarifies the need for Jews and Christians to confront the past as a means for meeting the challenges of the present and future.

Christians, Fleischner notes, must be willing to search their souls when they embark on the study of the Holocaust. She reminds us that Hitler and other Nazi officials never repudiated their Christianity and that Pope Pius XII never made an official statement condemning the Nazi policy toward Jews. While admitting there were "shining examples" of church men and women who assisted Jews during the Holocaust, Fleischner emphasizes that a study of the Holocaust leaves the unavoidable conclusion that the "churches failed." She is not referring only to Christian leaders but also to the wider community of churchgoers, the rank-and-file of the Christian community, who neglected their responsibility to the Jews.

What explains this phenomenon? Fleischner attributes it to the "teaching of contempt" that went on over hundreds of years in Christian communities. From the first and second centuries A.D. the Church used negative stereotypes about Jews, and they were perpetuated over the centuries. An examination of the gospels reveals the antisemitic attitudes that became embedded in Christian tradition. If the gospel writers had foreseen what their writings would lead to, Fleischner believes, they would have written differently. While it would be inappropriate to say that Christianity caused the Holocaust, Fleischner states that the "teaching of contempt" in Christian tradition did "prepare the soil" for the Holocaust. "The deafening silence," she explains, "would have been broken had it not been for deep-rooted antisemitism."

Having studied the attitudes among German Christians between 1945 and 1960, Fleischner is disappointed to find that little changed in Christian theology about Jews in the fifteen-year period immediately following the war. Nevertheless, in the 1960s and 1970s she has begun to note efforts for greater understanding between Christians and Jews. To continue this, Fleischner argues, it is critical for Christians to confront what occurred during the Holocaust and begin building stepping stones to break down the centuries of antisemitism embodied in Christian dogma and practices.

A facing of the Holocaust will lead to taking greater responsibility. By looking at the past, we will be better able to face the abyss of which humans are capable [of emerging] . . . with a stronger sense of human dignity.

Confronting the Complicity of Churches in the Third Reich: Observations for Teachers and Students

Father Robert Bullock

Supplements "Antisemitism, A Case Study in Prejudice," in the Resource Book.

Father Robert Bullock, Pastor of Our Lady of Sorrows Church in Sharon, Massachusetts, and Chairman of the Facing History and Ourselves Board of Directors, discusses the need for people of all backgrounds to confront not only the complicity of the churches in the Third Reich but also the implications of that involvement in our lives today. In the first part of this tape Bullock explains to teachers at the 1982 Facing History Summer Institute how he introduces students to the issue of antisemitism; in the second part he demonstrates with a lesson to eighth graders at the Driscoll School in Brookline, Massachusetts.

Bullock's Remarks for Teachers

Why is it important to teach the Holocaust and have it remembered? From Bullock's perspective, teaching about the Holocaust, especially in the manner that Facing History approaches the subject, is "good education" because it compels people to search for moral balance in their thinking. Learning about the Holocaust, Bullock explains, is crucial for counteracting the current fascination with violence in American society. That fascination, Bullock says, even corrupts contemporary language. "We have leaders who are talking a nuclear language that is unspeakable and unthinkable." Further, Bullock reminds us that our society has become accustomed to little lies that distort the truth.

> *My function with students is to talk about antisemitism and the roots of antisemitism. In teaching about the Holocaust we must not show it as some aberration of German history and a result of the personality of Hitler. We must see it as a part of European history, religious history, that has deep roots in Christian understanding.*

Bullock prefaces this section of his discussion by noting that when he was a seminary student none of this history was included in the curriculum. He and his colleagues did not study the Holocaust or racism or prejudice; they never heard of pogroms or went into details about the Inquisition. Yet, as Bullock reiterates, it is vital to face this history. "The awesome, compelling fact is that the destruction of six million took place in the heart of Christian Europe and that there was no organized opposition from the churches; the pope took no official stance against the persecution and massive death of Jews." Despite the examples of heroic individuals in the churches, Bullock says, "the churches were complicitous in genocide." Why were Christians unable to move from their life-giving ideology to life-giving actions?

The church is now coming to grips with its antisemitic past. Church scholars are groping with the problems of anti-Jewish language in the scriptures and the way the gospels have perpetuated the charge of deicide.

From Bullock's perspective, one of the most effective ways to face the history of the Holocaust—and ourselves—is to examine moral examples of our daily lives. The Holocaust teaches us what it means to be human. One poignant example that Bullock uses in classes concerns a seventh grader who had cancer. She was undergoing chemotherapy treatments and when she could come to school she wore a wig to hide her hair loss—a side effect of the treatments. Her classmates teased her unmercifully and no one at the school did anything to stop them. "To be moral," Bullock concludes, "is to make choices on serious questions."

Bullock Speaks with Students

Bullock begins his classroom discussion on antisemitism by explaining why he does not use a hyphen in the word, ("anti-semitism" is a common spelling). A hyphen can only be used in antisemitism if "anti" precedes a real word, according to Bullock. "Semitism" is not a real word and therefore cannot be preceded by a hyphen. The word "anti-semitism" was originally coined by Walter Marr in the late nineteenth century and became part of radical right-wing vocabulary.

Christ, Bullock observes, never taught in terms of groups. He taught his lessons to individuals. However, over the centuries Christians began depicting Jews as a group in negative terms. Mistakenly, Jews were blamed for the death of Christ; the Romans were the real villains in this death. Bullock also argues that there is no such thing as collective guilt: one cannot blame all Romans for the death of Christ. But to this day, Jews are referred to as Christ killers. Statements in the gospels reflect tensions for Christians and Jews, but we do not have to inherit those tensions today. To be ecumenical is to respect the differences among people.

The Facing History Clergy Group meets annually to discuss how members of the clergy deal in classroom settings with such issues as Christian-Jewish relations and the Christian roots of antisemitism.

Investigating Anti-Jewish Attitudes in the Christian Scriptures

Reverend Spencer Parsons

Supplements "Antisemitism, A Case Study in Prejudice," and "Preparing for Obedience" in the Resource Book.

Reverend Spencer Parsons, former University of Chicago chaplain and currently a lecturer at Andover-Newton Theological Seminary in Newton, Massachusetts, offers an in-depth discussion of the scriptures in the early church that became the basis of the "teaching of contempt" which, in turn, nurtured generations of Christians in anti-Jewish attitudes and stereotypes. "Until we acknowledge the depth of the problems [in Christian–Jewish relations]," observes Parsons, "we cannot begin to alter attitudes of Christians."

The Gospels, explains Parsons, charged Jews with the killing of Christ. Statistically, Jews are referred to in negative terms sixty-eight times in the Gospel of John and only three times in each of the other gospels of Matthew, Mark and Luke. The death of Jesus is qualitatively different from that of any other human being. If one believes that Jesus is God or the son of God through whom salvation is guaranteed, then it is not surprising that those responsible for the death of Jesus would be seen as "the most despicable of the human race." These types of views, according to Parsons, provided the root for the charge of deicide.

Jew *qua* Jew in Christian reflection became symbolic of every negative that Christians encountered in the Greco-Roman world. Going through the works of the church fathers of the fourth and fifth centuries—Saints Hilary, Ambrose, Jerome, Augustine, and Andrew—Parsons cites quotations that demonstrate the persistence of anti-Jewish statements. St. Andrew, for example, did not want to stain his honor by discourse with Jews. St. Hilary would not acknowledge the greeting of a Jew in the street, and St. Ambrose gave orders for the burning of a synagogue. In the sixteenth century Martin

338

Luther carried on this tradition of denigrating the Jew, although he thought he would be more successful than Paul in converting the Jews. It was Luther's intention to "make Moses speak so you would never know he was a Jew."

"The deicide charge became deeply embedded in Christian conscience." It was not necessarily spoken, but it was nonetheless deeply believed. At times of extreme pressure and tension in societies, prejudices against Jews would surface.

In the light of the Holocaust, it is imperative that Christians and Jews look to one another, understanding how the stereotypes have acted on their relations. While Christians and Jews may not be in agreement on the meaning of the crucifixion, the Holocaust may illumine Christian traditions to bring an end to anti-Jewish, anti-Moslem, and anti-Arab sentiments. Religious communities must also confront hard questions: What does it mean for Jews to be religious after Auschwitz? What does it mean to be a Christian after Auschwitz? What part did Christians in the recent and distant past play in preparing the background for the Holocaust? What role has sacred scripture played in directly feeding prejudice against Jews?

Like Eva Fleischner (see "The Teaching of Contempt" earlier in this Appendix), Parsons sees optimistic signs in the post-Auschwitz era that Christians are beginning to confront the strains of anti-Jewishness in their tradition. "I firmly believe," concludes Parsons, "[in] the cycle of healing by those who remember and embody the biblical injunction to love God and thy neighbor."

The Weimar Era, 1919-1933

Sol Gittleman

Supplements "German History" in the Resource Book.
Professor Sol Gittleman, Provost of Tufts University, examines the background to the Weimar Republic and the thinkers who had an impact in shaping public opinion in the interwar years.

Weimar, according to Gittleman, must be seen in the context of the intellectual forces that grew out of Darwinian ideas in the late nineteenth century and the mass brutalization that occurred during World War I. The ideas of Charles Darwin, popularized as Social Darwinism by such thinkers as Marx, Wagner, and Nietszche, accustomed Europeans to think about ways to make their respective nations prevail as the most powerful in Europe. At the same time that intellectuals were advocating these concepts, soldiers who took part in World War I became accustomed to brutality and violence on a mass scale never before imagined.

In the aftermath of World War I, Germans created a republic with a democratic constitution, but no constituency. Not only did the people associate the defeat on the battlefield with the republican leaders, but they also associated the republic with economic deprivation and German humiliation in international affairs. Particularly hard hit were the members of the middle class, who could not tolerate poverty and the embarrassment of Germany's military defeat.

Amid the widespread criticism and discontent of the Weimar Republic, the National Socialist German Workers' Party was formed in 1920, drawing together anti-Weimar individuals and groups from the right and left of the political spectrum. Josef Goebbels, Hitler's Minister of Propaganda, carefully crafted the image of a puritanical leader dedicated to the cause of rejuvenating Germany. Jews were singled out for weakening Germany's position in the world community. The economic depression beginning in 1929 fed on the National Socialist rhetoric, enhancing the popularity of the Nazi Party and its leader.

The Third Reich, continues Gittleman, was an era in which Germans sought to escape from freedom. They entrusted their welfare to Hitler, who made them feel good, and the culture of the Third Reich deliberately sought to make Germans take pride in their powerful nation-state, destined to prevail in the world community. The artistic and intellectual forces that characterized the Weimar society were discredited in favor of nationalistic art that lionized the purity and power of the Aryan race.

The Rise of Nazism

Henry Friedlander

Supplements "German History" and "Nazi Philosophy and Policy" in the Resource Book.

Henry Friedlander, Professor of Judaic Studies at Brooklyn College (City University of New York), discusses the intellectual, political, and social trends that contributed to the popularity of Nazi thought in the Weimar Era.

Friedlander does not make a direct link between antisemitic thought in the nineteenth century and the "Final Solution." Nevertheless, he stresses that antisemitism was a noticeable trend in European thought in the century before the rise of National Socialism. The emancipation of Jews, which began with the French Revolution in 1789 and spread to other western and eastern European states in the course of the nineteenth century, enabled Jews to gain legal equality with non-Jews and more economic opportunities than in previous centuries. Despite these gains, Jews never became totally assimilated in European societies. Among European states, explains Friedlander, there is greater homogeneity than is known in the United States, where pluralism is tolerated. In the late nineteenth and early twentieth centuries European leaders such as Karl Lueger of Vienna and Eduard Drumont of France were able to create popular movements that forged diverse groups around a common platform of antisemitism. The belief that nations composed of pure races are stronger and therefore better able to survive in the international community gained popularity in these decades.

In Germany a racial myth grew up around the concept of the *Volk* (the people). The German nation was composed of pure Aryans; the existence of impure racial groups such as Jews and Gypsies weakened the essence of the *Volk*.

Popular as these ideas of racial harmony were in the late nineteenth and early twentieth centuries, Friedlander continues, they would not have prevailed had there not been World War I. The Great War was the event that accustomed Europeans to dehumanization. In the Battle of Verdun alone, more than a million men died. Europeans had never before been involved in a modern war of this magnitude; in fact, a century had elapsed since Europeans had been engaged in any major conflict. World War I undermined the political stability of Europe. The three major empires—the Austro-Hungarian Empire, the Russian Empire and the Ottoman Empire—were destroyed, and revolution in

Russia led to the establishment of the Soviet Union and civil war. In Germany, the revolution of 1918-1919 was aborted, and there was an enormous price paid for this failure.

The Weimar Republic, created in Germany after her defeat in World War I, was based on a democratic constitution. However, the birth of Weimar amid military defeat and humiliation meant that it had little popular support. Because of economic difficulties, the new officials had no time to establish viable democratic institutions. The Germans, according to Friedlander, disliked the freedom of Weimar. They considered the Republic promiscuous and blamed it for the proliferation of new ideas and opinions. They were especially critical of theatrical productions such as "Cabaret," based on Christopher Isherwood's *Berlin Stories*. Groups critical of Weimar freedom held on to tradition: they demanded order and discipline in German society. While there are historians who emphasize the Versailles Treaty as a reason for the unpopularity of Weimar, Friedlander stresses that it was not so much the terms of the treaty as the loss of the war that distressed Germans.

The Nazis were only one of many groups in the 1920s that called for the union of all German peoples in the *Volksgemeinschaft* (society). This concept, which had always been popular with Germans, held a special attraction in the interwar years with the hardships of inflation and political divisiveness. The people were ripe for listening to the call for a new reich. The First Reich had existed in the Middle Ages around the leadership of Frederick Barbarosa; the Second Reich had been created by Otto von Bismarck in the late nineteenth century; and the Third Reich, the one the Nazis promised, was destined to save Germans from the disruption, uncertainty, and freedom of Weimar. The Third Reich was to be established by a charismatic leader, and Hitler was to be that leader. He was a master of propaganda and organization. Hitler spoke in the language of the lower middle classes, and he knew how to organize to get the ultimate effect.

Nazism as a body of thought, observes Friedlander, contained numerous contradictions and was never as consistent an ideology as Marxism. For example, the Nazis glorified the pastoral past while at the same time they were fascinated with technology.

Friedlander's closing point is that the Nazis never achieved the total control of German society that they intended. The old legal order remained; there also remained areas of privacy in family life that the Nazis were never able to destroy. The basic family structure remained intact throughout the Third Reich.

The World of Anne Frank: Historical Background

Paul Bookbinder

Supplements "Victims of Tyranny" and "The Holocaust" in the Resource Book.

Paul Bookbinder, Professor of History at the University of Massachusetts/ Boston, discusses the political, social and cultural milieu of Germany and Holland in the 1930s. His presentation, which provides background for the *Diary of Anne Frank*, divides into three principal sections: 1) conditions for Jews in Frankfurt before the Franks decided to emigrate to Amsterdam; 2) conditions for Jews in Holland before the war; and 3) Nazi occupation of Holland and the destruction of Dutch Jewry.

The Weimar Republic, which preceded the Third Reich, offered German Jews more opportunities for legal equality than had ever before existed in Germany. Jews gained prominence in professions such as medicine and law and made modest inroads into the civil service. Yet antisemitism was still evident in the Weimar era—high posts in the armed forces and universities were closed to Jews. And political parties to the right and center openly expressed antisemitic views: only the Social Democratic Party took a clear position against antisemitism. In the many political demonstrations that occurred during Weimar, Jews were frequently the victims of violence. The 1922 assassination of Walter Rathenau, an economics expert and member of the Weimar government, exemplified the anti-Jewish sentiment widespread in the interwar years, especially in periods of economic hardship. Because Jews often were excluded from prestigious academic posts such as named chairs in universities, they worked in privately-funded independent research institutes. Such intellectuals as Hannah Arendt, Theodore Adorno, Herbert Marcuse, and Erich Fromm were involved with these institutions.

There were approximately 500,000 Jews in interwar Germany, representing one percent of the total population of fifty million. Almost half of the German Jews sought to flee Germany after Hitler came to power in 1933. As greater numbers sought to leave, the major question became where they would be able to find refuge. Quotas in England, the United States, and Palestine restricted the entry of Jews. The results of the Evian Conference and the Wagner-Rogers Bill further attest to the obstacles German Jews encountered as they sought asylum from Nazi persecution.

The decision of the Frank family to emigrate to the Netherlands in 1933 seemed a prudent one at the time. The Dutch Jewish community of approximately 140,000 was a mixed one of Sephardic and Ashkenazic Jews who were fairly well assimilated within the population. In contrast to Jews in eastern European societies, Dutch Jews spoke Dutch and lived among Christians. Of the twenty newspapers published by the Jewish community, all used Dutch rather than Yiddish. The 30,000 German and Austrian Jews who sought refuge in Holland after 1933 also blended into the Dutch population.

The Nazi movement in the Netherlands had not flourished in the prewar years. Although there was initial enthusiasm between 1933 and 1935, support for the Dutch Nazi Party declined significantly after 1935 because the Dutch people were basically opposed to overt expressions of antisemitism. Only after the German invasion and occupation of the Netherlands in the spring of 1940 did the Dutch Nazi Party gain significance in the political life of Holland. Restrictions against Jews in the Netherlands proceeded rapidly in 1940-1941. By October 1940, Jews were required to register all their financial holdings; in January 1941, all Jews had to register and demonstrate their racial identity.

The antisemitic legislation of 1940-1941 was a prelude to plans for the destruction of Dutch Jewry. Transports of Dutch Jews from transit camps began in the summer of 1942 and continued until 1944 when Allied forces liberated the southern provinces. The Frank family was on the last transport leaving the transit camp at Westerbork in the early fall of 1944. It is estimated that at least eighty percent of Dutch Jews did not survive the war.

In the final tally, 105,000 Jews were deported from the Netherlands. Of those transported, one person of 1,750 returned from Mauthausen; nineteen of 34,300 from Sobibor; more than 1,000 of 60,000 from Auschwitz; and approximately 4,000 of 8,650 from Thereisenstadt and Bergen-Belsen. To the 100,000 dead deportees must be added 2,000 who were killed, committed suicide, or died of privation inside the country, particularly in the transit camps Vught and Westerbork.

The testimonies of Marion Pritchard (T-754) and Steven and Marion Hess (T-542, T-543, and T-544) at the Fortunoff Video Archive for Holocaust Testimonies provide additional detail on conditions for Dutch Jewry in hiding.

1941: Turning Point in World War II

Steve Cohen

Supplements "Victims of Tyranny" and "The Holocaust" in the Resource Book.

Steve Cohen, program associate at Facing History and author of curricula on Vietnam and the American civil rights movement, speaks to eighth graders about the events of 1941, the turning point of World War II. Dr. Cohen, who uses the Socratic method, suggests a number of questions that help the students recreate the events of 1941 and consider their implications for subsequent developments in the war.

Cohen's initial series of questions deals with the European theater of war in 1941. What is a theater of war? Where are battles fought? What countries were still at war with Germany in 1941? What was happening outside the theater of war? The students establish that the major power still fighting Germany in 1941 was England; France, the Netherlands, Scandinavian countries, and Poland had already come within the German orbit.

The class next explores a set of questions about what it was like for people living in conquered countries of the Third Reich. What does it mean to be conquered? What options were available for conquered people during the Nazi era? What were the attitudes of collaborators? Resisters? In order to facilitate this discussion, Cohen reads from an article in the *New York Times* about a Belgian collaborator who admired Hitler as a great leader. What, asks Cohen, would have caused someone in a conquered country to be so enamored of Hitler?

The students then review Hitler's accomplishments between 1933 and 1941. They conclude that in 1941 Hitler had reached the apogee of his power: if he had died in that year, his obituary would have enumerated diplomatic and military conquests as well as the economic recovery of Germany.

Hitler's success, Cohen explains, ended in the summer of 1941. On June 20 the Germans launched the invasion of Russia with Operation Barbarosa. At the time, Hitler referred to Russia as Germany's Africa. What did Hitler mean by this analogy? Why were Russians considered inferiors? Why did Hitler refer to inferior people inside and outside Germany as "useless eaters"? How did the war on the eastern front affect the German military situation after the summer of 1941? What was so devastating about the Russian "General

Winter"? Why was Hitler so intent on eliminating the threat of Jews in the East? Why did the "war within a war" begin with the German invasion and occupation of Russia?

Cohen also reminds the students of the American entry into the war after the Japanese invasion of Pearl Harbor in December 1941. He asked students to consider how this action strained the German war machine, already enmeshed in the war on the eastern front.

Cohen concludes the lesson by asking students to think about the consequences of Germany's defeat in World War II. Will there be another treaty similar to that of Versailles? What would it be like to be free after living in a conquered country? How will Germany be reintegrated into the international community?

Women in the Resistance and in the Holocaust

Vera Laska

Supplements "Victims of Tyranny" in the Resource Book.

Vera Laska, Professor of History at Regis College, Weston, Massachusetts, took part in the Czech resistance during World War II. She was captured and sent to Auschwitz in 1944. In her presentation she describes her wartime experiences and those of other women survivors, whom she interviewed for her anthology *Women in the Resistance and in the Holocaust*.

Dr. Laska opens by explaining why her most current research has focused on the experiences of women in the Holocaust and resistance. So little has been written about the Holocaust from the female perspective that some work on the subject was needed to balance the numerous memoirs and studies of men. She did not embark on this research because she felt strongly about feminist ideology.

The subject of resistance during the Holocaust years is not as thoroughly studied in the United States as it is in Europe, where there are still organizations of survivors who meet to discuss their experiences. Laska believes it is important that Americans be aware of two forms of resistance in particular: the resistance of Germans from the time Hitler came to power and the first concentration camps were erected, and the resistance of Jews. Countering the oft-repeated comment that Jews went like sheep to the slaughter, Laska points out that in a bibliography she has prepared on Holocaust materials, one chapter (of twelve) is devoted exclusively to the subject of Jewish resistance.

Laska focuses on the activities of four women who are featured in her book: the head of Noah's Ark, a spy network (Marie Fourcade); a Belgian woman (Andrea de Jong) who helped save more than 800 Allied pilots; a Dutch woman who served as a courier and who wrote of her experiences in *The Tulips Are Red*; and a Polish woman (Vladka Meed) who served as a liaison between the Warsaw Ghetto inhabitants and the Polish resistance.

Following these vignettes, Laska comments on the situation for women inmates in the concentration camps. A survivor of Auschwitz, she often refers to her personal experiences. She also speaks of the physical and psychological conditions, especially in the all-female camps such as Ravensbruck, that interviewees have related to her.

Laska comments particularly on the super-organization of the Nazis in the concentration camps, exemplified by their extreme efficiency and their use of criminal prisoners to keep other inmates in line.

Forms of Mass Slaughter in Human History: Background to Twentieth Century Genocide

Eric Goldhagen

Supplements Overview and "The Holocaust" in the Resource Book.

Eric Goldhagen, Professor of History at Harvard University and an associate of the Institute of Russian Research, analyzes three forms of mass slaughter known to history: the Machiavellian, the Visionary, and the Predatory. He prefaces his descriptions of each form by explaining there are no pure types; the different types overlap. This presentation places twentieth-century genocide in the context of world history.

Predatory mass slaughter is the form in which one group aspires to take over the property and possessions of another. Before the creation of universal morality, the universe for a particular group ended at the boundary of the tribe.

With the advent of Christianity there was a need to justify slaughter. Among justifications used were: 1) those we want to slaughter would slaughter us if given the chance; 2) victims are wicked and subhuman; and 3) the deity has invested us with power (religion invoked to justify mass slaughter).

The visionary form of mass slaughter has predominated in the twentieth century. Genocidal mass murder springs from ideology that says that the world is awry, unjust, and misshapen and avows that the elite can make it right again. The mass murderer thinks of himself as selfless. Heinrich Himmler, for instance, mentioned in October 1944 how difficult it was for the SS to engage in the elimination of the Jews but that they must endure so the Aryan race could emerge "pure and decent." More recently, a Cambodian general instigated mass murder in the name of a vision of an equal and just society. Why, asks Goldhagen, do such visionaries predominate in modern times?

The Machiavellian approach has also been prevalent in modern times. The guiding philosophy for this approach is that the ruler must kill enemies all at once and then dispense favors among followers over a long period of time. Killing the elite is necessary to eliminate potential leadership of one's political rivals. Such an approach has been seen in Latin American countries such as Chile and Argentina. Similarly, Stalin ordered the capture and slaughter of Polish officers in World War II in order to eliminate potential rivals.

An exaggerated form of the Machiavellian approach occurs when the leader becomes a tyrant and tries to live above society. Omnipotent dictators act with impunity, without restraints, disregarding rules and laws in order to preserve their absolute domination.

Goldhagen concludes by enumerating characteristics of the Holocaust that make it unique among the forms of mass slaughter he has described. First, the quantitative nature of the Holocaust sets it apart from other instances of mass slaughter. Second, there was the desire to kill all enemies even at the risk of losing military engagements. Finally, the Holocaust represented "the most profound mutation of western civilization." It set out to turn the whole moral world upside down, to write a new version of the ten commandments.

Appendix

Imagining the Unimaginable

Lawrence Langer

Supplements "Victims of Tyranny" and "Who Knew" in the Resource Book.
Lawrence Langer, Alumnae Professor of English at Simmons College and
author of works on literature of the Holocaust, discusses his observations
based on viewing over 250 of the video testimonies in the Fortunoff Video
Archive for Holocaust Testimonies. Dr. Langer divides his discussion into
three sections: suggestions for reading the texts and subtexts of video
testimonies; a description of the moral universe of Holocaust survivors; and
selected excerpts from video testimonies, illustrating moral decisions of
several survivors and a bystander.

According to Langer, in listening to the survivor testimonies, one hears both
the text (the story of what happened to the survivor) and the subtext or
subtexts—the meaning of the Holocaust experience for life after Auschwitz
when survivors reenter the normal world. Langer urges students of the
Holocaust to listen carefully for both the texts and subtexts to get a fuller
grasp of the total Holocaust experience. Langer uses the following graphic
example of a text and subtext in a testimony: a survivor of the *Einsatzgruppen*
[Nazi mobile killing units] actions on the Russian border relates how he was
among those who buried Jews in pits outside his town. From the pit he heard
the voice of his mother, but not being in a position to do anything for her, he
continued to perform his tasks at the pit rather than risk being thrown in
himself—this is the text of his story. The subtext consists of how he has
thought about this event and dealt with it in the post-Auschwitz world.

For the last twenty years, Langer has studied and written about the testimonies
of Holocaust survivors. What comes across for him again and again is that
victims of the Third Reich—Jews in particular—did not have the option of
making moral choices as we know them in the normal world. Thrust into
situations of starvation, filth and crowding, survivors placed acts for their
survival over consideration for the well–being or safety of others, whether
they were strangers or close friends and relatives. Students, Langer stresses,
must understand that the victims were not responsible for their treatment in
the Third Reich: they had been classified as non-human, worthy of
extermination and treated according to the classification rather than their
specific actions or deeds. Langer also points out how difficult it is for

Holocaust survivors to review their actions during the Holocaust when they committed deeds that today, in a normal environment, they would consider morally reprehensible. How can and do survivors cope with knowing of their past actions which are so antithetical to their present behavior and values?

In order to illustrate some features of the moral universe inhabited by Holocaust survivors, Dr. Langer selected excerpts from testimonies of Edith P., Mrs. W., Hannah B., and Alex. Edith describes a time when she looked outside a transport train at the normal world of sun and babies in a German station. For Edith, who had survived in abnormal conditions at Auschwitz, the scenes of normal life seemed very distant, almost unbelievable. Mrs. W. talks about how difficult it is to convey the reality of her experience and her fundamental pessimism about human behavior. Hannah B. and Alex relate painful memories of stealing from other prisoners in order to provide for their own survival.

While victims of the Holocaust had no real choices in their circumstances, witnesses did have the opportunity to intervene on behalf of the victims. Many of these witnesses, however, chose not to act on behalf of the victims. The excerpt from Father S. illustrates this point: he recalls that he was a seminary student when the Holocaust was taking place in Czechoslovakia. He describes in detail what he knew and what he failed to do upon that knowledge. Today, Father S. hopes he would do more than he did in the war years to help victims of persecution.

The Armenian Genocide: History and Legacy of the Forgotten Genocide

Richard Hovannisian

Supplements "The Forgotten Genocide: A Case Study in Denial" in the Resource Book.

Richard Hovannisian, Professor of History of Near Eastern Studies at U.C.L.A. and a member of the Facing History Board of Directors, presents a lecture on the history of the Armenian genocide and its meaning for contemporary society.

350

Appendix

The Armenian people date back to 3,000 B.C. but the first organized state originated around 500 B.C. in an area in the eastern portion of Turkey known as the Armenian Plateau. For the next 2,000 years Armenians lived in kingdoms—at times they had an independent kingdom and at other times they were part of larger kingdoms. In the eleventh century A.D. the Turks first arrived on the plains of Central Asia. Over the centuries the Turks had become Muslims and had driven back the Byzantine State. In 1454 Constantinople became the capital. Over the next 200 years the Ottoman Empire expanded and incorporated Armenian lands, and the Armenians became a minority Christian group. As Christians they had the right to practice their faith while accepting status as second-class citizens.

Minorities were not abused as long as the Turkish Empire was expanding. However, in the course of the nineteenth century, the Ottomans could no longer keep up with Europe and began losing territories. Ethnic minorities such as the Bulgarians and Rumanians demanded their national sovereignty and broke away from the empire. The weakened empire went into debt to western Europe and increasing corruption ended the Ottoman bureaucracy.

Throughout these decades the Armenians began a cultural revival. Christian missionaries encouraged their cultural and intellectual expression. Late in the nineteenth century the Armenians attempted to reform the laws of the empire, as evidenced by the 1894 and 1896 disturbances. The Ottoman government imposed harsh measures on the Armenians for their rebellious behavior.

The Young Turks feared that the weakened Ottoman Empire would fall. They embraced the pan-Turkish ideology for the creation of a new, strong Turkey and spoke about the need for a pure homogeneous society. When the Young Turks seized power in 1908 their liberal views of the need to create a strong state through liberal measures and a democratic constitution seemed to prevail. By 1912-1913, however, the direction of the regime was increasingly authoritarian. Even before World War I there had been talk of the need to eliminate the Armenian minority.

Orders for the actual deportation of the Armenians came during World War I, in the spring of 1915. A series of military reversals against Germany and her allies in the first year of the war precipitated the call for eliminating Armenians. The propaganda of the Turks stressed that the Armenians were an untrustworthy minority in cahoots with the Allies.

There was a pattern to the process of relocation. First, most Armenians in the army were segregated from the army and worked to death. Then all potential leaders in the villages and towns were segregated so that there would be no group to organize resistance. The Turks demanded that all Armenian-owned guns and other weapons be confiscated.

The deportation took one to three days to prepare—the people were not told they were to be killed. Males were separated from the general caravans, each caravan with about 5,000 people at the outset. The men had the most "merciful death" in that they were taken and shot immediately. The women, children, and old people were taken into the desert on death marches in hundred-degree heat, where they were pushed on until they died. Of the 5,000 in an original caravan, approximately 200 would survive. Deportations did not take place in the two cities of Istanbul and Smyrna.

The Armenian genocide was ruthlessly successful. It destroyed a people and their monuments so that even the memory of the people was erased. By the end of World War I the elimination of the Armenian population was nearly complete—there were survivors and limited resistance took place. Most uprisings, however, were not successful.

The Versailles Treaty and affiliated treaties guaranteed that an independent Armenia would be created. However, the promise on paper never materialized. Kemal Attaturk's Turkish resistance movement and the infighting among allies allowed the Turkish resistance to solidify. All that was salvaged was a small area known as the Soviet Republic of Armenia. Today there are approximately three million living in this area.

In the early 1920s Western powers were somewhat embarrassed about abandoning the Armenians, and the new Turkish government rationalized what had taken place in the war years as a result of imprudent leadership on the part of the Young Turks. By the later 1920s and 1930s, the denial process superceded the rationalizations—the Turkish government officially denied there had been a policy of genocide.

The fiftieth anniversary of the genocide sparked outbreaks of Armenian political violence. Meanwhile, the Turkish government considers the denial campaign a priority and tries to create a gulf between Armenians and other minorities who might be sympathetic to Armenian claims.

Appendix

The Stages of the Final Solution

Henry Friedlander

Supplements "Victims of Tyranny" and "The Holocaust" in the Resource Book.

Henry Friedlander, Professor of History at Brooklyn College and the City University of New York, outlines the stages of the "Final Solution" between 1933, when the Nazis first came to power in Germany, and the winter of 1941-1942 when the Nazi administration began to implement the "Final Solution." Friedlander does not view the "Final Solution" as inevitable from the beginning of the Third Reich, but as the culmination of a series of stages in which Hitler and officials of the Nazi regime sought to solve the "Jewish Question." Friedlander also stresses that Hitler did not mastermind every detail of the "Final Solution." Hitler gave overall direction to policies for dealing with the Jewish minority, but he permitted his bureaucratic chiefs to work out the details and jockey among themselves for positions of power in implementing anti-Jewish legislation.

The initial policies for dealing with Jews in the Third Reich occurred in the spring of 1933 just after Hitler became Chancellor. The April law for the Rejuvenation of the Civil Service called for the dismissal of those civil servants who were out of step with the direction of the Nazi Party— communists, radical socialists, and Jews. Because the definition of "Jew" had not yet been fully clarified, there remained many exceptions to the civil service legislation. Moreover, the Nazi order for a one-day boycott of Jewish businesses on April 1 met with little response. Germans at this time refused to comply with such harsh antisemitic policies. Also, during these months, the right wing still did not believe that Hitler intended to go through with the reforms set forth in his civil service regulations.

The Nuremberg Laws of September 1935 marked the next stage in antisemitic legislation. These laws clarified the definition of "Jews" based on hereditary grounds and set the stage for eliminating Jews from the public arena and cultural life of German society.

By the latter half of the 1930s, the regime imposed additional steps to eliminate Jews from the German economy and applied great pressure to compel Jews to emigrate. Nevertheless, as the Evian Conference and the voyage of the SS *St. Louis* demonstrated, plans for the emigration of German

Jews were unsuccessful. Nations were unwilling to alter immigration legislation to facilitate the entry of greater numbers of German and Austrian Jewish refugees.

Kristallnacht, on the night of November 9-10, 1938, presented a major dilemma for the Nazi bureaucracy. On November 12, when Göring met with party chiefs to consider how to deal with the damage of the November pogrom, German insurance companies insisted that their Jewish shopkeeper clients who had sustained property damages from *Kristallnacht* be reimbursed because the companies could not afford the loss of prestige that would ensue if claims were ignored. Eventually, it was determined that the insurance companies would pay claims to Jewish shopkeepers. The government then would levy a fine on those receiving the claims so that Jewish shopkeepers would be forced to pay to have their property repaired and would not benefit from insurance reimbursement.

The flight of Jews from Germany and Austria accelerated after *Kristallnacht*. By the outbreak of World War II in the fall of 1939 more than half the population of German Jews had left, and Jews in the occupied area of Czechoslovakia also had fled. With the onset of war, the policy of forcing Jews to leave became almost impossible to carry out. And in September 1939 the Reich inherited more than two million additional Jews living in Nazi-occupied Poland.

The Nazi bureaucracy was uncertain about the most effective policy for dealing with Jews in 1939-1940. Two main plans were considered: the Madagascar Plan, which proposed transporting Jews to the island of Madagascar, was not feasible due to the presence of the Free French and the British navy; the Lublin Reservation Plan, which envisioned concentrating the Jews in the area of the Lublin Reservation, was opposed by Hans Frank, the Governor of the General Government, because there was too large a population of Poles living there.

By the spring of 1941, as Hitler prepared for the invasion of the Soviet Union in Operation Barbarosa, he had decided on the plan for killing the Jews. No written documents of this order survive. Yet, as Friedlander maintains, most reputable historians agree that Hitler did, in fact, give the order. And there does exist some documentation on the existence of the order.

Initially, the method for eliminating Jews involved the use of gas vans, but this proved inefficient for dealing with the large numbers of Jews to be killed. The Nazis then decided on the establishment of permanent extermination centers.

354

The extermination camps erected in Poland used methods developed for the euthanasia program that had operated in German mental hospitals in 1939-1940. Some of the personnel involved with the euthanasia centers were assigned to the extermination camps. The first extermination camp, Chelmno, used gas vans. After Chelmno, three centers were opened at Belzec, Sobibor and Treblinka. These three centers shared the following characteristics: they were operated by personnel of the euthanasia program; stationary gas chambers replaced gas vans; exhaust from diesel motors (carbon monoxide) was used to kill Jews by pumping it into the chambers; corpses were buried in mass graves (later they were burned in open pits); and Ukrainian volunteers assisted Germans in running the camps.

Two million people were killed in the three extermination camps.

The concentration camps of Auschwitz and Maidanek combined the gas chambers of the extermination centers with labor camps. Fifteen percent of the victims arriving at these camps were selected for slave labor. In these camps, Zyklon B or prussic acid in crystalline form was the chemical used for killing. A subsidiary of I.G. Farben produced the Zyklon B; in the process the irritant was removed so that the gas was odorless. In contrast to the three extermination camps, Auschwitz and Maidanek used crematoria instead of burning corpses in an open pit. By late 1943, only Auschwitz and Maidanek were still in full operation and Jews from all parts of Europe were brought to these sites for extermination.

The "Final Solution" did not apply only to Jews in eastern Europe. From the start in the winter of 1941, Jews from western Europe were transported to extermination centers in the East because the Nazi hierarchy knew that they would never get away with the program in Western Europe. Careful planning was necessary for transporting Western Jews to the East.

A particularly knotty problem arose in this process with regard to the transport of German Jews, who were, after all, German citizens and therefore entitled to certain rights. To "legalize" their actions, the Nazi bureaucracy passed a law stipulating that any Jew who emigrated from Germany was automatically to be stripped of all rights as a citizen.

Why did the Nazi bureaucracy bother with the law? They flagrantly abused all existing laws and ignored rights of citizens whom they considered inferior. Friedlander brings some insights to this question in his presentation "The Rise of the Nazis." He points out that in a modern technological nation state of the twentieth century it is impossible to extirpate the existing bureaucracy and body of laws; a modern society is just too complex for this to occur.

Confronting the Holocaust: The Role of the Churches and Universities in the Third Reich

Franklin Littel

Supplements "Who Knew" in the Resource Book.

Franklin Littel, Professor of Religion at Temple University and Founder and Honorary Chairman of the National Institute on the Holocaust, discusses the ways in which the churches and institutions of higher education were responsible for the emergence of the Third Reich.

Littel opens his presentation by recalling his wedding day in May 1939. He reflects on how unmoved he and others were with the reports of Nazi brutalities against minorities. Dr. Littel has always been distressed by the response of American churches and universities to the news of the Holocaust. Intimately involved with these institutions, he believes it is imperative for church and university leaders today to consider the complicity of their institutions in events and to use this information of the Nazi era to insure that another Holocaust will never take place.

The issue of the role of the churches is like "a field strewn with mines." There are Holocaust survivors in American society. In the presence of those survivors, how do we square the involvement of Christendom? One particularly worthy response in teaching the lessons of the Holocaust must come from the groups like Action Reconciliation, a group of young Germans seeking to build understanding between the German people and peoples of other nations. How do we go about making a balance of the monstrous wrong of the Holocaust?

The first thing we must do, stresses Littel, is not to vacillate. We must approach the topic with a moral earnestness. As Elie Wiesel reminds us, this is the task not only of the survivors. Others, too, must be able to speak out. Hitler said he was only carrying out what the Fourth Lateran Council had decreed should be done with Jews: Jews were condemned as a people outside God's providence in history. It is up to those of us who now study this history to correct Christian teaching. According to Littel, this is the essence of the matter. If "we are born again, let us see the fruit."

The second credibility crisis is that of education. Death camps were not built by savages, Littel reminds us. Educated persons with good university backgrounds built these camps. Raul Hilberg's *The Destruction of the European Jews* offers evidence of the manner in which competent, professionally trained people carried out the events of the Holocaust, believing that they were acting legally. "What kind of university produced these people? The Holocaust will always evoke the most profound questions of ethics and morals."

How do we deal with this event in our teaching? Littel suggests that the movie, *The Voyage of the Damned*, a documentary on the fate of the SS *St. Louis*, and Henry Feingold's *Politics of Rescue*, a study of the response of the U.S. Department of State to the Holocaust, are useful resources for teachers and students as they begin to raise questions about responsibility.

The Search for the Evidence of the Holocaust

Martin Gilbert

Supplements "The Holocaust" in the Resource Book.

Martin Gilbert, the official biographer of Winston Churchill and an author of several works on the Holocaust, has two particular interests: locating the evidence of the Holocaust and verifying documents that have been located.

Gilbert breaks down evidence on the Holocaust into two major categories: evidence from contemporaries and evidence for the postwar years, 1945 to the present. From his perspective, both forms of evidence are worthwhile to the historian if the historian is properly trained to evaluate the evidence. He has a special interest in the postwar oral testimony that he believes is unique in comparison to oral testimonies for other historical events.

Contemporary evidence derives from three major sources: the German records, accounts by non-Jewish bystanders, and accounts by Jewish victims.

The German records are voluminous, but they are primarily the records of bureaucrats and are not always fully expressive of intentions or underlying rationales for behavior. Typical of the German records are the files of Colonel Jaeger of the *Einsatzgruppen* in Lithuania. Jaeger left a precise count of those murdered in the actions in which he was involved. Included in one of his accounts is the listing of Jewish victims along with one Armenian and one Lithuanian Communist. The most we can glean from such accounts, however, is that Jaeger was an efficient bureaucrat. We know nothing of his own background, training, or reasons for involvement with the Third Reich. In fact, Gilbert has come across very few German documents that disclose much about the intentions of the Final Solution. One rather unusual and important document in this regard that may be representative of many more similar (but as yet undiscovered) documents is the transcript of Hitler's meeting with the Hungarian Regent Admiral Horthy on April 17, 1943, in which Hitler carefully set forth reasons why the Jews must be destroyed. The Führer argued that those nations that had failed to eliminate their Jews, such as Persia, had suffered a tragic history.

It is equally difficult to procure bystander evidence in a systematic fashion. Those who witnessed the events and did nothing were not likely to set down an account of their behavior.

Jewish contemporary evidence presents similar fragmentary and incomplete records. There are literally thousands of communities, and many of them have left no records at all. After June 1941, Jews did sense the need to record what was taking place, and some of these records have survived. Yet it must be kept in mind that such records are at best fragmentary. Many of these records were hidden, and Gilbert speculates that some ninety-five percent of these records have never been recovered. For this reason the account by Yakov Grojanowski in the Ringelblum Archive is particularly remarkable: it is the first contemporary record of the mass murder of Jews by gas that has come to light, and it details the atrocities in Chelmno that occurred between January 6 and 19, 1942.

Gilbert concludes his discussion of contemporary Jewish evidence by mentioning that at present, archeological expeditions are planned at several ghetto and camp sites to uncover additional evidence that may have been hidden.

As with the contemporary evidence, Gilbert divides his discussion of postwar testimonies into evidence from German records, bystander accounts, and Jewish accounts. He also notes that, as with the contemporary evidence, post-1945 accounts are fragmentary, so historians must be content with what can be pieced together.

The testimony of Kurt Gerstein, Chief of Technical Disinfection Services, written just after the war and shortly before Gerstein's suicide in 1946, is a remarkable document by a Nazi, describing the killing process at Belzec and Treblinka. Gilbert reads Gerstein's description of an abortive gassing at Belzec to illustrate the wealth of detail that can be gleaned from the former Nazi technician. Embedded within Gerstein's detailed and technical account of the killing operation at Belzec are details that remind one forcefully of the involvement of well-educated and respected scholars and professionals in the Third Reich. Gilbert illustrates this point with a passage from Gerstein's diary.

Gerstein had originally tried to give his testimony to a Swedish diplomat during the war, but the Swedes decided not to release the information. However, Gerstein remained determined to disclose what he had witnessed, and for this reason he gave his testimony in France a short time before taking his own life.

The Nuremberg Trials had a number of important postwar German testimonies. According to Gilbert, only forty or fifty of these accounts survive. That of Hermann Graebe, describing two of the *Einsatzgruppen* actions, is particularly important. Graebe's disclosures had a tremendous impact at Nuremberg.

In addition to testimonies by Nazi leaders at Nuremberg, several non-Jewish bystanders also testified. The testimony of Madame Vaillant Courturier had an enormous impact because she spoke in elegant French and was Catholic: it was from her testimony that the world first learned details of the orchestra at Auschwitz.

The Jewish memoirs and recollections of the postwar years are so numerous that Gilbert knows of no scholar who has mastered the entire body of these accounts. These materials are not always of value to the historian because the survivors rely so heavily on memory of events and because fantasy is at times interwoven into the survivors' memory of events. Another problem is that the survivor accounts are dispersed in archives and private collections throughout the world, and there is no central clearinghouse for locating all of them.

Although Gilbert admits that there are certain limitations in the accuracy of survivor testimonies, he argues forcefully for historians to apply their training and experience in analyzing and interpreting written documents to oral history. From his perspective, historians ignore evidence from oral history at their own peril, since these documents can fill in omissions and enrich the evidence found in more traditional written sources.

Witnesses to the Holocaust

Henry Feingold

Supplements "Who Knew" in the Resource Book.

Henry Feingold, Professor of History at the City University of New York and author of *Politics of Rescue*, discusses the response of the American government and American Jews to the Nazi persecution of the Jews before and during World War II.

Feingold believes there were many opportunities for Americans to help European Jewry between 1938 and 1941. Reviewing the history of the Evian Conference and the Wagner-Rogers Bill, he points out that the Roosevelt administration avoided taking any deliberate steps to help Jews. The International Government Committee, set up after Evian, never once referred to Jews in discussing refugees—the response to the Jewish problem was a wall of silence. It was only in 1939 that the full quota of German and Austrian Jews was filled. Otherwise, the bureaucratic wall that kept out Jewish refugees served as a deterrent for any influx of refugees from Hitler's Europe.

For example, when the Blitz bombings threatened London in the spring of 1940, Americans immediately responded to the appeal for rescuing British children who were not in imminent danger. Conversely, the Wagner-Rogers Bill for the rescue of French Jewish children in the spring of 1939 received no positive response, even though it was known these children were in imminent danger.

Complicating the situation in the months before the outbreak of war was the response of American Jews themselves. Roosevelt's aid and confidante, George Rublee, opened negotiations with Göring in March 1939 for the ransom of German Jews to be paid by wealthy Jewish financiers. For three months the Jewish community debated whether to participate in such a scheme: they feared that if they cooperated in the ransom of German Jews, similar ransoms would be demanded for Jews in every other European nation. Moreover, the fear among Jews was that cooperating in this scheme would reinforce the stereotype that Jews were wealthy and controlled the major financial institutions in the international community. Thus, after months of debate the ransom notion was dropped: the opportunity to rescue German Jews before the war disappeared.

One of the major obstacles in the early days of the war was credibility: it was impossible to convey to people that Jews were being slaughtered in eastern Europe when members of the Jewish community themselves could not be convinced of the reports. On the other hand, Jews did develop tactics to mobilize public opinion to help European Jews once they became aware of what was taking place.

Initially, these tactics were fruitless. Breckinridge Long in the State Department was an outspoken antisemite whose diaries read like those of Goebbels. It was not until the winter of 1944 that Long was replaced by Henry Morgenthau, Jr., whose aides prepared a report informing the President of the situation of Jews. Within four days of reading the report, Roosevelt created the War Refugee Board which worked with representatives of the Swedish Government and the Vatican to save half of the Hungarian Jewish population in the closing months of World War II.

Feingold notes two warnings in closing. First, the study of American response to the Holocaust warns us of the fact that the nation state has a negative legacy primarily—more ill-will has come from the modern nation state than good. Second, if we fail to study the response of America and other Allied nations, we are as remiss today as those who failed to speak out during the Third Reich.

The Politics of Remembrance

Raul Hilberg

Supplements "Victims of Tyranny" and "Facing Today and the Future" in the Resource Book.

Raul Hilberg, Professor of Political Science at the University of Vermont and author of *The Destruction of the European Jews* as well as numerous scholarly articles on Nazi policy and bureaucracy, discusses how the United States and other nations have dealt with the memory of the Holocaust in the postwar decades. Dr. Hilberg looks at three major developments: memory of the destruction of European Jewry in the immediate postwar years; memory of the destruction of European Jewry in the new states of West Germany and Israel in the 1950s and 1960s; and memory of the Holocaust in the United States and Europe in the 1970s and 1980s.

In the immediate postwar years, there was no recognition of the mass destruction of European Jewry between 1942 and 1945. There was no language to describe the enormity of the atrocity, nor were governments in the international community willing to prosecute Nazis for their domestic policies against Jews. There were two principal causes for this reticence: first, continued respect for the principle that states not interfere with domestic matters of other states; and second, respect for the act of state doctrine that maintains that officials acting in behalf of their respective states are immune unless they have committed acts that could be considered war crimes. In fact, the word "holocaust" did not come into use until sometime around 1960.

During the 1950s the reconstituted West German state and the newly formed state of Israel began to approach the problem of memory of the destruction of European Jewry.

In West Germany the first stages of this process began with programs for reparations to victims of Nazi persecution. Although recipients of monetary reimbursement objected strenuously to the notion that their losses could be quantified, it was essential for West Germany to offer these payments in compliance with treaty regulations set by the Allies. Moreover, it was essential for West Germany to acquire its post-Auschwitz identity and somehow acknowledge what had occurred during the Third Reich. While financial arrangements were made with victims of the Nazis, myths soon built up in the new Germany that Germans had resisted during the Third Reich and that the Nazi usurpers did not represent the German people but had ruled only in the name of the German people. Hilberg claims that it became essential in writing official histories of various German agencies not to mention Jews in the index, for to find them in the index would be to find them as victims of this agency.

The new state of Israel also had difficulties. Its founding generation perceived itself as the toughest Jews, who had survived the onslaught of the Nazis. They would not recognize the eighteen centuries of history between 70 A.D. and 1948—these intervening years were dispensable in their history. It was this very omission that compelled the Israeli government to create Yad Vashem in 1953 by enacting the "Martyrs and Heroes Remembrance Law." It was essential to think of the dead as martyrs and of the survivors as heroes. What was to be remembered is disaster and heroism. Even in the Holocaust, Israel needed role models for its youth. Interestingly enough, the young Israel idolized martial arts and agriculture in its heroes: traditionally, these occupations had been denied Jews in Europe. Thus, the commander of the

Warsaw Ghetto Uprising was remembered as a young Greek god out of the pages of some epic.

However, true remembrance depends on the discovery of facts. It was bound to come as a new generation asked the question of what had happened. It is particularly difficult to examine critically what human decision–makers did in the era.

Why did this desire for true remembrance emerge so forcefully in the 1970s? Why were there new courses? Why was there suddenly a discovery of the Holocaust? Hilberg claims it is a search for meaning, and it is a search by a generation that has not been through the Holocaust.

In 1978, President Jimmy Carter reflected this concern by establishing a commission to create a Holocaust memorial. The creation of this commission was to introduce a new element in the politics of remembrance—the survivor. Survivors were a major presence on the newly established commission, and they decided to visit Holocaust sites in Europe and to learn what people in the world were thinking about the Holocaust. The commission visited sites in Poland and in the Soviet Union.

Two incidents during the trip stood out most vividly to Hilberg. First, there was the visit to Babi Yar. He remembers how short a bus ride it was, only two or three kilometers, from the hotel in the center of Kiev to the Babi Yar memorial park, site of the ditch where 33,000 Jews were killed in two days in September 1941. It would have been impossible for the inhabitants of the town not to know what was happening. Second, there was the informal gathering of the American members of the Holocaust commission with members of the Moscow Writers Union. Despite restrictions imposed on the Soviet writers, they wanted to know and record the truth. This was most clearly illustrated by the writer Anatoli Rubakoff, who spent three years recording historical truth in his novel, *Heavy Sands*, about a Jewish couple living through the Holocaust. Embedded in this novel is a passage by the narrator calling attention to the fact that circumstances precluded armed resistance by Soviet Jews. This is an extraordinary passage, explains Hilberg, because the Soviet Union does not value people who do not resist and the official Soviet line on World War II is that Russians valiantly resisted Hitlerism at all costs.

"Remembrance," Hilberg concludes, "is not a simple matter." In the immediate postwar era we remembered a special disaster without calling it the Holocaust. Today we tend to refer to every atrocity as a holocaust. In any case, a monumental and terrible historical event—the mass murder of European Jewry—will not vanish because people ignore it. It lives in memory; it affects the lives of all peoples. Today, as in the past, there are disasters. We must always hear them, distinctly and clearly.

The Belarus Secret: Activities of Nazi War Criminals in the United States

John Loftus

Supplements "Who Knew" and "Judgment" in the Resource Book.

John Loftus, a former attorney for the Office of Special Investigations of the Justice Department, summarizes his investigation of 300 Nazi collaborators from Byelorussia. Based upon his research, culled from vaults of army records, Loftus maintains that certain members in the State Department and individuals in the intelligence community knowingly facilitated the entry into the United States of the Nazi collaborators and helped cover this up so the collaborators could remain. In a number of instances the former Nazis smuggled into the United States were given jobs with government agencies. Initially, Loftus disclosed his discoveries during an interview for the television show *60 Minutes* in May 1982; his book *The Belarus Secret* relates the details of his investigation as well as reactions from the American public and government officials.

At the close of World War II, the State Department regarded the Communists as our main enemies and engaged in recruiting Nazis to hunt down Communists. A detailed discussion of the career of Stanislaw Stankievich serves to illustrate Loftus's thesis. Stankievich, a doctor of humanities who was enlisted by a special section of the SS when the Nazis came through Byelorussia in 1941, spied for the *Einsatzgruppen* forces. He also helped in the roundup and massacre of all Jews in his area in October 1941. Stankievich carefully calculated how many Jews could be killed and fit into the mass graves. Later, he became part of the Nazi puppet government of White Russia, where native volunteers carried out most of the killing of Jews. After the war the British anticommunist section viewed the puppet government of Byelorussia as an asset for an anticommunist crusade even though many of the members of the puppet regime had been placed on the list of Nazi war criminals. Stankievich was one of those on the list.

Nevertheless, American intelligence agencies helped smuggle Stankievich into the United States and secured a position for him as a broadcaster with Radio Free Europe. He lived undisturbed in the United States for over three decades and died in the early 1980s. Files about Stankievich were classified top secret, as were the *Memoirs of a Jew* by Solomon that related in detail the atrocities that Stankievich and other Byelorussian collaborators perpetrated against Jews in White Russia.

According to Loftus, the careers of men like Stankievich constitute one of the tragedies of modern history. Did we fight World War II, he queries, in order to bring into our country known mass murderers?

The American public, Loftus concludes, must face the fact that our government gave sanctuary to Nazi criminals. He is not optimistic that much will be done about this. Forty years from now the files he read will be released to our children and they will ask why we did nothing. Loftus says he wants the history books to record that we were not indifferent but we kept hunting to the end. Some crimes are too awful to be forgiven; men who murdered children should be hunted. The Holocaust is not solely a Jewish issue.

Anne Frank's Legacy: We All Have a Capacity to Make a Difference

Liv Ullmann

Supplements "Facing Today and the Future" in the Resource Book.
In an interview with Margot Stern Strom, actress and author Liv Ullmann describes how she became involved with UNICEF. For the last ten years Ullmann has been an ambassador for the United Nations, visiting children in oppressed circumstances throughout the world and urging individuals and governments to help save these children. Ullmann's first role in the theater was playing Anne Frank. Anne's diary entry on June 6, 1944—"[I]n spite of everything I still believe that people are really good at heart"—has had an enduring influence on her career. Ullmann does not view Anne as an

unrealistic optimist; rather, she interprets Anne's assessment of human nature as, "We all have the capacity to do good."

Ullmann works with UNICEF because it is important to her to try to make a difference. "Fifty years from now I don't want people to say we let children die. Because finally you and I are going to be defined by what we did for the children." She feels it is particularly important for people such as she, "privileged people," to do something about the plight of poor and oppressed children. She shares the frustrations of Elie Wiesel and other Holocaust survivors about those individuals who deny the Holocaust. "We must struggle against indifference and ignorance."

Strom notes that Julius Streicher of Nazi Germany published propaganda that deliberately incited neighbor turning against neighbor. The propaganda machine was aimed toward audiences of children as well as adults. Ullmann points out that a recent survey of children in areas of war indicates that many of these children live for revenge. They have been nurtured in hatred.

Toward the end of the interview Ullmann returns to factors which motivated her concern for children. Perhaps the event that left the greatest impression on her was her visit to refugee camps in Thailand. When she left she knew there was no way she could deny what she had learned. Her privileged life is at odds with reality in much of the world. She must face the fact that unfairness exists, but instead of despairing about the discrepancy she is determined to use her resources to help those in need.

Strom recalls Bill Moyers' comment that so many students today do not see themselves as historically significant. In many ways, Strom continues, it would be useful for students to hear Ullmann talk of her work in Ethiopia and Thailand.

Liv Ullmann concludes by saying that her efforts for UNICEF parallel the work being done in the Facing History program.

Lessons to be Learned From Studying the Holocaust and Nuremberg Trials

Bill Moyers

Supplements "Preparing for Obedience," "Judgment," and "Facing Today and the Future" in the Resource Book.

Bill Moyers, television journalist and producer of historical documentaries, discusses in an interview with Facing History Executive Director Margot Stern Strom the lessons to be learned from studying the Third Reich. The interview covers three principal topics: the way in which people look selectively at the past; the significance of confronting the truth of the Nazi era as revealed at the Nuremberg Trials; and how to help today's students think of themselves as people who have the potential for making a difference and preventing abuses of human rights and injustice.

Moyers' opening comments focus on the way in which people select facts from the past so as to screen out disturbing or painful events. American textbooks reflect this process, omitting the harsh treatment of Native Americans, the brutal behavior of Puritans, and the manifestations of hatred that have occurred throughout American development. Strom mentions that textbooks in the American South, where she grew up, presented a distorted version of the Civil War and the civil rights movement. Moyers, who grew up in East Texas, concurs.

Propaganda in the Third Reich, as Moyers explains, offers a poignant example of how selective use of the past can be used to distort reality. Referring to his documentary "The Propaganda Battle," Moyers compares how Nazi filmmaker Fritz Hippler used the media to celebrate death and martial values while American filmmaker Frank Capra applied his talents to celebrating values that opposed Nazism's tenets of death and destruction. With diametrically opposing goals, each of the filmmakers had immense power to shape public opinion; they both played a major role in the era of World War II.

The potential for distorting reality in modern states convinces Moyers of the importance of having accurate and objective public records of the past. For this reason he believes that the Nuremberg trials, which disclosed the perpetrators and the deeds of the Third Reich, should be an integral part of high school and college education in America.

Moyers thinks that prevention of the atrocities and abuses of human rights that occurred in the Third Reich require that people become aware of what they can do to promote civic conscience and caring in their society. To this end, he believes it is essential for young people to learn that change is often the product of a long, arduous process. They must "work at being informed."

Social Responsibility of the Artist: Problems of Visual Literacy and Analysis

Sybil Milton

Supplements "Preparing for Obedience," "Victims of Tyranny," and "Who Knew" in the Resource Book.

Sybil Milton, historian and archivist presently consulting for the U.S. Holocaust Memorial Council, describes the qualities of art approved by the Nazis and anti-Nazi art produced before the war and in the ghettos and concentration camps of the war years. She uses slides to illustrate salient features of Nazi and anti-Nazi art, and she develops two major themes: 1) the Nazis used the political state to popularize and disseminate art that was compatible with the goals and ideology of the Nazi regime; and 2) the art of opposition groups, which has survived on a variety of media (toilet paper, edges of newspaper, etc.), provides an invaluable visual documentation attesting to the attitudes and spirit of opponents and victims of the Third Reich.

The Reich Chamber of Culture, begins Milton, controlled the production and distribution of all forms of popular culture and sought to guarantee conformity with standards set by the Third Reich. This was a branch of the Ministry of Propaganda and Popular Enlightenment, headed by Dr. Josef Goebbels, and it controlled every aspect of an artist's life. Themes that received the greatest encouragement from the Chamber were those that illustrated Nazi ideals of the perfect society: romantic landscapes, peasants tending to large families, infants suckling at their mothers' breasts, Nazi personalities in guises of classic heroes and heroines— classical allegories and works that glorified the deeds of the Nazi state.

Milton shows slides representing various aspects of official art of the era, beginning with Nazi architecture of public buildings—massive scale, use of Nazi symbolism, and classical motifs are prominent features on these buildings. Milton next shows a painting by artist Richard Klein of a figure with the characteristics of a perfect Aryan. In addition to the physical features of the male figure, Klein's painting incorporates Nazi ideals of pastoral life and symbols of the strong Nazi state and a prosperous economy. Slides of works by artists Carl Diebitsch and Adolf Ziegler represent art that conforms to Nazi standards, while Nazi social realism is seen in the slide of the sculpture *Comradeship* by Joseph Thorack. Other slides show pictures in the children's books published by Julius Streicher—the Jews are vilified in the books and often are portrayed as the corrupters of womanhood. In another slide Milton shows the game "Juden Raus" that sold a million copies in the Third Reich and popularized the notion that it was appropriate for the state to hunt down and imprison useless and unwanted individuals. The language of deportation is introduced to players: deporting, collecting and ghettoizing people.

Poster art was particularly important for propaganda in the Third Reich. This is epitomized by the poster *The Eternal Wandering Jew* which encompasses all imaginable negative stereotypes.

After showing art that represented support of the Third Reich, Milton discusses characteristics of art considered unacceptable in the prewar years. This work was designated "degenerate" or "decadent" because it failed to conform to standards set by the Reich Chamber of Culture—its artists experimented with new non-classical forms and styles, used their works to criticize policies and leadership of the Reich, or made mockery of the goals of Nazism and pressed for peace and understanding through their works.

Several of these artists were able to seek refuge outside Germany in the 1930s. Others remained in the Reich but were forbidden from showing their works publicly or renting studio space necessary to do their work. Some artists were detained in prewar concentration camps inside Germany.

During the war there was a more concerted effort to detain recalcitrant artists in concentration camps. In such settings, artists found innovative ways to continue their work, although much of their work was eventually lost or damaged. These artists were endlessly creative in finding materials to use for their work—virtually anything available was used to replace paper, brushes and paints. Art done at camps such as Gurs and Theresienstadt illustrates the variety of ingenious ways artists found to express themselves while under strict supervision of the SS guards.

Milton concludes with the following generalizations:

1) "The Nazis were able to use the political state to reinforce the world of art." They touched all media. For instance, in 1940 a film was made entitled "The Eternal Jew" which depicted the themes seen in the earlier poster by that title.

2) The Nazis sought to destroy "degenerate" art, first in Germany and later in all parts of Europe under Nazi control. Works that fell under the rubric of degenerate or decadent were: all works produced by Jewish artists; works with Jewish themes; works with pacifist subjects and art that did not glorify war; works with socialist or Marxist themes and works by other political enemies; works and objects with ugly faces and distorted figures; all expressionist works; all abstract art; and works that any Nazi bureaucrat found objectionable.

3) At least 11,000 pieces of art survive from the concentration camp artists. They are important documents attesting to the life and attitudes of victims of the Third Reich. Unfortunately, many of these pieces are in a state of disrepair.

Degenerate Art in the Third Reich

David Joselit

Supplements "Preparing for Obedience" in the Resource Book.
David Joselit, curator of the Institute of Contemporary Art in Boston (ICA) discusses the background to the exhibition "The Expressionist Challenge," held at the ICA between December 1985 and February 1986. During the Third Reich expressionism and other forms of modern art were considered "degenerate art" because they did not conform to the artistic standards and cultural values of the Nazi State. Between 1939 and 1945 the ICA regularly displayed works of the so-called degenerate artists; these works were again displayed during the fiftieth anniversary of the ICA.

Joselit's central question is, "How does the artist have influence beyond the field of art?" He begins by discussing the relationship between the artist and society. Then he focuses on this relationship in the Third Reich, explaining the role played by "degenerate" artists.

The artist, begins Joselit, always works from a series of cultural values. In earlier centuries art was primarily an expression of religious beliefs colored by political reality. More recently, political realities and secular beliefs have tended to have more significance in many cultures. The artist either formulates or resists the dominant cultural values.

The Degenerate Art Exhibition mounted by the Nazis in 1937 provides a concrete example of the relationship of art and society in the Third Reich. Very deliberately the Nazis displayed pieces of art that did not conform to their artistic canons as a way of instructing the taste of the German public. The 1937 Exhibition was arranged as a parody of an art museum: paintings were hung askew and mock inflation prices were given. Joselit illustrates with seven slides of works shown at the exhibition and the Nazi commentaries that accompanied the paintings:

Slide 1: Emil Nolde's *South Sea Islander* (1914)—a painting that Nazis used to illustrate the degenerate nature of racial ideals in modern art. The Nazis considered Nolde's work as propaganda for Bolshevism.

Slide 2: Lionel Fineberg's architecture in the interwar years. The Nazis regarded Fineberg's work, which represented the Bauhaus movement, as a deterioration of the technical foundations of classic art and architecture.

Slide 3: Eric Heckel, *Landscape with Bathers*. The Nazis regarded this work as another example of the technical degeneracy of modern art forms.

Slides 4 and 5: Otto Dix, War Series, 1924. The Nazis thought Dix's new realism an example of decadence in German culture in the modern era.

Slide 6: Otto Dix, *Child with Doll*. Another example of Dix's new realism, which the Nazis condemned for its "grotesque and bizarre" forms.

Slide 7: Max Beckman, *Old Actress*. The figure in this painting was the antithesis of the feminine beauty extolled by the Nazis, who believed that a perfect woman was a child-bearing mother whose existence revolved around pleasing her husband and bearing healthy children.

Many of the artworks condemned by the Nazis belonged to the expressionist movement, with its emphasis on externals, that had begun in the first decade of the twentieth century. For instance, the portrait of the novelist Alfred Doblin is the artist's interpretation of the writer's inner life, and Josef Scharl's

371

The Uniform evokes the inner being of the soldier rather than details of his physical appearance.

While they exhibited the "degenerate art," the Nazis organized a House of German Art with examples of model Nazi art. Otto Ziegler, who formulated rules for Nazi artistic taste, emphasized three characteristics: glorification of the German military tradition; glorification of the beauty of women who performed their roles as wives and mothers; and glorification of traditional German culture.

Joselit concludes by observing that art in any culture can be used to buttress or criticize cultural values. The ICA displayed expressionist art during the period of the Third Reich as a means of rejecting Nazi political and cultural ideals.

The Facing History Resource Center has a special information packet of art in the Third Reich and the exhibition on "The Expressionist Challenge," including slides used by David Joselit and articles from art journals of the 1930s and 1940s that discuss the relationship between art and society.

Helping Students Interpret Propaganda Art

Barbara Halley

Supplements "Preparing for Obedience" in the Resource Book.
Barbara Halley, an art instructor in the Brookline (Massachusetts) Public Schools, co-taught a Facing History unit with Chris McDonnell, an eighth grade social studies teacher. Halley and McDonnell planned that during the final five weeks of the course the students would work in the art studio to design monuments to their study of Facing History and Ourselves. During the earlier weeks of the semester Halley sat in on the classes, contributed to class discussions, and shared insights with McDonnell. In the fifth week while the class was discussing topics in the chapter "Preparing for Obedience", Halley conducted a class on propaganda art to help students think about how such art influences perceptions and behavior. The class discussion that examines the techniques and purposes of propaganda is useful in considering how Nazis indoctrinated Germans and inhabitants of occupied territories; it also raises

questions about how propaganda influences our contemporary lives in the late twentieth century.

Chris McDonnell opens the class by reminding students of the previous day when they watched the film *Obedience*, and she asks students to provide a working definition for propaganda. The students mention several characteristics of propaganda: it stresses only one side of an issue, and it advances goals that can be positive or negative. When McDonnell is satisfied that they have a working definition for the term, she asks students to interpret Goebbels' quote on the board: "Nothing is easier than leading people on a leash. I just hold up a campaign poster and they leap through it." The students point out how Goebbels regards people as animals and how the manipulation with propaganda will lead them to follow whatever line is tossed out to them.

Halley outlines the three main steps that should be used in examining propaganda art: description, analysis, and interpretation. Description focuses on telling about what one sees in a neutral fashion so that all can agree on the image itself. Analysis pertains to finding the ways that the elements of the image—size, shape, color, lettering—are related or are organized. Students should be encouraged to look for things that are repeated or varied in the poster or how certain elements fit with one another. Interpretation seeks to answer the three questions: Who is sending the message? Who is the message for? What is the message? The facts derived from the description should provide for the basis for answering these three questions of interpretation. Halley points out that the description is particularly difficult at first because people are often tempted to want to move to interpretation without agreeing on the description.

Halley then shows the students four slides of propaganda art. With each slide the students go through the three stages Halley outlined at the beginning of her presentation.

Propaganda posters and slides of propaganda used in the Third Reich are available at the Facing History Resource Center.

Adolf Eichmann: Nazi Bureaucrat or Slavemaster

Paul Bookbinder

Supplements "Judgment" in the Resource Book.

Paul Bookbinder, Professor of History at the University of Massachusetts/ Boston, prepares Facing History docents for the Exhibition on the Judgment of Adolf Eichmann with a lecture on Eichmann's career and trial.

Bookbinder's central argument is that Eichmann was not a mere cog in the Nazi bureaucracy. Rather, Bookbinder describes him as an ardent Nazi who delighted in exercising his power and took pride in his efficiency as head of Bureau IV B 4, an agency in charge of the deportation of Jews between 1942 and 1945.

Bookbinder opens by tracing the activities of Eichmann from 1945 until his capture and trial in 1960-1. Several witnesses at the International Military Tribunal at Nuremberg, explains Bookbinder, referred to Eichmann's crucial role in the implementation of the Final Solution, and for the next sixteen years Eichmann managed to elude Israelis seeking to bring him to justice. Bookbinder also explains the legal precedents for the trial being held in Israel, even though Eichmann's crimes against humanity were committed in Europe.

Bookbinder then examines the evidence of Eichmann's Nazi career as it was revealed during the 1961 trial. Eichmann's successful career as a bureaucrat was closely tied to the success of National Socialism. Joining the party in 1932 Eichmann quickly established his reputation as a devoted party member and developed an expertise in the "Jewish Question." By 1938 he was in charge of programs for Jewish emigration and at the beginning of the war he took charge of operations or isolating and removing Jews from the Aryan community. During the Final Solution, Eichmann as head of Bureau IV B 4 was in charge of the transport of Jews to the death and labor camps.

Bookbinder cites two specific incidents which illustrate that Eichmann enjoyed his powerful position and had no remorse for victims of the Third Reich. Bookbinder takes exception with Hannah Arendt and other scholars who maintain that Eichmann epitomized the "banality of evil."

Videotaped testimonies of the Eichmann Trial and the Channel 7 special "Force of Evil," highlighting Eichmann's role in the Final Solution are available at the Facing History Resource Center. Also available is "Witness to the Holocaust," a 90-minute compilation of videotaped testimonies of the Eichmann Trial.

374

Appendix 2: Proceedings of Facing History Annual Conferences

The Facing History Annual Conferences examine in depth certain topics in the Resource Book that have elicited the greatest interest from teachers and students using the program. Speakers and panels at these conferences survey the latest research in Holocaust studies and suggest its relevance to the present. Available at the Facing History Resource Center are copies of the transcripts of keynote addresses, summaries of panels and presentations, and sample packets of materials distributed at the conference.

First Annual Conference, 1985, Boston College Law School

"The Impact of Nuremberg: Today and the Future"

Supplements "Judgment" in the Resource Book.

Opening Session and Keynote Address: Why Study Nuremberg

Margot Stern Strom, Executive Director of Facing History and Ourselves, welcomes conference participants and explains why Facing History views the topic of Nuremberg as central to the study of the unique and universal lessons of the Holocaust. Elizabeth Holtzman, district attorney in Brooklyn and a former member of Congress, explains why she took the vanguard in Congress to press for funds to pursue Nazi war criminals in the United States. Robert Conot, keynote speaker, reviews the dominant themes in his book *Justice at Nuremberg*.

Panel: Precedents and Principles of Nuremberg

Participants are two former members of the Nuremberg prosecution, Telford Taylor and Benjamin Ferencz; and two prominent human rights advocates, Alan Dershowitz and Father Robert Drinan.

Panel: Reminiscences of Nuremberg

Former participants in the Nuremberg Trials—Telford Taylor, Walter Rockler, Drexel Sprecher, Benjamin Ferencz, Thomas Lambert, and John Fried—recall episodes of their time at Nuremberg. In these informal presentations, participants provide glimpses into the social dynamics of the trials.

Panel: Medical Ethics

Dr. Robert Lifton opens the session with a twenty-minute paper on Nazi doctors. Respondents Stephen Chorover (Department of Psychology, Massachusetts Institute of Technology), Dr. Lavonne Veatch (physician and member of a Boston-area hospital's medical ethics panel), and Dr. George Annas (George R. Utley Professor at Boston University School of Medicine) comment on various aspects of Lifton's presentation, pointing out that the study of Nazi doctors has direct relevance for decision-making among contemporaries of the medical and health care professions.

Panel: Prosecuting Nazi War Criminals

Allan Ryan, director of the Office of Special Investigations between 1980 and 1983 and author of *Quiet Neighbors*, which examines the work of the OSI, presents the principal paper discussing the efforts since World War II to prosecute Nazi war criminals in the United States. Ruti Teitel, an advocate for human rights, and Irwin Cotler, professor of law at McGill University, comment on Ryan's presentation.

Panel: International Law

Richard Hovannisian, professor of Near Eastern Studies at U.C.L.A., discusses the aftermath of the Armenian genocide of World War I and compares it with the Nuremberg trials that followed World War II.

Concluding Session: Theological Implications of Nuremberg

The concluding session examines the impact of Nuremberg on contemporary theology. Rabbi Irving Greenberg delivers the principal address, enumerating the benefits and limitations of Nuremberg. Reverend Spencer Parsons and Father Robert Bullock respond to Rabbi Greenberg's presentation, pointing out how Christians in the post-Auschwitz world must confront what happened during the Holocaust and examine those parts of their traditions that contributed to the persecution of Jews.

Second Annual Conference, 1986, Boston University

"Making a Difference in the Shadow of History: Avenues to Participation"

Supplements "Victims of Tyranny," "Who Knew," and "Facing Today and the Future" in the Resource Book.

The conference explores the notion that a strong democracy depends on the informed participation of citizens from all sectors of society in thinking and action which prevent violations of human rights and promote care and attachment.

Opening Remarks: Making a Difference

The Conference opens with remarks by Margot Stern Strom, Executive Director of Facing History, and two members of the Board of Directors, Robert Sperber and Carol Gilligan. Each points out how the theme of the conference relates to the overall goals of Facing History and Ourselves.

Keynote Address and Panel Response: Prophecy, History, and Civic Action

Lawrence Fuchs, professor of political science at Brandeis University and a former director of the Peace Corps in the Philippines, discusses the prophetic tradition in America, a tradition which stresses that Americans should be committed to justice. Fuchs highlights how the postwar generation has made significant gains in pursuit of justice since World War II. William Sullivan (co-author of *Habits of the Heart*), Dr. Deborah Prothrow-Stith (Boston physician), and Frank Jones (president of the Boston Committee) respond to Fuchs' address.

Presentation: Making a Difference in the Local Community

Kip Tiernan, the founder of Rosie's Place (a shelter for homeless women) and other organizations for the poor of Boston, discusses ways that the community can deal with the moral and ethical problems posed by the poor.

Presentation: Motivations for Helping Others

Nechama Tec (professor of sociology at the University of Connecticut) and Ervin Staub (professor of psychology at the University of Massachusetts/ Amherst) each speak about their research on motivations for caring. Both have become interested in what motivates caring behavior because of personal experiences in which individuals helped them survive the Holocaust. The session provides insights into why people are inclined to help others and what types of upbringing and incentives people need to develop a caring attitude.

Presentation: Modes of Resistance

Peter Hoets and Hermann Field speak about their personal experiences with resistance in World War II and the postwar years. Each reflects on how his experience affected his subsequent activities. Their presentations raise important questions about the various types of resistance, and the moral ambiguity of acts of resistance that threaten the security of individuals and groups not involved in the resistance activity.

Third Annual Conference, 1987, Boston Public Library

"Child in War: 'Seed for the Sowing Shall Not be Milled'"

Supplements "Victims of Tyranny," "Who Knew," and "Facing Today and the Future" in the Resource Book.

The Conference explores the unique and universal lessons to be learned from listening to the voices of children who have lived through periods of extreme abuse.

Opening Session

Margot Stern Strom, Executive Director of Facing History, begins by reminding the audience of Hannah Arendt's pleas for people to exercise careful judgment to combat inhumanity and abuse of human rights. Harold Raynolds, Jr., Massachusetts Commissioner of Education, welcomes the participants with a challenge to speak out on behalf of human rights. Christine McDonnell, an English teacher and author of several children's books, stresses the value of using personal journals and multimedia approaches to promote human rights.

Presentation and Panel: Arn Chorn, A Child of War

Arn Chorn, a survivor of the Cambodian genocide and a freshman at Brown University, relates his own experiences as a child in Cambodia under the regime of the Khmer Rouge. Chorn cries out on behalf of all children in all cultures, past and present, who must endure the pain of war and genocide.

Dr. Michael Rothenberg (Seattle pediatrician and psychiatrist, co-author of the fifth edition of Dr. Benjamin Spock's *Baby and Child Care*), Samuel Betances (professor of sociology at Northeastern Illinois University), Robert Coles (professor at the Harvard Graduate School of Education and author of books examining political realities and perceptions of youth in a variety of cultures), and Carol Gilligan (professor at the Harvard Graduate School of Education whose writings call attention to gender differences in moral development) comment and elaborate on Chorn's remarks.

Address: Children in History

Richard Lyman, professor of history at Simmons College in Boston, reviews the methodology for studying the history of children in war and suggests sources on children who were contemporaries of Anne Frank.

Fourth Annual Conference, 1988, Harvard Graduate School of Education

"Facing History in Perspective: From Theory to the Classroom"

The Conference explores the ways in which historical research is made usable and exciting for the classroom. Sessions focus on how research and classroom practice have helped educators teach about the Holocaust, civic and multicultural education, and critical thinking.

Welcome and Overview

Dr. Richard Hunt, Marshall for Harvard University and a member of the Facing History Board of Directors, welcomes participants to the Conference. Margot Stern Strom, founder and executive director of Facing History, presents an overview of where the program has been in the last twelve years and some projects it is planning to embark upon in the next decade.

Panel: Using Video Testimonies in the Classroom

Panelists describe the Elements of Time project.

[See the Introduction for a fuller description of this panel session.]

Panel: Teaching the Armenian Genocide

Rouben Adalian (education director of the Armenian Assembly), Joyce Kazanjian (Program Associate for Facing History), and Phredd Wall (member of the Facing History Teacher Training Team) discuss approaches for teaching "The Forgotten Genocide" in the Resource Book.

Presentation: The Impact of Facing History and Ourselves in Classrooms

Bill Miller (an eighth grade social studies teacher at the Concord Middle School, Concord, Massachusetts), discusses three major advantages he has gained from working with the Facing History program. The program, he says, enables him to embark on a journey of learning with his students, enhances students' critical thinking skills, and encourages students to make links between their own lives and lessons of the Third Reich.

Presentation: The Impact of Genocide Studies on Adolescents

Dr. James Herzog (psychoanalyst and psychiatrist, Harvard Medical School faculty member, and former psychiatric consultant for Boston-area schools) focuses on two principal questions raised by participants when they mentioned their interest in the impact of genocide studies at the outset of the session: 1) What is the intention of a curriculum like Facing History?; and 2) What is the effect of such a curriculum on adolescents? He presents his findings based on data collected from students studying the Holocaust, and comments on the relationship between age and the effect of the curriculum, as well as the major influence of the teacher who presents the material.

Fifth Annual Conference, 1989, Boston Public Library

"The Judgment of Adolf Eichmann: Evil, the Media & Society"

The conference compares the ways in which the media covered the trial of Adolf Eichmann in 1961 with recent media coverage of human rights abuses. The central question is: Does modern media play an educational role? A group of scholars and professionals in the fields of communications and journalism participate in the panels and workshops.

Welcome

Margot Stern Strom, Executive Director of Facing History and Ourselves, welcomes the audience, explaining how sessions in the conference relate to themes in the exhibition on the Judgment of Adolf Eichmann, appearing in the main hall of the library.

Keynote

Elizabeth Minnich, Professor of Philosophy at Union Graduate School, opens the day with a philosophical discussion on judgment and emphasizes that the media should help citizens in exercising their skills of critical thinking.

Panel: Perceptions of Adolf Eichmann: The Media and the Trial

The panelists explore how the media, television in particular, covered the Eichmann Trial and explain why this trial marked a turning point in the history of modern media. Elizabeth Minnich is the facilitator. Speakers are: Milton Fruchtman, the coordinator for videotaping the Eichmann Trial for Capital Cities Broadcasting; Martin Agronsky, NBC-TV Correspondent at the Eichmann Trial; Alvin Rosenfeld, Special Correspondent for NBC at the Eichmann Trial; Raul Hilberg, Professor of Political Science, University of Vermont. The panelists who attended the trial shed light on what it was like to witness this event; Dr. Hilberg explains how he was one of the few scholars studying the Holocaust at the time of the Eichmann Trial.

Panel: Media and the Coverage of Injustice

This session expands upon the morning discussion of the Eichmann Case to examine how modern media in general deals with issues of injustice. Central questions are: Has the media coverage changed in the quarter century since the Eichmann Trial? Do contemporary media provide sufficient information for citizens to make sound judgments on current issues? Ted O'Brien, television talk show host, opens the session. Daniel Schorr, Correspondent for National Public Radio is the facilitator. Panelists are: Henry Hampton, Executive Producer for the Eyes on the Prize Series; Anthony Lewis, journalist for the *New York Times*; Richard Hovannisian, Professor of Near Eastern and Armenian Studies at U.C.L.A.; and Joshua Rubenstein, Northeast Director for Amnesty International.

Workshop: The Role of Journalism in Monitoring Human Rights Abuses

Richard Hovannisian, Anthony Lewis, and Daniel Schorr open discussion with the audience on what guidelines media should follow in covering injustice and human rights violations. Father Robert Bullock, Chairman of the Facing History Board of Directors, facilitates the workshop.

Acknowledgements

A number of authors, publishers, and archives have agreed to permit the quotation of copyrighted material and are acknowledged here with thanks.

American Congress of Jews from Poland: Roman Mogilanski, ed., *The Ghetto Anthology* (1985).

Samuel Bak: A. Kaufman, "Conversation with the Artist," in *Bak: Paintings of the Last Decade* (1974).

Behrman House: Lucy Dawidowicz, ed., *A Holocaust Reader* (1976).

Walter Bieringer: Letter of Rosa Feri to the Oregon Emigree Committee (n.d.).

Bildarchiv Preussicher Kulturbesitz: Roland Klemig, *The Jews in Germany Under Prussian Rule* (1984).

Center for Holocaust Studies, Brooklyn: Yaffa Eliach and Brana Gurewitsch, eds., *The Liberators* (1981).

Rose Eisenberg: Azriel Eisenberg, ed., *Witness to the Holocaust* (1981).

Facing History and Ourselves: Lawrence Langer, "Preliminary Reflections on Using Videotaped Interviews in Holocaust Education," *Facing History News* (1984); Lawrence Langer, "The Act of Recall: A Variety of Voices," *Facing History News* (Spring 1985); Lawrence Langer, "Making Distinctions: The Ultimate Challenge," *Facing History News* (Summer 1985); Lawrence Langer, "The Missing Voices of the Killers: What Could They Tell Us?" *Facing History News* (March 1986); Lawrence Langer, "Interpreting Oral and Written Texts," *Facing History News* (Winter 1988); Alan Filreis, "Learning to Hear a Voice: Learning to Find One's Own Voice," *Facing History News* (Summer 1987).

Farrar, Straus & Giroux: Saul Friedlander, *When Memory Comes* (1979); Fred Uhlman, *Reunion* (1977).

Fortunoff Video Archive for Holocaust Testimonies, Sterling Memorial Library, Yale University: Samuel Bak (T-638); Daniel F. (T-153); Edith P. (T-107); Elizabeth D. (T-95); Eva L. (T-71); Eva S. (T-29); "Flight from Destiny" (A-30); Frank S. (T-30); Helen K. (A-35); Krystyna S. (T-10); Menachem S. (T-152); Paul D. (A-41); Rachel G. (A-62); Selma E. (T-42); Shari B. (T-66); Walter K. (T 197); Zezette L. (T-100).

Abraham Foxman: note on resistance in "Abraham Foxman to Head ADL," *Together* (October 11, 1987).

Friendly Press: Malgorzata Niezabitowska and Tomasz Tomaszewski, *Remnants: The Last Jews of Poland* (1986).

Peter Gay: Video Testimony of Peter Gay in the Fortunoff Video Archive (T–51), conducted in 1981.

Martin Gilbert: Martin Gilbert, *The Holocaust: A History of the Destruction of European Jewry During the Second World War* (1985).

Brana Gurewitsch: "Transforming Oral History: From Tape to Document," (1989).

Hebrew Immigrant Aid Society (HIAS): "Walter Bieringer Demands Better Immigration Laws," *New Neighbors* (March 1953).

Holmes and Meier: Raul Hilberg, *The Destruction of the European Jews*, Vols. I and III (1985).

International Publishers: Fred Wander, *The Seventh Well* (1976).

Dori Katz: Dori Katz, "Hiding;" "The Return;" "Photographs."

Nora Levin: Nora Levin, *The Holocaust: The Destruction of European Jewry* (1973); and "The Importance of Survivor Testimony," (1986).

Midstream: Dr. Paul Heller, "A Concentration Camp Diary," *Midstream* (April 1980).

Moment Magazine: "A Moment Interview with Marion Pritchard," *Moment Magazine*, Vol. 9, No. 1 (December 1983).

George Mosse: George Mosse, ed., *Nazi Culture* (1981).

Oxford University Press: Robert Abzug, *Inside the Vicious Heart* (1985); Michael R. Marrus, *The Unwanted: European Refugees in the Twentieth Century* (1985); Nechama Tec, *Dry Tears: Story of a Lost Childhood* (1984).

Pucker-Safrai Gallery: Paul Nagano, ed., *Samuel Bak: The Past Continues* (1988).

Simon and Schuster: Primo Levi, *The Drowned and the Saved* (1987).

Stein and Day: Isaiah Trunk, ed., *Jewish Responses to Nazi Persecution* (1979).

U.S. Holocaust Memorial Council: Brewster Chamberlin and Marcia Feldman, eds., *The Liberation of the Nazi Concentration Camps, 1945* (1987).

Viking Press: Jeremy Noakes and Geoffrey Pridham, eds., *Documents on Nazism* (1975).

Sonia Weitz: "Fragments of Darkness: Journal at Bindermichel," (1986); *The Poetry of Sonia Schrieber Weitz* (1983).

Gisella Wyzanski: Mrs. Charles E. Wyzanski, "Vignettes of My Years as Youth Aliyah Chairman," Address to the National Youth Aliyah Committee of Hadassah (1958).

Yad Vashem: Yitzak Arad, Yisrael Gutman, Abraham Margaliot, eds., *Documents on the Holocaust* (1981).

Sources of Illustrations

Source	Page
Alternative Pictures	51
American Congress of Jews from Poland	31
Samuel Bak	8-9
Leon Bass	82
Walter Bieringer	72,75
Boston Jewish Times	71
Center for Holocaust Studies, Brooklyn	191
Elizabeth Dopazo	222, 224
Facing History and Ourselves	116, 178, 255
Rina Finder	26, 29
Leo Goldberger	53
Hebrew Immigrant Aid Society (HIAS)	73
Interpress Publishers	36
Leo Baeck Institute, New York	102, 138
McMillan Publishing Company	229, 239, 240
Rose Murra	205
National Center for Jewish Film, Brandeis University	157
Marion Pritchard	206
Pucker-Safrai Gallery	4
Liane Reif-Lehrer	196-197
State Museum Auschwitz-Birkenau	31, 128
U.S. Army Signal Corps	83, 121
Sonia Weitz	11, 20-21
Yad Vashem Museum	146, 147

Bibliography

Aarvik, Egil. "The Nobel Peace Prize, 1986." *Together: American Gathering/ Federation of Jewish Holocaust Survivors*, vol. 2, no. 1 (1987).

Abzug, Robert H. *Inside the Vicious Heart*. New York: Oxford Univ. Press, 1985.

Ainsztein, Reuben. *Jewish Resistance in Nazi-Occupied Eastern Europe*. London: Paul Elek, 1974.

Anne Frank Museum, Amsterdam. *Anne Frank in the World 1929-1945*. Exhibition catalogue. Amsterdam: Uitgeveril/Bert Bakker, 1985.

Arad, Yitzhak, Yisrael Gutman, & Abraham Margaliot, eds. *Documents on the Holocaust*. Jerusalem: Yad Vashem, 1981.

Bak, Samuel. "Self Portrait of the Artist as a Jew." In Paul Nagano, ed., *Samuel Bak: A Past Continues*. Boston: David Godine, 1988.

Barmash, Isadore. "The YIVO Story." *Moment Magazine* Vol. 10, No. 10 (November 1985).

Bauer, Yehuda. *The Holocaust in Historical Perspective*. Seattle: Univ. of Washington Press, 1978.

Bieringer, Walter. "Demands New Immigration Legislation." *New Neighbors*, Vol. 6, No. 1 (March 1953).

Bock, Gisela. "Racism and Sexism in Nazi Germany: Motherhood, Compulsory Sterilization, and the State." *Signs* 8 (Spring 1983), pp. 400-420.

Braham, Randolph L. *The Politics of Genocide: The Holocaust in Hungary*. 2 vols. New York: Columbia Univ. Press, 1981.

Breitman, Richard, & Alan M. Krant. *American Refugee Policy and European Jewry 1933-1945*. Bloomington, IN: Indiana Univ. Press, 1987.

Chamberlin, Brewster, & Marcia Feldman, eds. *The Liberation of the Nazi Concentration Camps, 1945*. Washington: U.S. Holocaust Memorial Council, 1987.

Conot, Robert. *Justice at Nuremberg*. New York: Carroll & Graf, 1984.

David, Kati. "Learning From Testimonies of Child Survivors." *Facing History News*, Spring 1987.

Dawidowicz, Lucy S. *The Holocaust and the Historians*. Cambridge: Harvard Univ. Press, 1981.

Dawidowicz, Lucy S., ed. *A Holocaust Reader*. New York: Behrman House, 1976.

Delbo, Charlotte. *None of Us Will Return*. Translated by John Githens. Boston: Beacon Press, 1982.

Denneny, Michael. "The Privilege of Ourselves: Hannah Arendt on Judgment." In Melvin A. Hill, ed., *Hannah Arendt: The Recovery of the Public World*. New York: St. Martin's Press, 1979.

Des Pres, Terrence. *The Survivor: An Anatomy of Life in the Death Camps*. New York: Oxford Univ. Press, 1976.

Dinnerstein, Leonard. *America and the Survivors of the Holocaust*. New York: Columbia Univ. Press, 1982.

Distel, Barbara, & Ruth Jakusch, eds. *Concentration Camp Dachau 1933-1945*. Brussels: Comite Internationale de Dachau, 1978.

Dobroszycki, Lucjan. *Chronicle of the Lodz Ghetto, 1941-1944*. New Haven: Yale Univ. Press, 1984.

Eisenberg, Azriel, ed. *Witness to the Holocaust*. New York: Pilgrim Press, 1981.

Eisenhower, Dwight D. *Crusade in Europe*. New York: Doubleday, 1948.

Eliach, Yaffa, ed. *I Too Had Dreams of a Bright Future*. Brooklyn, NY: Center for Holocaust Studies, 1988.

Eliach, Yaffa, & Brana Gurewitsch. *The Liberators*. Brooklyn, NY: Center for Holocaust Studies, 1981.

Engelmann, Berndt. *In Hitler's Germany: Everyday Life in the Third Reich*. Translated by Krishna Winston. New York: Pantheon Books, 1986.

Fein, Helen. *Accounting for Genocide*. Chicago: Univ. of Chicago Press, 1979.

Feingold, Henry. "The Government Response." In *The Holocaust Ideology, Bureaucracy and Genocide: The San Jose Papers*, edited by Henry Friedlander and Sybil Milton. Milwood, NY: Kraus International Publishers, 1980.

Feingold, Henry. *Politics of Rescue: The Roosevelt Administration and the Holocaust*. New Brunswick, NJ: Rutgers Univ. Press, 1970.

Ferencz, Benjamin. *Less Than Slaves*. Cambridge: Harvard Univ. Press, 1979.

Filreis, Alan. "Learning to Hear a Voice: Learning to Find One's Own Voice." *Facing History & Ourselves News*, Summer 1987.

Fischer, Julius. *Transnistria, the Forgotten Cemetery*. Cranburg, NJ: Thomas Yoseloff.

Fourcade, Marie-Madeleine. *Noah's Ark*. Translated by Kenneth Morgan. New York: Dutton, 1974.

Friedlander, Saul. *When Memory Comes*. New York: Farrar, Straus & Giroux, 1979.

Fry, Kay. "Holocaust Survivor Shares Memories of Concentration Camp." *Vermont Catholic Tribune*, December 15, 1987.

Garlinski, Josef. *Poland in the Second World War*. New York: Hippocrene Books, 1985.

Gay, Peter. *The Outsider as Insider: Freud, Jews and Other Germans*. New York: Oxford Univ. Press, 1978.

Gay, Peter. *Weimar Culture*. New York: Harper & Row, 1968.

Gilbert, Martin. *Auschwitz and the Allies*. New York: Holt, Rinehart & Winston, 1981.

Gilbert, Martin: *The Holocaust: A History of the Jews of Europe During the Second World War*. New York: Holt, Rinehart & Winston, 1985.

Goldberger, Leo, ed. *The Rescue of the Danish Jews: Moral Courage Under Stress*. New York: New York Univ. Press, 1987.

Goleman, Daniel. "Is Altruism Inherited?" *Baltimore Jewish Times*, April 12, 1985, pp. 66-70.

Goleman, Daniel. "Great Altruists: Science Ponders Soul of Goodness." New York Times, March 5, 1985, C1.

Gross, L. *The Last Jews of Berlin*. New York: Bantam Books, 1983.

Hájková, Dagmar. *Ravensbruck*. Prague: Nase vojsko, 1960.

Hallie, Philip. *Lest Innocent Blood Be Shed.* New York: Harper & Row, 1979.

Harris, Whitney. *Tyranny on Trial: Evidence at Nuremberg.* Dallas, TX: Southern Methodist Univ. Press, 1954.

Heller, Paul. "A Concentration Camp Diary." *Midstream*, April 1980, pp. 31-32.

Hersh, Gizelle, & Peggy Mann. *Gizelle, Save the Children!* New York: Everest House, 1980.

Hilberg, Raul. *The Destruction of the European Jews.* Vol. 1. Rev. ed. New York: Holmes & Meier, 1985.

Hilberg, Raul. *The Destruction of the European Jews.* Vol. 3. Rev. ed. New York: Holmes & Meier, 1985.

Hilberg, Raul, Stanislaw Staron, & Josef Kermisz, eds. *The Warsaw Diary of Adam Czerniakow.* New York: Stein & Day, 1979.

Hillinger, Charles. "A Systematic Study of Altruism: Motives of Rescuers who Aided Jews in WWI Examined." *Los Angeles Times*, August 22, 1984, part 5, p. 3.

Hoffmann, Peter. *German Resistance to Hitler.* Cambridge: Harvard Univ. Press, 1988.

Hunecke, Douglas, Samuel Oliner, Pierre Sauvage, Philip Hallie, & Manus Midlarski. *Altruism and Prosocial Behavior.* Special issue of *Humboldt Journal of Social Relations* 13:1-2 (1986).

International Military Tribunal, Nuremberg. *Official Text.* English Edition. Volume 5, 10 January 1946.

Jerome, Jerome K. *Three Men on the Bummel.* Third edition. London: Arrowsmith, 1924.

[Johnson, Mary]. "Rena Finder: Schindlerfrau." *Facing History News*, Summer 1985.

Johnson, Paul. *Modern Times.* New York: Oxford Univ. Press, 1983.

Karski, Jan. "Polish Death Camp." *Collier's Magazine*, October 14, 1944.

Karski, Jan. *Story of a Secret State.* Boston: Beacon Press, 1944.

Kater, Michael. "Problems of Political Reeducation in West Germany, 1945-1960." In *Simon Wiesenthal Center Annual*, vol. 4, edited by Henry Friedlander and Sybil Milton. White Plains, NY: Kraus International Publications, 1987.

Kaufman, A. "A Conversation With the Artist." In *Bak: Paintings of the Last Decade*. New York: Aberbach, 1974.

Keneally, Thomas. *Schindler's List*. New York: Simon & Schuster, 1982.

Klarsfeld, Serge, ed. *Les Enfants d'Isieu: Une tragedie juive*. Paris: Les Fils et Les Filles des Deportés Juifs, 1983.

Klemig, Roland, ed. *The Jews in Germany Under Prussian Rule*. Exhibition catalogue. Berlin: Bildarchiv Preussischer Kulturbesitz, 1984.

Koslowski, Maciej. "The Mission That Failed: An Interview With Jan Karski." *Dissent*, Summer 1987.

Kugelmass, Jack, and Jonathan Boyarin. *From a Ruined Garden*. New York: Schocken, 1983.

Kuper, Jack. *Child of the Holocaust*. New York: New American Library, 1967.

Laska, Vera, ed. *Women in the Resistance and in the Holocaust*. Westport, CT: Greenwood Press, 1983.

Levi, Primo. *The Drowned and the Saved*. New York: Simon & Schuster, 1987; Summit Books, 1988.

Levi, Primo. *Survival in Auschwitz*. Translated by Stuart Woolf. New York: Collier, 1969.

Levin, Nora. *The Holocaust: The Destruction of European Jewry*. New York: Schocken Books, 1973.

Lipstadt, Deborah E. *Beyond Belief: The American Press and the Coming of the Holocaust*. New York: Free Press, 1986.

Lockstein, Haskel. *Were We Our Brothers' Keepers? The Public Response of American Jews to the Holocaust, 1938-1944*. New York: Hartmore House, 1986.

Lukas, Richard. *The Forgotten Genocide: The Poles Under German Occupation*. Louisville, KY: Univ. of Louisville Press, 1985.

Mann, Erika. *School for Barbarians*. New York: Modern Age, 1938.

Marrus, Michael R. *The Holocaust in History*. Hanover, NH: Univ. Press of New England, 1987.

Marrus, Michael R. *The Unwanted: European Refugees in the Twentieth Century*. New York: Oxford Univ. Press, 1985.

Mayer, Milton. *They Thought They Were Free.* Chicago: Univ. of Chicago Press, 1955.

McKee, Ilse. *Tomorrow the World.* New York: J.M. Dent, 1960.

Meinicke, Friedrich. *The German Catastrophe.* Translated by Sidney B. Fay. Boston: Beacon Press, 1950.

Meltzer, Milton. "Schindler's Jews." *Chapter 3 in Rescue: The Story of How Gentiles Saved Jews in the Holocaust.* New York: Harper & Row, 1988.

Mermelstein, Mel. *By Bread Alone: The Story of A-4685, A Survivor of the Nazi Holocaust.* Huntington Beach, CA: Auschwitz Study Foundation, 1979.

Mogilanski, Roman, ed. and comp. *The Ghetto Anthology.* Los Angeles: American Congress of Jews From Poland, 1985.

"A Moment Interview With Marion Pritchard." *Moment Magazine*, Vol. 9, No. 1 (December 1983).

Morse, Arthur. *While Six Million Died: A Chronicle of American Apathy.* 1967. Reprint. New York: Overlook Press: 1985.

Mosse, George L., ed. *Nazi Culture.* New York: Schocken Books, 1981.

Nagano, Paul, ed. *The Past Continues.* Boston: David Godine, 1988.

Niezabitowska, Malgorzata, and Tomasz Tomaszewski. *Remnants: The Last Jews of Poland.* New York: Friendly Press, 1986.

Noakes, Jeremy, & Geoffrey Pridham, eds. *Document on Nazism, 1919-1945.* New York: Viking, 1975.

Nomberg-Przytyk, Sara. *Auschwitz: True Tales From a Grotesque Land.* Chapel Hill: Univ. of North Carolina Press, 1985.

Oliner, Samuel, and Pearl Oliner. *The Altruistic Personality: Rescuers of Jews in Nazi Germany.* New York: Free Press, 1988.

Paldiel, Mordecai. "The Altruism of the Righteous Gentiles." *Holocaust & Genocide Studies* 3, no. 2 (1988).

Prague Museum. *I Never Saw Another Butterfly.* New York: McGraw Hill, 1964.

Richter, Hans Peter. *Friedrich.* Holt, Rinehart & Winston, 1970. Reprint. New York: Puffin Books, 1987.

Ringelheim, Joan, & Ester Katz. *Proceedings of the Conference on Women Surviving the Holocaust.* New York: Institute for Research in History, 1983.

Rubenstein, Richard, & John Roth. *Approaches to the Holocaust.* Atlanta: John Knox Press, 1987.

Rudachevski, Y. *Diary of the Vilna Ghetto.* Tel Aviv: Ghetto Fighters Museum, 1973.

Rupp, Lelia J. "'I Don't Call That Volksgemeinschaft': Women, Class and War in Nazi Germany." In *Women, War, and Revolution,* edited by Carol Berkin and Clara Lovett, pp. 37-53. New York: Holmes & Meier, 1980.

Ryan, Allan, Jr. *Quiet Neighbors: Prosecuting Nazi War Criminals in America.* New York: Harcourt Brace Jovanovich, 1984.

Sauvage, Pierre. "A Most Persistent Haven: Le Chambon-sur-Lignon." *Moment Magazine,* October 1983.

Schleunes, Karl A. *The Twisted Road to Auschwitz: Nazi Police Toward German Jews 1933-1939.* Urbana: Univ. of Illinois Press, 1970.

Segal, Nancy. "Holocaust Twins: Their Special Bond." *Psychology Today,* August 1985, pp. 52-58.

Shirer, William L. *20th Century Journey: The Nightmare Years 1930-1940.* Boston: Little, Brown & Co., 1984.

Sichrovsky, Peter. *Born Guilty.* New York: Basic Books, 1987.

Smith, Marcus J. *Dachau: The Harrowing of Hell.* Albuquerque: Univ. of New Mexico Press, 1972.

Stendig, Jakob. "Execution in Plaszow." In *Anthology of Holocaust Literature,* edited by Jacob Glatstein et al. New York: Atheneum, 1976.

Stern, Fritz. *The Politics of Cultural Despair: A Study of the Rise of Germanic Ideology.* New York: Doubleday, 1965.

Stille, Alexander. "Primo Levi: Reconciling the Man and the Writer." *New York Times Book Review,* July 5, 1987, p. 5.

Syrkin, Marie. *The State of the Jews.* Washington: New Republic Books, 1980.

Tec, Nechama. *Dry Tears: The Story of a Lost Childhood.* 2nd ed. New York: Oxford University Press, 1984.

Tec, Nechama. "Sex Distinctions and Passing as Christians During the Holocaust." *East European Quarterly* 18 (March 1984), pp. 113-123.

Tec, Nechama. *When Light Pierced the Darkness: Christians Rescuing Jews in Nazi-Occupied Poland.* New York: Oxford Univ. Press, 1986.

Thallman, Rita, & Emmanuel Feinermann. *Crystal Night.* New York: Coward, McCann & Geoghegan, 1974.

Trunk, Isaiah, ed. *Jewish Responses to Nazi Persecution.* New York: Stein & Day, 1979.

Uhlman, Fred. *Reunion.* New York: Farrar, Straus & Giroux, 1977.

U.S. Army War Crimes Team. *Report on Dachau Concentration Camp: U.S. 7th Army Report of War Crimes Investigation of Dachau Concentration Camp.* #6823, APO 887, U.S. Army.

Wander, Fred. *The Seventh Well.* New York: International Publishers, 1976.

von Weizsäcker, Richard. Speech during a commemorative ceremony in the Plenary Room of the German Bundestag (May 8, 1985). *Remembrance, Sorrow and Reconciliation: Speeches and Declarations in Connection With the 40th Anniversary of the End of the Second World War in Europe.* Press & Information Office of the Government of the Federal Republic of Germany, n.d.

Weinstein, Lewis H. "The Liberation of Nazi Death Camps by American Army—1945: The Report of a Witness." *Facing History News,* Summer 1987.

Weitz, Sonia S. "Flashbacks of Darkness: Journal at Bindermichel." Author's unpublished papers.

Weitz, Sonia S. *Poetry of Sonia Schreiber Weitz.* Brookline, MA: Facing History & Ourselves National Foundation, 1983.

Wheeler-Bennet, J.W. *The Nemesis of Power: The German Army in Politics 1918-1945.* London: Macmillan & Co., 1964.

Wiesel, Elie. *Legends of Our Time.* New York: Holt, Rinehart & Winston, 1968.

Wiesel, Elie. *Night.* New York: Hill & Wang, 1960.

Wiesel, Elie. "What it Means to be Stateless." *New York Times,* July 6, 1986.

Wiesel, Elie. "Wiesel's Speech at Nobel Ceremony." *Together: American Gathering/Federation of Jewish Holocaust Survivors,* vol. 2, no. 1 (1987).

Wise, Helen M. "Making Sense of Risking All to Help Another." *The Alumnus* 16, no. 4 (Univ. of Massachusetts, Amherst, 1985).

Wundheiler, Luitgard. "Oskar Schindler's Moral Development During the Holocaust." *Humboldt Journal of Social Relations* 13:1-2 (1985-86).

394

Wyman, David. *The Abandonment of the European Jews: America and the Holocaust.* New York: Pantheon, 1984.

Wyman, David. *Paper Walls.* Amherst: Univ. of Massachusetts Press, 1968.

Wyman, David. *Abandonment of the Jews.* New York: Pantheon, 1984.

Young, James. *Writing and Rewriting the Holocaust.* Bloomington, IN: Univ. of Indiana Press, 1988.

Ziemer, Gregor. *Education for Death: The Making of a Nazi.* Oxford University Press, 1941. Reprint. New York: Octagon Books, 1972.

Index